PROPHETS DENIED HONOR

Puerto Rican Day Parade, New York 1978
(courtesy Migration Today)

PROPHETS DENIED HONOR

An Anthology on the Hispano Church of the United States

Antonio M. Stevens Arroyo, C.P.

ORBIS BOOKS

Maryknoll, New York 10545

Orbis 12,95/10.36/12/7/82

The Catholic Foreign Mission Society of America (Maryknoll) recruits and trains people for overseas missionary service. Through Orbis Books Maryknoll aims to foster the international dialogue that is essential to mission. The books published, however, reflect the opinions of their authors and are not meant to represent the official position of the society.

Library of Congress Cataloging in Publication Data

Main entry under title:

Prophets denied honor.

Bibliography: p.
Includes index.
1. Catholic Church in the United States—Addresses, essays, lectures. 2. Hispanic Americans—Religion—Addresses, essays, lectures. I. Stevens Arroyo, Antonio M.
BX1407.H55P76   282'.73   79-26847
ISBN 0-88344-395-3

Manufactured in the United States of America

To my grandparents
Antonio and María
who taught me to love my patrimony

CONTENTS

Chapter Two:
The Puerto Rican *Pensadores* 47

Chapter Three:
Pan-American Currents 64

Chapter Four:
Solitary Efforts toward a Hispano Church 76

PART II
GENESIS OF THE HISPANO CHURCH   97

Chapter Five:
Liturgical Battlefronts   100

Chapter Six:
Militancy   117

PART III
THE FORGE OF UNITY   175

PREFACE

This book is not a sociological treatise, nor does it pretend to be a much needed history of the Hispanos in the United States. It is an anthology of writings, documents, speeches, poetry, prayers, and hymns, along with information about important personalities and dates within a reality I have termed "the Hispano church." The intention was to allow people to speak for themselves and to offer to the patient reader a profile of the powerful forces summoning the Latin American people of the United States to a new articulation of their Catholicism. Any vibrance and power to be found in this collection, therefore, comes from the people themselves and their cause.

I wanted to show the different ways Hispanos in the United States have come to affirm both their faith and their cultural identity. This is something relatively new in the Catholic church and, from my point of view, it is theology. In these readings, Hispanos describe the catechetical, liturgical, and pastoral ways in which one can be Catholic and Hispano at the same time. Unfortunately, not every leader is given the attention and the space he or she deserves. Non-Hispano people have not been given much space, nor have Hispano Protestants. Moreover, I have left out many lay persons who, despite their silence, have accomplished more than some of the spokespersons included here.

However, in the assemblage of an anthology, there must be considerable selectivity exercised, and this implies interpretation. I trust that I have been fair. In the three-year process of gathering materials, I became aware of the rich pluralism within the Latin American community of the United States. No doubt I reflect the lights that illumine my own way, and it is not at all unlikely that this book will engender some reservations toward the value I implicitly place on certain events, concepts, and personalities. But with the intention of slighting no one, let me say that the modest scope of this book is meant to create curiosity for more information and to give a framework in which to understand a historical development in the Catholic church of the United States.

A historical overview opens the book. Following that, the book is divided into four sections, each of which is prefaced with an essay supplying sociological, anthropological, historical, and theological background. At least some of the materials included in each section are offered to an English-speaking audience for the first time. The bibliography at the end of the book provides a list of resources for more intensive study of the themes and topics touched upon.

I want to thank Pablo Sedillo of the Spanish-speaking Secretariat of the United States Catholic Conference (USCC) for his aid in supplying documents and other resources. In great part, the events described in this book have been his concern through the years of his administration. Archbishop Roberto Sánchez and Bishops Raimundo Peña, Juan Arzube, and René Gracida have helped me clarify concepts. Sister Mario Barrón, C.S.J., Fathers Mundo Rodríguez, S.J., Virgilio Elizondo, Juan Romero and, in a special way, Roberto Peña, O.M.I., have supported me in this process, particularly in questions about the Mexican American and Chicano realities. Finally, I wish to thank Ana María Díaz Ramírez, who with acumen and patience reviewed my interpretations, adding her own valuable insights. Most importantly, let me thank the people whom I have cited in the book for having had the courage to speak and act as Hispanos. All of them are, in one way or another, prophets who frequently serve with minimal recognition. Indeed, the Lord himself reminds us that a prophet is "not denied honor, except in his own country" (Mt. 13:57).

PROLOGUE

A HISTORICAL OVERVIEW

One point in ecclesiology generally agreed upon since the publication of Avery Dulles's *The Models of the Church* is that our understanding of church is conditioned at different historical moments by models. The Hispano phenomenon in the Catholic church of the United States demonstrates the emergence of a particular "model" of church. Let it be said from the outset that the Hispano church is not schismatic or separatist. It is a rather large and increasingly important sector of the church in the United States which has generated a new kind of liturgy and pastoral theology by reflecting upon its cultural heritage.

The genesis of the Hispano church is complex. There is, after all, no nationality group of "Hispanos" (Greeley, 1972, pp. 28ff.). There are only Mexicans, Puerto Ricans, Cubans, Guatemalans, etc. "Hispano" (the term preferred in this book) or "Hispanic," like "Spanish-speaking," is an adjective describing a cultural or linguistic common denominator. At times, even the Hispanos themselves reject this term. For instance, in some parts of New Mexico "Hispano" refers to the descendants of European-Spanish stock who never lived in modern-day Mexico. They are the original Spanish-speaking New Mexicans, who intermarried neither with the native Indians nor with the invading Anglos—the term applied to non-Hispanos from the United States (Acuña, 1972, pp. 56ff.). Naturally enough the other groups of Spanish-speaking in New Mexico feel that the term "Hispano" excludes them.

Another example of regional interpretation of terminology can be found with "Latino." The Midwest and most of the Southwest and California are accustomed to using this term with reference to the Spanish-speaking. Yet in the Northeast, "Latino" includes Italians, Portuguese, French, and even Romanian peoples. And so, while New Yorkers might refer to themselves in Spanish as *latinos,* they would not do so in English for fear of being confused with all Romance-language groups. The list of such words is long: "Spanish-surnamed," "Latin American," "South American," etc.

As a general rule, "Hispano" or "Hispanic" and sometimes "Hispanic American" have entered into the general vocabulary of the Catholic church as terms that refer to all those peoples who live in the United States who were themselves born in a country where Spanish is the national language or whose forebears came from these places.

It is much harder, however, to define "Mexican," "Mexican American," and "Chicano." These terms carry different connotations and the choice of one or

1

another discloses something of a personal option. Juan Hurtado (1975, pp. 15-16), who can be considered an expert, defines the terms as follows:

> *Mexican American.* Refers to persons living in the United States who are themselves of Mexican origin or whose parents or more remote ancestors came to the United States from Mexico or whose antecedents resided in those parts of the Southwestern United States which were once part of the Mexican nation.
>
> *Mexican.* Citizen of Mexico residing in Mexico or resident in the United States, who has not acquired United States citizenship and has chosen to remain a Mexican citizen.
>
> *Chicano.* A popularly used term by Mexican Americans who are conscious of being part of a people who are proud of their history and of ethnic and racial identity.
>
> The origin of the term "Chicano" is uncertain. Its meaning and significance remain to be clearly defined and understood by the majority of the Spanish-speaking people. One explanation is that Mexican Indians pronounced "Mexicano" as "Meh-chee-cano" and in time it was shortened and pronounced "Chicano." For many persons the word "Chicano" conveys a pejorative meaning. Some people believe that Chicano depicts the lower socio-economic class of Mexicans or Mexican Americans. Many Mexican Americans see no difference between *Chicano* and *Mexican American.*

I have preferred to use the term "Mexican American" myself. I have employed the term "Chicano" only where it is to be distinguished from "Mexican American" because of ideological meaning. Of course, the authors in this anthology use the words as they wish. I leave it to the reader to distinguish how much importance can be placed on the nuances of each author.

Of similar importance is the definition of the term "Puerto Rican." As traced in the selections of Chap. Twelve, persons born in the United States of Puerto Rican ancestry are sometimes called "Neorican" or "Niurican" in order to distinguish them from persons born on the island. These terms are used less and less today, nor has the hyphenated "Puerto Rican-American" ever found much acceptance. The 1970 census counted as Puerto Rican only those born on the island or their children. However, if the term "Puerto Rican" were to be used in the same way as "Mexican American," Puerto Ricans would not be limited to first or second generation alone.

For this anthology, the definition of Puerto Rican includes both those on the island and those on the mainland. Since Puerto Rico is a territory of the United States, individual Puerto Rican bishops have always been legal members of the National Council of Catholic Bishops (NCCB, *Directory,* 1976, p. 12). However, after the reforms of Vatican Council II, the Puerto Rican bishops decided to join the Latin American Episcopal Conference (CELAM) basically for questions of liturgical legislation. This jurisdictional compromise in terms of church government does not alter the ties of Puerto Rico to the United States. Puerto Ricans in New York City generally know more about politics in Puerto Rico or the lastest hit song there than Mexican Americans know about such things in Mexico. Moreover, there are many more Puerto Ricans today who travel back and forth between Puerto Rico and Manhattan than Mexican Americans who travel between Texas and New Mexico or California. And because Puerto Ricans on the Caribbean island have been citizens of the United States since 1917, migration to the United States mainland carries none of the immigration restrictions that Mexicans encounter upon crossing the border. In short, it is necessary to recognize that until Puerto Rico is an independent country like Mexico, Puerto Ricans on the island are part of the Hispano population of the United States.

The question of Puerto Rico is important for the statement of Hispano presence in the United States. First, by adding the 3 million Puerto Ricans on the island to the 12 million Hispanos of the 1970 census, United States Hispanos grow to 15 million. Second, Puerto Ricans become numerically more important. If we leave Puerto Rico out of the definition of Hispano, Mexican Americans with 6.7 million persons represent 56 percent of the Hispano population, while 1.7 million Puerto Ricans in the continental United States are only 14 percent of this total. By counting Puerto Ricans on the island, however, the Mexican American percentage drops to 45 percent and the Puerto Rican percentage rises to 32 percent of the Hispano population. If the figure of 2 million Mexican nationals in the United States is given credibility, then the Mexican Americans with citizenship amount to 4.7 million persons, the same number as Puerto Ricans.

Third, considering Puerto Rico as a part of the Hispano reality of the United States means that the first Hispano bishop was a Puerto Rican, Luis Aponte Martínez, ordained in 1960 as auxiliary in Ponce. He is also the first ordinary (1963), first archbishop (1964), and first cardinal (1973) of the United States Hispano church.

Fourth, the possibility of Puerto Rican independence gives the Hispano church an international importance which ought not be trivialized by describing it as the fruit of ethnic politics. Hispano identity includes the legitimate desire for Puerto Rican nationhood, so that the role of the Hispano church is not limited to fostering integration into United States society. Rather, the church concentrates on identity as a moral and personal quality that passes judgment on politics and society. When Puerto Rico is included in the definition of the Hispano church, so too is the aspiration to carry Hispano identity to its ultimate expression: separation from the United States of America and establishment of a separate Latin American nation. Those who would deny the Hispano church this responsibility do not properly understand that theology seeks to define the kingdom of God even if that implies criticism of political and social systems.

The Hispano church, then, is not to be defined territorially or linguistically. Nor is it some modern-day version of a "national parish" or even a "national diocese." The Hispano church is a mode of thinking about oneself, the Catholic faith, and the church that emphasizes historical and cultural expression of religion that are common to Hispanos. Their tradition-transmitted religion has become more important to them than the model of church that comes from non-Hispano experience. This emphasis, it should be noted, is generally not a rejection of clerical and hierarchical authority, but rather, a delimitation of its competence.

The differences of tradition and culture have been present for centuries.

What has happened in the past ten years is that these differences have been described as elements which define the role of the church. The struggle to articulate these differences for the sake of Hispanos and then to sensitize the rest of the United States Catholics to this reality has been part of the process of "liberation" that has enlisted the energies of many Hispano Catholics. In this struggle, the Mexican Americans have assumed the leadership, borne the brunt of the battle, and earned the laurels of victory. And so, despite any chronological sequence of events, Bishop Patricio Flores is the first Hispano bishop in the sense that he was the first to articulate what has become the Hispano model of church (see pp. 187–95). It is to Bishop Flores's credit that today his senior in date of ordination, Luis Aponte Martínez, cardinal archbishop of San Juan, Puerto Rico, is also involved in the Hispano church. Likewise, the active participation of Antulio Parrilla Bonilla, the Puerto Rican auxiliary bishop, in the process of the Hispano church, enlarges rather than diminishes the importance of Bishop Flores.

The conceptual model of the Hispano church is uniquely dependent upon Puerto Ricans and Mexican Americans. It is not that the other 3.5 million Hispanos are any less a part of the Hispano reality than the 11.5 million Puerto Ricans and Mexican Americans. It is just that they have not contributed to the forgoing of the conceptual models of the Hispano church to the degree that the two largest groups have. Nor is it coincidental that Puerto Ricans and Mexican Americans are born as citizens of the United States, while most other Hispanos are not. Citizenship is related to the participation in church as well as civil society.

It is unnecessary here to demythologize the Mexican-American and Spanish-American wars with the details that are available to the serious student. Both wars gave the United States extended territories that fulfilled internal economic needs. These territories were populated by people who had not been hostile to the United States, who were Spanish-speaking, Catholic, and lived in stratified agricultural semifeudal societies. Both had few native clergy, both underwent Protestantization efforts backed by the United States government, and both gradually came to realize a separate identity in the face of discrimination and the claims of a new Latin American consciousness. Both peoples are counted as "minority groups" and have taken increasingly active participation in the civil rights movement of the past decade.

While other Hispano nationalities have left behind their homelands to enter the United States, for Puerto Ricans and Mexican Americans it was the United States that entered their homelands. Thus most Puerto Ricans and Mexican Americans have never had to make a conscious decision to leave their nationality behind in order to become United States citizens.

Since they have been legally entitled to the rights and prerogatives of citizenship and nonetheless have suffered from discrimination and even repression, Puerto Ricans and Mexican Americans are more likely to be militant than immigrant nationalities from Latin America. The latter, while often sharing in the consciousness of Puerto Ricans and Mexican Americans, do not enjoy the protection of the United States Constitution. Frequently these Hispanos find upon entry into the United States that immigration and residency laws blunt their activism.

The Cuban exile community seldom identifies its social and political interests at a national level with those of Puerto Ricans and Mexican Americans. Recently it has become apparent that there is a drift within the Cuban community toward more solidarity with other Hispanos, particularly on questions of bilingual education. But this is a gradual transition and within the Catholic church has not yet found major spokespersons. And so, for better or for worse, the other Hispano groups within the United States will have to borrow and perhaps improve upon the model of church that is being created by the Puerto Ricans and the Mexican Americans.

Virgilio Elizondo (b. 1936) is a native son and priest of the Archdiocese of San Antonio, Texas. After his ordination in 1963, his academic preparation included graduate study abroad, with specialization in catechetics at the East Asian Pastoral Institute until 1969. He served the Latin American bishops at the historic pastoral conference at Medellín, Colombia. He was a logical choice to direct the Mexican American Cultural Center (MACC), a training and pastoral center which he helped to found in 1972. Located on the seminary grounds in San Antonio, MACC has attracted worldwide attention for its creative programs of theological and pastoral education. In 1978 Virgilio Elizondo completed his doctoral studies at the Institute Catholique in Paris.

The following selection from a paper by Elizondo deals with the Mexican American struggle against cultural oppression and the similarity of this experience to the Exodus tradition. In these efforts to achieve cultural independence, Elizondo sees the Mexican American contribution to a transformation of the church in the United States.

1. The Mexican American as Seen from Within

Virgilio P. Elizondo

From "A Theological Interpretation of the Mexican American Experience," a paper presented at an ecumenical symposium held at the Perkins School of Theology, Southern Methodist University, Dallas, Texas, March 28-31, 1973. Used by permission.

It is a sad phenomenon that until very recently and even to the present moment, the Mexican Americans have been denied the right of existence as a unique human group which is emerging and which exists among other groups in the United States. But the Mexican Americans today are awakening and emerging as a new people, a people who are proud of their origins and who are proud of their present condition. We are a people who are realizing that, even though we have been an oppressed people, as the people of God were led out of the bonds of slavery in Egypt to become a people in the process of liberation on the road to the promised land, we too are realizing ourselves to be in the process of liberation. We are not leaving the United States but we are leaving the state of oppression. We will no longer tolerate being laughed at by the Mexican or by the North American. We will no longer feel inferior. We realize that we are the bearers of a promise, a promise to form a new people, a people which truly unites in its very blood the greatness of two cultural parents—the Latin American with its combination of Indian and Latin European Catholicism, and the North American with its background of northern Europe transplanted to a new land called America with its strong Protestant tradition of work and discipline. We see the Mexican Americans as a people who form a bridge, who combine in themselves the best of these two cultural groups and, sad to say, often the worst.

Recognizing our uniqueness, there is a growing determination to preserve purity, to develop and share with our fellow citizens the substance of our culture and our language. It is true that for practical reasons we accept certain forms of acculturation and the language of this country, but at the same time we retain the essence of that which constitutes us as a bilingual and bicultural minority. We are not ashamed of what we are. On the contrary, we are proud of the heritage we have received from our parents and ancestors. We are proud to be descendants of our great Indian and European forebears. We are proud of the fact that we are truly a "new people," and as such, we shall serve as a prophetic people to our fellow North American citizens who for the most part are transplanted Europeans and not truly a new people in the New World, as indeed is the mestizo.

This growing consciousness is helping us to discover our self-identity. Rather than forgetting the past, there is a growing desire among us to preserve and share with the rest of America the best of our cultural traditions and language. This phenomenon is of the utmost importance when we consider the integration of our people and our active participation in the social, religious, economic, and political structures of our country.

We do not think of liberation as taking place overnight, in a year, or even within the lifetime of those of us who are young, healthy, and alive today. The liberation of the people of Israel included not only the exit from Egypt, but the forty years of struggle and sacrifice in the desert. Even the arrival in the Promised Land was but the beginning of a long process of ups and downs before the final phase of liberation was initiated by Jesus of Nazareth. So we feel that we are beginning our exit from the Egypt of today and expect to persevere in the long process.

Our Exodus is from the state of personal, social, economic, educational, religious, and political oppression. It will take the *movimiento* years of struggle, of strife, of sacrifice, of holy impatience, of encouragement, of doubt, of security, of commitment, of total dedication. A great faith, hope, and love will be necessary for us to continue to move forward unto the day when we can truly share our greatness and bring others into the ranks of the new people which today is emerging through the Mexican American group. In liberating themselves, Mexican Americans do not want simply to exchange places with the oppressing group, for that would mean accepting a new kind of oppression: the oppression of the competitive-consumer mentality of the impersonal business world, which makes up a great part of our society.

The following excerpt from an article on the Spanish-speaking published by the Bicentennial Committee (for the American Bicentennial) of the National Conference of Catholic Bishops (NCCB) was prepared for a general United States audience by Mexican American Virgilio Elizondo and Puerto Rican Antonio M. Stevens Arroyo.

2. The Spanish-speaking in the United States

Antonio M. Stevens Arroyo and Virgilio P. Elizondo

From "Liberty and Justice for All: A Discussion Guide" (Washington, D.C.: NCCB Committee for the Bicentennial, 1975), pp. 37-41. Used by permission.

Explaining the situation of Hispanics in the United States is a double task. One must explain the principles of interpretation, as well as little-known facts. As an example of the problematic, consider these questions: Why do people exclude Latin Americans when they talk of "Americans"? Why are Hispanics considered a "problem" for the country and the church, when their presence in this country preceded the arrival of the *Mayflower* at Plymouth Rock? Why have the Spanish-speaking been so invisible to the American church when they were the first Catholics here, practicing the faith for more than 150 years before the Constitution allowed freedom of religion? The answers to these questions will bring us closer to an understanding of how "liberty and justice for all" applies to the Spanish-speaking in the United States.

SOCIOLOGICAL BACKGROUND

U.S. Hispanics number approximately 12 million. The United States has the fifth largest Spanish-speaking population in the world. The number of Hispanic Catholics is estimated at more than 10 million, second only to Italians among ethnic groups. The largest group of Spanish-speaking Catholics, the Mexican Americans, are concentrated in the Southwest and on the West Coast; approximately 42 percent of all Hispanics are in this area. The Mexican, or Chicano, population reaches into Detroit and Chicago where it meets the second largest group of Hispanics in the United States, the Puerto Ricans. The Mexican population grows thinner as one moves eastward from Chicago, and the Boricuas, as they call themselves, grow more numerous. Puerto Ricans are the majority of the Spanish-speaking in the crescent stretching from Boston to Camden, New Jersey, with the largest concentration at the geographical center, New York City.

Yet alongside the Puerto Ricans is an almost equal number of Latin Americans from the continent, Central America, and the Caribbean islands of Cuba and Santo Domingo. Florida's Cuban population in Miami is well known, and at harvest time migrant farm workers from Mexico, the Southwest, and Puerto Rico swell the Hispanic population in the Southeast.

CULTURAL DISCRIMINATION

The Hispanics in the United States have been given a demeaning stereotype. History books downgrade the quality of the Spanish colonization; cartoons show a fat, mustachioed Mexican, sombrero pulled down over his eyes, sleeping in the middle of the day. Hispanics are perceived as inferior because they live outside the basic ethos of the North American republic. The tale has been so convincing that some Spanish-speaking have believed it themselves and have rejected their deepest traditions, including the Catholic faith, to become "red-blooded" Americans.

Americans of Latin ancestry have a unique culture and tradition not shared with Americans of northern European ancestry. Their Latin, Catholic heritage challenges the republic and the church in the United States today. While making due allowance for possible oversimplification, the comparison and contrast of values and attitudes in the North American Protestant and Latin American Catholic traditions as shown on page 9 is worth pondering.

Of course, not every North American or Latin American fits neatly into these categories, but this outline does represent many contrasting values which undeniably characterize the *modus vivendi* of both cultures.

North America	*Latin America*
Society based on individual rights. Identification by occupation.	Family the basic unity of society. Identification by family names (both mother and father); place of origin important.
Accumulation of wealth is power over events.	Wisdom, the articulation of truth, insures fame.
The non-productive are burdens to society.	The aged are sages; they deserve title "don" (sir).
Trading-commerce is the way to success. Horatio Alger succeeds by "pluck," aggressiveness.	Production from the land is the ideal occupation. Success depends upon "harmony" with people and nature.
Competition is the source of growth and expansion.	Harmony depends upon generous contribution to the common good, each in his or her own order.
Egalitarian society.	Hierarchical or corporate state.
Separation of church and state: life is divided between sacred and profane.	A holistic concept of society and obligation to fellow persons.
Work and activity is an end in itself; wealth manifests God's grace: art, self-expression are vain and presumptive.	Work is a necessary quality of human existence, a punishment for sin; leisure, however, is freedom to be spiritual and contemplative.
Emotions are to be suppressed; enjoyment in this life is frivolity and sinful.	Feeling bestows dignity; sensitivity to life dictates celebrations of joy and sorrow.

The bicentennial of this country, a time of reflection, provides an opportunity for a courageous self-examination of our attitudes and values—especially those attitudes and values which so negatively affect the oppressed people of our country, which certainly includes the Spanish-speaking themselves. . . .

MIGRATION

Migration is today a universal phenomenon. There are Pakistanis in Britain, Turks in Holland, Spaniards in Germany, Italians in Denmark. The United States has glorified the experience of immigration, but has not appreciated the importance of migration. While immigrants come to a new land to cut ties with their past, to learn a new language and to begin over again, migrants move from one country to another looking for some slight advantage to make life better in their true homeland. (The pastoral letter of Pope Paul VI, *Pastoralis migratorum*, of August 15, 1969, concerns the welfare of migrants.)

In the United States, migration caused by economic problems has created an "urban crisis." Migration of large numbers of families from the farms to the cities, the result of increased agricultural mechanization, is the brutal national application of the law of supply and demand. As long as there are more workers than jobs, workers will be forced to labor for low wages. Today's unions defend and protect their own and citizens have recourse to the ballot to choose legislators. But business interests often import workers who cannot join unions or vote; they do this to avoid paying a just wage.

The pope is keenly aware of the effects of neglect of the working class which devastated the church in Europe in the nineteenth century. The attention of the church to the rights of the poor and neglected is crucial in cities like Los Angeles and New York, where the majority of Catholics are or soon will be Hispanic migrants. But first the church must change patterns of thought established for and controlled by people of European ancestry. Moreover, the flow of migration into the United States is affected by policies of economic imperialism abroad. The oil industry, for instance, is anxious to exploit the island of Puerto Rico for refineries which will improve the quality of life in the United States at the expense of the environment of that tropical island.

In other Latin American countries the same process is underway. Thus any true statement on the situation of Spanish-speaking migrants in this country must include an awareness of international dimensions. It makes no sense in one breath to show anger at Latin Americans who supposedly come here to "take jobs away from Americans" or to "collect welfare," and in the next to complain of nationalization of United States industries in Latin America. The slogan "America: love it or leave it" is not very different from "Yankee, go home" and is every bit as ugly.

CUBAN POLITICAL MIGRATION

The migration of the Cuban exiles is a complicated case. Few if any of the earliest refugees from Cuba in 1958–60 came to these shores with the idea of staying. Miami, Tampa, and New York City had long been incubators for new revolts and triumphant returns to Cuba. However, it is now fifteen years after the Cuban revolution. It is presently a time of détente with Russia and China, and United States foreign policy regarding Cuba appears on the verge of change. Indeed, it is safe to say that the United States appears ready to end the current trade embargo against Cuba and recognize the Castro government.

Surely such a reversal of policy will pose many grave questions of justice.

THE "ILLEGAL" IMMIGRANTS

The question of migration is particularly important to Mexican Americans, since the majority of "illegals" in this country are Hispanic, and the majority of these, approximately 90 percent, are Mexicans. However, this problem also touches the lives of almost every non-Puerto Rican Hispanic in New York City, particularly the Dominicans. As Christians, we must ask the question: "Who owns the earth and its goods?" If we answer, "Its inhabitants," what right does the United States have to the land of Texas and California, since the original inhabitants were the same Mexicans and Indians who now come across the Rio Grande? Who really owns United States business holdings in the Romana province of the Dominican Republic? If we answer, "All persons, regardless of national origin," we strike at the basis for this nation.

The consistent doctrine of the church, from the time of the Middle Ages through the nineteenth century to the present, is indeed revolutionary, for it asks people to share with one another. All men and women belong to one human family, and the earth is for all. The evangelical declaration that "in Christ there is neither Jew nor Greek, free man nor slave, male nor female" is not just a pious platitude. As long as 6 percent of the world's population controls 50 percent of the world's wealth, migration remains a right and even a necessity.

What is true internationally is also true at home. The drama of the United Farm Workers, and subsequent efforts to unionize farm workers, is part of the struggle for a just distribution of wealth.

LATIN AMERICANS ARE AMERICANS

Latin Americans are examples to the rest of the American people. They know the meaning of revolution, not in a narrowly individualistic sense, but as a reflection of the scholastic-based principles of society and justice. Their integrated culture and their ancestry have created what one Mexican philosopher has called "the cosmic race."

LATIN AMERICANS ARE NOT IMMIGRANTS

Mexicans and Puerto Ricans in the United States are here because of the territorial expansion of past generations of North Americans. Their lands have been taken from them and annexed to the United States, and their citizens have been guaranteed rights under treaties with our government; these treaties have often been broken or ignored, and the people have been forced to assimilate "American ways" to exist. Today they have the right to continue to speak their own language and to live according to their culture. Other American Catholics must assist them in obtaining bilingual education programs and more use of Spanish, particularly in the church, including catechetical materials in Spanish and liturgical celebrations that reflect the culture of the Spanish-speaking.

LATIN AMERICANS ARE CATHOLICS WITH A NEW CATHOLICISM

In Latin America the clergy have never been as numerous as in Europe because the church did not foster native priests. Political considerations restricted the development of a native clergy with influence. The role of the criollo priest in the revolutionary movements against Spain was obviously in the minds of the invaders of New Mexico and Puerto Rico when English-speaking bishops and seminary staff were imported.

Also, the Indian and African roots of the Latin people give a different rhythm to their religious practices. The Cursillo movement has been the accepted form of Hispanic Catholic Pentecostalism with roots that go back centuries before the charismatic movement.

Adherence to Catholic ritual as a means of national identity, characteristic of the Irish and the Polish, is not a Hispanic experience. Latin American Catholicism is founded upon identity with *el pueblo*, a phrase meaning both the people and the town.

Latin American Catholics have a rich theological contribution to give to the church in the maturing discussion of the theology of liberation. While European and North American theologians reexamined fundamental truths of revelation, Latin American theologians of this decade have been reflecting on the lived experience of the Christian community. Similarly, American Hispanics have been able to plan a National Pastoral Encounter with only the concept of *La Raza* (the common Hispanic heritage) to bind them together. The Encounter offered far-reaching conclusions and pastoral recommendations for the North American church. In this and in later regional encounters the social, economic, liturgical, and catechetical dimensions of life were reflected on by laity, religious, and clergy. It is this experience of family community which the Spanish-speaking share with all their brothers and sisters in the United States during the bicentennial. This community is one people, prophetic and priestly, royal and Christian in the Spirit of God.

The following excerpt is from a talk delivered by Antonio M. Stevens Arroyo to the New York Archdiocesan Assembly held on April 8, 1972. The unity of the Caribbean, or Antillean, people from the islands of Puerto Rico, Española, and Cuba was the theme of the talk. The author believes that Puerto Ricans, being the largest and most established of this Antillean population in New York, will lead the way in asserting new challenges to the church of the United States in the coming generation.

As the author suggests, the Puerto Rican and Cuban flags are identical, except that the colors are inverted so that where the Cuban flag has blue, the Puerto Rican flag has red, and vice versa. It should also be noted that the term "Neorican" was popular at the time this address was given.

3. Caribbean Unity

Antonio M. Stevens Arroyo

From Address to the New York Archdiocesan Assembly, Mount St. Vincent's College, New York City, April 8, 1972.

It is a coincidence that this historic meeting of all the elements of Hispano leadership of the church of the Archdiocese of New York is assembled here on April 8. Yet this coincidence carries with it a profoundly symbolic meaning to our deliberations today. On this same date in the year 1827, in the town of Cabo Rojo, Puerto Rico, the illustrious patriot Ramón Emeterio Betances was born (d. 1898). In his lifetime of service his efforts touched all the people of the Antilles—the Cubans, the Puerto Ricans, and the Dominicans—the same groups that have come together for this meeting. Betances rooted his life in the hope of achieving the Antillean Federation. He strove to bring together the Spanish-speaking—and indeed all people—of the Caribbean islands into one great federation. He stressed the common heritage, background, and history in order to create greater unity among our forebears. But he never minimized the differences and he urged the federation as the crowning expression of unity in diversity. He was a member, right here in New York City, of the famous Cuban-Puerto Rican Revolutionary Committee, which celebrated its meetings on 14th Street in Manhattan. This unity explains the similarity between the flags of these two countries. . . .

Here in New York, as we gather to consider our reality as the Hispano church, we ought to reflect on our common past in order to appreciate how God is calling upon us "exiles" to achieve his plan of unity for the world, joined together in Christ. As we work toward this, let us share some of the insight of Betances that destiny has bound our futures together and that, far from separating according to our differences, we must work together to realize spiritually what always remained in politics nothing more than a dream of Betances's. . . .

The young generation of Puerto Ricans, sometimes called the "Neorican" generation, is in great visibility in New York City today. More ambitious than their parents, attuned to the vibrations of the great city, the young are conscious of their Puerto Rican nationality (a nationality which they claim even though they may not have been born on the island). They are not as interested in institutions as in personal values, and they have little loyalty toward non-Puerto Rican authority. They are interested in politics, in the independence of the island, and in the progress toward power in the city. They dabble in Spiritism—a folk religion for communication with the dead—because it symbolizes the potpourri of all Puerto Rican religions, and also because it suffers from very few ethical imperatives and no institutionalization.

The evangelization of these young Puerto Ricans, difficult as it may be for any traditional missionary approach, may well hold the key to the future of Christianity in New York City. What happens to these Neoricans will set the pattern for the second-generation Dominicans and Cubans. And one day these Caribbean Hispanos will form a majority in many churches, as they already do in the Catholic church of New York.

Although these nationalities—the Puerto Rican, the Dominican, and the Cuban—seem headed for a common future, one should not too hastily group them together. Indeed, in the work of Christian formation, it would be a mistake to attempt to form community one with another without first redeeming those facets of life in ourselves and in our brothers and sisters that still separate us culturally.

Published in 1967, "I Am Joaquín" was the first of a growing list of poetic and artistic expressions of the Chicano cultural renaissance. The poem has been dramatized and filmed and sums up a vital expression of militancy among Chicanos today. It is available in a convenient and attractive illustrated bilingual edition (Bantam Books).

The author, Rodolfo "Corky" González was born in Denver, Colorado, in 1928, the son of migrant workers. In his varied career he has been a packing-house worker, national AAU boxing champion and later professional boxer, a lumberjack, a farm worker, and a businessman. Currently he is director of the Crusade for Justice, a civil rights organization based in his native Denver.

Following are excerpts.

4. Yo Soy Joaquín
(I Am Joaquín)

Rodolfo González

From González, I am Joaquín (New York: Bantam Books, 1972).

Yo soy Joaquín,	I am Joaquín,
Perdido en un mundo de confu- sión,	Lost in a world of confusión,

Enganchado en el remolino de una
    sociedad gringa,
	Caught up in a whirl of a
	        gringo society,

Confundido por las reglas,	Confused by the rules,
Despreciado por las actitudes,	Scorned by attitudes,
Sofocado por manipulaciones,	Suppressed by manipulation,
Y destrozado por la sociedad mo- derna.	And destroyed by modern soci- ety.
Mis padres	My parents
perdieron la batalla económica	have lost the economic battle
Y conquistaron	and won
la lucha de supervivencia cultural.	the struggle of cultural survival.
¡Y ahora!	And now!
Yo tengo que escoger	I must choose
En medio de la paradoja del	Between the paradox of
Triunfo del espíritu,	Victory of the spirit,
a despecho del hambre física	despite physical hunger
O	Or
existir en la empuñada	to exist in the grasp
de la neurosis social americano,	of American social neurosis,

esterilización del alma
  Y un estómago repleto.

Sí,
Vine de muy lejos a ninguna parte,

desinclinadamente arrastrado por ese
  gigante, monstruoso, técnico, e
  industrial llamado
      Progreso
Y éxito angloamericano . . .
  Me miro a mí mismo.
    Observo a mis hermanos.
      Lloro lágrimas de desgracia.
        Siembro semillas de odio.
  Me retiro a la seguridad dentro
  del
Círculo de vida . . .
                MI RAZA

Yo soy Joaquín
Cabalgué con Pancho Villa,
  tosco y simpático.
Un tornado a toda fuerza,
alimentado e inspirado
  por la pasión y la lumbre
  de su gente mundana.
Soy Emiliano Zapata
    "Este terreno
     Esta tierra
        es
          NUESTRA"
Los Pueblos
  Las Montañas
    Los Arroyos
        pertenecen a los Zapatistas.
        Nuestra vida
          O las Vuestras
es el único cambio
por tierra blanda y morena y por
  maíz.
Todo lo que es nuestro regalo,
  ¡Un credo que formó una con-
      stitución

sterilization of the soul
  and a full stomach.

Yes,
I have come a long way to no-
    where,
Unwillingly dragged by that
  monstrous, technical
  industrial giant-called
      Progress
and Anglo success . . .
  I look at myself.
    I watch my brothers.
      I shed tears of sorrow.
        I sow seeds of hate.
  I withdraw to the safety within
  the
Circle of life . . .
                MY OWN PEOPLE

I am Joaquín.
I rode with Pancho Villa,
  crude and warm.
A tornado at full strength,
nourished and inspired
  by the passion and the fire
  of all his earthy people.
I am Emiliano Zapata.
    "This Land
     This Earth
        is
          OURS."
The Villages
  The Mountains
    The Streams
        belong to Zapatistas.
        Our life
          Or yours
is the only trade
for soft brown earth and maize.

All of which is our reward,
  A creed that formed a constitu-
      tion

para todos los que se atreven
a vivir libre!
"Esta tierra es nuestra . . .
Padre, Yo te la doy devuelta.
Méjico debe ser libre . . ."

Mi tierra está perdida
y robada,
Mi cultura ha sido desflorada,
Alargo
la fila a la puerta del bene-
ficencia.
y lleno las cárceles con crimen.
Estos son
pues los regalos
que esta sociedad tiene
Para hijos de Jefes
y Reyes
y Revolucionarios sangri-
entos.
Quienes
dieron a gente ajena
todas sus habilidades e ingen-
geniosidad
para adoquinar la vía con Sesos y
Sangre para
esas hordas de Extranjeros hambri-
entos
por Oro
Quienes
cambiaron nuestro idioma
y plagiaron nuestros hechos
como acciones de valor
de ellos mismos.
Desaprobaron de nuestro modo
de vivir
y tomaron lo que podían usar.
Nuestro Arte
Nuestra Literatura
Nuestra música, ignoraron
así dejaron las cosas de valor verda-
dero
y arrebataron a su misma destruc-
ción

for all who dare live free!
"This land is ours . . .
Father, I give it back to you.
Mexico must be free . . ."

My land is lost
and stolen,
My culture has been raped,
I lengthen
the line at the welfare door

and fill the jails with crime.
These then
are the rewards
this society has
For sons of Chiefs
and Kings
and bloody Revolution-
ists.
Who
gave a foreign people
all their skills and ingenuity

to pave the way with Brains and
Blood for
those hordes of Gold-starved

Strangers
Who
changed our language
and plagiarized our deeds
as feats of valor
of their own.
They frowned upon our way of
life
and took what they could use.
Our Art
Our Literature
Our music, they ignored
so they left the real things of value

and grabbed at their own destruction

con su Gula y Avaricia.
Disimularon aquella fontana purifi-
cadora de
    naturaleza y herman-
    dad
La Cual es Joaquín.
    El arte de nuestros señores
    excelentes
        Diego Rivera
        Siqueiros
        Orozco es solamente
otro acto de revolución para
    la salvación del género hu-
    mano.
    Música de mariachi, el
    corazón y el alma
    de la gente de la tierra,
    la vida de niño
    y la alegría del amor.
    Los Corridos dicen los cuen-
    tos
    de vida y muerte,
      de tradición,
    Leyendas viejas y nuevas,
    de alegría
      de pasión y pesar
    de la gente . . . que yo soy.

Yo fui parte en sangre y espíritu
    de aquel
      padre aldeano y valiente
      Hidalgo
que en el año mil ochocientos
    diez
repicó la campana de independencia
Y dio el constante:
    "El Grito de Dolores, ¡Qué
    mueran
    los Gachupines y que viva
la Virgen de Guadalupe!" . . .
Yo lo condené a él
    que era yo.
Yo lo excomulgué a él mi sangre,

by their Greed and Avarice.
They overlooked that cleansing
fountain of
    nature and brotherhood

Which is Joaquín.
    The art of our great señores

        Diego Rivera
        Siqueiros
        Orozco is but
another act of revolution for
    the Salvation of humankind.

    Mariachi music, the
    heart and soul
    of the people of the earth,
    the life of a child,
    and the happiness of love.
    The Corridos tell the tales

    of life and death,
      of tradition,
    Legends old and new,
    of joy
      of passion and sorrow
    of the people . . . who I am.

I was part in blood and spirit
    of that
      courageous village priest
      Hidalgo
in the year eighteen hundred and
    ten
who rang the bell of independence

and gave out that lasting cry:
    "El Grito de Dolores, ¡Que
    mueran
    los Gachupines y que viva
la Virgen de Guadalupe!" . . .
I sentenced him
    who was me.
I excommunicated him, my blood.

Lo desterré del púlpito para enca-
bezar
una revolución sangrienta para
él y yo . . .
        Yo lo maté.
Su cabeza,
que es mía y de todos los que
pasaron por aquí,
La puse en la pared del fuerte
para esperar la Independencia.
¡Morelos!
    ¡Matamoros!
        ¡Guerrero!
Todos Compañeros en el acto, se
pararon
ENFRENTE DE AQUELLA
        PARED DE INFAMIA
a sentir el arrancón caliente de
plomo
que mis manos hicieron.
Yo morí con ellos . . .
    Viví con ellos . . .
        Viví para ver mi patria libre.
Libre
de regla española, en
    mil ochocientos veinte y uno
        ¿Méjico esta Libre? ?

Y ahora suena la trompeta,
La música de la gente incita la
        Revolución,
Como un gigantón soñoliento len-
tamente
alza su cabeza
al sonido de
        Patulladas
        Voces clamorosas
        Tañido de Mariachi
        Explosiones ardientes de
        tequila
la aroma de chile verde y,
Ojos morenos, esperanzosos de
una
        vida mejor.

I drove him from the pulpit to lead

a bloody revolution for him and
me . . .
        I killed him.
His head,
which is mine and all of those
who have come this way,
I placed on that fortress wall
to wait for Independence.
Morelos!
    Matamoros!
        Guerrero!
All compañeros in the act,

STOOD AGAINST THAT WALL
        OF INFAMY
to feel the hot gouge of lead

which my hands made.
I died with them . . .
    I lived with them . . .
        I lived to see our country free.
Free
from Spanish rule in
    eighteen-hundred-twenty-one.
        Mexico was Free? ?

And now the trumpet sounds,
The music of the people stirs the
        Revolution,
Like a sleeping giant it slowly

rears its head
to the sound of
        Tramping feet
        Clamoring voices
        Mariachi strains
        Fiery tequila explosions

    The smell of chile verde and
Soft brown eyes of expectation
for a
        better life.

Y en todos los terrenos fértiles,
      los llanos áridos,
los pueblos montañeros,
ciudades ahumadas
      Empezamos a AVANZAR
   ¡La Raza!
¡Mejicano!
   ¡Español!
      ¡Latino!
         ¡Hispano!
         ¡Chicano!
o lo que me llame yo,
      Yo parezco lo mismo,
      Yo siento lo mismo
      Yo lloro
      y
      Canto lo mismo

Yo soy el bulto de mi gente y
Yo renuncio ser absorbido
      Yo soy Joaquín
Las desigualdades son grandes
pero mi espíritu es firme
      Mi fe impenetrable
      Mi sangre pura
Soy príncipe Azteca y Cristo Cristiano
      ¡YO PERDURARE!
      ¡YO PERDURARE!

And in all the fertile farm lands,
      the barren plains,
the mountain villages,
smoke-smeared cities
      We start to MOVE.
  La Raza!
Mejicano!
   Español!
     Latino!
       Hispano!
       Chicano!
or whatever I call myself,
      I look the same
      I feel the same
      I cry
      and
      Sing the same

I am the masses of my people and
I refuse to be absorbed.
      I am Joaquín
The odds are great
but my spirit is strong
      My faith unbreakable
      My blood is pure
I am Aztec Prince and Christian
Christ
      I SHALL ENDURE!
      I WILL ENDURE!

Right: Pancho Villa (left) and Emiliano Zapata
(courtesy Aultman Collection)

El Pachuco, from the play Zoot Suit by Luis Valdés
(courtesy Visitante Dominical)

Above: Puerto Rican Pensador José de Diego
Below: Puerto Rican Pensador Pedro Albizu Campos
(courtesy Claridad)

PART I

THE *PENSADORES*

... Ignoramos, en estos históricos reveses,
la lengua y el sentido de los pueblos ingleses.
Hablamos otra lengua, con otro pensamiento
en la onda del espíritu y en la onda del viento,
y os estamos diciendo hace tiempo en las dos,
¡que os vayáis con el diablo y nos dejéis con Dios!

... We have not grasped in these historical events
the meaning and the speech the Anglo mind invents.
We speak another language our world to extol
On the wings of the wind and in·the depths of the soul.
In both of these we have long since said with a nod
That you should go to the Devil and leave us with God!

José de Diego Martínez, from "Aleluyas: a los caballeros del Norte"
(Hallelujahs: to the Northern Cavaliers) (Puerto Rico, 1916).
Used by permission. Trans. A.M.S.A.

In the Latin American tradition, great leaders are *pensadores*. The word literally means "thinkers," but in Latin America a *pensador* is always more than just an intellectual. The best analogy within the United States experience is the example of the Founding Fathers. Benjamin Franklin, Thomas Jefferson, and Alexander Hamilton were more than just intellectuals. They were complex combinations of philosophers, statesmen, generals, diplomats, scientists, artists, bankers, businessmen, and patriots. And a Latin American *pensador* parallels the spirit of a Founding Father. Leadership depends upon both deed and theory.

With the exception of the military dictator, or *caudillo*, whose presence stands like an ugly shadow behind the *pensadores*, Latin America's presidents were expected to be "complete" men. They depended upon what political analysts today call "charisma." For those who did not have the talents for fiery

23

speechmaking, the written word of journalism was powerful enough. Very often they generated as well the image of the *macho*, a human capable of acts of heroism and bravery.

In the first decades of the twentieth century, some of the *pensadores* articulated a type of Catholicism that was uniquely Latin American. They used traditional Catholicism as a tool of resistance to European secular atheism and United States Protestantism. Although similar to the Neo-Thomists led by Jacques Maritain in Europe, the Latin American *pensadores* went beyond questions of abstract philosophy in their Neo-Catholic revival. They insisted, in a variety of ways, that the Latin American reality was created when Spanish religion merged with native Indian beliefs. The popular Catholicism of the masses rather than the slavish imitation of European and North American societies was the true basis for Latin American cultural identity. The following two chapters offer excerpts from Mexican and from Puerto Rican *pensadores*. At times, these men risked unpopularity and even death by going against the stream of political and intellectual thought. For example, in Mexico there was an armed revolt (1926–1929) called the Cristero Religious War, which defended the Catholic faith against the official anticlericalism of the Mexican government. (Graham Greene wrote his popular novel *The Power and the Glory* with this revolt as the historical background.) Moreover, the *pensadores* made a distinction between Catholicism as the cultural and religious expression of the people and the church as institution.

Church leaders with the ability to speak and act as *pensadores* were not common while Spain ruled Mexico and Puerto Rico. The famous Padre Miguel Hidalgo (1753–1811), who led the first revolt against Spain in Mexico in the year 1810, could be classified as a *pensador*. But like Padre José Morelos (1765–1815) who followed him, Hidalgo met with ecclesiastical excommunication and military execution. The tone and style of repression was changed when the Southwest and Puerto Rico became territories of the United States. This condition will be examined in Chapter Four, which describes the solitary figures who articulated the need for a Hispano church.

However, as Chapter Three will demonstrate, there were always currents of popular song and poetry that echoed the themes of the *pensadores*. These currents accompanied the waves of Hispano migration in the decades before and after World War II. The migration from Puerto Rico, Mexico, and the Southwest diffused Hispano presence throughout the United States. And since the migration increased nostalgia for the *patria*, or homeland, Spanish-language recordings and radio broadcasts multiplied wherever there were Hispano barrios. Frequently the different nationalities brushed shoulders in crowded urban centers like New York, Chicago, and Los Angeles. A cultural Pan-Americanism expressed in music was born. The Argentine tango, the Cuban rumba, the Mexican *ranchera*, and Puerto Rican bolero became common property of all Hispanos in the United States. These musical styles were frequently accompanied by lyrics that contained a powerful social message.

Hispanos in the United States were alienated from their surroundings. They used certain figures of speech in the songs and poems to demonstrate dissatisfaction with the United States way of life. They sang of coldness, they lamented the change of flora and fauna, contrasting the barren city with mountains or beach, or the workers' camp with hearth and home. The migrants expressed a desire to return to where they came from, reflecting upon discrimination and hoping to keep others from suffering the same fate. They sometimes promised a sort of revenge by a display of anger or by a strike against the employer. Most of all, the homeland was given a sense of sacredness and religious value, while the situation in the United States was seen as profane and even sinful. The simplest Mexican *campesinos*, like their Puerto Rican counterparts, philosophized with the concepts of the *pensadores* by singing these songs, which become hymns of liberation filled with faith and hope and love. These people are the most authentic of the prophets denied honor.

Don Miguel Hidalgo y Costilla
(courtesy Visitante Dominical)

CHAPTER ONE

THE MEXICAN *PENSADORES*

The cultural identity of the Mexican American is unavoidably touched by the long shadow cast by Emiliano Zapata (1879 –1919). Born into a peasant family of Anenecuilco in the state of Morelos, the young Zapata took up the cause of agrarian reform in the chaos of the first days of the Mexican Revolution in 1910. At first easily satisfied by the promises of the different elitist governments of Mexico, Zapata grew in understanding as well as reputation. Along with his contemporary, Pancho Villa, Zapata was successful in defending the ideals of the revolution for the poor peasants. In 1915, after having defeated the armies of the ruling classes, he triumphantly entered the capital, Mexico City, with Villa. But he suddenly returned to his native Morelos, leaving the complicated questions of national government to others, and contented himself with land reform among the people he knew and loved best.

The saga of Zapata is often seen through the eyes of Hollywood. In *Viva Zapata,* Marlon Brando is the horseman hero. His thick moustache means *macho.* With gunbelts across the chest, wide sombrero, and high-heeled boots, he has become the stereotyped Mexican male, the *bandido,* who never washes, takes what he wants when he wants, and always finds time for a siesta.

Beyond this unfortunate image is the reality. Erick Wolf (1969, p. 195) sees Zapata's crusade as a romantic but anachronistic form of revolution, one that is capable of seizing power but not of holding it. Another commentator described the heroic failure in this way: Zapata "did not conceive of Mexico as a future to be realized, but as a return to origins" (Paz, 1961, p. 144). Octavio Romano (*Voices,* 1973) in his marvelous essay, "The Historical and Intellectual Presence of the Mexican-Americans," says that Zapata's identity with the land was a reaffirmation of an American Indian philosophy. Likewise, the armed struggle of the peasants against professional armies demonstrated the essential need of the Mexican for historical confrontation. These two basic elements, Indian philosophy and historical confrontation, were united by the religious symbolism of Our Lady of Guadalupe, who is the patroness of Mexico. Zapata ordered his men to put the blue sash of Our Lady as bands around their sombreros in an action reminiscent of what the revolutionary Padre Miguel Hidalgo had done in 1810 against the Spaniards. Thus the revolution became a "Holy War."

Simultaneous to the efforts of Zapata in Morelos, an exiled Mexican writer, Ricardo Flores Magón (1873–1922), struggled to raise a cry of solidarity from

26

within the United States. Publishing a newspaper, *La Regeneración,* from Los Angeles and later from San Antonio, Flores Magón articulated an ideology that deepened the straightforward romanticism of Zapata (Wolf, 1969, p. 25). He advocated an anarchist socialism based on the ideas of Bakunin, Malatesta, and Kropotkin and, true to the role of the pensador, not only wrote and gave speeches, but led an invasion into Baja California. He helped form the International Workers of the World (IWW), or "Wobblies," a workers' union which shared his anarchist and anticlerical views. Repeatedly jailed for his efforts to unionize Mexican farm workers in the United States, Flores Magón died mysteriously in his cell on the eve of a pardon and repatriation as a hero to Mexico. Unlike Zapata, he never appealed to traditional Catholicism in his organizing efforts: perhaps this explains his limited success as a military and union leader. His contribution was in polemical writing.

Flores Magón has a threefold importance to Mexican American leadership. First, he expresses solidarity between the Mexicans in the United States and those in Mexico struggling against injustice. Second, he involved Mexican Americans in the labor movement, particularly with farm workers. And third, he is the ideological expression of Zapata's attachment to the earth and to the need for historical confrontation. Any articulation of Mexican values in terms of the common people, the workers of the land, will echo the words of Flores Magón the moment it evokes the image of Zapata.

In each of the three selections that immediately follow, Zapata and Flores Magón demonstrate a desire to defend the common people against the tyranny of the government which hypocritically makes unjust laws in the name of the common good. This disregard of legal authority when it conflicts with the needs of the people is a facet of the historical confrontation that characterizes the Mexican national identity.

The "Open Letter to Carranza" was the declaration Zapata made in 1919 from the state of Morelos upon his reentry into national Mexican politics. Zapata intended to lead his men in armed combat against President Venustiano Carranza, who had taken advantage of Zapata's military prowess to eliminate opposition and take power himself. Less than a month after writing this letter, on April 10, 1919, at Chinameca, Zapata was betrayed and murdered in a trap set for him by a Carranza ally.

5. An Open Letter to Carranza, March 17, 1919

Emiliano Zapata

From James W. Wilkie and Albert L. Michaels, eds., Revolution in Mexico: Years of Upheaval, 1910–1940 *(New York: Alfred A. Knopf, 1969), pp. 116-120. Used by permission.*

I am not addressing the President of the Republic, whom I do not know, nor the politician, whom I distrust. I speak to the Mexican, to the man of feelings and reason, whom I find impossible to conceive as a man not capable of being stirred sometime (even for an instant) by the anguish of mothers, the suffering of orphans, the anxieties and desires of the nation.

I shall say bitter truths; but I shall not express to you anything that is not true, just, and honestly said.

From the moment that the idea of making revolution, first against Madero and then against Huerta, germinated in your brain . . . the first thing you thought of was to further yourself, and for that purpose you set yourself to use the Revolution for your own improvement and that of a small group of friends or opportunists who helped you to rise and who are ready to help you to enjoy the booty: wealth, honor, business, banquets, sumptuous parties, bacchanals of pleasures, satiating orgies of ambition, power, and blood.

It never occurred to you that the Revolution should be beneficial to the great masses, to that immense legion of oppressed whom you attempted to sway with your speeches. . . .

Nevertheless, in order to triumph you had to proclaim great ideals and principles and to announce reforms.

But in order to prevent popular commotion (a dangerous, double-edged weapon) from turning against him who used it and in order to restrain the semifree people, . . . a tyranny was created to which the novel name of "revolutionary dictatorship" was given. . . .

In order to win the vindicating goals of the Revolution, a dictator was necessary—it was then said. Autocratic proceedings were inevitable in order to impose new principles on an obstinate society.

In other words, the formula for the so-called Constitutionalist policy was this: "To establish liberty one must use despotism."

It was on these sophisms that your authority, absolutism and omnipotence were founded. . . .

Nobody believes in you or your ability to pacify anymore, nor in your greatness as a politician or governor.

It is time for you to retire, it is time to leave your post to more honorable and honest men. It would be a crime to prolong the situation of undeniable moral, economic, and political bankruptcy.

Your remaining in power is an obstacle to union and reconstruction.

---

6. The Outlaws

Ricardo Flores Magón

From Adolfo Sánchez Mascuñan, ed., La revolución mexicana *(Mexico City: Editorial Grijalbo, 1970), pp. 15-17. Used by permission. Trans. A.M.S.A.*

The true revolutionary is an outlaw par excellence. The man who adjusts his actions according to the law can be, after all, only a good domesticated animal. But he cannot be a revolutionary.

The law preserves, the revolution renews. If it is necessary to renew, then it is necessary to begin by breaking the law. To claim that the revolution can be carried out within the law is crazy; it is nonsense. The law is a yoke, and whoever wants to free himself from the yoke has to break it. Whoever preaches to the workers that we can achieve the emancipation of the proletariat within the law is an impostor because the law prohibits our taking from the hands of the rich the wealth they have stolen from us. The expropriation of wealth for the benefit of all is the condition without which it is impossible to achieve human emancipation.

The law is a brake, and it is impossible to arrive at freedom by using brakes. The law castrates and the castrated cannot aspire to be men. The freedom achieved by the human race is the work of all the outlaws of history who took the law into their own hands and broke it into pieces. The tyrant dies by blows, not by articles of law. Expropriation is achieved by trampling upon the law, not by carrying it on the shoulders.

This is why revolutionaries like ourselves have to be outlaws. We have to leave the road well-marked by conventionality and open new ways in the furrows of old flesh made by the whippings we have suffered.

We carry the torch of the revolution in one hand, the program of the

Liberal Party announcing war in the other. We are not moaning messengers of peace: we are revolutionaries. Our electoral ballots are going to be the bullets fired by our guns. From now on, the pickaxes of the mercenaries of Caesar will not find the passive chests of citizens who go about their civic functions, but rather the bayonets of the rebellious ready to return blow for blow. It would be insane to respond by law to those who do not respect the law: it would be absurd to open up a lawbook to defend ourselves from the aggression of a knife. . . . They want to defeat us by bullets? Let us defeat them by bullets too!

Now, to work! Let us separate the cowards: we don't want them. The revolution will enlist only the brave. Here we are, as always, in our combat positions. Martyrdom has made us stronger and more resolute. We are ready for greater sacrifices. We say to the Mexican people that the day of their liberation is drawing near. There is a splendid dawn of a new day; we hear the rumblings of the salvific storm soon to be unleashed. The revolutionary spirit seethes. The whole fatherland is a volcano about to spew angry fire from its belly.

"No more peace!" is the cry of the brave; it is better to die than to live in infamous "peace." The long hair of future heroes waves in the wind at the first breezes of the approaching tragedy. A bitter, strong, and healthy breath of war invigorates an effeminate world. The apostle announces how and when the catastrophe will begin. Rifles are impatient to abandon their holsters and burn brightly in the sun of battle. Mexicans, to war!

7. *I Will Not Be a Slave*

Ricardo Flores Magón

From a speech delivered on June 1, 1912. Reprinted in Adolfo Sánchez Mascuñan, ed., La revolución mexicana *(Mexico City: Editorial Grijalbo, 1970), pp. 107-111. Used by permission. Trans. A.M.S.A.*

This is social revolution. It is not made from the top down, but from the bottom up. It has to run its course without leaders and in spite of leaders. It is the revolution of the disinherited, who raise their heads at the banquet of the surfeited, demanding their right to live.

It is not the vulgar turnabout that ends with the dethronement of one bandit and the rise to power of another. It is, rather, a battle of life and death between two social classes, between the poor and the rich, the starving and the satisfied, the landless and the landowners. Its end will surely be the destruction of the authoritarian capitalist system by the formidable effort of the brave who give their lives under the red banner of Land and Freedom.

This sublime struggle, this holy war, whose goal is to free the Mexican people from the capitalist yoke, has powerful enemies. Disregarding any risk and with all kinds of means at their disposal, they attempt to put obstacles before its development. Freedom and the common good—just aspirations for Mexican slaves—are bothersome for the sharks and vultures of Capital and Authority. What is good for the oppressed is bad for the oppressor. The interests of the lamb are diametrically opposed to the interests of the wolf. The welfare and the freedom of working-class Mexicans signify the downfall and death of exploitation and tyranny. So when Mexicans lay strong hands upon the law to shatter it into pieces and when they snatch the land and machinery of production from the hands of the rich, cries of terror arise from the bourgeois sector and they seek to drown in blood the generous efforts of a people who wish to free themselves.

Mexico has been prisoner of the rapacity of adventurers from all countries who have invested in this rich and beautiful land, not to benefit the Mexican proletariat, as has been falsely asserted all along by the government, but rather to carry out the most criminal exploitation the earth has ever seen. Mexicans have seen their lands, their forests, their mines, everything, go from their hands into the hands of foreigners who were assisted by our government. Now the people will bring justice by their own hands, having despaired of finding it elsewhere. Now the people have understood that it is by force and by their own hands that they must recover everything that the bourgeoisie of Mexico and of every country have taken from them. Now they have found the solution to the problem of hunger. Now the horizon of their future is clear and they dream of days of good fortune, of abundance, and of freedom. And so now the international bourgeoisie and the governments of all those countries pressure the government of the United States to intervene in our internal affairs, under the pretext of guaranteeing the life and interests of the foreign exploiters. This is a crime! This is an offense to humanity, to civilization, to progress! They want 15 million Mexicans to starve, to suffer humiliations and tyranny, in order that a band of thieves live on, satisfied and contented. . . .

Nothing nor anyone will be able to stop the triumphal march of the revolutionary movement. Does the bourgeoisie want peace? Then let them become working class! Do those in authority want peace? Then let them take off their Prince Albert coats and like men pick up the pick and shovel, the plow and hoe.

As long as there is inequality, as long as some work so that others can eat, as long as the words "bourgeoisie" and "people" exist, there will be no peace. There will be war without quarter. And our flag, the red flag of the people,

will continue challenging the enemy machine guns, raised high by the brave
who cry, "Long Live Land and Freedom!"

It is impossible to understand Mexican culture and nationalism without
analyzing the meaning of *mestizaje*, or "mixed blood," as elaborated in the
book *The Cosmic Race*, which was written by the Mexican statesman and
educator José Vasconcelos (1881–1959). The description of *pensador* fits
Vasconcelos as if it were a suit of clothes tailored to his personal order. Exiled
as a young man to Los Angeles in the repressive years before the Mexican
Revolution, he later took up the theme of cultural identity as minister of
education under President Alvaro Obregón (1920–1924). His book was published in 1925 and carried the subtitle "The Mission of the Iberoamerican
Race." He broke philosophically with the positivism of the old regime that had
attempted to manipulate the Mexican soul into a factory for foreign profits
under the banner of scientific progress (Jorrín and Martz, 1970, pp. 216ff.).
Vasconcelos was influenced by Bergson's philosophy, which stressed the
creativity of intuition. The *élan vital* of the French philosopher was not, however, sterilely translated into Spanish (Sánchez 1949, passim). Vasconcelos
was able to discover manifestations of this elemental creative force in the
mestizaje of the Mexican nation. He thus incorporated the popular concept of
Indianism, which had propelled the revolution in its pristine vigor toward a new
nationhood, with a philosophical expression of complexity and richness.

Vasconcelos surpassed the Latin American *pensadores* of an earlier decade
in discerning the basic differences between Anglo-Saxon and Latin American
cultures. These others were called *Arielistas* after a mythological hero, Ariel,
who represented artistic humanism in opposition to the demigod of science,
Calibán. By analogy, the *Arielistas* suggested that while Anglo-Saxon science
was worthwhile, the Latin American sensitivity toward humanistic values
would allow an importation of North American science without a risk to Latin
American cultural identity. The Mexican *pensador*, however, did more than
make analogies with mythological figures: he scientifically proved the
superiority of the Latin American people.

Vasconcelos linked culture to biology. He held that cultural patterns were
pre-existent ideas genetically innate in the races. These cultural forces were
controlled by the laws of biology. The mixture of all races in Latin America
would eventually produce a synthesis of previous world civilizations. And just
as the cosmic race is the ultimate expression of biological perfection, the
cosmic culture is destined to supercede all other civilizations. This triumph
would not require a violent or antagonistic battle. The conflict was not social
between classes of bourgeoisie and proletariat, but among cultures. Echoing
Benedetto Croce, who took a similar tack in pre-Mussolini Italy, Vasconcelos
reduced Marxism to purely economic terms and preferred his dialectical
idealism to dialectical materialism.

Vasconcelos's writings gave him an international reputation, and in 1929 he ran for president of Mexico. His failure to achieve this honor disappointed him. He dedicated himself to teaching and writing, spending time at the University of Puerto Rico as a visiting professor. From time to time he entered into polemics with the secularist trends of Mexican politics. In all his writings, the symbols of Catholicism become a special property of the cosmic race, so that the eventual triumph of Latin American culture is also to be the enthronement of a universal Catholicism in its Hispano manifestation.

8. *The Cosmic Race*

José Vasconcelos

From La raza cósmica: la misión de la raza iberoamericana *(Barcelona: Espasa Calpe, 1925), pp. 26–28, 30–31, 35, 43– 49. Used by permission. Trans. A.M.S.A.*

Let us recognize that it was a misfortune for Latin America not to have proceeded with the cohesion demonstrated by North America. North Americans are a prodigious race, even if we are accustomed to pour opprobrium upon them simply because they have beaten us in every facet of secular struggle. Their race has triumphed because it unites practical abilities with a clear vision of a great destiny. It preserves an intuition of a defined historical mission, while we lose ourselves in a labyrinth of verbal chimeras. It seems that God himself guides the steps of the Anglo-Saxons, while we murder each other for dogmas and then proclaim ourselves atheists. How these mighty builders of empires must laugh at our stumbling and our Latin vanity! They do not put importance on a Ciceronian sheen of phraseology, nor does their blood carry the contradictory instincts of a mixture of dissimilar races. They, however, committed the sin of destroying these races, while we assimilated them to ourselves. This gives us new rights and hope for a mission without historical precedent.

Hence our adversities do not mean that we shall lose our way. Vaguely we feel that they can help us to discover our route. Precisely in our differences do we find our way. If we merely imitate, we are lost; if we discover, if we create, we triumph. The advantage of our tradition is that we possess a greater facility for getting along with foreigners. This implies that our civilization, with all its defects, can be the one chosen to assimilate and convert all people into a new type. Our civilization thus prepares in itself the weave, the multiple and rich mold of the humanity of the future. This mandate of history began to be apparent in the abundance of love that permitted the Spaniards to create a new race with Indians and blacks. The white race flourished through the soldiers who engendered Indian families and western culture. The doctrine and example of missionaries placed the Indians in a position to penetrate the new stage, that is, the stage of One World. Spanish colonization created *mestizaje*, which marked the character of colonization, fixed its responsibility, and defined its future.

The English married only whites and exterminated the natives. They continued to exterminate them in a silent economic war, more efficient than armed conquest. This demonstrates their limitations and is an index of their decadence. It is the equivalent, writ large, of the incestuous marriages of the pharaohs, who undermined the hardiness of their race. It contradicts the ultimate purpose of history, which is to achieve the fusion of peoples and cultures. To make the world English, to exterminate the redmen, so that all America would be another northern Europe made up of pure whites, is nothing more than to repeat the victorious process of a conquering race. This is what the redmen once did; and this is what has been done or what has been attempted by all mighty and homogenous races.

But this does not solve the human problem. Latin America did not lie in wait for five thousand years for such a tarnished objective. The task of the New World and the Old is much more important. It is predestined to be the cradle of a fifth race in which all peoples will be fused, in order to replace the four that have made history isolated from each other. The diaspora will end on the American continent; here unity will be consummated by the triumph of a fruitful love and by transcending all racial stocks.

In this way a synthesizing type will be produced, combining all the treasures of history and expressing the aspirations of the whole world.

The peoples called Latins, because they have been the most faithful to their divine mission in America, are those called upon to bring it to conclusion. And such fidelity to this hidden design is the guarantee of our triumph.

Even in the chaotic period of independence that deserves so much criticism, one nonetheless catches glimpses of that quest for universality that announced even then the desire to fuse the human being into a universal synthetic type. Even then, Bolívar, partly because he was aware of the danger of dividing into isolated nationalities, and partly because of his gift for prophecy, formulated his plan for an Iberoamerican Federation, which yet today certain foolish people still discuss.

The rest of the leaders of Latin American independence generally did not have a clear concept of the future. They were motivated by a provincialism that today is called "patriotism" or by the limitation that today is entitled "national sovereignty"; each busied himself with no more than the immediate fortune of his own people. So it is all the more surprising to observe that almost all felt motivated by a universal human sentiment that coincides with the destiny we today ascribe to the Iberoamerican continent. Hidalgo, Morelos, Bolívar, Petion in Haiti, the Argentinians in Tucumán, Sucre—all were concerned with freeing the slaves, with declaring the equality of all by natural right, with social and civil equality for white, black, and Indian. Under the pressure of historical crisis, they formulated the transcendental mission assigned to our part of the globe: to fuse all races ethnically and spiritually.

In this way, the Latins did what no one even thought about doing on the Anglo-Saxon continent. In the North, they continued operating on the contrary thesis, with the confessed or tacit purpose of purifying the land of Indians, Asians, and blacks, for the greater glory and fortune of the whites. In reality, from that time there have been two clearly defined systems, which to this day place the two civilizations in opposed sociological camps: one that fosters the exclusive predominance of the white race and the other that involves the formation of a new race, a race of synthesis that aspires to encompass and express all that is human in a program of constant improvement. If it were necessary to introduce proofs, it would be enough to observe the increasing and spontaneous mixture that has been operative among all peoples throughout the Latin continent, and, on the other hand, the inflexible wall that separates blacks from whites in the United States and the ever stricter laws to exclude the Japanese and Chinese from California. . . .

So it will soon be seen that we are tomorrow's people, just as they are yesterday's. The Yankees will form the last great empire of a single race: the last empire of white might. In the meantime, we will continue to suffer in the immense chaos of a race in formation, afflicted with the leavening of all types, but assured of being the embodiment of a better stock. In Spanish America, nature will not repeat again one of its partial efforts. There will not be a race of a single color and a particular dimension, like one that might have emerged from a long-forgotten Atlantis. The future race will not be either a fifth or a sixth new race, destined to prevail over its predecessors. What is going to emerge is a definitive race, a synthesizing and integral race, made up of the genius and the blood of all people. Because of that, it will be the most capable of true fraternity and a really universal vision.

In order to draw close to this sublime purpose, we must go on creating, as it were, the cellular fabric that will serve as flesh and support the new biological apparition. And in order to create this malleable, profound, ethereal, and essential prototype, the Iberoamerican race must comprehend its mission and embrace it as a mystique.

Perhaps there is nothing useless in the processes of history. Our very material isolation and the mistake of creating too many nations, together with the original mixture of blood, has prevented us from falling into the Anglo-Saxon limitation of establishing pure-blooded castes. History demonstrates that prolonged and rigorous selection produces specimens of physical refinement, interesting in form but lacking in vigor. They are beautiful with a strange beauty, like that of the Brahman chiliastic caste, but the end result is decadence. Never have they had an advantage over other people, neither in talent, nor in goodness, nor in energy. The path that we have undertaken is much more daring. It breaks ancient prejudices. It can scarcely be explained, except that it is founded in a kind of far-off cry, one not of the past, but of the mysterious beyond whence come presages of the future.

If Latin America were only another Spain, as the United States is another England, then the age-old battle of the two races would only repeat the same episodes in a broader land, and one of the two rivals would come to dominate the other. But this is not the natural law of conflict, either in mechanics or in real life. Opposition and struggle, particularly when transferred to the realm of the spirit, serve better to define opposites and carry each to the culmination of its destiny, finally uniting both in a mutual and victorious higher stage. . . .

Naturally, the fifth race will not try to exclude white people, just as it does not propose to exclude any other peoples. The norm of its formation has been precisely to profit from all abilities for a greater integration of power. Its purpose is not war against whites, but rather war against any kind of violent domination, whether by white people or, for example, yellow people, as would be the case if Japan were to become a continental threat. The fifth race will utilize the contributions of white culture and, indeed, awaits still further contributions from white genius. Latin America owes what it is to white Europe and it is not about to turn its back upon it. For the most part it owes its railroads, bridges, and industry to the North Americans; and in the same way it needs all the other races. We accept the superior ideals of the whites, but not their arrogance. We wish to share with them, as with other peoples, a free land where they can find a home and refuge, but not a prolongation of their conquests. The white people themselves, unhappy with the materialism and social injustice into which their race has now fallen, have a good antecedent for creative achievement of love. But that love must be a work of art in itself and not an escape for desperate persons. If parents are going to communicate only stupidity, then what joins them is not love, but shameful and destructive instinct. . . .

Because of isolation and war, the human species lives, in a certain sense, according to Darwinian laws. The English, who see only the present of the external world, do not hesitate to apply zoological theories to the field of human sociology. If the false translation of physiological law to the realm of the spirit were acceptable, then to speak of the ethnic incorporation of blacks would be tantamount to defending retrogression. The English theory supposes, implicitly or explicitly, that blacks are a missing link, closer to monkeys than to whites. Hence there is no recourse left to blacks other than to disappear. On the other hand, the whites, particularly the whites who speak English, represent the sublime goal of human evolution. To cross them with another race would be equivalent to contaminating the line. But such a viewpoint is only the illusion created by every nation that has come into power. Every one of the great peoples of history has believed itself the best and the chosen ones. When such infantile arrogance is considered in a comparative way, we see that the mission each people assigns to itself is at the core nothing more than the desire for plunder and the urge to exterminate a potential rival. Even official science in each period is a reflection of the arrogance of the dominant race. . . .

Every imperialism needs a philosophy to justify it, but this science that has invaded us along with the artifacts of the conquerors' commerce is to be combated, like all imperialisms, by confronting it with superior science, with a more vigorous and far-reaching civilization. . . .

Every race that arises needs to constitute its own philosophy, the *deus ex machina* of its success. We have educated ourselves under the humiliating influence of a philosophy of our enemies' invention. It was fashioned with a sincere sentiment, but with the purpose of exalting its own ends and nullifying ours. In this way we ourselves have come to believe in the inferiority of the mestizos, in the irredeemability of the Indians, in the damnation of the blacks, in the irreparable decadence of the Orientals. The rebellion of arms was not followed by a rebellion of consciousness. We rebelled against the political power of Spain, but we did not realize that, like Spain, we had fallen under the economic and moral domination of the race that had ruled the world after the decline of Spanish grandeur. We shook off one yoke to fall under another. The trend of substitution which victimized us could not have been avoided even if we would have understood it in time. There is a certain fate in the destiny of nations, just as there is in the destiny of individuals. But now that a new phase of history has begun, we must reconstitute our ideology and organize the life of our entire continent according to a new ethnic doctrine. We will then begin to forge our own life and our own science. If the spirit is not first set free, we will never be able to redeem matter.

We have the duty of formulating the basis of a new civilization. And precisely because of this, we must remember that civilizations are not repeated either in substance or in form. The theory of ethnic superiority has simply been a tool of combat common to all warring peoples. But the battle that we must undertake is so important that it does not allow any deceitful ruse. We do not believe that we are or that we shall become the leading race of the world, or the most enlightened, or the mightiest, or the most beautiful. Our purpose is higher and more difficult to achieve than any temporary excellence. Our values are of such potential that we are still nothing compared to it. The Hebrew race was nothing more to the arrogant Egyptians than a vile caste of slaves, and from that stock was born Jesus Christ, the author of history's greatest movement, which announced love to all humankind. This love will be one of the fundamental dogmas of the fifth race that will be produced in America. Christianity frees and fosters life because it contains a universal revelation, not a national one. Because of this, the Jews had to reject it, since they had decided not to communicate with Gentiles.

But America is the homeland of the Gentiles, the true Christian Promised Land. If our race proves itself unworthy of this consecrated land, if it is lacking in love, it will be supplanted by people more capable of realizing the inevitable mission of these lands—to be the seat of a humanity composed of all nations and races. . . .

Christianity preached love as the basis for human relationships, and now it is becoming apparent that only love is capable of producing an exalted humanity. The politics of the state and the positivist science directly influenced by these politics say that antagonism, not love, is the law. The law is struggle and the survival of the fittest, they say, and there is no other criterion to judge ability than the curious begging of the question contained in the thesis itself, for the fittest are those who survive, and only the fittest survive. Thus all the modest knowledge that enlightened revelation discloses is reduced to vicious verbal formulas of this kind, in order to substitute for truth generalizations based on nothing more than the sum of details.

It could be said that Christianity is going to be fulfilled, not only in souls, but in the root of all being. As the instrument of transcendental transformation, it has continued to form on the Iberian continent a new race, full of vices and defects, but gifted with malleability, rapid comprehension, and easy emotion—fertile elements for the germinal matrix of a future species. Now grouped together in abundance are the biological materials, the predispositions, the characteristics, the genes of which the Mendelians speak. The only thing still lacking is the organizing impulse, the plan of formation for the new race. What will be the traits of this creative impulse?

If we were to proceed according to the law of pure, confused energy of the first period, according to primitive biological Darwinism, then blind force, by an almost mechanical imposition of the most vigorous elements, would decide selection in a simple and brutal manner, exterminating the weak or, better said, those who did not fit into the plan of the new race. But in the new order, by its own law, the lasting elements will not be sustained by violence, but by good taste. The selection will be accomplished spontaneously, as in the case of the artist who puts on the palette only those colors that are appropriate for the portrait. . . .

There are many obstacles to this plan of the spirit; but then, obstacles are common in any process. And some ask how the different races are going to unite in concord if not even the children of a single racial stock are able to live in peace and happiness within today's oppressive social and economic order. But this state of affairs will have to change rapidly. All the tendencies of the future are found in the present: Mendelism in biology, socialism in government, a growing sensibility in humanity, general progress, and the emergence of a fifth race that will fill the planet with the triumphs of the first really universal culture, one that is truly cosmic.

Octavio Paz (b. 1914) is an ideological successor of Vasconcelos. Born in Mexico, Paz was a child of the revolution. A writer and poet, he left a promising university career to join other intellectuals of his age who fought on the Republican side in the Spanish Civil War.

During his career, he has published a dozen volumes of poetry and prose essays. He has been a member of the Mexican diplomatic corps, serving as ambassador to India from 1963 until 1968. He resigned his post in protest over the murder of Mexican university students in October of that year. He has since traveled to foreign universities, as did Vasconcelos before him, serving as Charles Eliot Norton Lecturer at Harvard in 1972.

His writings on a wide range of topics demonstrate his ability to synthesize anthropological and psychological science with themes of politics and culture. Paz is a contemporary *pensador*. In the following excerpt from the most famous of his books, *The Labyrinth of Solitude*, first published in 1950, he picks up Vasconcelos's theme of cultural identity and develops insightful psychological dimensions.

A basic question for Paz when he lived in Los Angeles in 1944 was the Mexicanness of the California ghettos. Here he found alienated youth, formed into the juvenile gangs of that era, who called themselves *pachucos*. They claimed a Mexican cultural identity independent of accepted Mexican models. Paz dipped into Freudian terminology and developed a coherent explanation of Mexican identity that included both the *pachucos* and their counterparts in Mexico.

According to Paz, Mexicans use social roles as "masks" because these roles disguise contrary currents within the soul. National identity has been paralyzed without adequate expression, and Mexicans are alienated from their own culture. The need to be free and unshackled by foreign convention is necessary for a Mexican's fulfillment, even if it entails seemingly superstitious activity or self-defeating violence. Accordingly, the contradictory elements of the national character, such as those which characterized the Mexican Revolution, were all masks, each expressing a yearning to reclaim a lost element of national culture. Romanticism and pragmatism are both authentic Mexican traits, as are gentleness and cruelty, because they are different masks for the true Mexican character, which is still unsure of its instincts. However, while the energies of these instincts move in different directions, they search for a common middle ground. Consequently, the modern quest for Mexican identity is a struggle for equilibrium.

Paz avoids the biological causality of Vasconcelos, preferring a psychological explanation for culture. Romano, the insightful commentator on contemporary culture, criticizes Paz, however, for attempting to find the "pure Mexican." There is not one person with many masks, says Romano; rather, there are "different life styles which represent different historical trends, a variety of individual experiences and multiple intellectual currents—in short, many Mexicans, just as today there are many Mexican Americans" (1973, p. 167). Romano sees Paz as a romantic who relativizes the life experiences of real people into psychological abstractions. Despite the power of his expression and the depth of his insights into Mexican culture, Paz believes, as he states in his poem "Aquí," "Nothing is real but the fog."

9. *Aqui*
(Here)

Octavio Paz

From *John Frederick Nims*, Sappho to Valéry *(New Brunswick, N.J.: Rutgers University Press, 1971), pp. 234-235. Used by permission. Trans. John Frederick Nims.*

Mis pasos en esta calle	My footsteps in this street
Resuenan	Re-echo
En otra calle	In another street
Donde	Where
Oigo mis pasos	I hear my footsteps
Pasar en esta calle	Passing in this street
Donde	Where
Sólo es real la niebla	Nothing is real but the fog.

10. *Three Excerpts from The Labyrinth of Solitude*

Octavio Paz

From *Paz*, El Laberinto de la soledad *(Mexico, D.F.: Fondo de Cultura Económica, 1959). Used by permission. Trans. A.M.S.A.*

THE *PACHUCO* AND OTHER EXTREMES

At the beginning of my stay in the United States I lived for a time in Los Angeles, a city with a population of more than a million persons of Mexican origin. At first sight, the visitor is surprised—not only by the purity of the sky and the ugliness of the scattered and showy buildings—but also by the vague Mexican atmosphere of the city, which is impossible to grasp with words and concepts. This Mexicanness—a flair for decoration, carelessness and magnificence, negligence, passion and reserve—floats in the air. And I say "floats" because it neither mixes nor fuses with the other world, the North American world, made up of precision and efficiency. It floats, but it does not impose itself. It hovers, blown by the wind, sometimes being torn apart like a cloud, and again moves stiffly like an ascending skyrocket. It creeps, it collapses, it expands, it contracts, it dreams, it sleeps like a tattered beauty. It floats, it never quite evolves, it never completely disappears.

Something similar occurs with the Mexicans that you see in the street. Even though they have lived here for many years, use the same clothes, speak the same language, and feel ashamed of their origin, no one ever confuses them with genuine North Americans. And do not think that physical traits are as important as is commonly believed. It seems to me that what distinguishes them from the rest of the population is the furtive and restless spirit like that of creatures that disguise themselves. They are like a people who fear an alien glance that can strip them naked and catch them with their pants down. When you speak with them you notice their sensitivity, which seems like a pendulum that has lost its bearings and oscillates violently and wildly.

This state of spirit—or lack of spirit—has spawned what has come to be called the *pachuco*. Everyone knows the *pachucos* are juvenile gangs, generally of Mexican origin, of those who live in Southern California cities and are identifiable as much by dress as by behavior and language. They are instinctive rebels, and North American racism has vented its anger against them on more than one occasion. But the *pachucos* do not reincarnate their race or the nationality of their ancestors. In spite of the fact that their attitude reveals an obstinate and almost fanatical willpower, this will does not affirm anything concrete except a decision—ambiguous as we shall see—to be different from all others about them. The *pachuco* does not wish to return to his Mexican origin; nor—at least apparently—does he wish to blend into the North American way of life. Everything in him is an impulse to deny himself, a knot of contradictions, an enigma. And the first enigma is his very name: *pachuco*, a noun of uncertain origin that says nothing and says everything. How strange a word, which does not have a precise meaning! Or, more exactly, a word laden, like all popular creations, with a set of meanings! Whether we like it or not, these persons are Mexicans, one of the extremes at which the Mexican can arrive.

Incapable of assimilating a civilization that rejects them, the *pachucos* have not encountered a better response to their hostile surroundings than this exasperated affirmation of their personality. (In the last few years, many youth gangs have sprung up in the United States that recall the *pachucos* of the postwar period. It could not be any other way. On the one hand, North

American society is closed to the alien; on the other, it is inwardly petrified. Life cannot penetrate it. Rejected, it squanders itself purposelessly on the extraneous. It is a marginal, formless life, but a life in search of its true form).

Other communities react in different ways. The blacks, for example, persecuted by racial intolerance, summon courage "to walk over the line" and enter into society. They wish to be like other citizens. The Mexicans have suffered a less violent rejection, but instead of attempting a problematical adaptation to current lifestyles, they affirm their differences, flaunt them, and try to make them more noticeable. By means of grotesque dandyism and anarchic behavior, they demonstrate not so much the injustice or incapacity of a society that has not been able to assimilate them, as their personal desire to remain different.

It is not important to know the causes of this conflict and even less to know if they have a remedy or not. Everywhere there are minorities who do not enjoy the same opportunities as the rest of the population. What we are talking about is characterized by the stubborn desire to be different, in this painful tension with which the deprived Mexicans—orphaned by value-makers and values—affirm their differences from everyone else. The *pachuco* has lost all his heritage: language, religion, customs, beliefs. All that is left to him is a body and soul in the open, defenseless before every glance. This disguise protects him and, at the same time, distinguishes and isolates him; it hides him and puts him on display.

With his suit—deliberately aesthetic and upon whose obvious significance it is not necessary to dwell—he does not seek to show his allegiance to any sect or association. *Pachuquismo* is an open society—in a country full of cults and tribal attire—destined to satisfy the desire of ordinary North Americans to feel part of something more vital and real than the abstract morality of the "American way of life." The suit of the *pachuco* is not a uniform or a ritual costume. It is, simply, a fad. Like all fads, it is made out of novelty—the mother of death, as Leopardi said—and out of imitation.

The novelty of the suit lies in its exaggeration. The *pachuco* carries fashion to its ultimate consequences and makes it into the aesthetic. One of the principles that reigns in North American fashion is comfort; when he makes fashion aesthetic, the *pachuco* becomes "impractical." Thus he denies the very principles that inspired his model. This is the source of his aggressiveness.

The rebellion is no more than a vain gesture, since it is an exaggeration of the models against which he tries to rebel and not a return to the attire of his ancestors or the invention of new styles. Generally eccentrics use clothing to emphasize their decision to separate from society—sometimes to constitute new and more exclusive groups, other times to affirm their idiosyncrasy. In the case of the *pachucos*, an ambiguity is noted. On the one hand, their clothes isolate and distinguish them; on the other, the clothes themselves constitute homage to the society they try to deny.

This duality is also expressed in another way, perhaps more profound: the *pachuco* is a stoic and sinister clown who does not try to amuse others but to terrorize them. This sadistic attitude combines with a desire for self-humiliation, which seems to me to constitute the basis of his character. He knows that it is dangerous to be the exception and that his conduct irritates society. It does not matter to him, for he seeks and attracts persecution and scandal. Only in this way can he establish a more vital relationship with the society that he aggravates. As a victim he will be able to take his place in the world that only recently ignored him; as a delinquent he will be one of its cursed heroes. . . .

By secret and risky paths, the *pachuco* attempts to enter into North American society. But he denies himself the access. Detached from his traditional culture, the *pachuco* affirms himself as both solitude and defiance. He denies the society from which he came as well as North American society. The *pachuco* sets himself face to face with the exterior, not to fuse with what is around him, but only to defy it. It is a suicidal gesture, since the *pachuco* does not affirm anything, does not defend anything, except his exasperated will to "not-be." His is not an intimacy shared, but rather a sore exposed, a wound exhibited. The wound is a primitive ornament, both grotesque and capricious; it mocks itself and bedecks itself for the hunt. The *pachuco* is the prey who is to attract the hunter's attention. Persecution redeems him and breaks through his solitude: his salvation depends on access to the very society he seems to negate. Solitude and sin, communion and health, these become synonymous terms.

If this is the case with persons who abandoned their homeland long ago, who hardly speak the language of their ancestors, and for whom the secret roots that bind them to their culture have almost completely dried up, what can be said about the rest of the race? . . .

It seems to me that for North Americans, the world is something to be perfected; for us, it is something to be redeemed. They are modern; we, like their Puritan ancestors, believe that sin and death constitute the ultimate basis of human nature. But the Puritans identify purity with salvation. Hence their asceticism and its consequences that purify: the cult of work for work's sake, the somber life—bread and water—the nonexistence of the body to the point of never losing—or finding—itself in another body. All contact contaminates. Races, ideas, customs, bodies of foreigners carry in them germs of perdition and impurity. Social hygiene is achieved in soul and body. Mexicans both ancient and modern, on the contrary, believe in communion and fiesta; there is no salvation without contact. Tlazoltéotl, the Aztec goddess of impurity and fertility, of earthly and human feelings, was also the goddess of the steam baths, of sexual love, and of confession. And we have not changed that much for our Catholicism, which is also communion. . . .

MEXICAN MASKS

Old or adolescent, Creole or mestizo, military general, worker, lawyer, the Mexican seems to me like a creature who closes in upon himself for protection. His face is a mask and his smile is too. Set in his arid solitude, biting and polite at the same time, he uses everything to defend himself: silence and speech, courtesy and disdain, irony and resignation. As jealous of his own intimacy as that of others, he doesn't even dare to look at his neighbor; a glance can unleash the anger of souls thus charged with electricity. He goes through life like a man who has been flayed. Everything can wound him: talk, and the suspicion of talk. His language is filled with the reticence of figures of speech and allusions, of ellipses. In his silence are retreats, nuances, large storm clouds, sudden rainbows, indecipherable threats. Even in disputes, he prefers veiled expressions to direct insult: "A word to the wise is sufficient." In sum, between reality and his person stands a wall of impassivity and distance, which although invisible is still impenetrable. The Mexican is always distant, distant from the world and from others. Distant also from himself. . . .

Sometimes forms suffocate us. During the past century the liberals vainly tried to force the realities of the country into the straitjacket of the Constitution of 1857. The results were the dictatorship of Porfirio Díaz and the Revolution of 1910. In a certain sense, the history of Mexico, like that of every Mexican, consists of a struggle between the forms and formulas which try to encapsulate our being and the explosions with which our spontaneity takes vengeance. A few times the form has been an original creation, a balance arrived at not at the expense of, but thanks to, the expression of our instincts and wishes. Our juridic and moral forms, on the contrary, frequently mutilate our being, impede us from expressing ourselves, and deny satisfaction to our vital appetites.

Without doubt the masculine vanity that we have inherited from Indians and Spaniards enters into our conception of feminine modesty. Like almost all people, the Mexican considers the woman an instrument, whether for the wishes of man, whether for the fulfillment of the goals assigned her by law, society, or morality. Goals, it has to be said, for which her consent has never been sought and in whose realization she has participated only passively as repository of certain values. Prostitute, goddess, grand lady, lover, the woman transmits or preserves, but does not create the values and energies that nature or society has confided to her. In a world made in the image of men, the woman is only a reflection of the masculine will and desire. When passive, she becomes a goddess, loved, a being that incarnates the stable and ancient elements of the universe: the land, mother, and virgin. When active, she is always a function, a medium, a channel. Unlike masculinity, femininity is never an end in itself.

In other countries these functions are realized publicly and in broad daylight. In some, prostitutes, and also virgins, are reverenced; in others, mothers are rewarded. In almost all, the *grande dame* is adulated and respected. We prefer to hide these gifts and virtues. Secrecy ought to accompany the woman, who not only ought to hide herself, but in addition ought to offer a certain smiling impassibility to the exterior world. In the face of erotic titillation she ought to be "modest"; in the face of adversity, "long-suffering." In both cases, her response is neither instinctive nor personal, but conforms to a generic model. And that model, as in the case of the *macho*, tends to underline the defensive and passive aspects, in a gamut running from innocence and modesty to stoicism, resignation, and impassibility. . . .

Some say that by transforming into virtue something which ought to be the cause for shame, we only try to unburden our conscience and cover an atrocious reality with illusion. This is true, but it is also certain that in attributing to woman the same invulnerability for which we aspire, we clothe her evident anatomical debility with moral immunity. Thanks to suffering and her capacity to endure without protesting, the woman transcends her conditions and acquires the same attributes as man.

It is curious to notice that the image of the "evil woman" almost carries with it a concept of activity. Contrary to the "sacrificing mother" and the "girl friend who waits" and the heretical idol—static beings every one—the "evil woman" comes and goes, seeks men, leaves them. Through a mechanism analogous to the one described above, her extreme mobility makes her invulnerable. Activity and promiscuity are united in her and in time petrify her soul. The "evil woman" is as hard, impious, and independent as the *macho*. By different routes, she also transcends her physiology and closes herself off from the world. . . .

THE DAY OF THE DEAD

Religion and fate ruled the Aztecs' life as morality and freedom rule over ours. We live beneath the sign of freedom where everything is choice and struggle, even Greek fate and the grace of the theologian. For the Aztecs, the problem was reduced to investigating what might be the not always clear will of the gods. Hence the importance of divination. The only free beings were the gods. They were able to choose and were thus, in a profound sense, the only ones able to sin. Aztec religion is full of great sinful gods, Quetzalcóatl, is the best example. These were gods who failed and were able to abandon their believers, in the same way that Christians sometimes denied their God. The conquest of Mexico would be inexplicable without the betrayal of the gods who denied their people.

The advent of Catholicism radically changed the situation. Sacrifice and the idea of salvation, which previously were collective, became personal. Freedom was humanized, incarnated in people. For the ancient Aztecs the essential was to secure the continuity of creation. For the Christian, the individual is what counts. The world—history and society—is condemned beforehand. The death of Christ saves each person in particular. Each one of us is human and in each one are deposited the hopes and possibilities of the species. Redemption is a personal task.

Both attitudes, as opposed as they seem to be, possess a common note: life, collective or individual, is open to the perspective of a death which is, in its way, a new life. Life is justified and transcended only when it is fulfilled in death. And death also is a transcendence because it consists in a new life. For the Christian, death is a transit, a moral leap between two lives, the temporal and the extraterrestrial: for the Aztecs, death was the deepest way to participate in the continual regeneration of creative forces, always in danger of being extinguished if blood, the sacred food, were not provided. In both systems, life and death lack autonomy. They are the two faces of the same reality. All their significance comes from other values, which rule them. They are references to invisible realities.

Modern death does not possess any significance which transcends it or refers to other values. In almost all cases, it is simply the inevitable end to a natural process. In a world of facts, death is just another fact. But as it is a disagreeable fact, a fact that brings down the curtain of judgment on all our conceptions and the very sense of our lives, the philosophy of progress (progress toward what and from what? asked Scheler) pretends to hide its presence from us. In the modern world everything functions as if death did not exist. No one counts on it. Everything suppresses it: the preaching of the politicians, the ads of the merchants, public morality, customs, low-cost happiness, and health at everyone's fingertips offered by hospitals, drug stores, and athletic fields. But death, not now a transit but a great empty mouth which nothing satisfies, dwells in everything that we undertake. The century of health, of hygiene and contraceptives, of miracle drugs and synthetic foods is also the century of concentration camps, of the police state, of atomic extermination, and of the "murder story." Nobody thinks about death, about his own death, as Rilke wished, because no one lives a personal life. The collective butchery is nothing more than the fruit of the collectivization of life. . . .

CHAPTER TWO

THE PUERTO RICAN *PENSADORES*

The intellectual history of Puerto Rico's Catholicism in the nineteenth century is similar to that of Mexico, although the absence of a successful revolution in Puerto Rico has not given the same edge to national identity. In 1898 Puerto Rico was ceded to the United States by Spain as compensation for the expenses incurred by the victorious country in the Spanish-American War. At that time Puerto Rico possessed its own autonomous government. In a desperate attempt to persuade Cuba to avoid total separation, Spain had granted to Puerto Rico in 1897 a political status similar to the former commonwealth arrangement of Canada with Great Britain. The Spanish hoped the Cubans would accept a similar arrangement. Unfortunately, the United States callously denied the validity of Puerto Rican autonomy and used the internal squabbling of various political factions as a pretext to impose its own formulas (Wagenheim, 1970, pp. 61ff.).

Three distinct political ideologies related to the question of status have existed in Puerto Rico. There are those who want independence from the United States, just as their forerunners labored for separation from Spain. There are those who advocate annexation to the United States as a state of the Union, just as before them others had argued for the incorporation of Puerto Rico as a province of Spain with rights equal to those of, for example, León or Cataluña. Finally, there are those who advocate a middle-course of autonomy, or the commonwealth status, a diluted version of the autonomy granted by Spain in 1897.

There is a temptation to compare Puerto Rico today with New Mexico in 1900 before it was a state. But there are important differences. Since it is an island, Puerto Rico has a sense of territorial self-determinateness, whereas New Mexico was permeable to hosts of outside settlers. Also, Puerto Rico is densely populated; its 3.1 million inhabitants are more than twice those of New Mexico today, although in size New Mexico is thirty-five times larger than Puerto Rico. This lends to the island a sense of being a complete and intact national territory with recognizable distance and differences from the rest of the United States. Most Puerto Ricans think of themselves as a nation.

The rest of the world views the United States' role in Puerto Rico unfavorably. In 1973, by a vote of 104 to 5, the United Nations General Assembly approved a resolution ratifying the Decolonization Committee's report that

Puerto Rico was a colony of the United States. By 1978 there was not a single major political leader in Puerto Rico who would deny the charge of imperialism against the United States, and in the Decolonization Committee's hearings in August 1978, the island's leaders unanimously urged the immediate decolonization of Puerto Rico. The question of political status is crucial to national identity: Puerto Ricans cannot define their reality as Hispanos without reference to it.

Among the *pensadores* of Puerto Rico the most ardent defenders of Puerto Rico's Catholic identity are those in favor of independence. The leading spokesman of the independence cause during the first decade of United States military occupation was José de Diego (1866–1918). Reconverted from anti-clerical positivism to the religion of his youth, de Diego was an activist in politics, fighting for the ideal of Puerto Rican independence. He argued that since Puerto Rico had a national culture, it logically had a right to a national sovereignty. However, in 1917 United States citizenship was imposed upon Puerto Ricans without a plebiscite and against the unanimous vote of the insular legislature. Since the legal struggle to avoid citizenship had been lost, a weary and sick de Diego withdrew from direct political activity. He launched a cultural crusade to ensure that Puerto Rico would continue as a distinct Latin American nation. In this effort he resurrected an idea that had circulated in the intellectual circles of the *pensadores* of a previous generation—the concept of an Antillean, or Caribbean, Federation, in which Cuba, Puerto Rico, and the Dominican Republic would become three states of one country.

De Diego's poetry has survived his cultural union and his dream of a federation. Modernist in his technique, he refused to accept the "art for art's sake" of the Latin American modernists. Although a mystic, he never lost sight of the practical and concrete historical moment. To paraphrase his most celebrated critic, Margot de Arce Vásquez, "de Diego mysticizes politics and politicizes mysticism." As a result, there is very little that de Diego wrote that did not express his romantic attachment to Catholicism as an assertion of national identity. He uses the themes of resurrection, virginity, the crusades, and chivalry over and over again in reference to Puerto Rico's independence.

José de Diego died in New York City in 1918, almost in despair about the prospect of eventual independence for Puerto Rico. However, his speeches, his writings and, most of all, his poetry helped weave together the twin concepts of independence and a Catholic national identity for Puerto Ricans.

11. *Ultima Actio*

José de Diego

From Carmen Gómez Tejera, Ave Maria Losada, Jorge Luis Paras, eds., Poesía puertorriqueña *(México, D.F.: Orión, 1957), p. 288. Trans. A.M.S.A.*

Colgadme al pecho, después que muera,
mi verde escudo en un relicario;
cubridme todo con el sudario,
con el sudario de tres colores de mi bandera.

Sentada y triste habrá una Quimera
sobre mi túmulo funerario. . . .
Será un espíritu solitario
en larga espera, en larga espera, en larga espera. . . .

Llegará un día tumultuario
y la Quimera, en el silenciario
sepulcro erguida, lanzará un grito. . . .

¡Buscaré entonces entre mis huesos mi relicario!
¡Me alzaré entonces con la bandera de mi sudario
a desplegarla sobre los mundos, desde las cumbres del Infinito! . . .

* * *

Clasp upon my chest the day on which I die
my green escutcheon to a relic-box endowed;
and cover me completely with the shroud,
the shroud of those three colors of the flag I glorify.

A Phantom Dream will settle nigh
and sit upon my grave, sad and cowed. . . .
And there will be one more lonely spirit vowed
to drawn-out standing-by, to drawn-out standing-by, to drawn-out
standing-by. . . .

At last will come that day of tumultuous crowd
and in the soundless crypt that Phantom Dream, long bowed,
will straighten up and cry out lustily. . . .

Then will I seek among my bones that relic-box endowed!
Then will I be raised up with the flag, my shroud,
to unfurl it over worlds from peaks of an Infinity! . . .

12. For God and Country

José de Diego

From Obras completas *(San Juan, P.R.: Instituto de cultura puertorriqueña, 1966), vol. 2, pp. 85–88. Used by permission. Trans. A.M.S.A.*

Soon a plebiscite,[1] or an electoral count, will determine exactly the number of those in favor of independence. But just as one can judge the brilliance of light by the contraction of the pupils, so too the value of ideas can be gauged by the dilation of the spirit. As far as public opinion is concerned, a moral criterion is worth as much as a statistic. And it is here one sees, hears, feels, breathes, glows, bounces, moves, soars, burns, suffers, shouts, sings of all that is involved. This is how one penetrates into and lauds the gigantic and powerful soul of a rebellious people that—free and proud—struggles to raise itself above the earth that brings affliction, to raise itself as high as the heavens offering refuge.

The majority of Catholics are in agreement with a majority of all the elements genuinely Puerto Rican. Concerning the sacred ideal of independence, it can be stated that only a majority of Protestants (because they are Americans and foreigners) oppose the national aspiration of the partisan and total majorities of the inhabitants of our land.

One could scarcely conceive that a Catholic magazine truly interested in the welfare of the Catholic church in Puerto Rico would oppose our desire for emancipation.[2] More than any other institution, the Catholic church would enjoy the benefits of a sovereign government in Puerto Rico.

We do not intend to establish here a Pontifical State, a Theocratic Republic, or some other form of government in which Catholicism would be

1. The plebiscite was never held.—Ed.
2. The reference is to an article in which the bishop of San Juan explained that the Catholic church was absolutely neutral in political matters.—Ed.

recognized as the official or established church. The Puerto Rican people are Catholic, but the Puerto Rican nation, as with every republican form of government, will properly maintain freedom of worship, freedom of conscience, and all other civil liberties. It could not be otherwise today, given the spirit of generous and reciprocal tolerance that inspired the venerable Leo XIII to publish his encyclical *De Immortale Dei,* instructing the clergy and people to recognize the institutions of the French Republic.

As is found today in Puerto Rico, the Catholic church of *Propaganda Fidei,* by the universality of its pure doctrines, by the nobility of its dogmas, by the unity of its cult, by its spirit of love, by its irresistible attraction toward revealed Truth and discernible Beauty, loves by its own inner force and stretches its heavenly empire to the ends of the earth.

Thus, in the United States, where some fifty years ago Catholics formed only 1 percent of the population, that is, some thirty or forty thousand of three million inhabitants (according to Brumetiere), in the last published census they have grown to be one-seventh. At any rate, the assurance of official support in other countries has produced a decline in religious practice. Antagonistic impiety has pitched its battle tent. Christ did not need the help of Caesar. He was insulted, persecuted, killed. And he alone—in his short life, humble, passive, poor, wandering, set against emperors, armies, philosophers, poets, artists, and all their combined forces—gave up his life and saved all humanity.

It is unnecessary and perhaps even harmful to Catholicism to be proclaimed the official or established state church. Its spiritual power triumphs more beautifully in the freedom of conscience. It commands allegiance above and beyond political power. But in the circumstances and relationships between the United States and Puerto Rico under the present regime, our church suffers here the plague of the 189 heretical sects which Max O'Rell counted on the continent of Jonathan. They are here, and while they do not make progress in their catechetical mission, they still divide the solidarity and the energy of the Puerto Ricans. They add to the confusion of spirit and, through hidden ambassadors in the United States, spread the false concept of our inability for self-government. These ministers and pastors judge the failure of their religious mission as an indication of Puerto Rican ineptitude to control our own destiny! . . .

The Republic of Puerto Rico will not have an official religion; it will leave free the means to propagandize and it will respect the practice of worship according to the laws, rights, and privileges due to the responsibilities and service of all citizens. The Catholics of Puerto Rico will live under a sovereign government of Puerto Rico, without the prejudices and omissions held against them by the government and policy of the United States. A Puerto Rican priest will be able to be bishop in his homeland; a Catholic Puerto Rican will be able to be head of his country. The Catholic church of Puerto

Rico is of God and is at the same time, as it ought to be, of Puerto Rico. In those countries which stuggle for their emancipation, our country is faith and Faith is in our country, and God blesses both.

Cayetano Coll y Toste (1850–1930), a distinguished doctor in Puerto Rico at the time of the Spanish-American War, was selected by the United States military government to represent Puerto Ricans in the administration. After his retirement from public life, this gentle and generally nonpartisan man spent many years in collecting historical information on leaders of the island. This selection reflects what a nonseparatist thought about the Catholic church in Puerto Rico.

13. *Celebrated Puerto Ricans*

Cayetano Coll y Toste

From "Puertorriqueños ilustres," Boletín Histórico, *ed. Isabel Cuchi y Coll (New York: Las Américas Press, 1957). Trans. A.M.S.A.*

Spiritual directors are able to revive or extinguish the patriotism of a people. Men of state, sensing this great truth, do not lose sight of the people dedicated to religious worship and always try to attract them to their side. Rome had to destroy the Druids in order to take over the Gauls and the spirit of the Gallic peoples; they had to destroy the temple in Jerusalem and deport the Hebrew population in order to dominate the Jewish people as well, whose patriotic spirit was sustained by the priests of Jehovah.

The Puerto Rican people should not forget that priests are generally able to render them a great service in achieving the goals of political redemption. In this sense, the creation of the Conciliar Seminary was most useful, and we very much lament that, after the way it was founded, it has had to disappear. The idea of the Puerto Rican Arizmendi and the Peruvian Gutiérrez de Cos was that the young men who could follow a priestly career would not have to leave their country. Thus they founded an ad hoc institution with this purpose and this alone. But they also extended this bread of knowledge to other classes of society; indeed, the educational work of the seminary has been most brilliant.

A great deal of the adversity that a people has to undergo originates from within. The key to all great success, then, is forged in the mettle of strong character in the persons who are to be followed, since the ideal is not behind us, but before us.

"Give to God what is God's and to Caesar what is Caesar's," said the Rabbi of Nazareth; but the apostles of Christ know what this refers to and what exactly belongs to Caesar: the sovereignty of peoples comes from God and belongs to God, not to Caesar.

We respect the apostles of all the creeds who come to Puerto Rico to evangelize the religion of Christ in the different sects which have been born within Christology. But we believe and understand that the public religious positions which may have something to do with politics should be occupied by priests who are genuinely Puerto Rican. Each and every post is one of honor in defense of our homeland, and when a city is besieged, each inhabitant has a place on the ramparts.

Luis Muñoz Rivera (1859–1916) and his son, Luis Muñoz Marín (b. 1898), played an essential part in defining the autonomist or commonwealth status of Puerto Rico. Seldom in history have a father and son reflected such similar careers with such striking parallels. The struggles of the elder Muñoz against Spain were repeated in the efforts of his son Muñoz Marín to achieve autonomy for Puerto Rico from the United States.

Both father and son believed in independence (Maldonado, 1969, p. 118). But being pragmatists, they saw little chance for revolution to bring it about. They looked for halfway independence, called commonwealth status. Theirs was a hybrid political status, with some of the aspects of independence and some of assimilation. In many ways, they represent a direct line to the *pensadores* who believed that Anglo-Saxon know-how could be wedded to Latin American sentiment and culture. Catholicism was an appendage to national identity, although the institutional church proved to be an obstacle for Muñoz Marín, (cf. p. 89).

When in 1916 United States citizenship for Puerto Ricans was totally opposed by the House of Delegates on the island, it fell to Muñoz Rivera to make this opposition known in Washington. All the parties of Puerto Rico, including those in favor of statehood, felt that there should be a plebiscite to determine the issue, rather than unilateral action by Congress. On May 5, 1916, Muñoz Rivera spoke in Congress in an effort to derail the bill bestowing citizenship. But just as when statehood was granted to New Mexico (1911) and Arizona (1912) during the Mexican Revolution, the principal purpose of citizenship was related to national security (Wagenheim, 1970, pp. 126–36). The bill was filtered through a Congress woefully ignorant of Puerto Rico. A senator from North Dakota, for example, added an amendment that extended prohibition to the island despite the fact that the rum industry was one of the major sources of income to the impoverished economy.

The words of Muñoz Rivera went unheeded, and on May 23, 1916, the Jones Act, as it was called, passed the House vote. On September 19, a depressed Muñoz Rivera left for San Juan looking for peace in his mountains and his beloved hometown of Barranquitas , where he died November 15, 1916.

The poem "Nulla es redemptio" by the elder Muñoz reveals his frustration in rallying the Puerto Rican people into some sort of collective action against the colonial situation imposed upon them by imperialistic power. He had achieved the autonomist status in 1897 from Spain, only to have it taken away by the United States. He left to his son the task of achieving autonomy once again.

Critics (e.g., Silén, 1970, pp. 59–62) have noted Muñoz Rivera's characterizations of the common people of Puerto Rico as "submissive and unlucky," as without hope "to be free or respected." On this basis Muñoz Rivera has been accused of despising the peasant Puerto Ricans. This is probably an exaggeration, but the style of this Puerto Rican *pensador* contrasts sharply with the ringing words of the Mexicans Zapata and Flores Magón. The younger Muñoz Marín was to found the Popular Democratic Party, which has always enjoyed substantial electoral support from Puerto Rico's rural poor. But this brand of populism appealed to moderation rather than to heroism.

Eventually, passivity and nonviolence were identified as the model for religious conduct in Puerto Rico. The peasant or *jíbaro*, was expected to prefer reconciliation to confrontation, rhetoric to reprisal, pious prayer to apostolic zeal, peace to martyrdom. This complex of being ineffective and wishy-washy on all issues is characterized in Puerto Rico with the epithet *blandengue*.

The reader should compare the patriotic fervor of the speech of Muñoz Rivera which follows with the conformism of his poem. It should be remembered, moreover, that his son, Luis Muñoz Marín, has fostered the same ambivalence toward Puerto Rican national identity.

14. Speech before the United States Congress, May 5, 1916

Luis Muñoz Rivera

From The Congressional Record 53 (64th Congress, 1st Session, 1916): 7470-7473.

On the 18th day of October, 1898, when the flag of this great Republic was unfurled over the fortresses of San Juan, if anyone had said to my countrymen that the United States, the land of liberty, was going to deny their right to form a government of the people, by the people, and for the people of Puerto Rico, my countrymen would have refused to believe such a prophecy, considering it sheer madness. The Puerto Ricans were living at that time under a regime of ample self-government, discussed and voted by the Spanish Cortes, on the basis of the parliamentary system in use among all the nations of Europe. . . .

You, citizens of a free fatherland, with its own laws, its own institutions, and its own flag,[1] can appreciate the unhappiness of the small and solitary people that must await its laws from your authority, that lacks institutions created by its will, and who does not feel the pride of having the colors of a national emblem to cover the homes of its families and the tombs of its ancestors.

Give us now the field for experiment which we ask of you, that we may show that it is easy for us to constitute a stable republican government with all possible guarantees for all possible interests. And afterwards, when you acquire the certainty that you can found in Puerto Rico a republic like that founded in Cuba and Panama, like the one you will found at some future day in the Philippines, give us our independence and you will stand before humanity as the greatest of the great; that which neither Greece nor Rome nor England ever were, a great creator of new nationalities and a great liberator of oppressed peoples. (*Applause.*)

15. Nulla es redemptio

Luis Muñoz Rivera

From Obras completas: Poesías *(San Juan, P.R.: Instituto de cultura puertor-riqueña, 1960), pp. 137-140. Used by permission. Trans. A.M.S.A.*

Born on this tropical rock,
I never thought that unhappy colonists
would surrender their own dignity to ob-
livion. . . .

Submissive and unlucky masses,
who live and die in servile ignorance,
willingly, fearfully, traditionally

1. The Puerto Rican flag was prohibited as a political symbol until 1952—Ed.

prostrate themselves before the hand that wounds them!
A people whom victory hands over to humiliation,
they hope neither to be free nor respected.

This was not the people who one day
fashioned my fantasy, the dreamer of light,
in its rash and blind longing.

It was a manly people, with soul of fire,
with the tenacious bravery of a Spartan
and the indomitable nobility of a Greek.

An intelligent and sovereign people
who would reject the severe lashing
energetically and actively with ready hand.

How can I find the potent ingredient
to give back to our frozen blood
its ancient strength and native heat,

if a glance upon this land which bemoans its ills
only finds itself absorbed
in the absolute emptiness of nothingness?

There is no redemption! Anemia devours us,
inaction unnerves and scourges us;
fever colors our cheeks

and in military combat, the mind doubts
its rights, the pulse does not throb,
the lips fall silent, the heart does not beat. . . .

It is the divine power of ideas,
by whose impulse, in a shaken suddenness
the altar trembles and the throne sways,

while here, with suicidal calm,
Borinquen is handed over to its bitterness,
—pariah which finally forgets its slavery—

thus she withers, the virgin without fortune,
the insignificant atom in human endeavor
like a sterile spot of green growth
lost in the middle of the ocean.

* * *

En esta roca tropical nacido,
jamás pensé que el infeliz colono
su propia dignidad diese al olvido. . . .

¡Sumisa y desdichada muchedumbre
que en servil ignorancia vive y muere,
por voluntad, por miedo, por costumbre

se posterna ante el brazo que la hiere!
Pueblo que el triunfo a la humildad confía,
ni libre ser ni respetado espere.

No era ese el pueblo que fingió algún día
en su anhelar irreflexivo y ciego
soñadora de luz, mi fantasía:

Era un pueblo viril, de alma de fuego,
con el valor tenaz del espartano
y la altivez indómita del griego:

Un pueblo inteligente y soberano
que rechazara, enérgico y activo
el rudo azote con resuelta mano.

¿Cómo hallar el potente reactivo
que restituya a nuestra sangre helada
la antigua fuerza y el calor nativo,

si sólo encuentra, absorto, la mirada
en esta tierra que sus males llora,
el vacío absoluto de la nada?

¡No hay redención! La anemia nos devora,
la inacción nos enerva y nos abate;
la fiebre nuestros pómulos colora,

y del derecho en el marcial combate
la mente duda, el pulso no palpita,
el labio calla, el corazón no late. . . .

Es el poder divino de la idea,
a cuyo impulso, en brusca sacudida
tiembla el altar y el trono bambolea,

mientras aquí, con calma suicida,
se entrega Borinquen a su amargura,
—paria que al fin su servidumbre olvida—,

Y así se agosta, virgen sin ventura,
átomo leve en el esfuerzo humano
como una mancha estéril de verdura
perdida en la mitad del océano.

The independence issue, begun as a political and patriotic cause, was expanded into an economic issue as well (with anticapitalist and anti-Yankee overtones) by Pedro Albizu Campos (1891–1965). Like de Diego, he had been converted to Catholicism from positivism in his early manhood. He was influenced by Vasconcelos in Mexico and by other leading *pensadores* in the decade after World War I when, as vice president of the Puerto Rican Nationalist Party, he spent three years traveling in Latin America in order to build support for Puerto Rican independence. His was the age of resurgent nationalism and severe internal crisis for the capitalist system. It was an age that witnessed the end of colonialism in Ireland and the Balkans, as well as anticolonial stirrings in India and the Orient. It marked the triumph of many kinds of socialist movements, including the Mexican Revolution of 1910 and the Russian Revolution of 1917. The response of the Catholic church to these crises was an anticapitalist theory of society based on Neo-Thomism as articulated by Jacques Maritain, among others.

Albizu Campos entered into the spirit of his age and, with the fervor of his religious conversion, used Neo-Thomist philosophy to explain the cause of Puerto Rican independence. A graduate of Harvard Law School, he used his considerable legal skills to seek a juridic confrontation with the United States. He sustained the natural-law theory of nationhood and argued that a court of international law should intervene in the Puerto Rican situation. He attempted to question the legality of the treaty signed at the end of the Spanish-American War. In a brief filed with the Court of Appeals in Boston, he used an argument from constitutional law. The United States had no moral right to the island, he said, since the treaty in 1898 had "given" Puerto Ricans to the United States as a *res in commercium*, to pay for the war debt. Clearly this is slavery, and the Constitution of the United States prohibits slavery. Therefore, the United States occupation of Puerto Rico is unconstitutional.

Perhaps because Albizu was black himself, he went further. He asserted that this treatment of Puerto Ricans as political slaves was natural for a racist nation like the United States. And he blamed this racism on Protestantism. Influenced by the writings of James Connolly, who was a hero of the Easter Rebellion that led eventually to Irish independence, Albizu compared the Protestant United States to England and Catholic Puerto Rico to oppressed Ireland. Moreover, he used the just-war theory to legitimize armed resistance, when all legal recourse to rectify injustice had failed. His firm conviction that a state of war existed between the Puerto Rican people and the government of the United States led him to encourage the transformation of his political party into a paramilitary force. Branded alternately as fascist and as communist, Albizu was neither, but his frequent equation of violence with heroism became the Achilles' heel of the Nationalist Party.

Jailed repeatedly and harassed mercilessly by the police, Albizu spent most of his life after 1937 in prisons, until his death in 1965. To Mexican Americans, Albizu's career should be strongly reminiscent of Ries López Tijerina, who insists that the United States has no legal title to much of the American Southwest (Acuña, 1972, pp. 237–241). The considerable oratorical skills of both men, together with their religious fervor, have given them great appeal among the common people. Both men found their efforts at legal settlement cut short by imprisonment after trials of doubtful justice (see pp. 67ff.).

Even though recent political events in Puerto Rico have altered the relationship between Catholicism and the independence cause, the strongest tradition of Catholicism as a source of national identity is found among those Puerto Ricans who share the ideals of Albizu Campos's Nationalist Party. Even if the Nationalists are guilty of romanticism, the nobility of their aspirations is profoundly influenced by Catholicism. The following selection is from one of Albizu's famous speeches on Columbus Day, or *Día de la raza*. Despite a spontaneous oratorical style that loses its impact in print, this speech demonstrates Albizu's understanding of Hispano Catholic values in opposition to the racist, materialistic North American Protestantism. He utilizes the themes of Vasconcelos, his friend, but translates them into a Puerto Rican experience.

16. Columbus Day Speech, Ponce, Puerto Rico, October 12, 1933

Pedro Albizu Campos

Full text appears in Manuel Maldonado Denis, ed., La conciencia nacional puertorriqueña *(Mexicò, D.F.: Siglo XXI, 1972), pp. 191 et passim. Trans. A.M.S.A.*

WOMEN IN THE PUERTO RICAN NATION

... After undergoing other invasions and finally destroying the Arab civilization, Spain achieved its greatest work ... under the inspiration of a woman —Isabela the Catholic. And that is because a people's sense of unity has to come from women.

Where women are divided, the nation is pulled apart. Where the white woman is not a sister to the black woman, there is no nationhood, there is no civilization; there is only barbarity, opposition, ruin, murder. The woman nurtures the unity of a race, the unity of a civilization, the unity of a people. The principles of this glowing, inspired unity in Spain were crystalized in Isabela the Catholic. The moral engine of unity was a woman, just as the engine of unity in Puerto Rico has to be Puerto Rican women.

Puerto Rico will be free, Puerto Rico will be sovereign and independent, when the Puerto Rican woman feels free, sovereign, and independent. And for the Puerto Rican woman to achieve this unity, she has to feel it in her bones. . . .

Gentlemen, where women do not feel in their bones sisterhood with other women, without distinction of creed, race, or material aspirations, nationhood has not been formed. It has not been formed because woman is the intimate mover of man. Men believe they are very strong and the almighty on earth. They demand obedience from women, and women always say Yes to men—if it suits them. . . .

There is a myth that the male is the stronger sex and another that the female is the weaker. Yet women have governed the world from the beginning. Women are the great statespersons, the dictators par excellence, ruling over the most critical moments of life. They allow men to govern when it suits them and they assume dictatorship when it suits them, but always with great diplomacy. And I say that women possess not only feminine talents, but also the talents of all the diplomats that ever were or will be.

Women in Puerto Rico must begin to think seriously of the enormous dignity they represent in this country. They must not let themselves be guided by movements that degenerate and reduce them to beasts of burden and that make them objects of man's most vulgar passions. . . .

THE ECONOMIC EXPLOITATION OF PUERTO RICO

Puerto Rico is the fifth largest market in the world for the great country of Mr. George Washington; the fifth largest market on this planet is Puerto Rico. And we are only a mission of six hundred thousand souls! Figure how much we're worth in dollars and cents! The balance of trade of our nation, that is, the value of what Puerto Rico exports compared to what Puerto Rico imports, for three hundred years favored Puerto Rico. Now the value of what is sold compared to what is bought, the balance of trade, amounts to one million two hundred and fifty thousand dollars against us.

There are those who say that Puerto Rico cannot be independent because it is very poor. I say you shouldn't be so stupid. You should read your own history and know these matters and know who were your fathers and mothers so that you can speak about the independence of your homeland.

Where is all this Puerto Rican money, gentlemen? Where is it? Each one of you ought to have something like one hundred pounds sterling in gold here, right? (*Laughter.*) The pack of bills you carry in your pocket is enormous, right? (*Laughter.*) We're all very rich here right?

Well, the Yankees have robbed all this from the people of Puerto Rico. They have it over there! (*Gesture. . .*)

THE STRUGGLE IS INTERNATIONAL

I have spent five years making speeches in this place, analyzing each week the problems of Puerto Rico and of Ponce. I am not one of those who says, "I am not a Nationalist because I am an internationalist, because I love humanity." This fellow who insists he loves humanity is murdering his Puerto Rican brother. Charity begins at home. Those who love their own kind, love their neighbor. Those who don't love their own kind, don't love their neighbor. Such persons are hypocrites.

Do you wish to be worthy of a celebration like this one? You have to demand respect for the symbols of your origins. You have to punish severely those who come to disrupt an event such as this. And it is only this kind of event that will win respect from our enemy, because it shows the enemy that you're not completely hopeless.

Do you want to be respected by your own brothers and sisters? Stand here in this plaza surrounded by the sacred heroes of our race, by Isabela the Catholic, by Ferdinand, by patriots like Bolívar, Sucre, Rius Rivera, Betances. Then you will understand what these flags stand for. You will understand what a flag is and what a day of *la raza* is. . . .

CATHOLICISM VS. RACISM

The fundamental principles of which I speak constitute the Christian aspiration of a people. In the United States there is no Christianity. So when a black man sits down on the train where he is not supposed to, the Yankees simply grab him by his rear end and drag him off so that the other blacks can see what awaits them. (*Laughter and applause.*) Don't laugh! Silence! That is what ruins our people. They are forever being dragged around by the feet and they don't defend themselves.

If Christianity existed in the United States, there would be no lynchings, because if there were a Catholic priest there, he would defend the black person. They admire this; the best of the Yankees are surprised at these things in Puerto Rico. (*Gesture to the church.*) They admire our interior peace—they say "interior peace"—but we tell them it is the renovation of our soul and blood. And we tell them that we are the depository of their salvation.

And now our hour begins. We must not abandon our people to those who do not know the grandeur of the civilization that courses through our veins. Even as the Spaniards saved the Iberian peninsula, we will save our lands from profane hands. Puerto Rico must begin to yank out by the roots this economic invasion, this political and cultural invasion: nationalism involves every aspect of nationhood.

Each one of you has to become a landowner, each one of you has to own at least a tiny plot, so that you know what land is worth. You do not defend your freedom because you do not know what the land is worth, because you do not know what it is to be on a piece of land where a law of dispossession cannot throw your wives, your children, your mothers into the street with nothing but the shirts on their backs. . . .

ELECTORAL FARCE IN PUERTO RICO

There is no act more contemptible than placing the independence of Puerto Rico on public auction. The man who sells his vote is unworthy of living there.[1]

They said we had an election. What election? They are elections of sheep, of pigs! That kind of election is like a herd of pigs who run to put their garbage into the ballot box. They were offered a piece of sausage and were guided by their smell.

Citizens? Citizens of Hell! Slavery has no citizenship; it is death for everyone who embraces the goddess of shame. You want freedom? You want to be masters of your lands? Then rise up! Lift up your heads, if you want to have the right even to speak Spanish. But no one has the right to speak any human language to defend slavery.

I am going to finish, gentlemen, because my time is running out. I am going to speak to my beloved people, to this piece of the earth most beloved by me of all my homeland. To it I have been consecrated ever since I was a small boy. Ever since I was in school, I have contributed to the uplifting of the spirit of my people. I tell you now that you are the owners of a great treasure. . . .

THE REASON FOR THE CELEBRATION

Here today, gentlemen, we honor the memory of all that is great. There is an obligation laid upon every person who possesses anything to share it with one's brothers and sisters, even with one's enemy, because one's enemy is also one's brother. Nationalism is the teacher of world brotherhood and is the affirmation of one's own dignity. Nationalism expresses the principle that we are always bound to our enemy by right—even though we struggle and cross swords in a duel to the death. We are not going to kill a fallen enemy, we are not going to attack an enemy unfairly, because our movement is inspired by the Christian civilization of our people. We do not recognize assassination.

We have something good to breathe into America. Let us begin by assuring our own civilization to our posterity in Puerto Rico. And let us, together with the other people of the Antilles, carry our civilization to North America, so

---

1. Impoverished peasants were often pressured to sell their votes to the wealthy landowners.—Ed.

that it will cover the world from pole to pole. Thus will we be forever affirmed on this planet.

Nationalism postulates four beautiful principles: the independence of Puerto Rico, the Antillean Confederation, Pan-American unity, and the hegemony of the Iberoamerican people for the glory of all of us before history. In the Tribunal of the Hague they have just finished rendering homage to the greatest jurist of the modern age, the father of international law, the priest Friar Vittoria.

Spanish art, all the science of our race, above all the spiritual values, the values of the soul of our race are our aspirations, the supreme aspirations in a welter of material ambitions. The orgy of the golden calf is carrying humanity toward chaos and destruction. And I tell you that it will carry us to a world war as disastrous and fatal as the last one.

Puerto Rico has to play its role in history, and in order to look posterity in the face, it has to be free.

There then is our history, our flag, the flag of our forebears, the flag of our brothers and sisters. There is our flag that is also the flag of the future of Puerto Rico! Unfurl the flag and die shoulder to shoulder for it!

Gentlemen, I have finished.

CHAPTER THREE

PAN-AMERICAN CURRENTS

The poverty of the depression years leading up to World War II fell heavily on Puerto Ricans and Mexican Americans. Economic necessity forced greater and greater numbers of Hispanos looking for jobs to migrate to different parts of the United States. But despite the separation from their homelands, ideas of a national identity remained alive. Whether it was an intellectual like Mercedes Negrón Muñoz, known as Clara Lair, reminiscing about Puerto Rico while in New York, or an anonymous Mexican laborer working on the railroad, the love of homeland was counterpoised to the sense of loneliness and hardship in the United States. The two different sentiments—one of nostalgia for the homeland, the other of anger against the United States system—were to explode in the Nationalist attack on the United States Congress in 1954.

---

17. Tres Nocturnos de Nueva York
(Three New York Nocturnes)

Clara Lair [Mercedes Negrón Muñoz]

Trans. A.M.S.A.

¡Islita en que he nacido, Puerto Rico . . . !
Pobre tierra cedida y entregada;
Leve paisaje, brisa de abanico,
Día calcinador, noche extasiada. . . .

¿Tierra ansiosa de qué? ¡Nadie lo sabe!
Tierra sin rumbo, sin nivel, sin meta. . . .
Eres igual a mí, fija e inquieta.
Eres igual a mí, estanque y ave. . . .

No queriéndolo ser, soy a tu modo.
Sueño de lucha, despertar de entrega. . . .
Y en mi siembra y mi flor como en mi siega,
Dejas tu inútil pequeñez en todo.

* * *

Little island where I was born, Puerto Rico . . . !
Poor land, delivered and surrendered;
Delicate scenery, fresh breezes,
Daytime furnace, nightime rapture. . . .

A land eager for what? No one knows!
Land without direction, without balance, without goal. . . .
You are the same as me, fixed yet restless,
You are the same as me, the pond yet a bird aflight. . . .

Not wishing to be, I am made in your mold.
A dream of struggle, a wakening up to surrender. . . .
And in my sowing, in my flower, and in my harvest,
You leave your useless smallness in everything.

This song was composed in the 1920s during the period of heavy Mexican immigration to the United States. The title "Los Enganchados," meaning literally "The Hooked," refers to contract laborers.

18. *Los Enganchados*
(The Hooked)

Anonymous

From David F. Gómez, Somos Chicanos *(Boston: Beacon Press, 1973), p. 57,* citing *Manuel Gamia,* Mexican Immigration to the United States *(Chicago: Univ. of Chicago Press, 1930), pp. 84-86. Used by permission.*

Cuando salimos de El Paso	When we left El Paso
A las dos de la mañana,	At two in the morning,
Le pregunté al "reenganchista"[1]	I asked the boss contractor
Si vamos para Louisiana.	If we are going to Louisiana.
Llegamos a la Laguna	We arrived at Laguna
Sin esperanza ninguna.	Without any hope.
Le pregunté al "reenganchista"	I asked the boss
Si vamos para "Oclajuma."	If we are going to Oklahoma.
Unos descargaban rieles	Some unloaded rails
Otros descargaban "tallas."	And others unloaded ties.
Y otros de los compañeros	And others of my companions
Echaban de mil malallas.	Threw thousands of curses.
"Más valiera estar en Kansas	"It would be better to be in Kansas
Que nos mantenga el gobierno."	Where the government would support us."
"Valía más estar en Juárez	"It would be better to be in Juárez
Aunque sea sin trabajar."	Even if we were without work."
Estos versos son compuestos	These verses were composed
por un pobre mexicano	By a poor Mexican
Pa'[2] ponerlos al corriente	To spread the word about
Del sistema americano.	The American system.

1. *Reenganchista*=boss contractor; *ganche* literally means "hook"; here it refers to a contract for migrant work, or *enganche*.
2. *Pa'*, for *para*.

Pedro Albizu Campos and other leaders of the Nationalist Party of Puerto Rico were tried in 1937 for sedition against the United States. When the first trial resulted in a hung jury, the government saw to it that for the new trial the jury was composed of ten North Americans living on the island and two Puerto Ricans who worked for United States banks. After the guilty verdict was rendered, the Nationalists were sent to Atlanta Federal Penitentiary. Public protests against the trial were widespread, but repression was swift and brutal. On March 21, 1937, Palm Sunday, in the southern Puerto Rican city of Ponce, twenty-one Puerto Ricans were killed by the National Guard and 105 persons were injured while participating in a peaceful march to the central plaza. The incident is known as the Ponce Massacre, and the military was condemned by a special United States investigation panel.

Released ten years later (1947), Albizu returned to a Puerto Rico that was heading toward a political destiny involving a new autonomist status as designed by Luis Muñoz Marín. On July 4, 1950, President Harry S. Truman signed Law 600, which permitted a Puerto Rican Assembly to draft a constitution for a limited amount of self-government on the island. Hounded by police, and persecuted by the Law of the Muzzle, a Puerto Rican version of the Smith Act (anti-subversive act passed during the McCarthy era), Albizu and the Nationalists realized that they were unable to operate by any normal political process. They decided on armed rebellion.

On October 30, 1950, the Nationalists attacked several island towns and the governor's mansion in San Juan. They captured the municipality of Jayuya and proclaimed the establishment of the Second Puerto Rican Republic. By November 1 the revolution had been quashed and all Nationalist sympathizers were rounded up and jailed. On November 3 two Puerto Rican Nationalists from New York City, Griselio Torresola and Oscar Collazo, made an attack on Blair House, where President Truman was living during the renovation of the White House (Maldonado Denis, 1969, pp. 197ff.). Torresola and a federal guard died in the shooting, and Collazo was seriously wounded. Collazo was sentenced to death for the attack, but the sentence was commuted to life imprisonment.

Albizu Campos was jailed once again. In 1952 the Puerto Rican Common-wealth was established with Muñoz Marín as governor. The United Nations, however, looked upon the new commonwealth suspiciously. In an era of liberating former colonies throughout the world, the legal status of Puerto Rico's self-government was not comparable to the independence granted new nations in Africa and the Caribbean. The vote to approve the removal of Puerto Rico from the list of colonies was passed by the Decolonization Committee 26 to 16, with 18 abstentions. The United States, however, guaranteed United Nations inspection of the island and eventual improvement in the juridic powers of Puerto Rico (EPICA, 1976, pp. 22–24).

On March 1, 1954, the eve of the thirty-seventh anniversary of the passage of the Jones Act (in 1917), the Nationalists from New York again demonstrated on behalf of the sovereignty they claimed for Puerto Rico. During a vote upon a bill that would have authorized a continuation of the Bracero program admitting Mexican laborers to the United States, the Nationalists in the gallery prayed the

Lord's Prayer together, stood up waving the Puerto Rican flag and shouting, "¡Viva Puerto Rico libre!"—and began to shoot. According to an account in the *Washington Post,* some congressmen thought it was "a demonstration with blanks." However five representatives were wounded by shots from the pistols of the Nationalists, although none died or was permanently injured (Wagenheim, 1970. pp. 204–207).

The following note was found in the purse of the leader, Lolita Lebrón:

> Before God and the world, my blood claims the independence of Puerto Rico. My life I give for the freedom of my country. This is a cry for victory in our struggle for independence which for more than half a century has tried to conquer the land that belongs to Puerto Rico.
>
> I state forever that the United States of America are betraying the sacred principles of mankind in their continuous subjugation of my country, in violation of our rights to be a free nation and a free people, and in their barbarous torture of our apostle of independence, Don Pedro Albizu Campos.

José Vasconcelos, the Mexican *Pensador,* wrote the following in defense of the Puerto Rican Nationalists.

19. The Puerto Rican Nationalists

José Vasconcelos

From Novedades, *as quoted in Federico Rives Tovar,* Albizu Campos: Puerto Rican Revolutionary *(New York: Plus Ultra, 1971), pp. 146–150. Used by permission. Trans. Federico Rives Tovar*

In my first reflections on what had happened in the House of Representatives of the United States, there was a sentiment of repulsion, perhaps of condemnation. Afterwards, only afterwards, did I feel pity and, with it, the feeling that there are, in Man, despite his usual wretchedness, possibilities so great that they cannot be perceived by the eyes of the pygmies who form the commonality of each generation. The day following the events, I studied a photograph: that of Lolita Lebrón, the slender young lady dressed correctly and in a way to set off her Spanish type. Graceful and serene, she held in both hands, as she paraded before the UN in New York, a poster which read: "We demand the complete independence of Puerto Rico."

The grave representatives of the imposing and useless United Nations doubtless had no time to look at the poster; probably, some felt themselves briefly attracted by the beauty of the bearer of that silent patriotic demand. The Great Ones of the earth do not put themselves out for anything so trivial as the caprices of a supposed minority on a small island demanding the right to live in accordance with their race, their language and their religion. And they decide, without reflection: the United States has already granted them a national status. What more do they want? Why do they make a fuss? We must hurry and—taking out a watch—we have a couple of receptions after the assembly today, and a banquet tonight. A lot of work.

The indifference of the many, the treachery to their ideals consummated by governments given to compromise, cause desperation in courageous temperaments. "What can be achieved by desperation?" the prudent, the Pharisees, are apt to ask. Doubtless nothing immediate. But that same nothing may be a solution, for nothing is preferable to ignominy; nothing sometimes surprises us with the treasures that lurk in its depths. In any event, it is a refuge when the moment comes when death is preferable to a life without honor. Worse is the fate of those who deliver themselves to the nothing that is the worldly life, expecting to find in it satisfactions which content only the unworthy.

Because of a desperation which was superhuman, three or four island patriots, led by Lolita Lebrón, took the road from New York to Washington. They made the trip by bus, because it was cheaper. The UN officials who failed to read Lolita Lebrón's posters travel high above in jet planes; they could not discern the humble caravan headed by Lolita Lebrón. The island girl, like her comrades, bought only a one-way ticket. Partly for economy, no doubt, but also because they realized that they were on a trip from which there was no return.

When a people suffers military occupation without having provoked it; when Puerto Rico was wrenched away from the motherland, in which it had five deputies and one senator, like any other free province of Spain; when a people has given hundreds of thousands of lives in all the wars of its new masters; when, in exchange for all this, they seek to satisfy it with a constitution which does not give it control even over the internal administration of its revenues, nor its customs, nor its foreign affairs; when the group of men who represent the best of a nationality sees that all roads are closed to it and that its struggle is hopeless, because it has to confront a Colossus which is almost omnipotent, for the moment that group of patriots has no other path to follow but that of desperation, nor any other program but the sometimes fruitful program of the absurd.

There are not many who sympathize with the cause of Puerto Rico. Not all those leftists who issue intellectual manifestoes and raise their fists in the political fronts are prepared to commit themselves to such a cause. The leftists are cautious. They do not go against what really affects the interests of the rulers of the United States. They denounce imperialism, but are always careful not to annoy the heirs of Mr. Roosevelt and Mr. Truman and the Good Neighbor policy. Puerto Rico's nationalism, which is not communist nor liberal in the style of *The New York Times* and *The Nation*, is outside all that. In the last analysis, the leftists seldom commit themselves to the attack.

The Puerto Rican Nationalists, who are, in their majority, Catholics, demand for their country the maintenance of its language and the customs of their Spanish ancestors. The case which can be compared with that of the Nationalists of Puerto Rico is that of Ireland. And history knows no more heroic example of desperate struggle through the ages to final victory. We sincerely believe that it is within the United States itself that the Puerto Rican Nationalists may find loyal friends.

At any rate, the act of desperation in the gallery of the American Congress has already moved the consciences of two or three American Congressmen, who, with all the reserves of generosity and righteousness that inspire the American people, have cried, in response to the involuntarily criminal bullets of their Puerto Rican assailants: Why do we not grant these Puerto Ricans their independence once and for all?

The atmosphere of distrust and suspicion that prevails in the Pan-American Assembly in Caracas, which began on the same day as the events in the House of Representatives in Washington, is no secret to anybody. In an instant and as if by a miracle, the United States would earn the confidence, the gratitude, the affection of the twenty nations of this continent by an action which would cost them nothing: the granting to Puerto Rico of an authentic sovereignty, accompanied by a general amnesty, as was demanded in Cuba by the representatives of Spanish-American thought in connection with the Maritime Congress of last year. . . .

The eerie symbol of an attack upon the House of Representatives by Puerto Rican Nationalists during the vote on the *Bracero* program was just one of the auguries during the 1950s of the growing currents toward solidarity among Hispano people. The writings of international *pensadores* like Vasconcelos expressed this solidarity for the educated classes. Communication for working-class people was less sophisticated. Folk songs, hastily recorded on phonograph records and played on radio broadcasts, had been available for some time to Hispano migrants in the United States. Now added to radio were the cinema and eventually television. The themes of the songs were more defiant, describing discrimination or a workers' strike for higher wages. The places linked together, such as Texas to Pennsylvania, gave proof that regional distances were shrinking. Public personalities were known from coast to coast. Movie stars like Libertad Lamarque and Jorge Negrete were idolized. Hispanos laughed together with North American movie audiences at the antics of Mexican comedian Cantinflas in the production *Around the World in Eighty Days.* The Puerto Rican José Ferrer won an Academy Award in 1950. Carmen Miranda frolicked through a Bing Crosby-Bob Hope special. Xavier Cugat was a celebrity while the *mambo* and the *cha-cha-cha* were the rage. In sports, Cuban welterweight Kid Gavilán thrilled TV boxing audiences from Brooklyn to the Golden Gate with his bolo punch, and the Puerto Rican baseball players Roberto Clemente and Orlando Cepeda achieved stardom in the middle 1960s.

The tragic side of the Hispano migration to northern cities was graphically dramatized in the Broadway musical *West Side Story.* This visibility helped to mature what would eventually become a national Hispano consciousness.

This popular song, a *seis*, was composed and sung by Baltasar Carrero. It allows a Puerto Rican working man to criticize a system which, he feels, he can escape by returning to Puerto Rico.

20. El Jíbarito de Adjuntas
(I'm Going Back to My Shack)

Baltasar Carrero

Used by permission. Trans. A. M. S. A.

Si yo vine a Nueva York con el fin de progresar,	If I came to New York I came with the idea of getting ahead.
si allí lo pasaba mal aquí lo paso peor. Unas veces el calor y otras el maldito frío, a veces parezco un lío por la nieve patinando, esto no me está gustando yo me vuelvo a mi bohío.	If things are bad there they are worse here. Sometimes the heat and then the damn cold, at times I look like a mess slipping along in the snow, I'm getting to dislike this I'm going back to my shack.
Fui por el Parque Central me estuvo muy divertido, y me preguntó un amigo que si sabía "caminar," "yo estoy aprendiendo a andar,"	I went by Central Park I was really having a good time, and a friend asked me if I knew how to get along, "I'm learning to get around

le contesté, "amigo mío."
Pero me siento aturdido
oyendo tanto alboroto,
y por no volverme loco
yo me vuelvo a mi bohío.

Ay, no sigo de esta manera
porque no me está gustando
de estar subiendo y bajando
las malditas escaleras.
No sé qué suerte me espera,

cuándo saldré de este lío.
En ver donde estoy "metío"[1]
no puedo hablar con certeza.
Esto es un rompecabeza
yo me vuelvo. . . .

Ay, llega el día de cobrar,
llega el día de cobrar,
me pongo a sacar cuenta.
Después de pagar la renta
¿cuánto me puede sobrar?
Y el resto se va en pagar
lo poco que me he comío.[2]
Con el bolsillo vacío
no sé a dónde iré a parar.

Si nunca a mí me sobra un real
yo me vuelvo. . . .
Compadre Ladí,
yo me vuelvo a mi bohío.

my good friend," was my answer.
But I get rattled
hearing so much noise,
And in order not to go crazy
I'm going back to my shack

Oooo, I'm not continuing this way
because I'm getting to dislike it,
This going up and coming down
the damn stairways.
I don't know what kind of luck
   awaits me
when I can get out of this mess.
In seeing where I'm stuck
I can't say for sure.
This is a puzzle
I'm going back. . . .

Oooo, come pay day,
come pay day
I start to take account.
After paying the rent
how much will I have left?
And the rest goes to pay for
the little I got to eat.
With my pocket empty
I don't know where I'm going to
   end up
If I ever have a buck left over
I'm going back. . . .
Old buddy, Ladí,
I'm going back to my shack.

1. *metío:* for *metido*
2. *Comío:* for *comido.*

A Mexican balladeer, a migrant worker recruited from across the border for foundry work (*worque*) in the Pennsylvania steel mills, composed this *corrido* in 1955.

21. Corrido

Anonymous

From Armando B. Rendón, Chicano Manifesto *(New York: Collier Books, 1971), p. 150. Trans. A.M.S.A.*

El veintiocho de abril
a las seis de la mañana
salimos en un enganche[1]
pa'l[2] estado de Pensilvania.

Adiós, estado de Texas,
con toda tu plantación,
yo me voy para Pensilvania
por no pizcar[3] algodón.

Al llegar al "steel mill worque"[4]
que vemos la locomotora
¡y salimos corriendo
ochenta millas por hora!

Ya con ésta me despido
con mi sombrero en las manos
de mis fieles compañeros
son trescientos mexicanos.

The twenty-fifth of April
at six in the morning
we left under contract
for the State of Pennsylvania.

Goodbye, State of Texas,
with all of your farming,
I'm off for Pennsylvania
to get away from picking cotton.

Getting to the steel mill foundry
We saw the locomotive
And we left running
at eighty miles an hour!

Now with this I bid farewell
with my hat in my hands
to my faithful companions,
the three hundred Mexicans.

1. *Enganche:* for *contrato.*
2. *Pa'l:* for *para el.*
3. *Pizcar:* instead of *recoger.*
4. *Worque:* for the English "steel works."

"¡Alo! ¿Quién Ñama?" is a *plena* that became a commercial hit in both Puerto Rico and New York during the 1950s. The singer, Mon Rivera, dramatized the experience of women on strike in a laundry. The telephone call represents the search for scab labor by the employers.

22. ¡Alo! ¿Quién Ñama?
(Hello! Who's There?)

Mon Rivera

Used by permission. Trans. A.M.S.A.

¡Alo! ¿Quién ñama?[1]
María Luisa Arcelay conectando con JohnVidal.
Dicen las planchadoras
que si no hay plata no van a
planchar.
¿Qué será, qué pasará? Que el taller de Ma'[2] Mary
que pide gente pa' trabajar.

Empezó la huelga.
¡Dios mío qué barbaridad!
Las trabajadoras, comenzaron a bembetear,[3]
que si cuchicú—que si cuchicá.[4]
¡Petra, apaga esa plancha,
no trabajemos ná![5]
¿Qué se cree esta gente?
No nos tienen piedad.
La lana[6] que aquí nos pagan
Ay, no nos da pa'[7] ná,
Ay que si cuchicú. . . .

*   *   *

Hello! Who's there?
María Luisa Arcelay talking with John Vidal.
The pressers say
that if there's no money they're not going to press.
What will be? What will happen? In the workshop of Ma' Mary
they're looking for people to work.

The strike began.
My God what a terrible scene!
The workers, they started to give us a lot of lip,
"That if doo-dee-dee, that if doo-dee-dah. . . ."

"Petra, turn off your iron!
We work no more!
What do these people think?
They don't have any feeling for us.
"The dough that they give us here,
it doesn't pay for anything.
That if doo-dee-dee. . . ."

1. *Ñama:* slang pronunciation for *llama.*
2. *Ma':* short for *Madre.*
3. *Bembetear: bembe* is a word of African origin used in Puerto Rico to refer to lips with negroid characteristics. *Bembetear* is a verb formed from that word and is similar to the English idiomatic expression "to give a lot of lip" in the sense of petulant response.
4. *Cuchicú, cuchicá:* nonsense sounds.
5. *Ná:* for *nada.*
6. *Lana:* means "wool," but used here in the sense of money.
7. *Pa':* for *para.*

The Puerto Rican Nationalists (see pp. 67ff.)   *(courtesy Claridad)*

CHAPTER FOUR

SOLITARY EFFORTS
TOWARD A HISPANO CHURCH

Puerto Rico is the birthplace of the Catholic church in the Americas; it was the first diocese in the New World to receive its bishop, Alonso Manso, who arrived in 1513. When the easy wealth of Indian gold evaporated, the island lost population and the episcopal see suffered diminished importance. Nonetheless, throughout the years of the Spanish colonial empire, Puerto Rico served as first step for new bishops, including a high percentage of Latin American-born prelates. Only one of these was a Puerto Rican, however (see p. 87).

In 1898, when the United States took control of Puerto Rico, Rome could have removed the island see from the Office of Propaganda Fidei and attached it to a continental ecclesiastical province, such as Florida. But the Vatican left things as they were. While some importance can be attached to the failure to annex Puerto Rico to a United States ecclesiastical province, it probably has more to do with Puerto Rico's small size than a pro-independence attitude from Rome. The bishops of the island, like all bishops of United States territories and possessions, belonged to the North American church. Indeed, Puerto Rico continued as a first step for prelates who went on to "greater things": Bishops James Blenck to New Orleans; George J. Caruana to the Vatican diplomatic corps; Aloysius J. Willinger, C.SS.R. to Monterey, California; Edwin Vincent Byrne and James P. Davis to Santa Fe, New Mexico.

In contrast, as the Franciscan historian Chávez describes, New Mexico did not achieve diocesan stature until the Mexican-American War made it necessary to separate the new United States territory from the Mexican Diocese of Durango. Thus ecclesiastical history for the Santa Fe Diocese begins with the intervention of the United States. Interestingly, the Holy See has viewed Puerto Rico as a training ground for at least two of the most recent ordinaries of Santa Fe.

Chapter Four presents some of the solitary efforts toward a Hispano church, beginning in the New Mexico settlement of the seventeenth century as described by twentieth-century historian Fray Angélico Chávez, O.F.M. Later, in the nineteenth century, the priest Antonio José Martínez (1793–1867) defended the Mexican American reality against an invading United States church that was not able to recognize the treasure of Catholicism in the Southwest.

The Puerto Rican reality has undergone a similar process, continuing into the present day with the forceful presence of Bishop Antulio Parrilla Bonilla (b. 1919).

These church leaders echoed the ideas of the *pensadores*, insisting that there was a unique Catholicism present in the national identity of Puerto Ricans and Mexican Americans despite the insensitivity of ecclesiastical leaders who favored a complete assimilation into United States structures. They lacked none of the talents required for authentic Hispano church leadership, but the people were not yet ready for their words. Their contributions remain as solitary efforts toward a Hispano church.

23. Native Hispano Vocations

Fray Angélico Chávez, O.F.M.

From Address at the PADRES Retreat, Santa Fe, New Mexico, delivered on February 2, 1970. Used by permission. Trans. A.M.S.A.

... The colony of New Mexico began anew, and once again through the missions. More priests came—but never enough, because the Hispano population increased; besides, the Hispanos in their charity celebrated fiestas with the pagan Indians, when they were not fighting with them. Some of these Indians fought among themselves; the Comanches fought with the Haiwas and with the Panamas, and they stole children from one another and then they came to sell them to the Hispano people of New Mexico. Thus they were called "Indians of ransom." The Hispanos took grain to them and they celebrated together. They exchanged it for a little Indian, boy or girl, and took care of these children in their own families and gave them their names. Then, when they reached marriageable age, they were let free and were not slaves. They married one another and they were called "Geniseros" because they were not Indians of some tribe, as we say, but they were of different tribes and of different tongues. They did not have their own language, but spoke Spanish. In time these Geniseros married with the Spanish people; because carnal love becomes divine love in that there are no distinctions of classes for those who are in love—whether the pope likes it or not—they marry. So it is that we of New Mexico are mestizo. Some of us are mostly Spanish, some mostly Indian, and some part Indian and part Spanish. But we are all Spanish-Americans. And we are all Catholics—but now I'm going off on a tangent and we were going to speak about vocations.

The population was so small that, in its first century, Santa Fe did not have more than six hundred persons. As for the rest of the town, there were no others; nor were there even Hispano villages; there were only ranches. Because the population was so small there never was a question of whether or not some of the native sons would be priests. There were no seminaries; how could they have had the inspiration? The Franciscan Friars had their headquarters in Mexico City, some 1,200 miles from here with nothing in between. Who could think about vocations? Thus there is no record of any New Mexican who became a Franciscan. I am the first since the Conquest. In the year 1724, Ignacio de Roybal, a Spaniard from Caldos de Reyes, a city of Compostela, came here as a soldier to New Mexico. (Many soldiers arrived at this time and married the women of New Mexico.) And the son of Ignacio de Roybal, Santiago de Roybal, went to Mexico to study. I don't know if he went to study for the priesthood, but in the end he was ordained. The archbishop of Mexico ordained him. The bishops at that time wanted to put a finger on what was happening here—I don't know why—because they were not able to govern from so far away. But there was always some dispute between the regular friars and the bishops, and the salvation of souls didn't matter as much as having jurisdiction. The friars were also guilty because they wanted to be in charge. Then the archbishop of Mexico, upon ordaining this young man of New Mexico, sent him to the bishop of Durango, Bishop Hesper, in order that he would set foot in New Mexico. He sent Señor Roybal as his vicar, but he got along well with the friars anyway. He lived for half a century as vicar and the only secular priest. At the end, when he died around 1764, the Franciscan priests of Santa Fe wrote: "Today we bury our most beloved curé who died upon finishing the Holy Mass." After finishing the Holy Mass, the old man returned to God. And I say "old man" because he is my uncle seven times removed, but he could be the first native priest within the limits of the United States. I never heard anything to make me believe otherwise. It is possible that in Florida, when it was a Spanish colony, some fifty years before New Mexico, some native Spaniard was a priest in Cuba, in Puerto Rico,[1] or on the continent; we don't know. But Reverend Vicar Santiago de Roybal without doubt is the first native Chicano priest in the United States—before the Irish, all the French, and everybody else. And he became a vicar right after ordination—and he was my uncle.

In the seventeenth century the population grew and there were fewer friars. Some of the poor priests died and replacements were not sent. Later there was more work for the poor friars and that was worse for the people,

1. The distinction of being the first native of all the Americas to become a priest belongs to Luis Ponce de León, the only male heir of Juan Ponce de León, first governor of Puerto Rico and discoverer of Florida. Luis was ordained as a Dominican, August 31, 1527, by Bishop Alonso Manso of San Juan, Puerto Rico. (See Vincente Murga Sanz, *Juan Ponce de León* [San Juan: Editorial Universitaria, 1971], p. 18 et passim.)

who were left without instruction. Religious instruction occurred only between parents and their children. Then at the end of the eighteenth century,
around 1799, the bishop of Durango sent three secular priests, but they did
not stay long because they came from civilization to a primitive place and they
could not stay. Once again, the old Franciscan priests had to take work as
interim pastors.

Even those bishops who wanted to have jurisdiction over the area never
came. More than a generation went by before a bishop came. In 1812, for
example, the one and only representative from New Mexico to the Spanish
Cortes[2] was old Don Pedro Pino. When he saw a certain bishop of Seville in a
procession in the court he said, "This is the first bishop that I have seen in my
whole life." And the poor old man with a long beard, who spoke the archaic
Spanish of New Mexico, was called in Spain "Our father Abraham of New
Mexico."

Later in the century, in 1833, a new bishop came to Durango, the Reverend
Antonio Laureano de Zubiría, who during his episcopate of twenty-three
years made three special trips to New Mexico. Inasmuch as the Franciscans
were pulling out, it helped the people to see the need for a native clergy.
From then on, various sons of New Mexico in that time went by horseback to
Durango, at great trouble, in order to get an education. And many of them
returned priests, and some of the best of priests. There was not one scandal.
They worked with their people and died among them. And because of this,
the Reverend Zubiría merited a statue in Santa Fe in the cathedral for having
done something that was necessary and that many others had not been able to
foresee. His last visit was in 1850 (shortly before the North American troops
took over New Mexico and New Mexico became North American territory).

The bishops in Baltimore decided to ask His Holiness if he would make
Santa Fe a diocese. They sent as the first bishop a Frenchman from Ohio, His
Excellency Bishop Lamy. He was a man of superior quality, but when he
entered New Mexico he knew nothing about its conditions. The native
priests, having been educated in Durango during the revolutions for independence, were very Mexican. There was a French invasion[3] and they were
very anti-French. Then the one sent to them was a Frenchman! But the Irish
hierarchy in Baltimore knew everything—they should not have done it this
way, but then, well. . . .

2. This Cortes was a parliament formed to rule Spain and its possessions in the name of the
king, who had been taken hostage by the invading armies of Napoleon Bonaparte. In another of
those coincidences whereby the paths of New Mexico and Puerto Rico cross, the vice president
of this Cortes was Ramón Power y Girault, a Puerto Rican admiral in the Spanish navy.
3. This was the invasion during the reign of Emperor Napoleon III to place the archduke of
Austria, Maximilian, on a Mexican throne, 1864–1867.

Antonio José Martínez (1793–1867), the parish priest of Taos, New Mexico, during the nineteenth century, has been offered as the prototype of all *padres* by Juan Romero, former executive director of the Hispano priest organization known as PADRES. In a precious gem of historical scholarship, called *Reluctant Dawn*, Romero has reconstructed the life of this controversial priest.

Antonio José Martínez was born in Abiquiu, a part of present-day New Mexico. In 1812 he married, but suffered the tragedy of having his young wife die in childbirth. After ensuring the well-being of his child, he entered the seminary in Durango, Mexico, and was ordained in 1822. He was sent to Taos in 1826 and became pastor of the first parish to be named in honor of our Lady of Guadalupe in what is today the United States. Skilled as a civil and canon lawyer, he founded a newspaper called *El Crepúsculo de la Libertad* (The Twilight of Liberty) and served as deputy in the Mexican Territorial Assembly at Santa Fe. He agitated against the corruption of the Mexican dictatorships of that period and advocated New Mexican separatism. After the Mexican-American War, he presided at the convention organizing the New Mexican Territory in October 1848. He also was president of the Constitutional Convention in 1850 and served three terms in the Legislative Assembly of the New Mexican Territory.

Padre Martínez's role of leadership was severely curtailed by Bishop Lamy, who became the ordinary of the new Diocese of Santa Fe, carved from the Durango See in 1850. In 1856 the new bishop suspended the older priest for criticizing (in the *Santa Fe Gazette)* the tithing instituted by the French-born prelate. As the selection from Romero's book describes, Padre Martínez was excommunicated. History has not dealt kindly with the native New Mexican priest, and the historical biography of Bishop Lamy by Willa Cather, *Death Comes for the Archbishop*, does Padre Martínez an injustice. But as Romero points out (p. 2), there was a deeper conflict hidden in the confrontation.

> The excommunication had therefore not been the death blow to the long-time pastor. It was merely one more step in a progressive alienation which divided the Hispanic community from the institutional Church in the Southwest. . . . [Martínez] retreated to his own private oratory, from which he continued to baptize and to minister to those who came to him until his death. In much the same way, the people of New Mexico retreated to their own internal village institutions rather than follow a Church leadership out of sympathy with their culture.

The excerpt included here from one of Padre Martínez's sermons illustrates his pride in history and culture, his powerful personality, and his admiration of Miguel Hidalgo—a padre who was a *pensador* and a leader of the armed rebellion against Spain in 1810.

Padre Juan Romero is himself a descendant, on his mother's side, of the famous Padre Martínez. Born on August 31, 1938, in Taos, New Mexico, Juan migrated with his family to Los Angeles in 1943. He entered the archdiocesan seminary there and was ordained in 1964. His first assignments as a young priest in the Archdiocese of Los Angeles under Cardinal MacIntyre did not provide him with an opportunity to serve the Spanish-speaking people. However, the quickening pulse of militancy in Los Angeles eventually brought Romero into active support of the farm workers and other Mexican American causes. He participated in the first meetings of PADRES and served as executive director of that organization from November 1972 until January 1976. His graduate studies include a master's degree in bilingual education and pastoral training at the University of Salamanca, Spain. He currently is a parish priest in Los Angeles.

24. Padre Martínez

Juan Romero

From Romero, Reluctant Dawn *(San Antonio: MACC, 1976), pp. 30-38. Used by permission.*

Damasio Taladrid arrived in Taos on May 8, 1856, with official letters from Bishop Lamy authorizing him to take over the parish. But within a week there was a serious confrontation between Taladrid and Martínez. Taladrid complained in a letter to Lamy on May 14 of trouble with the parishioners. Among other things, he said the people had been ill-trained by Padre Martínez. He also informed the bishop that Martínez claimed he had not resigned but only asked for an assistant. On the same day, Padre Martínez presented his case to the people in a letter to the editor of *La Gaceta.* He gave these reasons for his "resignation": (1) his age of 64, (2) worsening health, and (3) the bishop's pastoral letter concerning taxes.

During May, June, and July Father Taladrid kept spying on Martínez and generally harassing him. Within that time, he wrote at least five letters to Bishop Lamy to complain about Padre Martínez. Taladrid forewarned Lamy that friends of Martínez would very likely be asking permission to use a private oratory. He also reported that Padre Martínez was sick in bed, and that there were rumors that he was building a private chapel. Taladrid also complained against Martínez' friend and neighbor, Padre Lucero of Arroyo Hondo. On July 23, Taladrid reported that Martínez was working on an article for the *Gaceta* concerning the abolition of tithes, and that Martínez and Lucero were often seen together. The article by Padre Martínez was published in the *Gaceta* on September 3, 1856. Lucero was suspended on September 29 because of his close association with Martínez, although that reason was not explicitly cited. Three weeks later, Lucero wrote to Lamy saying, "I deny the allegations cited by you against me."[1]

Lamy's action against Lucero made Martínez fearful that the bishop would try to curtail his own activities even further by means of ecclesiastical censure. He wrote to the Bishop on October 1, shortly before the feast of St. Francis, patron of the church in Ranchos, to state that he had personal faculties from the Franciscan Custos, which were approved by Bishop Zubiría. These faculties empowered him to receive members into the Third Order of St. Francis and to celebrate Mass for them. Padre Martínez explained that these faculties could not be delegated to Father Taladrid. Martínez further charged that Taladrid was a real trouble maker in Taos, and then enumerated his reasons for celebrating Mass in his private oratory. Martínez explained that the sacristan had been instructed not to prepare for his celebration of Mass unless it was very late in the morning, but Martínez was not able to fast for very long, and wanted to fulfill the Masses promised to the people. He concluded his letter by recognizing Bishop Lamy as his legitimate prelate.

Taladrid then wrote to Bishop Lamy on October 23 saying that Martínez was celebrating Mass in his private oratory and that he was taking over some parish functions. He again complained about Padre Lucero. The very next day Bishop Lamy suspended Padre Martínez in a curt note depriving him of canonical faculties because he celebrated Mass in the oratory. It appeared that the Bishop was waiting for some pretext for which to suspend the aged and ailing Cura de Taos. Lamy further informed Martínez that his suspension would be in effect until he retracted his article which appeared in the *Gaceta*. It seemed strange that a sick priest celebrating Mass in his own home should merit such a severe ecclesiastical censure as suspension. This is all the more surprising when one considers that Bishop Lamy's mentor, Bishop Purcell, was celebrating Masses in private homes twenty years before.[2] Furthermore, Lamy himself as a young priest also celebrated Masses in private homes.[3]

Padre Antonio José responded to the suspension by taking the offensive against what he considered to be an unjust ecclesiastical censure which lacked the formalities of due process. In a strong and forthright letter written to Bishop Lamy on November 12, 1856, Padre Martínez went to great lengths in an effort to prove through Canon Law that the suspension was null and void. While Martínez conceded that his use of a private oratory without explicit permission may not have been excusable, he insisted his publication of letters on the matter of tithes was protected by guarantees of "republican free speech." However, Martínez agreed that Lamy had every right to have given a canonical warning for either celebrating Mass in his oratory or for publishing in the *Gaceta*, if either of these things did not seem right in his eyes. But Lamy never gave even one warning, much less the required canonical three warnings. Martínez was never cited nor given a hearing or trial as required by Canon Law. In the matter of his stand on the tithes, however, Padre Martínez was uncompromising: "The point is simply this: the faithful must be given the spontaneity and the freedom in the matter of tithing and the maintenance of your excellency and other priests under you." He continued as follows:

> Its total payment as you demand under most severe penalties is in violation of the rights of this my people among whom I first saw the light of day. . . . I beg your excellency to respect my viewpoint for what I am about to say. . . . The diocesan statutes invite the faithful to enter into mercantile agreements making the parish priests appear like hucksters or traders. They also make the sacraments, Masses, and other spiritual gifts as so much merchandise in a warehouse by order of Your Excellency. . . . Compare this way of acting with the account of Simon Magus in the Acts of the Apostles. . . .[4]

Father Phillip Cassidy of Santa Fe said over 18 years ago, "This lengthy letter reveals the soul of Padre Martínez, his acuity in logic, and his almost perfect defense which is devastating while not being angry. The letter is ignored by Lamy to whom Martínez was to write five more times without ever receiving a reply."[5] Subsequent letters by Padre Martínez are couched in much softer words indicating a certain retreat from his strong stand. They became overtures, and sometimes even pleas, for reconciliation, always with that sincere personal respect for the person of the bishop. Even Father Machebeuf had to admit "the truth obliges me to say that he has never failed in a show of personal respect towards the bishop."[6]

Within two weeks, Padre Martínez again wrote a long letter to Bishop Lamy reviewing the incidents that led to the present predicament. He expressed his views on Taladrid and reminded the Bishop how long a time he had been pastor of Taos. He suggested that his long tenure was equivalent to the canonical position of "permanent rector."[7] A short time later, Martínez deplored his "furious words"[8] to the Bishop and informed him that he had made peace with Father Taladrid. Four months later, Martínez reminded Lamy that he had been ignoring his letters. In reference to this suspension, Martínez called attention to the commentary on Canon Law by Murrillo (Vol. V, Sec. 31) entitled *Decretals Against Bishops' Excesses in Matters of the Rights of their Clergy*. He informed Bishop Lamy that the canonist Murrillo cited Pope Alexander III as his authority. Padre Martínez was suffering, and was not ashamed to let Bishop Lamy know it:

> Is it that you wish to treat me the way you treated and injured other priests who because of their candor suffered all exactly the same way I do? What you did to Father Manuel Gallegos, the pastor of San Felipe, the church in Albuquerque, who because he had made a trip to Mexico in 1852 with due letters from the Vicar General returned to find himself suspended, his books and property thrown out of his rectory,

and Father José Prospecto Machebeuf ensconced in his place. You did the same with the Vicar Forane, Father Juan Felipe Ortiz, the next year without canonical regard, dividing his parish, taking his rectory away from him, and finally suspending him.[9]

Receiving no response from Bishop Lamy, Martínez wrote to the next in command who was the Vicar General Father J. P. Machebeuf. It is substantially the letter of self-defense written shortly after the suspension, and now addressed to Machebeuf "so that you will understand." He continued:

Please do not destroy the peace and repose of my home, nor would I wish you to distress my faithful parishioners who come to me in their needs. The obligation to help them is imposed on me by reason of the Catholic religion I profess as by my position as their pastor. I recognize the duties which my conscience unfolds to me, as well as the help and consolation I have in Canon Law and in our liberal republican American government in which I believe so confidently. These I feel will not allow the machinations of others to trouble me. . . . I am yours with due regard to the protests I have made to you and I offer you my esteem and good will.[10]

This letter was sent in early May of 1857. Within the month, Bishop Lamy set in motion formal proceedings of excommunication. "Before the excommunications, Lamy had seen the necessity of replacing . . . Taladrid with Eulogio [Ortiz]—the young priest (brother of the belligerent vicar) who had in all loyalty, traveled abroad with the bishop."[11] Appointing a native Hispanic priest to replace the unpopular Basque before excommunicating Padre Martínez was seen as a necessary stratagem in order to avoid a popular riot.

Padre Martínez was unaware that formal excommunication procedures had begun and was under the illusion that a "reconciliation" was taking place. He joyfully welcomed Eulogio Ortiz to Taos on June 22, 1857. Besides being the younger brother of his old friend and mentor, the former Vicar Juan Felipe Ortiz, Eulogio was also a former pupil of Padre Martínez. This initial joy quickly turned to sorrow and disappointment when it became clear that the young priest, who had served as the Bishop's secretary and his traveling companion to Rome, was in Taos to implement diocesan policies in regard to tithes and to promote uncritical loyalty to the bishop. The conflict resumed, or better, continued. Within five months after the arrival of Father Ortiz, the formal excommunication of Padre Antonio José Martínez, Cura de Taos, had dramatically taken place in the parish church.

1. Archives of Archdiocese of Santa Fe: Lucero to Lamy (October, 1856).
2. Cf. Horgan, *Lamy of Santa Fe* (New York: Farrar, Straus and Giroux, 1975), p. 33.
3. Ibid., p. 39.
4. Cassidy, *Padre Martínez*, unpublished manuscript: Immaculate Conception Monastery, Santa Fe (1958), translation of letter, Martínez to Lamy (November 12, 1856).

5. Ibid.
6. Horgan, *Lamy,* p. 229.
7. Archives: Martínez to Lamy (November 27, 1856).
8. Ibid., December 17, 1856.
9. Ibid., April 13, 1857.
10. Ibid., Martínez to Machebeuf, (May 2, 1857).
11. Horgan, op. cit., p. 244.

25. Padre Hidalgo

Padre Antonio José Martínez

From a sermon preached in the Church of St. Francis, Santa Fe, New Mexico, September 16, 1832. Trans. A.M.S.A.

... I descry in these heroes persons who relived the Sacred History presented in the Books of the Maccabees, those valiant champions who resolved at all costs to sustain the rights of their nation and to authenticate their constancy with the blood from their veins, by struggling mightily for the cause of their homeland, of their temple, and of their laws. This is the way we see our Padre Hidalgo, who in order to accomplish his goals ordained to such a great undertaking, namely saving his beloved homeland, joined together ... with General Allende and formed an army. They gave it as patroness the Virgin of Guadalupe, exhorting the soldiers to act with the bravery that was heaven-sent according to the righteousness of the cause that they espoused and with all the other memories which naturally inflamed the brightness of their primal obligation. Once the war had begun, they sought to minimize the bloodshed. Thus the laws of nature and the precious rights of society were to be saved through the sacrifice of those committed to the struggle. But the unholy fury of Spain twisted these just intentions, rendering the spirit of peace unstable and setting in motion the devouring vortex that covered the fields with corpses, bedecked in mourning the tomb of our America, and raised sad lamenting, repeated moaning, from the parents who were left without their children, from those who had lost their parents, from wives who were left abandoned for having endangered their husbands, and from those who were beset with the misfortune of their consorts. In a word, when all saw the desperate need to let the avenging sword decide the controversy, the Mexicans gave of themselves to the utmost, even to death.

May they be witnesses of all this—that majestic mountain of Las Cruces, the wide fields of Acapulco, Guanajato, and Calderón—in those places which unfortunately saw the demonstration of butchery that, through bloody crimes and offenses, was offered in their holocaust for freedom. We are led to meditate upon the valor and glory of those who fought and thus gave on those fields of honor the example to be imitated. Their compatriots had to continue in that spirit afterward until achieving the victory that we celebrate today with great renown in thanksgiving to the Lord.

Read the annals of the peoples who encircle the globe, go through the records of history in times past, untangle the pomp surrounding great events, and you will find clearly that in no other time and for no other nation was a war waged with greater ardor, nor was the cause of freedom defended and proclaimed with more surety. Thus that resolution, supernatural in a certain way, was not cut short with bribes offered, or torture inflicted, or excommunications promulgated, or the many other judgments the Spanish fury was to invent. With none of these were the heroes made to waver. The just Hidalgo, our dear liberator, bent himself each day to his purposeful enterprise and with the same brilliance at the end as at the beginning followed faithfully to the death that they inflicted upon him.

Immortal Hidalgo! Glorious hero, author of the freedom of our America! What great deeds were conferred upon you by the Providence of the Most High, who always shapes and refines the destiny of creatures according to just designs! How many preparations, how many motives were prophesied by your splendid spirit of benevolence in order to save your beloved homeland, freeing it from the outrages of the tyrant! To you we render praises on this day in which, by recalling your deeds, we celebrate the successes with which the God above was pleased, the God whose decrees you faithfully executed! Your immortal memory will be carried from age to age, authenticated in the list of the most famous of heroes who have given glory to your name! Yes, my esteemed listeners, these very deeds prove that Hidalgo was one of the greatest men of this earth.

Do you perhaps think that when I compare him to the valiant Maccabees I attempt to exaggerate his merit and that of his companions? That I make them too much alike? Well, this is not my intention, but only to place him upon a high pedestal. The others were witnesses of Sacred Scripture of a valor and merit almost incomparable, and protected by the very God Hidalgo called upon. But they acted with commitment, I would say, because of the harsh and unavoidable need to defend themselves and repulse the aggressions against their ancestral lands. They moved against those who came to provoke them, with intentions of robbing them of their rights and extinguishing their existence. However, our Hidalgo put his hopes in the whole universe, raising war spontaneously against an almost omnipotent government which ruled our America, holding millions of men beneath its power, men who obeyed blindly, for the basis of their laws and government was laid upon most unseemly premises in order to quash any kind of murmuring. The Maccabees acted the way they did by dint of the unavoidable situation in which they found themselves: either to die at the hands of the enemy or to escape by force and be overcome again. But Hidalgo, bound to freedom, brought to the point of waging war or of forswearing it, had to embrace it at all costs. He was almost certain, or if I can say it, totally certain of the risks involved. To whom then can I compare him in order to reveal his glory? What term of reference is left to him? Ah! I have said it already in the exordium. I announced it in the beginning. I compare him to the Liberator of the whole world, to Jesus Christ, sent by his Eternal Father to bring spiritual salvation to the nations. To this Lord, he is comparable in his deeds and decisions. Jesus came into the world, preached his doctrine, denounced evil, gave us his example and, in the end, died persecuted by his enemies. He thus offered himself to the Eternal Father as a sacrifice for all men. Following in these footsteps, Hidalgo carried his doctrine into all his determinations. He attacked the tyrants, he gave us his example and, in the end, he died at the same cost for the sake of his homeland. In his death, Jesus accomplished the work of his mission, establishing the means by which people would have to be saved. But as far as reaching out to converts, Jesus was sent only to some peoples and not even to these in their totality, leaving the fulfillment of the extension and perfection of his kingdom to the arrangements of his apostles and gospel ministers who worked for many years, although this meant bloodshed in the crucible. Hidalgo, in his death, finished the work of fate because he left established the means to save his compatriots. Thus his eminent legacy endures in his worthy companions, apostles of our freedom. . . .

The crystallization of a Puerto Rican identity through Catholicism shone brightly in Juan Alejo Arizmendi (1760–1814), first native bishop of Puerto Rico. His episcopate coincided, however, with the wars of liberation on the Latin American continents. Thus upon the saintly bishop's death, Spain helped preserve its control over the island colony by preventing any Puerto Rican priest from ever again achieving leadership and prestige such as that of a bishop in his homeland.

Reminiscent of Milton's *Paradise Lost*, the epic poem *La Sataniada* by Alejandro Tapia y Rivera (1827–1882) reflects the religious feeling maintained in Puerto Rican culture, which was all that was possible in a church that refused to recognize native sons as legitimate pastors.

26. La Sataniada Canto XV, 25-26

Alejandro Tapía y Rivera

From *Tapia y Rivera*, Obras completas *(San Juan, P.R.: Instituto de cultura puertorriqueña, 1968). Used by permission. Trans. A.M.S.A.*

Cristo son los que sufren, los que lloran
y por su amor al bien son combatidos,
lo son los que a Satán jamás adoran
y son por no adorarle, perseguidos:
los que aman la verdad y los que moran
por no vender el alma, desvalidos:
Cristo es la Humanidad, cuando inocente
padece cual si fuera delincuente. . . .

Cristo es la Humanidad encadenada,
Cristo es el ideal sobre la Tierra.
Es la Humanidad cuando azotada
serena y firme a su verdugo aterra.
Cristo es la Humanidad crucificada,
es la tumba del mártir do se encierra
la libertad, que resucita un día
y postra de Satán la tiranía.

*   *   *

Christ is those who suffer, those who weep
and for the sake of love are sore distressed;
He is those who honor upon Satan never heap
and for not adoring him are more oppressed.
Christ is those who love the truth and those who reap
abandonment for bartering not a soul possessed:
Christ is Humanity which in innocence
will suffer as one punished for offense. . . .

Christ is Humanity in chains of slavery
Christ is the one ideal of man below.

Christ is Humanity scourged at pillory
whose peaceful strength unnerves the hangman foe.
Christ is a crucified humanity,
the tomb of martyrdom where hope can stow
the freedom which will rise and then one day
the tyranny of Satan sweep away.

The movement for independence from the United States as initiated by José de Diego and developed by Pedro Albizu Campos had a strong expression of Catholicism (see Chap. Two). After World War II, Catholics favoring independence formed the Arizmendi Society (named for the first Puerto Rican bishop) and wrote to the Holy See petitioning for Puerto Rican bishops. They saw a native episcopate as a necessary step toward a national consciousness. The 1960 elections in Puerto Rico proved to be a catalyst for the desired change.

The North American ordinaries on the island, Bishops Davis and McManus, let it be known that the government programs of birth control and sterilization made it a mortal sin for Catholics to vote for Muñoz Marín and his Popular Democratic Party (PPD). The bishops started their own Party of Christian Action (PAC), which was vigorously promoted everywhere from church steps to parochial classrooms. Blind obedience to the bishops in political matters might have been expected from the Irish in the Boston of Cardinal O'Connell or from Catholics in a Latin American country where there had always been a strong identification of the institutional church with the people. But this was not the case in the Puerto Rico of 1960. Moreover, the PPD had been in power for more than a dozen years. The election results were overwhelmingly in favor of Muñoz Marín and his party. The PAC disappeared by 1964 and so did the bishops. Bishop Davis went to Santa Fe, as had his predecessor, Bishop Byrne, and Bishop McManus retired to New York. Puerto Rican ordinaries were named to the sees of Ponce and San Juan (the latter became an archdiocese), and new sees were created in Caguas and Arecibo. When all was said and done, however, the new native hierarchy meant little to the independence movement.

In the aftermath of the Cuban Revolution and especially with the inability of the United States to thwart a communist government there, a radical shift took place within the independence parties. Bound together in an association called the Movement for Independence (MPI), *independentistas* reached out for some form of Marxist-Leninism as a model to achieve Puerto Rican independence from the United States. Marxist-Leninism is, of course, atheistic. This meant that the independence movement increasingly took on a radical, atheistic, anti-Christian image. This characterization was exploited by forces within the church with ideological commitments against a change in the status quo (Silén, 1970, pp. 175-176). Some of the more aggressive of these forces were identifiable as Cuban exiles in Puerto Rico, others were in movements such as the Cursillo, closely identified in Puerto Rico with the professional class and the Opus Dei (a clandestine Catholic society supporting the Franco Falangist government in Spain). The reasoning in these anti-independence church circles went something like this: Catholics must be anti-Communist; *independentistas* are Communists; therefore, Catholics must be anti-*independentistas*; moreover, the most anti-*independentista* position is to favor statehood; therefore, the most Catholic position is to favor statehood.

This conflict became division in 1971 when, in an action with ambiguous canonical precedent, four Dominican priests of the Dutch Province who administered to the Church of Christ of Good Health in Comerío, Puerto Rico, were expelled from the parish house and their faculties suspended. A similar action was taken in Yauco, where the Dominicans had maintained a parish since 1907. There was no official reason given for these actions other than the exercise of episcopal prerogative in the choice of pastoral assistants. (The Methodist Church took a similar action against a young minister in Comerío, replacing him with a Cuban exile.) The secular media were swift to allege the militant pro-independence convictions of the Dominicans as the real issue. Nor were these actions isolated. In time, Regina Cleri, the island's seminary on the campus of the Catholic University in Ponce, underwent a series of wrenching changes in administration that for all practical purposes shut down one of the most promising developments in over a hundred years toward the formation of a native clergy for Puerto Rico (Sáez, 1969). The reasons given for these drastic seminary changes included politicization caused by faculty members who favored Puerto Rican independence. As a result of these and other painful confrontations in Comerío, Yauco, and the seminary, the "official church" lost credibility as representative of *all* Puerto Rican Catholics. Obviously, the powers that be were putting all the blame for polarization on the *independentistas* and none on those who were anti-independence. The official Puerto Rican church had taken sides. Since the independence movement was constantly asserting the cause of Puerto Rican nationhood, the refusal to discuss this issue within the church was equivalent to a rejection of Puerto Ricanness. In an effort to remain neutral by separating church pastoral care and political status, the Puerto Rican hierarchy gave the impression of making politics more important than ever. Admittedly the bishops might have "backed into" this problem, in the sense that they did not seek to foster one or the other status but to transcend them all. But soon there were two sets of church leaders in Puerto Rico: a very small group, with many students and intellectuals, claiming continuity with Vatican Council II, Liberation Theology, and pastoral concern for the Puerto Rican nation; and the other, made up of practically everyone else, safeguarding neutrality in politics, emphasizing strictly "spiritual" concerns, and claiming for itself the responsibility for the common good.

The conception of a church responding to Puerto Rican nationhood was sustained because the church, small as it was, had a bishop to articulate its pastoral theology. Bishop Antulio Parrilla Bonilla was born in San Lorenzo, Puerto Rico, in 1919. Although his family was Protestant, he converted to Catholicism and became a priest in 1952. He later asked for acceptance into the Society of Jesus and spent several years of apostolate in the field of cooperativism, in which he had taken a graduate degree. He was ordained titular bishop of Ucres and auxiliary of Caguas in 1965. It should be emphasized that despite Parrilla's strong convictions about independence and his subsequent alienation from brother bishops on the island at no time has the division in the Puerto Rican church ever posed the threat of schism. Together with Marxist Father William Loperena (see pp. 243, 262), the Puerto Rican member of the parish staff expelled from Comerío, Bishop Parrilla Bonilla has insisted on a pastoral approach built solidly upon an effort to change the colonial status of Puerto Rico. This has made him a highly controversial figure, not only on the island, but in the United States and Latin America.

Bishop Parrilla Bonilla was the first Catholic bishop with United States citizenship to denounce the war in Vietnam. He visited the United States and made a tour of jails from coast to coast (see *National Catholic Reporter*, January 7, 1970), talking with the political prisoners: war protesters, Black Panthers, Chicano activists, and most especially the five Puerto Rican Nationalists (see Chap. Three). Unlike Loperena, Bishop Parrilla Bonilla represents the Nationalist tradition, which advocates for the independent republic of Puerto Rico a Christian democracy with some form of socialism modeled after the papal encyclicals.

After hearing of the expulsion of Mexican Americans from St. Basil's in 1969, Bishop Parrilla Bonilla flew to Los Angeles to celebrate a mass for the Hispano people on the front steps of the church (see pp. 123–33). Bishop Parrilla Bonilla was then the first prelate to act as a bishop in the name of solidarity among Hispanos in the United States. Ordained for Puerto Rico, he acted as a bishop for Chicanos because the Chicanos had no bishop of their own. His, however, was a solitary effort, too sudden and too dramatic to be more than a glimpse of things to come. He was literally a bishop without a church, for the Hispanos had not yet been awakened to the possibility of a Hispano church. The following selections from talks delivered by Bishop Parrilla Bonilla demonstrate both the fervor of his commitments and the breadth of his vision.

27. The Role of Christians in Puerto Rico

Bishop Antulio Parrilla Bonilla, S.J.

From Address to the Círculo puertorriqueño Conference, *Río Piedras, Puerto Rico, May 9, 1968. Used by permission. Trans. A.M.S.A.*

. . . What then is the role of the Christian in Puerto Rico under these circumstances? One has to assume clear and firm positions. I will indicate some of them here, and I assure you that I do not pretend to be exhaustive and that reflection will help you add others.

1. The first is the role of the prophet. The colonial problematic of Puerto

Rico is serious and dangerous, and the Christian has the right to denounce it to the four winds. The silence, even what is called the "prudent silence," of those who have the obligation and office of prophet is cowardice. This has to be denounced in Puerto Rico, in the United States, in the United Nations, in the hemisphere, and in the whole world. All sectors of our life have an obligation to condemn: the home, the school, the community at all levels— industry, commerce, agriculture, religion. The "sacred silences" are likewise culpable: "Do not sow, my son, in the furrows of wrongdoing, or you may reap it seven times over" says the book of Ecclesiasticus (7:3). It is useless then to wish to establish Christianity in a capitalist or colonial atmosphere.

2. The second position is that of affirming and reaffirming what is Puerto Rican in the present moment, seeking the authentic roots of our traditions in all things, in all the sectors of our life according to our profession or position, character, temperament, or vocation. Through Vatican Council II, the Catholic church is going to the primitive sources to obtain, by study of Christian practice in the first centuries of our era, the Christian authenticity with which we must orient our life today. We have to do this somehow both with politics and with our traditions. We have to look for and study our cultural roots to reaffirm what is Puerto Rican. Thus one can see the importance of our historians and biographers, and above all, what kind of objectivity is required. We don't have to fear that we will be called "Nationalists" pejoratively. We will never fall into exaggerations in defending what is ours, since our life as a people is in grave crisis.

3. The third task is to be an apostle of the ideal of independence, to be a crusader and a missionary. This imposes great sacrifice, renunciation, detachment, and withdrawal from other commitments. By word and deed in every situation, we must spread the true criteria of our cause to drive fear out of the world of confusion in which we live. We have to insist that to be a good Christian in the environment in which we live we must fight for the minimum—that is, for sovereignty—even though we do not necessarily indicate the form that freedom will take in the future, or the possible modification within that sovereignty which gives back to us the capacity to make free decisions as a political community and to participate in the universal political community.

4. The fourth position is to link ourselves to some *independentista* group of our choice as a militant; or, if by conviction one remains outside them, to collaborate with them as much as we are physically and morally able. The fragmentation that exists among the *independentista* sentiments in Puerto Rico is a terrible shame. As long as there are so many parties, groups, or movements acting uncoordinatedly, we will not be able to structure an effective and efficient instrument for national liberation. The Christian ought to promote a unity among the diversity of groups, unity that will help to obtain some long- and short-range achievements, both here and abroad. This unity has to base itself on various conditions that all will accept: no attack by

one group on other; respect for each other's criteria and political strategies; dialogue and cooperation among groups within the limits of what is possible. . . .

28. The Reality of the Present North American Society

Bishop Antulio Parrilla Bonilla, S.J.

From Address to the Ateneo of Puerto Rico, March 10, 1970. Used by permission. Trans. A.M.S.A.

. . . The leadership of the modern North American revolution is made up of men and women who know where they are going and have a social and political ideology. First, there are the socialists (not necessarily Marxists), who in politics are democratic integralists; that is, they understand political democracy only in terms of social and economic democracy.

Who are some of these leaders? One is Bobby Seale, who knows that his stay in prison is a way of advancing his cause. Another is César Chávez, a Gandhian, who with his long strike of resistance has demonstrated that it is possible to organize field workers and get collective contracts out of growers. Another is Terence Diabo, the son of a Mohawk chief, who refused to be drafted into compulsory military service, alleging that Washington and the Pentagon do not have the right to demand such service of him for the sake of the Native American people. Another is Jack F. McGuinn, a lawyer who has dedicated his entire professional career to defending conscientious objectors. Another is Mike Cullen, who is committed to the service of the poor, the persecuted, and the disowned in a free hospice. Another is Dorothy Day, a woman with charisma who has been distinguished for her thought and action in favor of every unpopular cause. Then there are priests like the Berrigans, Tony Mulvaney, Jim Harney and Larry Rosebaugh, and the Protestant minister Barry Lee Walley, resisters and prisoners for Christ. These are some of the leaders of this promising revolution.

The ideals are peace, reconciliation, concord among peoples, a humanist and personalist lifestyle, social justice for all, freedom for all people, and universal brotherhood. For such, they struggle against war, regimentation, militarism, the arms race, the draft, imperialism, capitalism, pollution of the waters and the atmosphere, ecological imbalance, and poverty. The changes they seek have to be political, social, economic, and religious. Their methodology is one of resistance to bad laws and bad structures, and since the former are not capable of correcting the latter with the necessary dispatch and flexibility, the methodology is also that of civil disobedience, demonstrations, symbolic protests, and the acceptance of prison as Christian and civic witness.

Thus, just as Puerto Ricans are part of the Latin American Revolution because we are a Latin people, we are not able to escape the coincidences that confront us and come to us by way of the North American Revolution. As a matter of fact, all revolutions of the world are similar. All humankind, especially those of the two-thirds of the poor world in developed and non-developed countries, have the same aspirations, according to the highlights of Paul VI's encyclical *Populorum Progressio* (On the Development of Peoples). All these people have very much in common. They struggle against the status quo and against those who sustain it for their own advantage. They struggle to be free. . . . It is fitting that the Puerto Rican revolutionary movement maintain good contacts with all revolutionary movements of the world, but particularly with those of Latin America and the United States.

Padre Antonio José Martínez,
"Father of New Mexico"
(courtesy Alberto Gallegos)

Above: Bishop Antulio Parrilla Bonilla of Puerto Rico marches with
Católicos Por La Raza around St. Basil's Church, Los Angeles (courtesy La Raza)
Below: César Chávez (left) and Antonio M. Stevens Arroyo

Above: Mexican American iron workers on strike
Below: Mexican American boy and portrait of Zapata
(courtesy Migration Today)

PART II

GENESIS OF THE HISPANO CHURCH

Caballeros, somos perdidos. Aquí no hay más recursos que ir a coger gachupines.

Gentlemen, we are lost. There is nothing to do except to go out and grab a Spaniard.

—Padre Miguel Hidalgo y Costilla,
Sunday, September 16, 1810,
the first day of the War for Mexican Independence

It is safe to say that before 1970 there was no national Hispano church leader. The office that later became the Spanish-speaking Secretariat, under the directorship of Pablo Sedillo, was a subdivision of the Social Services of the United States Catholic Conference (USCC), with regional offices in Michigan, Texas, and California. The main purpose of these offices was to serve Mexican American farm workers. There was no provision for the migrant laborers of the East Coast and the millions of Puerto Rican and other Hispanos in the cities. The Cubans in Miami had a refugee program, which dealt only indirectly with pastoral problems; but these efforts were not coordinated toward a national Hispano church.

One of the reasons for this state of affairs was simple:

Hispanos were supposed to be assimilated into the "mainstream" of the North American church, as had all other Catholic immigrant ethnic groups. Leadership was gained by Hispanos when they served the assimilationist ends of institutions. In this process the Hispanos who "made it" accepted the goals of society's institutions rather than the aspirations of their own people. Examples abound of putting as much distance as possible between one's success and the folks at home with their quaint ways. The principle at work has been called "Simmons' Law": Anglos tend to reward in practice those Mexican Americans who are most like themselves in ideas and action patterns (Simmons, 1961). A typical Spanish-speaking apostolate at that time consisted of social help, almsgiving, and paternalistic forms of Catholic Charities. Although

97

genuinely offered and really needed, this help was paternalistic because, until Vatican Council II, little attention was paid to self-development (McNamara, in Grebler et al., 1970). In New York the approach was guided by the national parish and the settlement house which had served as buoys for those immigrants who sailed into the city on their way to assimilation. Hispanos were expected gradually to abandon the structure of their ghetto communities and their own leadership, in the manner of other Catholic ethnic groups before them. The function of the church was to aid in that assimilation process and to reflect the goals and styles of the dominant society (Fitzpatrick, 1971, pp. 123-24).

Beginning in 1967, however, and flowering everywhere in the pockets of Spanish-speaking people in the United States, was a new expression of militant nationalism. This consciousness was eventually to overflow into the institutions of the church. Initially, however, mainstream Catholicism discounted the nascent Hispano militancy. Many Catholics, including Hispanos, saw only ugly agitation in the verbal and at times physical violence of groups such as the Puerto Rican Young Lords and the Chicano Brown Berets. These groups were castigated as being anti-American, Hispano versions of the Black Panthers, throwbacks to the *pachucos* or Nationalists. Because of Marxist-sounding rhetoric, they were labeled irreligious and atheistic groups. Initially these young militants had belonged to street gangs and they often suffered from lack of education, foresight, and internal discipline. Nonetheless these young Puerto Ricans and Chicanos were able to launch a new movement.

Instead of questioning the authority of the institutional system by philosophical argumentation, they took direct action to confront the powers that be. The militants discredited the constraints officialdom had exercised upon the natural leaders of Hispano communities for generations. Direct action, like "liberating" a traveling library and driving it into the barrio, captured headlines. The Lords and the Berets used the media to appeal to a public conscience. They sidestepped traditional institutional power and eventually generated new sources of influence based on affirmative-action quotas and political pressures (Levy and Kramer, 1972, p. 22). In the climate that had been created by the black civil rights movement, these efforts served as catalysts. Hispanos began to demand the same kinds of things granted to blacks.

When the Hispano university students became involved with these currents of nationalism, they were able to analyze with greater sophistication than the street groups. For students on the island of Puerto Rico, of course, the question of nationality was one of nationhood, centered entirely upon the question of independence from the United States. In a short time, Marxist terminology and sometimes communist organizational tactics were used. The Young Lords in New York separated from those in Chicago because of ideological differences. Other ideological groups such as El Comité (The Committee) were formed. Island-affiliated groups such as the Federation of Puerto Rican Students for Independence (FUPI) later appeared in New York. The Mexican American Youth Organization (MAYO) paralleled this ideological development. MAYO was to supply leaders for the Raza Unida Party, which rejects both the Republican and Democratic parties as vehicles for the political development of Mexican Americans.

The first influence upon the Catholic church was only indirect. Despite the radicalness of the militants, more and more people began to speak of *pueblo* and *patria* (people and homeland). Within the barrios from East Los Angeles to Spanish Harlem, the Hispanos were awakening to their national identity. The direct involvement of the Catholic church in these movements had to be left to Hispano Catholics.

Some of the first articulations of church consciousness came after the initiation of liturgical reform by Vatican Council II. It became common to write original eucharistic prayers (canons for the mass), which reflected the cultural aspirations of the people (see Chap. Five). At the same time, the ever-present church concern for social welfare was transformed into a struggle for peoplehood (see Chap. Six) and redefined the "problem" (see Chap. Seven). This was the genesis of the Hispano church.

Inscription on jacket of Puerto Rican teenager (courtesy Migration Today)

CHAPTER FIVE

LITURGICAL BATTLEFRONTS

Monsignor Robert Fox became the director of the Spanish-speaking Apostolate for the Archdiocese of New York in 1963 and remained at that post until 1969. A bright, handsome, and personable priest who had been trained in Uruguay before his appointment, Monsignor Fox was gifted with charisma. While he was head of the Archdiocesan Office he was able to effect important changes in ministry with the small army of clergy and religious who had received pastoral and cultural training at the Institute of Intercultural Communication in Ponce, Puerto Rico, directed by the gifted Father Ivan Illich. Monsignor Fox's leadership came at a crucial time for both the secular urban society and the church community.

The War on Poverty launched by President Lyndon B. Johnson showered federal funds upon the inner city and created a plethora of community-based agencies. At the same time, the liturgical and pastoral changes of Vatican Council II began to take effect. The emphasis of both was on cultural and national identity. Just as the new liturgy called for folksongs and a popular style of church celebration in the vernacular, the War on Poverty stressed the need for leaders from minority groups. In New York City, Puerto Ricans were expected to head Puerto Rican agencies in Puerto Rican neighborhoods. The leadership had to be taken from within the Puerto Rican community, thus breaking with the previous pattern of leadership personnel coming from outside the minority group. On the basis of race and nationality, Hispano leaders are labeled "internal leaders" and non-Hispanos, "external leaders."

In the process of putting the powerful New York Archdiocese at the service of the emerging Hispano community, Fox created levels of church leadership. There were roles and functions for both internal and external leaders, to enable them to work together in the common task of creating a new community (Sexton, 1965, pp. 71-91). The stages might be described as follows:

1. *Social and institutional needs for church leadership:* e.g., liturgy planning, catechetical classes, money-raising, census-taking, etc.; in short, things that the non-Hispanos found difficulty in doing because they did not understand the language or know the neighborhood.
2. *Professional and political community leadership for church neighborhood agencies:* posts on school boards, in poverty agencies, political clubs, etc. Some clergy took these posts themselves, but there were good numbers of Puerto Rican or internal leaders who also received this recognition. Occasionally emerging political leaders who already had these

posts sought church support in order to rise higher on the ladder of internal community leaders.

3. *Pastoral theologians:* the highest level of leadership and almost always reserved for non-Hispano clergy who worked as parish priests.

In terms of this description, many Spanish and Latin American priests in New York and Brooklyn, who comprised perhaps 35 percent of the clergy working with Hispano peoples, were able to function only at the first level of church leadership, i.e., as social-events experts: preachers, musicians, directors of pious societies, etc. The same was true initially in the Southwest and California. Since the majority of native Mexican American priests were relatively young, they were restricted from the more important kinds of leadership within diocesan structures. Likewise, petty rivalries between diocesan clergy and members of religious orders frequently impeded the full use of the talents of many Hispano priests in the United States. Since bishops generally trusted their own men more than clergy whose direct allegiance was to a religious congregation, the large percentage of Hispanos belonging to religious orders was unable to enter into the circles of church power as theologians.

Instead, Hispano consciousness was channeled into liturgical creativity at the first level of church leadership. There was production of eucharistic prayers borrowing from historical and cultural traditions. A collection of Chicano prayers with an excellent presentation by Pablo Sicilia is available through MACC in San Antonio. The Research Center for Evangelization and Ministry (CEMI) in New York has undertaken a similar project for Puerto Rican prayers.

Below (pp. 101-14) are examples of eucharistic prayers.

29. Anáfora mexicana
(Mexican Anaphora)

Anonymous

Used by permission. Trans. A.M.S.A.

. . . En la sangre generosa de los pueblos,
del Nuevo y del Viejo Mundo,
nos reuniste
para que a través del sufrimiento y del mestizaje

y bajo la mirada tierna y cariñosa
de María de Guadalupe
llegáramos a conocer la bondad de tu Hijo Jesucristo.

El, habiendo venido hasta nosotros,
se hizo humilde con los humildes,
hermano con el hermano,
libre con el que venciendo la esclavitud y la codicia,
alcanza en el amor la libertad verdadera.
El caminando con nosotros
el doloroso y fecundo camino de nuestras luchas patrias,
preparando para nosotros,
en la obra de nuestros héroes
una patria más justa y fraternal.

Y para que en adelante no vivamos en el egoísmo
sino en el servicio de aquel que por nosotros murió y resucitó,
nos ha enviado, Oh Padre,
al Espíritu Santo,
a fin de redimir y encaminar hacia Ti
nuestro pasado, nuestro presente y nuestro porvenir en este suelo bendito
y entre todas las naciones de la tierra.

Que este mismo Espíritu santifique, Señor,
estas ofrendas y sean para nosotros,
Cuerpo y Sangre de Jesucristo, Nuestro Señor. . . .

*   *   *

. . . In the generous blood of the peoples,
of the New and the Old Worlds,
you gathered us
so that through the suffering and the *mestizaje*
and under the tender and loving gaze
of Mary of Guadalupe,
we would come to know the goodness of your Son Jesus Christ.

Having come to us,
he was made humble with the humble,
brother with his brother,
free with him who in conquering slavery and avarice
reached true freedom in love.
Walking with us
the sorrowful and fertile roads of our patriotic struggles
he prepares for us
in the work of our heroes
a more just and brotherly homeland.

And so that in the future we might not live in selfishness
but in service of him who, for us, died and rose again,
He has sent to us, O Father,
the Holy Spirit
to redeem and set aright toward you,
our past, present, and future on this blessed land
and among all the nations of the earth.

May this same spirit O Lord, sanctify
these offerings, and may they be for us
the Body and Blood of Jesus Christ Our Lord. . . .

Padre Martínez, formerly pastor of a Franciscan parish in San Antonio, Texas, also served as executive director of PADRES from 1976 to 1978.

30. Anáfora chicana de liberación I
(First Chicano Liberation Anaphora)

Padre Manuel Martínez

Used by permission. Trans. A.M.S.A.

. . . Ahora, como peregrinos en marcha,
te suplicamos que envíes tu Santo Espíritu,
tu auxilio y valentía,
a tu pueblo aquí reunido
y extendido por todo el mundo.
Haz que el fuego de su amor nos haga vernos cara a cara
como hermanos y sepamos ayudarnos
con nuestras cargas y juntos encontremos el camino hacia Ti.

Nos alegra la palabra
de nuestra mestiza Madre de Guadalupe,
que se acercó al pobre y oprimido para dar aliento
a la nación mexicana.

Enviaste, Señor, a grandes hombres y mujeres a nuestra tierra, como:
    Bartolomé de las Casas,
    Martín de Porres,
    Rosa de Lima,
    Juana Inés de la Cruz
    Francisca Javier Cabrini,
    Fray Junípero Serra,
    Fray Antonio Margil de Jesús,
    Eusebio Kino
    [*se pueden escoger los que se quieran*]
que dieron una verdad perdurable:
que español, indio, mestizo
y todo americano son hijos de Dios.

Y de estas palabras tuyas, Señor,
surgieron hombres que rezaron y pelearon por
su mismo mérito como seres humanos:
    un Miguel Hidalgo,
    un Emiliano Zapata,
    y nuevamente unos Kennedys,
    un Martin Luther King,
y entre ellos muchos hombres y mujeres que trabajan incansablemente
por realizar día tras día tu reino de paz y justicia.

Que tus pastores sirvan a tu pueblo,
creyente y no creyente,
con sabiduría y valor:
el Papa, nuestros Obispos N. y N.,
y todos los que desempeñan responsabilidad en servicio nuestro.

En nombre de una hermandad más justa
clamamos por la liberación
de todas las minorías oprimidas en nuestro país y en todo el mundo. . . .

* * *

. . . Now, as pilgrims on the march,
we ask that you send your Holy Spirit,
your help and courage
to your people here assembled
and spread throughout the whole world.
In the fire of your love make us see ourselves face to face
as brothers so that we know how to help each other
with our burdens and so that together we will find our way to you.

You have made us happy with the Word
from our *mestiza* Mother of Guadalupe

who came to the poor and oppressed to give sustenance
to the Mexican nation.

You sent, O Lord, great men and women to our land like
        Bartolomé de las Casas,
        Martín de Porres,
        Rosa de Lima
        Juana Inés de la Cruz
        Frances Xavier Cabrini
        Junípero Serra
        Antonio Margil de Jesús
        Eusebio Kino
        [more names may be added as desired]
who gave a lasting truth:
that the Spaniard, the Indian, the mestizo
and all Americans are children of God.

And from these words of yours, O Lord,
came the men who prayed for and battled for
their worth as human beings:
        Miguel Hidalgo,
        Emiliano Zapata,
        and recently the Kennedys,
        Martin Luther King,
and among these many men and women who work unceasingly
to bring about daily your kingdom of peace and justice.

May your pastors serve your people,
the believers and the nonbelievers,
with wisdom and courage:
the Pope, our bishops [add names],
and all those who have assumed responsibility in our service.

In the name of a more just Brotherhood
we cry out for the freedom
of all the oppressed minorities in our land and in all the world. . . .

After his ordination as a Jesuit priest, Héctor Montes served on the faculty
and eventually became rector of the Puerto Rican seminary Regina Cleri. He
has since been laicized and lives and works in New York City.

31. Anáfora puertorriqueña
(Puerto Rican Anaphora: From the Preface)

Héctor Montes

Used by permission. Trans. A.M.S.A.

Diálogo
Sacerdote: Recordemos ahora las palabras del Señor: "Dondequiera que hay dos reunidos en mi nombre, allí estoy yo."
Pueblo: Por eso, Señor, sabemos que tú estás aquí entre nosotros.
Sacerdote: Démosle, pues, gracias por todos sus beneficios:
Pueblo: A ti, Señor, te damos nuestros corazones.
Acción de Gracias
Sacerdote: A ti, Señor, que lo creaste todo y dijiste que era bueno.
Pueblo: Te damos gracias porque es cierto.
Sacerdote: El azul del cielo y el verde del mar, la mata de plátano y la caña de azúcar, el yagrumo y el manantial, el pitirre y el buey.
Pueblo: Y todo es bueno porque es tuyo. Gracias, Señor.
Sacerdote: También nos diste el alma del jíbaro, el corazón de la madre, la preocupación del padre, el amor del novio, la fidelidad de la esposa, el celo del sacerdote.
Pueblo: Te damos gracias, Señor.
Sacerdote: Tu regalo es, Señor, el ritmo de la música, la alegría del baile, la televisión y el cine.
Pueblo: Gracias, Señor, por tu bondad.
Sacerdote: Pero Señor, no somos ingenuos y sabemos que a pesar de que todo es bueno, nosotros lo dañamos. De la paz hacemos guerra, del amor hacemos odio, de la esperanza hacemos desesperación, del bien hacemos mal.
Pueblo: Gracias, Señor, por hacernos caer en cuenta de esto.
Sacerdote: No somos, Señor, libres para amar. Intrínsecamente estamos incapacitados. Necesitamos redención.
Pueblo: Gracias, Señor, por oírnos.
Sacerdote: Y por eso enviaste a tu Hijo. Para libertarnos y enseñarnos a amar. Para enseñarnos el camino, la verdad y la vida.
Pueblo: Y contigo, Señor, sí podemos. Gracias.
Sacerdote: En este banquete eucarístico nos recuerdas que nos necesitamos

los unos a los otros. Que solos no podemos. Que por eso fundaste una comunidad de amor: la Iglesia.

Pueblo: Gracias, Señor, por darnos compañeros.

Sacerdote: Y para mantener esa llama de amor viva en tu pueblo enviaste al Espíritu Santo, el cual está entre nosotros.

Pueblo: Gracias, Señor, por mantener tu amor vivo entre nosotros.

Sacerdote: Y ahora cantemos todos en alabanza:

Pueblo: Santo, Santo, Santo. . .

* * *

Dialogue

Priest: We remember now the words of the Lord, "Wherever there are two or three united in my name, I am there in their midst."

People: By this, Lord, we know that you are here with us.

Priest: Then, let us give him thanks for all his benefits.

People: To you, Lord, we give our hearts.

Thanksgiving

Priest: To you, Lord, who created everything and said that all was good.

People: We give you thanks for it is true.

Priest: The blue of the sky and the green of the sea, the plantain tree and sugar cane, the *yagrumo*[1] tree and the brooks, the *pitirre*[2] and the ox.

People: And all is good because it is yours. Thanks, O Lord.

Priest: You gave to us the soul of the *jíbaro*[3] as well as the heart of a mother, the concern of a father, the love of a bridegroom, the faithfulness of a wife, the zeal of a priest.

People: We give you thanks, O Lord.

Priest: Your gift, Lord, is the rhythm of music, the television, and the film.

People: Thank you, Lord, for your goodness.

Priest: But, Lord, we are not foolish and we know that even though everything is good, we damage it. From peace, we make war, from love we create hatred, from hope we make despair, and from good we bring evil.

People: Thank you, Lord, for making us aware of this.

Priest: We are not free to love, Lord. We are intrinsically crippled. We need redemption.

People: Thank you, Lord, for listening to us.

Priest: And for this you sent your Son to free us and teach us how to love. To show us the way, the truth, and the life.

People: And with you, Lord, we are able. Thank you.

Priest: In this eucharistic banquet you remind us that we need one another. That by ourselves we are incapable. That on this account you founded a community of love, the church.

People: Thank you, Lord, for giving us *compañeros*.[4]

Priest: And in order to keep this flame of love alive in your *pueblo*[5], you sent your Holy Spirit who is among us.

People: Thank you, Lord, for keeping your love alive among us.

Priest: And now let us all sing in praise: Holy, Holy, Holy. . . .

1. *Yagrumo: Cecropia peltata*; also known as *yagrumo hembra*. This tree grows seventy feet high, and has a hollow trunk. Its big leaves resemble an umbrella, green on one side and white on the other. The wood derived from this tree is whitish and is used for the top part of musical instruments such as *el tiple, el cuatro*, and *el requinto*, all Puerto Rican variations of the guitar. This tree is plentiful (in the island) and the Indians used to make mats and ropes from the bark.

2. *Pitirre*: a kingbird, of which there are several species on the island. Although small, it is vocal and fearless; writers have used it to symbolize the Puerto Rican spirit.

3. *Jíbaro*: rural agricultural worker. The word came to mean "free mountain dweller." Etymologically it is closely related to *guajiro* and *naboria*, or *naborí*.

4. *Compañeros*: companions, comrades.

5. *Pueblo*: people, nation.

Monsignor Lonnie Reyes is a priest of the Texas Diocese of Austin, and a former vice president of PADRES. He presently serves as vicar general of the diocese, with title of Domestic Prelate.

32. Anáfora chicana II
(Chicano Anaphora II)

Padre Lonnie Reyes

Used by permission. Trans. A.M.S.A.

. . . ¿Por qué no darte gracias,
Señor Dios del universo,
tú que creaste y guías todas las cosas?
Desde el principio de los hombres,
en cada tiempo y a cada raza
fuiste favoreciéndoles con su propia tierra y país:
a tu pueblo de Israel
lo liberaste de la esclavitud y le diste su tierra.
To our forefathers,
Huemac y Quetzalcóatl,
les diste el destino de guiar al pueblo a la tierra

que les habías reservado con amor.
Así brotaron los grandes templos de Teotihuacán a Tzintzuntzán,
de Casas Grandes a Chichén Itzá.
To the Pilgrims les diste la entrada en Plymouth Rock
so that they would found a new nation,
conceived in revolution for the liberty of conscience of all men.
In the Mexican-American War,
no dejaste que venciera la codicia del hombre blanco
sino que you left a remnant de tu pueblo mestizo,
con el espíritu de Aztlán,
para no perderse el sentido humanitario.
En las fronteras de este nuevo mundo fuiste formando un pueblo nuevo
de mestizo y anglo
en Santa Fe, San Augustín, San Antonio, Los Angeles, Denver, Tucson,
y sobre todo el suroeste de la nación.
Nos hiciste una raza mestiza, enriqueciendo nuestra sangre
con la virtud de todos los pueblos.
For a long time we suffered the oppression,
discrimination y mesnosprecios de las otras razas en los Estados Unidos,
hasta llegar casi a perder nuestro idioma y cultura.
Pero siempre nos diste el orgullo de ser mestizos
y a través del sufrimiento
nos reuniste bajo la mirada tierna y cariñosa de nuestra Madre,
la Virgen María de Guadalupe.
Con su maternal protección
llegamos a ser un pueblo nuevo,
florecido de las fuentes de dos culturas y dos idiomas.
En tu designio divino,
Padre Celestial,
nos encontramos herederos de un mandato
para vencer el racismo y egoísmo
y hacerte
un pueblo de carnalismo y de verdad. . . .

* * *

. . . Why not give you thanks,
Lord God of the Universe,
you who create and guide all things?
From the beginning of all humankind
in each time and to each race
you favored them with their own land and country.
Your people of Israel
you freed from slavery and gave them their own land.

To our forefathers,
Huemac and Quetzalcoatl,[1]
you gave the destiny of guiding the people to the land
which with love you had set apart for them.
Thus flourished the great temples from Teotihuacán to Tzintuzuntzán,
from Casas Grandes to Chichén Itzá.
To the Pilgrims you gave entry to Plymouth Rock
so that they would found a new nation,
conceived in revolution for the liberty of conscience of all men.
In the Mexican-American War,
you did not allow that the avarice of the white man would triumph
but you left a remnant of your mestizo people
with the spirit of Aztlán[2]
so that a humanitarian sense would not be lost.
On the frontiers of this new world you formed a new people,
mestizo and Anglo,
in Santa Fe, Saint Augustine, San Antonio, Los Angeles, Denver, Tucson
and over all the southwest of the nation.
You made us a mestizo race, enriching our blood
with the strength of all people.
For a long time we suffered the oppression,
the discrimination, and disdain of the other races in the United States,
until we nearly lost our language and culture.
But you always gave us pride in being mestizos
and through suffering
you have joined us under the tender and loving gaze of our Mother,
the Virgin, Mary of Guadalupe.
With her maternal protection
we have come to be a new people,
flourishing from the sources of two cultures and two languages.
In your divine designs,
O Heavenly Father,
we recognize ourselves heirs to a command
to overcome racism and selfishness
and to make for you
a people of *carnalismo*[3] and of truth. . . .

1. Huemac and Quetzalcóatl: ancient gods of the Aztec peoples.
2. Aztlán: Aztec name for the present-day southwestern United States.
3. Carnalismo: brotherhood, friendship (see p. 137).

33. *Plegaria de añoranza puertorriqueña* *(Canon of Puerto Rican Nostalgia)*

Padre Antonio M. Stevens Arroyo

. . . Cuando nuestros padres pecaron
y perdieron al Edén precioso
no nos abandonaste,
sino nos prometiste el Nuevo Adán [*Gen. 3:15; Rom. 5:12ff.*],
Cristo, el único hijo tuyo.

El era rico pero se hizo pobre por amor de nosotros
para que nosotros fuéramos hechos ricos
por medio de la pobreza de él.
Juan era el nombre de su pregonero;
la Virgen María era Madre de él
y es Señora de la Providencia para todos nosotros.

Cuando su destino ameneció,
Cristo el Salvador salió loco de contento [*"Lamento Borincano"*]
desde las montañas de Galilea.
Pasando por las veredas del país,
llevó el cargamento de la buena nueva.
Burlado por ser de humilde cuna [*Isa. 53:2ff.; Mt. 26:73; Jn. 46:16-25*],
despreciado por sus parábolas y forma de hablar,
le rechazaron los soberios.
Fue como un jíbaro en una ciudad sin corazón.
Pero padeció sin violencia
ofreciendo su vida como rescate para todos.
Y nos dió este memorial de su muerte
para que nosotros también
podamos vivir con igual amor transformador. . . .

Acuérdate también de aquel pueblo fiel
que caminó en el valle de lágrimas peregrinando hacia ti;
de aquéllos que ganaron su pan por el sudor de su frente;
de aquéllos que trabajaron bajo el son tropical
y que cayeron en la flor de la vida como caña bajo el machete.

Y nunca te olvides de aquéllos que ofrecieron su vida
en búsqueda paciente de una libertad
que todavía nos queda como promesa.

Acuérdate de nosotros aquí presentes;
añoramos el lindo bohío, el alegre palmar
y la hamaca ondulante [*"Vida Criolla"*]
como Adán soñó con el Edén perdido.

Pero recordamos que llamaste a Abrahán de su patria,
que conduciste a Moisés en el Exodo,
y a Juan Bautista en el desierto.
Como Cristo suspendido entre cielo y suelo,
estamos crucificado en un Limbo
y ni somos de aquí ni de allá,
porque nos has dado servirte
como un espíritu solitario en larga espera [*"Ultima Actio"*].

¡Qué nuestro llanto sea alabanza tuya!
Porque no vemos el flamboyán
en esta jungla gris de cemento y acero
te buscamos con fe más pura.
Porque no oímos el canto del coquí
en el ruido de la gente en las calles,
te bendecimos con fidelidad comprobada.
Porque no bailamos ni en el barrio ni en el batey,
pintamos a un mundo mecanizado
con sonrisa perpetua.

Doblemente ausentes de la Tierra de Promesa,
te hablamos con la peleíta monga del niño
en vez de glorificarte abiertamente.

¡Ay bendito, Señor!
No podemos alabarte como mereces.
Pero si nuestra oración está unida a la de Cristo
tendremos canción para darte gracias.

Por Cristo
con él y en él,
a ti Dios Padre omnipotente
en la unidad del Espíritu Santo
todo honor y toda gloria
por los siglos de los siglos. Amén.

                              *   *   *

. . . When our forefathers sinned
and lost the beauty of Eden,
you did not abandon us,
but promised a new Adam [*Gen. 3:15; Rom. 5:12ff.*],
Christ your only Son.

Rich as he was, he made himself poor for our sake
in order to make us rich
by means of his poverty.
John was the name of his herald;
the Virgin Mary was his mother
and is Lady of Providence for all of us.

In the fullness of time,
with a happiness beyond reason [*"Lamento Borincano" by Rafael Hernández*],
Christ the savior set out from the mountains of Galilee.
Traveling by the footpaths of the countryside,
he brought the tidings of good news to the City of Man.
Scorned for his humble birth [*Isa. 53:2ff.; Mt. 26:73; Jn. 46:16-25*],
slighted for his parables and manner of speech,
he was rejected by this world's wisdom
as a *jibaro*[1] in a city of heartlessness.
But he bore his sufferings without violence,
offering his life as a ransom for many.
And he gave to us this memorial of his death
so that we too
might live with the same transforming love. . . .

Remember the faithful
who walked through the valley of darkness on their way to you;
those who earned their bread by the sweat of their brows,
those who toiled in the heat of the tropical sun
and who fell in their youth like cane under the *machete*.[2]
And do not forget those who offered their life's blood
in patient pursuit of a freedom
which still remains your promise to us.

Remember those of us here present.
We pine away for the lovely *bohío*,[3]
the happiness of the palm tree and the swaying *hamaca*[4] [*"Vida Criolla" by Luis Llórens Torres*]
even as Adam dreamed of Paradise Lost.

But we recall that you summoned Abraham from his homeland,
that you led Moses in the Exodus,

and John the Baptist in the desert.
As Christ hung on the cross between earth and sky,
we are crucified in a Limbo,
belonging neither here nor there
because you have given us the lot of serving you
as a solitary spirit in great expectation [*"Ultima Actio" by José de Diego*].

O that our plea would be your praise!
Because we do not see the *flamboyán*[5]
in this gray jungle of steel and cement,
we seek you with a faith more pure.
Because we do not hear the song of the *coquí*[6]
above the din of people in the streets,
we bless you with proven faithfulness.
Because we do not dance in the *barrio*[7] or *batey*,[8]
we paint a mechanized world
the color of an eternal smile.

Exiles twice-over from the Promised Land,
we speak to you with the stubborn badgering, *la peleíta monga*,[9] of a child
until we can glorify you with straightforwardness.

¡Ay Bendito,[10] Lord!
We will never be able to praise you as you deserve.
But if our prayer is united with Christ's,
we will have a song for thanking you.

Through him,
with him, in him,
Almighty Father,
in the unity of the Holy Spirit,
all glory and honor is yours,
forever and ever. Amen.

1. *Jíbaro*: the Puerto Rican peasant or mountain man.

2. *Machete*: a large knife used to cut sugar cane.

3. *Bohío*: Indian word for a shack or hut.

4. *Hamaca*: Indian spelling for the "hammock," taken to Europe from the Caribbean by Columbus.

5. *Flamboyán*: the flame tree, noted for its bright red-orange flowers; it is very common in Puerto Rico.

6. *Coquí*: small frog, native to Puerto Rico, noted for its high-pitched call.

7. *Barrio*: an outlying district.

8. *Batey*: an Indian word for the unpaved central plaza of the village; it has come to mean the area immediately surrounding a house where people gather to talk or socialize.

9. *La peleíta monga*: an idiomatic Puerto Rican expression for a way of "beating around the bush" in order to gain something.

10. *Ay Bendito!*: a traditional Puerto Rican exclamation that has been weighted with connotations of fatalism by contemporary commentators.

Mr. Angel Pérez is a talented composer and musician who worked with Monsignor Bob Fox and Father Robert Stern in the Spanish-speaking Apostolate Office of the Archdiocese of New York. The following excerpt is a tribute as much to Monsignor Fox's charisma as to Mr. Pérez's faith.

34. Angel Pérez

Mary Cole

From Cole, Summer in the City *(New York: P. J. Kenedy and Sons, 1968), pp. 141-142. Used by permission.*

Angel is a glowing man who speaks broken English poetically. He was trying to explain to the researcher how he happened to join Summer In The City and ended up explaining the kind of love and fulfillment he and many other people were getting out of it.

"I am a man who has lived two lives," he began. "My first life, which I lived for many, many years, was all money and fame and plauses—how you say, applause. When I was already a young boy in Spain I showed great talent for music and everyone watched me and said I would do big things. At sixteen I wrote an 'Alleluia' for Easter that was beautiful. It was my own but just the same I must say it—it was beautiful, magnificent! I said to myself, to sing this 'Alleluia' I must find the greatest chorus in the world.

"I graduated from the conservatory and I began to play with orchestras and to compose and conduct. I earned much money and I wore fine clothes. Always you would see me in a beautiful mohair suit, cut just so. I began to make tours throughout Spain and to France and Italy conducting orchestras and choruses, and every once in awhile I would think to give one of the choruses my 'Alleluia' to sing. Then I would say, No, maybe I can find a better chorus and for this 'Alleluia' I must have the greatest chorus in the world. I went to America and I conducted in Puerto Rico and Miami and New York. Still I loved money and applause and I thought, No, not yet, not this chorus for my 'Alleluia.' Then I met Monsignor Fox and my second life began.

"I have no money and I play on the street and I am so happy! The first summer I went to the Lower East Side and I didn't wear a fine suit for then how could I be close with the people? And that is what is beautiful in this program—to be close with the people. I took off even my shirt and I went with what you call, the T-shirt, and I strapped an accordion on my chest and I played and played and everybody sang. Before many times at parties people asked me to play the accordion and always I say, No! because in Spain it is the beggars who play the accordion on the street for *pesetas*. But now I play and sing with the people and I am so happy to be near the Puerto Rican people. Oh some days on the street it is so hot, terrible! But still I am happy, because the people love so much to hear me.

"Then on the Upper West Side near Broadway I formed a chorus with the people. And we did an Easter show with Monsignor Fox on Channel 47, the Spanish television station. Listen to the tape! You hear that with the guitars. They made a mistake. But I didn't take it out. I didn't do it again. Because this mistake too is beautiful. Because it is done with love. They love so much to play. They never played guitar before and in a few weeks they learned. The chorus, they never sang before, and they are so proud to sing. They are so happy. When people hear them, they cry, it is so beautiful, because this chorus sings with love. So even when they make mistakes it is still beautiful.

"When I saw how they loved to play and to sing, how they did it all with love, I gave them to do on this TV show my 'Alleluia' because I knew I had found the greatest chorus in the world."

PADRES Retreat-Workshop in Tucson, Arizona, April 1973. Helder Camara of Brazil speaks on "Justice and Chicano Ministry." (left to right) Juan Romero, Helder Camara, Bishop Patricio Flores, and Paul Sedillo.

CHAPTER SIX

MILITANCY

When he began in 1962 to organize farm workers, César Chávez (b. 1927) stressed the importance of internal or native leadership. Based on his training as a Saul Alinsky organizer, he profited from the resurgent sense of nationalism that was part of the political atmosphere created by the Chicano militants. But Chávez had an advantage over other secular leaders. He possessed an authentic Catholicism, almost mystical in quality. Moreover, he insisted on nonviolence, in spite of the dramatic visibility of the farm workers' oppression. He was an attractive alternative to radical forms of Hispano internal leadership. Accordingly, the strike at Delano, California, gathered clout and influence within liberal circles. With the support of the Kennedy family after 1966, the cause—La Causa—became national (Meier and Rivera, 1972, pp. 263ff.). It was only a matter of time before acceptance from the national Catholic church would be extended to Chávez. After all, this was an issue of labor organization, an experience of most Catholic ethnic groups in their process of assimilation. And so the issue of the Mexican American farm workers became for Catholic liberals an affirmation of the upward cycle of the American dream.

The boycott was a most important factor in the genesis of the Hispano church because Chávez allowed only Mexican Americans to speak for the Mexican Americans. Of necessity, Mexican American priests had a special role in representing the official church support for the strike and boycott. The role of internal leader became much stronger than that of external leader. That is to say, it was more important to be Mexican American and therefore a part of the people than to have status in the diocese and be a part of the institutional church, if one sought to support the farm workers. Because attention was given to the closeness of priest with his people, the Mexican American clergy involved in the strike and boycott for the farm workers enjoyed greater influence than their ecclesiastical superiors in the Southwest and California diocesan chanceries. The institutional non-Hispano church found itself viewed as an outsider. Even non-Hispano priests who served Mexican Americans in the poorer parishes of a diocese were considered more authentic spokesmen for Mexican Americans than chancery officials. Dunne describes the result as follows: "So many priests *(including non-Hispanos)* had pledged to help Chávez that if restrictions were placed on their involvement the church would find itself in an untenable position" (1967, p. 83).

This is a process called "cross-validation." It leapfrogs over the internal power structure of an institution like the church and gives clout to those whose previous standing has been low within the establishment. The public had altered the normal flow of power within the church because of its interest in the cause of the farm workers. There was an audience for new ideas on ministry at the grassroots, and some chancery officials were put into the unfamiliar role of listeners.

The following article, written by César Chávez, shows how a few priests could gain publicity and prestige for the farm workers and create a new role for the Hispano ministry.

This material, prepared by Chávez during his "spiritual fast," was first presented by him to the Second Annual Mexican-American Conference, held in Sacramento, California, March 8-10, 1968.

35. The Mexican-American and the Church

César E. Chávez

From Octavio I. Romano V., ed., Voices: Readings from El Grito (Berkeley: Quinto Sol, 1973), pp. 215-218.

The place to begin is with our own experience with the Church in the strike which has gone on for thirty-one months in Delano. For in Delano the Church has been involved with the poor in a unique way which should stand as a symbol to other communities. Of course, when we refer to the Church we should define the word a little. We mean the whole Church, the Church as an ecumenical body spread around the world, and not just its particular form in a parish in a local community. The Church we are talking about is a tremendously powerful institution in our society, and in the world. That Church is one form of the Presence of God on Earth, and so naturally it is powerful. It is powerful by definition. It is a powerful moral and spiritual force which cannot be ignored by any movement. Furthermore, it is an organization with tremendous wealth. Since the Church is to be servant to the poor, it is *our* fault if that wealth is not channeled to help the poor in our world.

In a small way we have been able, in the Delano strike, to work together with the Church in such a way as to bring some of its moral and economic power to bear on those who want to maintain the status quo, keeping farm workers in virtual enslavement. In brief, here is what happened in Delano.

Some years ago, when some of us were working with the Community Service Organization, we began to realize the powerful effect which the Church can have on the conscience of the opposition. In scattered instances, in San Jose, Sacramento, Oakland, Los Angeles and other places, priests would speak out loudly and clearly against specific instances of oppression, and in some cases, stand with the people who were being hurt. Furthermore, a small group of priests, Frs. McDonald, McCollough, Duggan and others, began to pinpoint attention on the terrible situation of the farm workers in our state.

At about that same time, we began to run into the California Migrant Ministry in the camps and fields. They were about the only ones there, and a lot of us were very suspicious, since we were Catholics and they were Protestants. However, they had developed a very clear conception of the Church. It was called to serve, to be at the mercy of the poor, and not to try to use them. After a while this made a lot of sense to us, and we began to find ourselves working side by side with them. In fact, it forced us to raise the question why OUR Church was not doing the same. We would ask, "Why do the Protestants come out here and help the people, demand nothing, and give all their time to serving farm workers, while our own parish priests stay in their churches, where only a few people come, and usually feel uncomfortable?"

It was not until some of us moved to Delano and began working to build the National Farm Workers Association that we really saw how far removed from the people the parish Church was. In fact, we could not get any help at all from the priests of Delano. When the strike began, they told us we could not even use the Church's auditorium for the meetings. The farm workers' money helped build that auditorium! But the Protestants were there again, in the form of the California Migrant Ministry, and they began to help in little ways, here and there.

When the strike started in 1965, most of our "friends" forsook us for a while. They ran—or were just too busy to help. But the California Migrant Ministry held a meeting with its staff and decided that the strike was a matter of life or death for farm workers everywhere, and that even if it meant the end of the Migrant Ministry they would turn over their resources to the strikers. The political pressure on the Protestant Churches was tremendous and the Migrant Ministry lost a lot of money. But they stuck it out, and they began to point the way to the rest of the Church. In fact, when 30 of the strikers were arrested for shouting Huelga, 11 ministers went to jail with them. They were in Delano that day at the request of Chris Hartmire, director of the California Migrant Ministry.

Then the workers began to raise the question: "Why ministers? Why not priests? What does the Bishop say?" But the Bishop said nothing. But slowly the pressure of the people grew and grew, until finally we have in Delano a priest sent by the new Bishop, Timothy Manning, who is there to help minister to the needs of farm workers. His name is Father Mark Day and he is the Union's chaplain. *Finally,* our own Catholic Church has decided to recognize that we have our own peculiar needs, just as the growers have theirs.

But outside of the local diocese, the pressure built up on growers to negotiate was tremendous. Though we were not allowed to have our own priest, the power of the ecumenical body of the Church was tremendous. The work of the Church, for example, in the Schenley, Di Giorgio, Perelli-Minetti strikes was fantastic. They applied pressure—and they mediated.

When poor people get involved in a long conflict, such as a strike, or a civil rights drive, and the pressure increases each day, there is a deep need for spiritual advice. Without it we see families crumble, leadership weaken, and hard workers grow tired. And in such a situation the spiritual advice must be given by a *friend*, not by the opposition. What sense does it make to go to Mass on Sunday and reach out for spiritual help, and instead get sermons about the wickedness of your cause? That only drives one to question and to despair. The growers in Delano have their spiritual problems . . . we do not deny that. They have every right to have priests and ministers who serve their needs. BUT WE HAVE DIFFERENT NEEDS, AND SO WE NEEDED A FRIENDLY SPIRITUAL GUIDE. And this is true in every community in this state where the poor face tremendous problems.

But the opposition raises a tremendous howl about this. They don't want us to have our spiritual advisors, friendly to our needs. Why is this? Why indeed except that THERE IS TREMENDOUS SPIRITUAL AND ECONOMIC POWER IN THE CHURCH. The rich know it, and for that reason they choose to keep it from the people.

The leadership of the Mexican-American Community must admit that we have fallen far short in our task of helping provide spiritual guidance for our people. We may say, "I don't feel any such need. I can get along." But that is a poor excuse for not helping provide such help for others. For we can also say, "I don't need any welfare help. I can take care of my own problems." But we are all willing to fight like hell for welfare aid for those who truly need it, who would starve without it. Likewise we may have gotten an education and not care about scholarship money for ourselves, or our children. But we would, we should, fight like hell to see to it that our state provides aid for any child needing it so that he can get the education he desires. LIKEWISE WE CAN SAY WE DON'T NEED THE CHURCH. THAT IS OUR BUSINESS. BUT THERE ARE HUNDREDS OF THOUSANDS OF OUR PEOPLE WHO DESPERATELY NEED SOME HELP FROM THAT POWERFUL INSTITUTION, THE CHURCH, AND WE ARE FOOLISH NOT TO HELP THEM GET IT.

For example, the Catholic Charities agencies of the Catholic Church have millions of dollars earmarked for the poor. But often the money is spent for food baskets for the needy instead of for effective action to eradicate the causes of poverty. The men and women who administer this money sincerely want to help their brothers. It should be our duty to help direct the attention to the basic needs of the Mexican-Americans in our society . . . needs which cannot be satisfied with baskets of food, but rather with effective organizing at the grassroots level.

Therefore, I am calling for Mexican-American groups to stop ignoring this source of power. It is not just our right to appeal to the Church to use its power effectively for the poor, it is our duty to do so. It should be as natural as appealing to government . . . and we do that often enough.

Furthermore, we should be prepared to come to the defense of that priest, rabbi, minister, or layman of the Church, who out of commitment to truth and justice gets into a tight place with his pastor or bishop. It behooves us to stand with that man and help him see his trial through. It is our duty to see to it that his rights of conscience are respected and that no bishop, pastor or other higher body takes that God-given, human right away.

Finally, in a nutshell, what do we want the Church to do? We don't ask for more cathedrals. We don't ask for bigger churches or fine gifts. We ask for its presence with us, beside us, as Christ among us. We ask the Church to *sacrifice with the people* for social change, for justice, and for love of brother. We don't ask for words. We ask for deeds. We don't ask for paternalism. We ask for servanthood.

---

36. *Viva la huelga en general*
(Long Live the General Strike)

Anonymous

From Armando B. Rendón, Chicano Manifesto *(New York: Collier Books, 1971), p. 122. Trans. A.M.S.A.*

El día 8 de septiembre	On the 8th of September
De los campos de Delano	From the camps of Delano
Salieron los filipinos.	Came the Filipinos.

Y después de dos semanas	And then after two weeks
Para unirse a la batalla	To join in the battle
Salieron los mexicanos.	Out came the Chicanos.
Y juntos vamos cumpliendo	And together we're fulfilling
Con la marcha de la historia	The march of history
Para liberar el pueblo.	To liberate our people.
Coro	*Chorus*
¡Viva la huelga en el fil![1]	Long live the farm strike!
¡Viva la causa en la historia!	Long live our historic cause!
¡La raza llena de gloria!	Our people crowned with glory!
¡La victoria va cumplir!	Will achieve the victory!

1. *Fil:* for "field".

The reaction from official church circles to increased Hispano militancy on behalf of Chávez differed according to circumstances and policies of the local ordinaries. In the Los Angeles Archdiocese, under Cardinal McIntyre, for instance, the tendency was to reject the importance placed on the strike and the boycott. This led to charges of racism in the secular media, which damaged the church's prestige. In self-defense, official leadership tried to lump together the efforts of Chávez with the "ugly" militancy of the more radical groups. The following excerpt describes how an incident at St. Basil's Church in Los Angeles led to a confrontation on Christmas Eve 1969.

Fortunately, the reaction in other dioceses was more favorable. Local churches, often with the support of non-Hispano clergy, validated the leadership of young Mexican American priests involved with Chávez. This valuable encouragement from the non-Hispano priests fostered the growing momentum of Hispano assertiveness.

With their role as religious leaders within the community secure, the Mexican American clergy began articulating the needs of their people. They soon went beyond the limitations of immediate social and political causes and began to speak in a prophetic voice about the Catholic church as an institution. The past ugliness of the confrontation at St. Basil's reinforced their credibility and they found themselves speaking as pastoral theologians to a growing audience of Hispanos and non-Hispanos alike.

37. El Movimiento Chicano

David F. Gómez

From Gómez, Somos Chicanos: Strangers in Our Own Land *(Boston: Beacon Press, 1973), pp. 155-170.*

Chicanos have learned the lessons of history. We have been in this country—our country—long enough to have identified the enemy. The enemy is variously labeled "*gabacho*," "Anglo society," "the Man," et cetera. The name is not important. The reality behind the labels is a system which creates desperately impoverished and underprivileged people on a regular basis. Invariably these poor people are Chicanos, blacks, and other visible minorities.

The Chicano movement is the collective understanding and concerted effort by Chicanos to eradicate the causes of our widespread poverty, discrimination, and economic oppression. By whatever means necessary! The analysts of nationalistic movements like to chart the progression of a militant people through stages of collective consciousness.[1] To some extent, this pattern is valid for Chicanos.

First, there is the primitive consciousness that nothing can be done about our plight. People come to think that poverty is a way of life, an undeniable fact that we must adjust ourselves to. A subtle variation of this attitude, one expressed by middle-class Mexican Americans, is that while poverty is indeed always with us, any Chicano can "make it" in Anglo society if he works hard enough and pulls himself up by his own bootstraps.

Second, there is the naive consciousness that although we've somehow been victimized, the blame as well as the solution rests with others. And so the people look to the government, the churches, poverty programs, et cetera, as their salvation. In the early stages of the movement, many Chicanos hid themselves behind posters of Emiliano Zapata and Pancho Villa, as if those dead warriors could now win victories for them in twentieth century Anglo society. We had not yet learned to trust ourselves and one another.

The final stage is when the people stop looking to others for their liberation and come to the critical awareness not only of who has been victimizing

1. See, for example, Paulo Freire's excellent work, *Pedagogy of the Oppressed* (New York: Herder and Herder, 1972).

them, but also of the fact that the power for liberation resides with the people. No one else. Leaders, the new Zapatas and Villas, will emerge when the people start fighting for their own cause.

Chicanos have been reaching this critical consciousness in ever-increasing numbers. This chapter illustrates how this Movement consciousness has provoked Chicano Catholics to overcome their early childhood fears and so-called religious training to challenge the most powerful church in this country and the world; how Chicano lawyers have repudiated Anglo values they learned in law school and have started to fight as part of the people; and how an obscure Chicano from East [Los Angeles] sacrificed his freedom and risked his life for the cause of Chicano liberation.

> How many churches, let alone million-dollar churches, did Christ build? We looked further and found that, although as a matter of faith all of us are members of the Catholic Church, nonetheless no Chicanos are able to participate in decisions within the Church, which are not of purely religious nature. Would you have voted for a million-dollar church? As Mexican-Americans, as Católicos, as Chicanos, it is our fault if the Catholic Church in the Southwest is no longer a Church of blood, a Church of struggle, a Church of sacrifice. It is our fault because we have not raised our voices as Catholics and as poor people for the love of Christ. We can't love our people without demanding better housing, education, health, and so many other needs we share in common.
> —*Open letter from CPLR to the people of the barrios*

The conflict between the Catholic Church and the Chicano was dramatically, almost surrealistically, acted out in violent confrontation on Christmas Eve 1969, in St. Basil's Church, Los Angeles.

The open conflict began to develop in the Fall of that year when Chicano activists, many of them college and university students and members of *Mecha,* raised the issue of the Church's flagrant neglect of its oldest, most faithful, and largest racial minority in the Southwest. "Any fool could see," said one of the *Mechistas,* "that the Catholic Church has done nothing for our people."

The activists, who called themselves *Católicos por la Raza* (CPLR), i.e., Catholics for the People, had little trouble proving their point. The Church, ever since the Southwest was annexed, has approached Mexican American people with the same colonialist, missionary attitude which motivated the Franciscan friars in their evangelization of the Indians during the mission era.

An instance of this approach is that there have never been many native Chicano vocations. In other words, Mexican Americans would have to be *gringo*ized (and very few of them were) to the point that the Church would seem attractive as a framework for a lifetime of ministry and service. Moreover, the Southwest Church has been dominated by French, German, and mainly Irish priests in top leadership positions, despite the fact that there have always been able Mexican or Mexican American priests available. Needless to say, the Irish, non-Spanish-speaking priests and bishops have traditionally been unable to fully identify with the needs, aspirations, and best interests of Chicanos.

And Chicanos, along with Indians, were treated like irresponsible children. The Church patronized them instead of defending them. The Church preached passivity and acceptance instead of resistance against evil. And they practiced what they preached: during the repatriations in the 1930s, the Church made no protest at the illegal and unconstitutional deportations of Mexican Americans. During the 1940s, the Church stood by silently while Chicano youth were made the object of a concerted campaign of racist propaganda and overt violence.

Besides recalling history, CPLR did extensive research into the Church's assets and came up with some startling statistics that most Catholic lay people and even priests would not be aware of. Through research into title records, they discovered that the Church owned property totaling more than a billion dollars in Los Angeles County alone.

This figure included churches, parochial schools, and convents, but four out of six of the properties listed were non-church related. These were businesses and residences which included a variety of holdings from slum property in the Pico-Union area to exclusive hi-rise apartments in Beverly Hills and West Los Angeles. "The Church is filthy wealthy," said one of the *Católicos,* "and it can say what it wants about the property not being negotiable or in liquid assets, yet the fact is that they have the land and that means power."

In 1969, the spiritual leader of Los Angeles's two million Catholics and the guardian of the billion dollars in real property was 83-year-old James Francis Cardinal McIntyre. *Católicos por la Raza* arranged an initial meeting with him in early September and another meeting was subsequently held in November. (At the second meeting, the *Católicos* had to push their way past the Cardinal's priest-secretaries because he had refused to see them at first.) "Both times we met," said Joe Razo, one of the CPLR spokesmen, "they said they sympathized with the Chicano's problems but that there was no money for the programs we proposed. Yet we knew they had given the blacks money. We told the Cardinal, 'If you're able to give the blacks money and we are a larger population, 65 percent of the Catholic population in the Southwest, then why don't you service the people through community action-oriented programs?' "

McIntyre told the group on both occasions that there was no money and even if there were, the Church could not get involved in such programs because the Church is apolitical. The only kind of programs being funded, he said, were like the mission downtown for derelicts and alcoholics. He also said the Church had already done a great deal for Chicanos by building parochial schools in the *barrios*. Which in fact was true. CPLR challenged this, however, because they said that Catholic schools, hospitals, et cetera were as racist and inadequate as similar public institutions. Which also was true.

"When the Cardinal told us, 'We give Easter baskets and Christmas baskets,'" said Joe Razo, "we challenged him again. The Church is a hopemaker. They give people hope by giving them a Christmas basket, hope that things will change next year. And sure as hell, next year the Church is bringing the same Christmas basket again. And they're giving hope but no social change just like the welfare, you give people a check and they hope things will change by next check but it doesn't. And it's just sucking them up on their hopes and aspirations and makes no political change."

Despite the Cardinal's statement to the contrary, the Church has never hesitated to enter the political arena, using whatever influence it has, whether to influence antiabortion legislation or state aid to parochial school education. What most angered the *Católicos* was that while Cardinal McIntyre was disavowing any involvement with political matters, he had recently invited Governor Ronald Reagan and President-elect Richard M. Nixon (both accepted) to a $100-a-plate fund-raising dinner for the Archdiocese.

The central issue that emerged from the two encounters with the Cardinal and other chancery officials was whether or not the Catholic Church in Los Angeles, with its tremendous wealth and power, would do anything for the political and social involvement of the Chicano people. The Cardinal from that point on refused to see the activists and labeled them "militants" and "rabble." At this point also the CPLR activists took to the streets with protests and demonstrations. They picketed the chancery office, and soon St. Basil's Church, a recently built, ultramodern church, the size of a basilica or cathedral, became the focal point of dissent. St. Basil's had cost four million dollars to build and was intended to be the Cardinal's showpiece for special occasions.

On the Sunday prior to Christmas Eve, CPLR staged a protest in front of the large church. About two hundred demonstrators stood outside with placards denouncing the Church's wealth and affluence, singing songs in Spanish *("Estas Son Las Mañanitas")*, and passing out leaflets to passers-by. At the end of the protest, the group's leaders told the Cardinal's representatives inside the rectory that unless their demands for more Chicano programs were met, they would be back again—and not to sing *"Estas Son Las Mañanitas"!* There was no apparent response from the Cardinal.

On Christmas Eve, at about 11:00 P.M., CPLR met in front of the chancery office on Ninth Street. About four to five hundred people showed up. Candles were distributed to all present, and a candlelight procession began wending its way toward St. Basil's, a few blocks to the north. The participants were mostly young Chicano students, but a great many family people— mothers, fathers, grandmothers, even infants—were also in attendance. Among the Chicano students, there were several *veteranos,* seasoned campaigners in the Chicano movement. For instance, at the head of the procession was a tall, heavy-set Chicano dressed almost completely in black. On his shirt, he wore several movement buttons ("Chicano Power," "Boycott Grapes," "Free Sal Castro," et cetera) in much the same way a soldier proudly displays campaign ribbons. Chosen as the standard bearer, he carried a large banner of *La Virgen Mestiza, La Madre de la Revolución*.[2]

When the procession reached the church, they staged their own Mass in Spanish, on the church steps. Three priests (all Anglos) who sympathized with the Chicano group, celebrated the eucharist. As this service of breaking bread was being conducted, people began arriving to attend Midnight Mass inside the church. CPLR people passed out leaflets and, by being present in front of the church in such a large group, made clear their point that Chicanos were critical of the rich white man's church.

By the time the *Católicos'* Mass outside had finished, the Mass inside was about to begin. Richard Cruz, CPLR Co-chairman, gave a short talk from the steps of the church, reminding the people of the Church's hypocrisy in building a four million dollar church while saying they were on the side of the poor. He also pointed out the symbolism of the *Católicos* being on the street while the white parishioners, most of them upper-middle-class types, were inside the sumptuous church. "The church is ours because we're Catholics, too, and anyone who wants to go to Mass can go to Mass," he said. "But we're through out here. So anyone who wants to go home, go home." Everyone stayed.

Then a nucleus of about fifty went up the concrete steps to enter the front doors of the church but found the heavy glass outer doors locked. "The thing was locked up real tight, like a coffin," said one participant. "And that's where it all started." The four to five hundred people outside, all of whom were Catholics, became very angry and frustrated because the doors had been locked against them. It was an insult to them, said one, because it was like calling them "rabble" or "troublemakers" who couldn't be trusted inside the church. The people began to shout for someone to open the doors and let them enter.

At this point, a white nun, a sister of the Immaculate Heart Order, who was inside worshiping at the back of the church, heard the noise and went back to see what was going on. She asked the ushers, who seemed to be standing guard at the large doors, "Why don't you let the poor people in?" And the Chicanos on the other side of the doors took up the cry, "Let the poor people in!" Soon all the demonstrators were chanting, "Let the poor people in!" And the sound of the chanting could be heard inside the church and was even

2. Our Lady of Guadalupe, according to Mexican Catholic tradition, appeared in a vision to Juan Diego, an *Indio,* in 1521. She appeared as a *mestiza,* a racial mixture of Spanish and Indian. Thus, as the *Mestiza* mother of God, she is the chief symbol and source of Mexican religiosity as well as a unifying symbol to Mexican people during times of adversity or revolution. Under her patronage and banner, peasants fought against Spaniards in 1810; and the armies of Zapata revered her as their patroness during the revolution of 1910.

picked up on the sound system of the television crews who were televising the Mass.

During the chanting, Chicanos went around to the side of the church looking for an entrance and found a way in. They went to the back of the church and opened the doors from inside. But when one of the Chicanos opened the doors, he was jumped from behind by one of the ushers. The ushers, it turned out, were undercover sheriff's deputies who later claimed they were "off duty." While they may have been officially off duty, each of them was fully armed with service revolver, night stick, handcuffs, and can of mace. As a burly deputy jumped the Chicano from behind, other deputies joined in to prevent the demonstrators from entering, but it was too late. The people had already started to stream in.

All of the ushers went to the back of the church with their night sticks drawn and cans of mace ready to use. They tried to force the people out of the church and only succeeded in starting a number of fights with the angry Chicanos who were determined not to be thrown out of their church. By this time the Gospel of the Nativity was being intoned by one of the priests in the sanctuary. Because of the chanting and noise from the fighting and scuffling in the back, the priest summoned two other priests to join in unison with him reciting the Gospel. In this way, they tried to drown out the sounds of the people being beaten by the deputies.

At this time, a prearranged signal had been given for the Los Angeles Police Department's crack riot squad to come to the aid of the deputies. Apparently the Cardinal had made special plans for stopping trouble before it could develop, because the riot squad troopers had been secretly hidden from view in the Cardinal's personal quarters at the rear of the church. Two full units took only moments to arrive on the scene. And they came dressed for action—helmets, face shields, riot sticks. They streamed into the vestibule, striking first with their riot sticks and asking questions later.

While this confrontation escalated with the arrival of the riot squad, Cardinal McIntyre, dressed in red velvet robes and seated on the high episcopal throne inside the sanctuary, did not once look toward the source of the disturbance but kept his eyes on the Mass as it continued without interruption.

The vestibule or antechamber was the battlefield that evening and morning. In St. Basil's, the vestibule is exceptionally large and can accommodate three to four hundred standing people. By the time the riot squad had arrived their work was cut out for them, because most of the demonstrators had gotten into the vestibule. The officers beat the people back into the street and allowed no one to get into the main part of the church. (The television cameras never caught a glimpse of what was happening, although the TV audience could plainly hear the battle sounds from the vestibule for a full fifteen minutes.) The demonstrators were beaten, kicked, clubbed, and maced by police in an effort to get them out into the street again.

The noises grew so loud that Monsignor Benjamin Hawks, who was acting as Master of Ceremonies, again attempted to drown out the anguished screams of the people by having the congregation sing (ironically) "O Come, All Ye Faithful"!

"They pushed us out onto the sidewalk," said Joe Razo. "I saw one person being beaten by three cops, and I went over there and before you know it, I got hit. Whacked me on the head and knocked me down. The first thing I did was bundle up and I tried to crawl under a car. And I heard one of the cops say, 'Give that bastard another head-shot.' And I was defenseless, I wasn't struggling. I was trying to protect my head. And before you know it, the lights went out. That head-shot took sixteen stitches." Another participant said, "I saw a pregnant woman down and being kicked. But I couldn't get over to help her."

Meanwhile, back in the church, Cardinal McIntyre was still absorbed in the Mass as worshipers approached the altar to receive holy communion.

Still more police reinforcements were called in. About twenty-one arrests were made and the remaining two to three hundred demonstrators were pushed down Wilshire Boulevard by club-swinging police until the crowd was dispersed. In the church, as the Mass ended, Cardinal McIntyre addressed the congregation for the first time: "We are ashamed of the participants and we recognize that their conduct was symbolic of the conduct of the rabble as they stood at the foot of the cross, shouting, 'Crucify him!' " Then he told the people, "Forgive them for they know not what they do."

"So that night and later," said Richard Cruz, "the whole posture and approach of the parishioners, Cardinal, and police was that we were 'rabble.' It was a once-in-a-lifetime type thing. I have been in lots of riots, you see riots and you can see them for what they are—individuals and passion and turmoil. But you don't always see the issue so clearly. Here you see Jesus being used like crazy, being used not by some flunky priest who's afraid of anybody, but by the Cardinal. It was a mind-blower, like seeing some sort of fantastic painting, or something like that, where you could see theory, political action, philosophy, and religion all at once."

While the Cardinal had generously made reference to Jesus' words of forgiveness, there was no forgiveness for those arrested or later charged. At first they were booked on conspiracy charges, but when the district attorney could not gather enough evidence for that, the charges became the misdemeanor of disrupting a religious service. In subsequent trials, only seven persons were actually found guilty and sentenced to ninety days in the county jail.

"McIntyre should have stood trial, not us," sayd Richard Cruz. "He incited to riot that night! If there's anyone who should have gone to jail it was the Cardinal. If the church doors had been open, only a few angry Chicanos might have gone in and said something or been otherwise so pissed off at the pomp and circumstance that they would have done something. So here you go and lock the doors and the police and riot squad are waiting in ambush for us; and we come in with our mothers and sisters and babies! And who laid the ambush? Cardinal McIntyre!"

In the aftermath of the Christmas Eve incident, *Católicos por la Raza* brought the issues of conflict into clearer focus by publishing and distributing in the *barrios* 200,000 copies of a four-page tabloid which factually itemized the Church's immense holdings in Los Angeles County and asked the readers to draw their own conclusions. The tabloid was printed in both Spanish and English. Mexican Americans, many of them unsympathetic to the irreverent troublemakers (as the press depicted them), were nevertheless drawn into the debate because the facts and figures spoke for themselves. Many went to their local parish priests and asked, "Father, is it true about the property?" The Church responded by using the Archdiocesan paper, *The Tidings*, to rebut the charges of hypocrisy. And the debate continued in that vein for two or three months.

Many observers still question whether *Católicos por la Raza* accomplished anything by their conflict with the institutional Church. Many will say it was good for emotional uplift but produced nothing substantial. Perhaps one reason people have been reluctant to give CPLR credit for anything is that the white press dismissed them as "rabble" and "agitators." Another reason is that the Church never admitted any wrongdoing or accepted any fault for the events which developed on Christmas Eve. The implication was that the CPLR was totally responsible for the bodily injuries, destruction of Church property, and arrests.

Directly or indirectly, however, *Católicos por la Raza* were responsible for the following:

The Fund for Human Development. This fund was started a few months after the incident at St. Basil's as a direct response to the CPLR charge that the Church had done nothing for the Chicanos in their struggle for self-determination. It is a nationwide collection taken up on a yearly basis in Catholic parishes in the United States. The money is distributed from a national office in Washington, D.C., to grass-roots organizations with almost no strings attached. Most of the money has gone to Chicano groups like Chicano Health Organization, *Abogados de Aztlán,* and so on.

Apparently the Church was afraid that the discontent would grow among Chicano Catholics. Indeed several churches—Catholic and Protestant—had been liberated by Chicano militants in the months following the Christmas Eve confrontation in Los Angeles. The Church wanted to take no chances of a trend starting in which they would continually be put in an embarrassing position. The fund was conscience money being offered to people who had accused the bishops and priests of hypocrisy; it was also a way to neutralize criticism and stem the growing tide of militant rebellion within the fold.

Resolution of the Grape Boycott. In 1969, the U.S. Conference of Catholic Bishops had entered the grape boycott dispute between César Chávez's

UFWOC [United Farm Workers of California] and the growers in Delano as a liaison. But the Church had not been pursuing a negotiated settlement with the influence and power at its disposal. According to CPLR spokesman Richard Martinez: "Some of us talked to César Chávez in Delano several months later and he said, 'If it wasn't for you people, although I may not agree with your tactics, the Church wouldn't have pushed so adamantly for a resolution.' " Six months after the St. Basil's affair, the grape boycott and strike were settled and the Church was rightly given much credit for helping to engineer negotiations.

Appointment of Chicano or Spanish-surnamed Bishops. In 1969, there was not a single Chicano bishop in the United States, nor had there ever been a Chicano member of the U.S. Catholic hierarchy. In the wake of the CPLR demand for representation, Bishop Patrick Flores was installed as auxiliary bishop of San Antonio, Texas. Also, Bishop Juan Arzube, an Ecuadorian by birth, was installed as auxiliary bishop of Los Angeles.

Cardinal McIntyre was forced to retire as head of the Los Angeles Archdiocese. Most of the speculation and educated guesses point to Cardinal McIntyre's being retired because of the bad publicity the Church received on Christmas Eve as well as his advanced age. Complaints were said to have been lodged in Rome, and the papal nuncio was also said to have suggested retirement to the Cardinal. "The reason they got rid of Cardinal McIntyre in my opinion," said Richard Cruz, "was because he was such a lousy tactician. As I said, he incited to riot that night and that doesn't look good for the Cardinal or the Church." Whatever the specific reason, McIntyre was retired, and Archbishop Timothy Manning was appointed to assume control of the Archdiocese. The atmosphere has greatly changed because Manning relates more easily to Chicanos.

Chicanos became more critically aware of their Church and of themselves. The major impact of the demonstrations and demands was the profound and far-reaching effect within the *barrios* and within Chicano families. The week of the Christmas Eve affair, almost every Chicano family had an argument about the nature of the Catholic Church and its role within the Chicano community. Even though it was the young on one side and the older parents and relatives on the other, families stayed together, discussed together, and as a result were stronger families for it.

Many Chicanos who grew up in fear and trembling at the Church and Church officials, were no longer afraid. They had stood their ground, challenged the Church, and made their demands known. And no lightning came down. Many liberal priests and nuns also had to take a stand for or against the Church and the *Católicos por la Raza.* "There's no end to the type of things that happen when men look critically at their church," one activist told me.

What CPLR accomplished, while very great in light of their small numbers, was only a beginning. Indeed most of the monies and programs and appointments have amounted to little more than token concessions. As one veteran activist put it: "The hierarchy still has not made a major decision to support the national liberation struggle of the Chicano people as a nationally oppressed minority." Chicanos remain the most neglected and forgotten people within the Church.

Chicano priests, moreover, are still passed over or ignored when bishops are chosen to head dioceses with large Mexican American populations, despite the fact that the people have repeatedly asked for Chicano bishops to lead them. In 1971, when the See of Brownsville, Texas, was open (and the area is nearly 90 percent Chicano!), *Raza* organizations urged the hierarchy to choose a Chicano and named possible candidates. Instead an Irish American was chosen.

Most tragic of all, the Church continues to deal with Chicanos on a largely superstitious basis, lulling them into being passive, accepting believers who never question. The Cursillo movement has given a needed shot in the arm to Mexican American Catholicism, but unfortunately the proportion of bishops and priests who have been exposed to Cursillos or are even aware of the Cursillo principles of co-responsibility and priest-lay people cooperation, is minuscule. This is one reason why priests are so far out of touch with their Mexican American parishioners.

Non-Spanish speaking American priests (mostly Irish-American) continue to dominate the organized religious life and worship of Chicano Catholics. The sermons I hear them preach in church today have not changed one word from those I heard as a boy growing up in Los Angeles. They still exclusively dwell on the three aspects of the "ideal" Christian life: creed, code, and cult. Proper individual moral behavior (code) and not social justice is repeatedly emphasized from pulpit and confessional. Steady Mass attendance (cult) is inculcated as a primary religious value, even prior to service of those in need. And one's formal, articulated knowledge of the catechism (creed) is held up as a means to sainthood, instead of urging that people become action-oriented in the selfless service of their own people and others less fortunate.

Never once have I heard a priest tell the people from the pulpit (in churches where the majority of the people are Chicanos) to be proud of who they are. Never have I heard a sermon on the Mexican's civil and human rights, and how to win them. To my knowledge no bishop or priest in Los Angeles has ever spoken in church on the Church's own social principles of equal distribution of wealth and the workingman's right to organize and fight for a just wage. There is no question that the code, cult, and creed are important in the life of organized religion; but unless man's social duties and rights are also taught and actively fostered, the Christian "ideals" become only another means to selfishness, not salvation.

The recently formed Chicano priests' organization, PADRES (acronym for [Padres Asociados para Derechos Religiosos Educativos y Sociales, or] Priests for Religious, Educational, and Social Rights) has suggested a radical and exciting idea, which for a time had the Irish American Church leadership scared stiff. They suggested the formation of a Chicano Catholic Church, a national church within the Roman Catholic Church but not under the control of the U.S. hierarchy. It would be accountable only to the Pope.

Such a national church would enable Chicano lay people and priests to assume more responsibility for meeting their own religious needs as well as for taking an active, decisive role in determining precisely what those needs may be at a given time. We would be able to create our own unique liturgy. Presently, the Mariachi Mass is popular, but it is only a stop-gap measure, using Mexican rhythms to cover up the obvious inadequacies of the Roman rite. And we would be able to develop our own theology—a theology of *la raza*!

But the idea of a Chicano Catholic Church remains only an idea. That's why top Church leaders dismiss it now as an idle threat of separatism. And many of the Chicano priests who were the founding fathers of PADRES and who most vigorously promoted the idea of a separate church have since left the active priesthood. This lets the hierarchy off the hook in one sense, but in another, it spells potential disaster when priests are saying the Church isn't even worth fighting about anymore. Apparently many of these men did not think they had a fighting chance because of the recurring opposition from Church superiors and mounting frustration of having good ideas which the Church opposes and won't allow to be implemented.

The only answer may be a complete break. "I think it's great when a priest leaves the Church," a friend of mine recently said. "Any priest who don't quit is going no place. I don't care who he is." In my opinion, if all the oppressed priests in the Church (which is almost all of them) were to leave the institutional Church, they would be in a far better position to see what's going wrong as well as be in a strong enough bargaining position to return to organized religion like decision-making men and not like the powerless subjects and subordinates they are now.

If priests and lay people ever start acting on ideas like that, or the hundreds of others which have been discussed since the Vatican Council, there will be far-reaching and meaningful changes for Catholics, Chicanos included. Until then, a lot of us Chicanos thank God the *Católicos por la Raza* are still around, angry as hell, and ready to deal with the issues.

José Angel Gutiérrez is a Texas militant and former president of the Mexican American Youth Organization (MAYO), a forerunner of many Chicano movements, such as the Raza Unida Party, which seeks to organize Hispanos into one political party in the United States, offering an alternative to the national Republican and Democratic parties. Gutiérrez was born in Crystal City, Texas, in 1945, and after graduating from high school there as an honor student, left the small Texas town of his birth for college and graduate school at St. Mary's University in San Antonio. Returning home with a master's degree in political science, he became involved in Crystal City politics in 1969 (Shockley, 1974).

Gutiérrez is the *béte noire* of those who see Mexican American political power only in terms of participation in institutional structures. According to Congressman Henry González (Dem.-Texas), the proposals of Gutiérrez "reflect the language of Castro and incorporate language that is alien to our area of the country" (Shockley, 1974, p. 125). For others, however, Gutiérrez is the authentic political prophet of Chicano militancy. The following excerpt, taken from a statement describing the early goals of MAYO, demonstrates differences from the United Farm Workers (UFW) of César Chávez in purpose and tactics. The poem by Richard Olivas, which follows it, echoes the Chicano sentiments of students who look to Gutiérrez for leadership and inspiration.

38. The Mexican American Youth Organization (MAYO)

José Angel Gutiérrez

From "Aztlán: Chicano Revolt in the Winter Garden Area," unpublished paper, Crystal City, Texas, 1970, in John Staples Shockley, Chicano Revolt in a Texas Town (Notre Dame, Ind.: Univ. of Notre Dame Press, 1974), pp. 123-124. Copyright 1974 by University of Notre Dame Press, Notre Dame, Indiana 46556. Used by permission.

. . . MAYO was not intended to be a mass membership organization; nor, a constipated civic group of reformists. . . .

We were not misguided and mal-informed VISTA volunteers; nor, were we white-knighted Latin Americans that sought to manage the affairs of the gringo for the gringo. We were young Chicanos who saw and felt things like Chicanos should. We loved and accepted our Mexicanismo and saw brighter things for La Raza. . . .

The primary goal was to force the educational system to extend to the Mexican student. . . .

The second goal was to bring democracy to those counties [where a majority of the people were Mexican-Americans]—in other words—rule by the majority. . . .

. . . our third goal was a direct confrontation with the gringo. We sought to expose, confront, and eliminate the gringo. We felt that it was necessary to polarize the community over issues into Chicano versus gringos.

Basically, the difference between the Chicano and gringo, aside from the bad guy-good guy criteria, is one of attitude. The attitude gringos have of racial superiority; of paternalism; of divine right; of xenophobia; of bigotry; and of animalism is well-known to La Raza.

After the gringo was exposed publicly, the next step was to confront their security-status, business, and morality in order to recognize the enemy in all their involvements of policies, roles and power manipulations. Once the Chicano community recognized the enemy, then he had the power to eliminate gringo attitudes by not voting for the gringo and not buying from the gringo. . . . Consequently, the Chicano would take power available to the gringo and then attack the [colonialist] states so evident in South Texas.

The fourth goal of our Aztlán model would be a program of rural economic development since colonialism still exists in South Texas. Under this economic development the first step would be to replace the existing white managerial functions with Chicano expertise. The transfer of existing businesses from gringo hands to Chicano hands would be the second step. In the last step, La Raza would set upon the agri-business, the oil and gas industry, and the modern day land and cattle barons—the real subversives in America today. . . .

---

39. The Immigrant Experience

Richard Olivas

From Octavio Romano V. ed., Voices: Readings from El Grito *(Berkeley: Quinto Sol, 1971), p. 174. Used by permission.*

I'm sitting in my history class,
The instructor commences rapping,
I'm in my U.S. History class,
And I'm on the verge of napping.

The Mayflower landed on Plymouth Rock.
Tell me more! Tell me more!
Thirteen colonies were settled.
I've heard it all before.

What did he say?
Dare I ask him to reiterate?
Oh why bother
It sounded like he said,
George Washington's my father.

I'm reluctant to believe it,
I suddenly raise my mano.
If George Washington's my father,
Why wasn't he Chicano?

When César Chávez's efforts became a national cause, the priests support-ing the Mexican American farm workers came to know each other through the various rallies and national meetings. Padre Ralph Ruiz, who has since left the active priesthood, took the initiative in October 1969 to call a meeting for February of the following year in Tucson, Arizona. That 1970 assembly started Padres Asociados para Derechos Religiosos Educativos y Sociales (PADRES; in English translation, Priests Associated for Educational, Social and Reli-gious Rights).

The next year, Mexican American religious women initiated the same type of process. In April 1971, Sisters Gloria Gallardo, a Holy Spirit sister, and Gregoria Ortega of Victory Knoll, organized a meeting in Houston, Texas. This led to a November assembly in Santa Fe, New Mexico. The name given to the women's organization was "Hermanas," which in Spanish means "Sisters." There was an important difference between the two groups, despite obvious similarities. PADRES had voted in a stormy congress to exclude all but Mexican Americans from full membership in their organization, while Hermanas opened itself up to include Puerto Ricans, Cubans, and all other Hispanos as full members. Be-tween these initial meetings and subsequent constitutive assemblies, Patricio Flores of Houston was ordained as auxiliary bishop of San Antonio, Texas on May 5, 1970.

In a relatively short period of time, the Mexican Americans had turned the recognition provided them by participation in Chávez's strike and boycott for the farm workers into a national platform within the church to promote a Mexican American dimension to pastoral care and theological reflection. They tested the sincerity of non-Hispanos toward Mexican American advancement by requiring a partnership not just for liturgical tasks or in social causes, but also for complete ecclesiastical leadership. In sum, the Mexican American clergy and religious rose to a level of leadership within the church that was new for them.

In articulating a theological role, the spokespersons of the Mexican Ameri-cans borrowed the concepts of the *pensadores*, especially Vasconcelos, Paz, and Zapata.

The giant shadow of the fearless Zapata was present in the support given to Chávez and his cause. The padre was on the picket lines, close to the people. He broke with the sacristan-like image of the village priest and became a *macho*. Longer hair, overalls, a moustache, the traditional poncho and sombrero, even coarser and more pungent language and manners became part of the new image. Behind these phenomena was an ideological commitment. It was directed not toward the kind of articulated socialism, sometimes Communism, of the Chicano student movements. Rather, the sense of revolution was in the call of Zapata in 1910 for land and bread and freedom through a revolution. A direct commitment to action was more important than political strategy against capitalism. This commitment came to be called *carnalismo*. It is a term found over and over in the vocabulary of the Mexican American leaders. It is not to be translated as "carnalism" with overtones of lust or sexuality. It refers to a concept of presence with the people and an incorporation as brother—a *carnal* of the experience of oppression and the struggle for freedom. Often Spanish words are interjected into an English-language presentation to dramatize the solidarity. Mexicans believe that in no case does *carnalismo* demand a previously devised plan, nor should it be spoiled with devious stratagems for achieving personal power at the expense of the people. This is the historical symbolism of Zapata's nobility and the articulated power of Magón's words in *La Regeneración* (see p. 28–32).

Vasconcelos's concept of *La Raza Cósmica* (see pp. 33–38) was also present in the movement. The Mexican philosopher, it will be remembered (see pp. 32–33), argued that the mixture of races as found in the Mexican people endowed them with a rich cultural aptitude that incorporated the best of other civilizations. When the right time was at hand, Vasconcelos theorized, the Cosmic Race would assume leadership over all others. Dialectical Idealism was the revolutionary force in the world, and the race with the best ideas bred into its peoples would inevitably become dominant. There was an indirect Messianism in this; also a subtle contradiction because Mexican Americans called for pluralism and equal rights while trusting in an underlying premise that eventually the superiority of *La Raza* would replace Anglo-Irish Catholicism as the dominant mode of United States Catholicism. In other words, pluralism was a temporary stage before the new cultural dominance by *La Raza*. Frequently one discovers in the elaboration of statistics about population a statement to the effect that one day Mexican Americans (or Hispanos) will be the largest nationality group in the church. They are, as some native poets have put it recalling the Mexican Revolution, the "Cockroach People" who are everywhere in plentiful numbers.

This sense of destiny inspired the ambitions of PADRES and Hermanas. They had the widest horizons as their goal and a drive based on a powerful optimism and confidence in ultimate victory over obstacles. Yet because these ambitions were couched in language of *La Raza* and *carnalismo*, individual successes served to strengthen the mass appeal rather than isolate the new leaders. For instance, Bishop Flores's ordination as auxiliary was seen as a triumph for all Mexican Americans; but far from assuaging a desire for a share in hierarchical power as leaders of the church, it intensified the call for more Hispano bishops. And the call became increasingly aggressive. As Coser points out (1956, p. 118):

. . . conflicts in which the participants feel that they are not merely fighting for self but for the ideals of the group they represent, are likely to be
more radical and merciless than those fought for personal reasons.

This aggressiveness in the name of the people was defended as a part of the
decentralization and democratization of church structures according to Vatican Council II.

The theme of Octavio Paz, the cultural search for identity, became another
armament of the Hispano church movement. Paz says that modes of being,
doing, thinking, and acting form the essence of culture. Individuals who are
culturally free produce political and social structures which are liberating.
Even if there are contradictions and confusion in the psychological understanding of one's culture, the process can be neither hastened nor interrupted,
for the freedom to be cultural is the ultimate freedom. Put in metaphysical
terms, act follows essence, so that achieving liberation for others can only be a
consequence of being free oneself.

A theological dimension was added to cultural freedom by viewing it as
conscientization, a type of educational process which had been developed by
the Brazilian educator Paulo Freire. Conscientization was very popular in
church circles at that time for its heightened sense of moral truth. Conscientization served as a bridge between being and doing.

However, in their rapid incorporation into the political battles of the people,
not a few of the Mexican American priests and religious had become sensitive
to their own relative ignorance about Mexican history and culture. Their
training in a preconciliar church had deprived them of contact with their roots.
At the same time that they campaigned for people's rights, they sought to
reflect Mexican culture and lifestyle within rectories and convents. To give
themselves a comfortable way of repairing the damage of inadequate cultural
sensitivity, it became necessary to establish a center for transmission of the
characteristics of the Mexican American culture to church personnel. This was
done in 1971 with the help of PADRES, and the Archdiocese of San Antonio.
Virgilio Elizondo, trained as a catechist, became the first executive director of
the Mexican American Cultural Center (MACC). If one compared the fledgling
MACC with the Institute of Intercultural Communication that had been
founded by Monsignor Ivan Illich in Puerto Rico for the New York clergy, MACC
would have been judged as second-best in practically every academic category. But the basic difference made all the difference: MACC was run by the
Mexican Americans themselves. As MACC grew, so did the consciousness of
many of the PADRES and Hermanas. Indeed, MACC grew *because* the people
running it were growing. The success of the center established the leadership
credentials of PADRES and Hermanas, of Virgilio Elizondo and Bishop Patricio
Flores.

40. PADRES: Who They Are and Where They Are Going

Padre Juan Romero

From a paper written for the PADRES Congress of 1975. Used by permission.

. . . In 1968 Chicano priests in San Antonio began to discover that they were sharing very similar anxieties and frustrations, and the same thing was going on in other places. For example, in my first parish in Los Angeles, I was not permitted to celebrate mass or preach in Spanish, although 80 percent of my confessions and about 90 percent of parlor calls were in Spanish. My experience was similar in subsequent parishes during the first five years after ordination.

In 1969 on the West Coast there was a group of militant people, mostly student activists calling themselves *Católicos por la Raza*, who were denouncing the church for not effectively relating to the Chicano. At the same time they were challenging the church to do so by fulfilling certain demands. Many Mexican American people, including several Chicano priests, could identify with that frustration voiced by *Católicos por la Raza*. It was a plaint that the church was somehow not effectively relating to the Chicano in his struggle for justice. It preferred to remain neutral, aloof, and uninvolved.

During 1969 Father Ralph Ruiz, the first national chairman of PADRES, contacted other Mexican American priests throughout the country. The first national gathering of people responding to these initial contacts took place in Tucson, Arizona, in February of 1970. Sisters, lay people, and priests—Anglo and Chicano—met. Among the twenty-five Chicano priests present was Father Patricio Flores from the Houston Diocese. After discussion and heated debate, a particular group emerged as a *priests'* organization, and specifically as a *Chicano priests'* organization. Other priests involved in the Spanish-speaking Apostolate were invited to be associate members of the newly formed group called PADRES, which is an acronym for Padres Asociados para Derechos Religiosos Educativos y Sociales [Priests for Religious, Educational, and Social Rights].

This fledgling group shouted for native Spanish-speaking leadership in the country, both in civil life and in the church. There was a specific demand for *Chicano bishops* and a call for some kind of *mobile team ministry* which could pastorally serve neglected Spanish-speaking areas.

Five months later, Cinco de Mayo [May 5], 1970, Patricio Flores was ordained as this country's first Mexican American bishop! That happy occasion was my personal introduction to Chicano priests who identified themselves with the organization of PADRES. I felt their *carnalismo* and immediately knew that we shared the same frustrations, hopes, joys, and anxieties as ministers in the church who were looking for more effective ways to serve the Mexicano in his total life in the land north of Mexico.

The next national meeting of PADRES was held in Los Angeles, one year after the first. By February 1971, some particular organizing efforts among Chicano priests had taken place in California and New Mexico. This meeting was calmer: It was in fact a retreat on "The Social Dimensions of St. Luke's Gospel." A senior Chicano priest-historian, Fray Angelico Chávez, O.F.M., gave his talk on the history of native Hispano vocations. Bishop-elect Juan Arzube of the Archdiocese of Los Angeles was with us. Bishop Flores and Father Virgilio Elizondo were two members of a task force that formalized the idea which, a year later, became the Mexican American Cultural Center in San Antonio with Father Elizondo as its president. We were still trying to refine the idea of the mobile team ministry which had been put forth the year before.

Another five months later, in May of 1971, PADRES sponsored a three-week symposium on the *Teología de Liberación y Pedagogía de Concientización.* I came only for the first two weeks, which were facilitated by a team of three Latin American priests: theologian, anthropologist, and sociologist. Hicimos un análisis de nosotros mismos y de nuestro pueblo—los hechos concretos de nuestra vida que es nuestra realidad. Este análisis, entonces, sirviría como punto de partida para una reflexión y acción pastoral.

This began our strong bond with Latin America, which has grown until today. We are part of the same American continent and have so much in common, although we are different countries. We were convinced that we had much to learn from our Latin American brothers and sisters, so we sent teams of priests to the Instituto Pastoral para Latino América in Quito, Ecuador, para una profundización en la teología de liberación y pedagogía de concientización. All of this was pointing toward getting in motion that mobile team ministry.

The most important insight for me during that symposium was to discover how so many things focused on one reality: falta de *conciencia crítica* de tan gran número de la raza. The purpose of the mobile team ministry was beginning to become more clear: to help develop the critical consciousness of Hispano poor throughout the country so that they could in fact become masters of their own destiny, and live in that freedom of the sons and daughters of God to which he calls all of us.

41. Hermanas

Sister María Iglesias and Sister María Luz Hernández

WHO ARE HERMANAS?

We of Hermanas are a group of religious women[1] of Hispanic or of Anglo-Saxon origin, who work for the spiritual and social well-being of the Hispanos in the United States.

WHAT IS THE PURPOSE OF HERMANAS?

Hermanas is an organization that wants to keep itself aware of the sufferings of our Hispano people. By reason of our heritage, and in response to the mind of Vatican Council II and the encyclical *Populorum Progressio*, we feel obliged to be faithful to the Christian message of hopeful creation for a Christian humanism within the context of the culture of the Hispano community. . . .

Our people find themselves in what sociologists call the "helpless cycle," that is, a vicious circle which entraps us in an inability to act for our own causes. It is clear that we would like to be free from this situation. We believe that we are the ones called to clear the way for our people because we are capable of understanding and appreciating them and their culture.

The Catholic church in this country has responded to the needs of its Spanish-speaking faithful only a few times. As part of this same church, we feel now the obligation to respond to these needs before it is too late. Lacking priests and religious who speak Spanish and who can help alleviate some of their problems, many Hispanos seek relief in other religious sects such as the Protestants, the Evangelicals, and the Jehovah's Witnesses among others.

TEAM GOVERNMENT

We have chosen team government for various reasons. First, so that it will be more representative of the constituted membership, and second, in order to distribute responsibility. There are three national coordinators. One is in Texas, the second in Colorado, and the third in New York. We have state and local representatives. All the Hermanas have something special to contrib-

1. Hermanas today admits women who are not members of a religious order or congregation.

ute. Also, we see as positive the idea of each one of us assuming individual responsibility, responsibility for our actions and responsibility to the group with which each works.

As a National Coordinating Team, our work consists in relating the activities and the goals proposed by the Hermanas General Assembly to national, regional, and state action.

SOME PROJECTS OF HERMANAS

1. Meetings of conscientization for religious or any group that is working in the Spanish apostolate.

2. The Mexico Project, which is an educational program for those religious who are doing domestic work as part of their Apostolate, but who have expressed a desire to take part in an Apostolate more related to parishes or dioceses.

3. The Orientation Center, which *(a)* provides a continuous orientation for candidates or postulants for the religious life who have intentions of serving the Spanish-speaking and *(b)* offers a program of renewal for those religious presently employed in this type of work.

---

42. The Status of Religion among Mexican Americans

Jorge Lara-Braud, Director, Hispanic-American Institute

From Address to Joint Meeting of the American Academy of Religion and the Society of Biblical Literature, Southwest Region, Texas Christian University, Fort Worth, Texas, March 19, 1971. Used by permission.

INDIGENIZATION AND PLURALISM

. . . The road to renaissance for Mexican-American Catholics and Protestants lies unmistakably in their willingness and ability to indigenize their leadership and their forms of church life in consonance with the spirit of self-assertion sweeping through the entire ethnic community. This spirit is one not of assimilation, not of separatism, but of pluralism. It is nourished certainly by the example of the black liberation struggle, but also by the claims which the many other subcultures are making upon society (Indians, Orientals, white ethnics, youth, women, hard-hats, suburbia, peace groups, and the like).

On the eve of the birth of a truly pluralistic society, the Mexican American is stirred by the richness of his own inner diversity. He is not only a Mexican–tough Mexicanhood lies at the core of his being. He is not only an American—tough Americanhood touches every particle of his life. He is a Mexican American. This means the human intersection of two histories, two nations, two cultures, two languages converging, colliding, blending, embracing, depending on one's location within the human geography evolved by one and a half centuries of relentless interaction. The interaction is by no means over. Through dogged determination more Mexican Americans carve out leadership roles in every public institution, formerly closed to people of color, or open only to those who would disguise their difference. Here and there appear counter-institutions of, by, and for Mexican Americans. Paradoxically, their long-range strategy is the return of their graduates to the traditional institutions, to reorient them toward the further empowerment of the ethnic community, and the larger pluralization of the entire national citizenry. In words reminiscent of New Testament eschatology, the Mexican American is speaking of himself as a new man—a man for whom there is no historical parallel, at least not in the experience of the United States. He speaks of his ethnic family as La Raza, a new family of man, the first fruits of a new humanity, where the color range of Mexican-American skin, from the darkest to the fairest, will itself be the visible sign of a new age of fraternity.

These are the large dreams and great visions that young and old Mexican Americans perceive as possible, with themselves as the vanguard to make them come true. Messianism? Utopianism? Most certainly so! Don Quixote lives again. He walks through barrios and colonias. But this is a collective Don Quixote, a community reviving and revived by Christian ideals kept alive by French Oblates, New England missionary ladies, authoritarian Spanish Claretians, scholastic Presbyterians, humble Franciscans, unlettered Pentecostals, and the myriad of their unsung successors.

An Instance of Indigenization

Religion lives among church and unchurched Mexican Americans as a pervasive spirituality. One does not have to be a theologian or a professor of religion to know that spirituality can easily become superstition instead of enlightenment, repression instead of liberation. Much depends on the forces that lead it. It is at this point that I am optimistic regarding the consonance of the new spirituality and the role of Mexican-American churches. Indigenization is the key factor. By indigenization I mean the embodiment of the new spirituality in leadership and structures which themselves correspond to it.

Perhaps the best example I can offer is the forces which led to the elevation of Patricio Flores as the first native-born Mexican-American bishop of the Roman Catholic Church in May of 1970. A nation wide association of Mexican-American priests, PADRES, had come into being in October of 1969. One of the chief concerns of PADRES (Padres Asociados para Derechos Religiosos, Educativos y Sociales) has been the participation of Mexican Americans on all levels of decision-making in the life of United States Catholicism. PADRES is also the strongest voice in the Catholic church for overall Mexican-American advancement.

The church heard that voice. Patricio Flores stands today as the best-loved and most respected church charismatic among Spanish-speaking Catholics. The Archdiocese of San Antonio, as a result, is in full renaissance. Many apathetic or even hostile Mexican-American Catholics have thronged back into the church following with enthusiasm the pastoral direction of the new auxiliary bishop. An Archdiocesan Office for Mexican-American Affairs has come into being. The marketplace and the church are thereby made responsive to each other in every area of human endeavor. The diocesan seminary, lately decimated of teachers and students, is on its way to full recovery, with new church vocations, and the possibility of becoming a national center for the study of the pastoral apostolate among Mexican Americans.

Other dioceses in the Southwest are pressing for similar developments. A compromise concession has been made in the Archdiocese of Los Angeles, where an Ecuadorean educated in England and the United States has been made auxiliary bishop.

INDIGENOUS ECUMENISM

Parallel movements to PADRES are to be found in Mexican-American Protestant caucuses among United Methodists, American Baptists, United Presbyterians, and Southern Presbyterians. Mexican-American Protestants are being employed in key positions of those same churches, and foreign and domestic boards and agencies search diligently for new Mexican-American members. Candidates for the ordained ministry are trickling back to denominational seminaries, which just three years ago were seriously doubting whether Mexican-American students would stop enrolling altogether.

Much of the renaissance of religion among Mexican Americans is the result of ecumenical cooperation by Catholics and Protestants in a common apostolate of redress for a long-suffering community. Illustrations abound, none more dramatic than the struggle of César Chávez and the United Farm Workers Organizing Committee to secure the right of collective bargaining for farm workers. Chávez's own genuine religious piety, commitment to nonviolence, and passion for social justice have naturally attracted the support of churches. In the process, sectarian interests have been put aside.

The practice of ecumenical solidarity with the poor of one's own ethnic family has also advanced a common quest for more indigenous forms of witness and service. Here and there liturgy, sermon, religious instruction, theological formulations, church buildings, and leadership style reflect genuinely Chicano features. Where this happens, it involves more than renaissance of religion. It is, rather, the rebirth of a unique spirituality whose saints are the black Peruvian San Martín de Porres, the brown Indian Virgin of Guadalupe, and the blonde European madonnas, and whose Lord is a mestizo Jew, Jesus of Nazareth. . . .

In New York City, where the Puerto Ricans were concentrated, there was practically no Puerto Rican clergy to follow the example of the Mexican Americans in the Southwest. Indeed, while the total Puerto Rican population of the area was estimated at 1.3 million, at no time between the years 1968–1972 did the number of Puerto Rican priests in the New York metropolitan region exceed six. The most important of these clerics was Peter Ensenat, who while still a very young priest, was given the directorship of the Institute of Intercultural Communication in Ponce. Although he followed Ivan Illich at his post and collaborated with Robert Fox, Peter Ensenat never achieved acceptance from the New York Archdiocese beyond the level of social and institutional needs for leadership. He was expected to administer the programs initiated by others, but was given no canonical powers beyond those shared by every parish priest.

Eventually Ensenat's position was as ambiguous as the continued purposefulness of the Institute of Intercultural Communication, which lost archdiocesan sponsorship in 1972. The New York Puerto Rican community did not protest the loss of this center. Caught up in the search for identity that characterized those years, New York's Puerto Ricans sought to differentiate themselves from the people on the island. Moreover, the issue of Puerto Rican independence or statehood found faint echo in the struggles of the people in New York City. There was, however, no other Puerto Rican political issue with the richness of the farm-worker strike and boycott. Hence there was no way that the Puerto Rican leadership of New York City, clerical or lay, could advance beyond the simplest kinds of church responsibility. And although celebrations such as the San Juan Fiesta had a political side, it was impossible to foster national unity with a mass in Central Park once a year (López, 1973, p. 309).

A transforming moment came under the direction of Father Robert Stern who had succeeded Monsignor Fox in 1969. Stern set about encouraging a native Puerto Rican and Hispano leadership in pastoral affairs. He invited Edgard Beltrán, a specialist from Latin America in the formation of fundamental ecclesial communities (comunidades de base), into New York. A series of workshops was held and Stern's organizing talents generated new perspectives of Hispano identity within the church. The selections taken from the proceedings of two of these conferences show the admirable theological depth that characterized the process and the concrete goals set forth.

These developments came at an opportune time because the stirrings of identity on the East Coast among the Puerto Ricans coincided with the Mexican American desire to influence policy within the church at a national level. Thus, June 1972 became the target date for a meeting of Mexican American leadership with those in the Spanish-speaking apostolate for Puerto Ricans, Cubans, and all the other Latin American peoples in the United States.

43. Lay People's Encounter Workshops

From Minutes of the Lay People's Encounter workshops, held at the Convent of Mary Reparatrix, New York City, in 1971, under the direction of Father Edgard Beltrán. Used by permission.

SATURDAY, SEPTEMBER 25, 1971

Theme: Man

Love towards others is manifested in actions rather than in mere words. Our love, or our lack of love, for our fellowmen, is made evident through our actions. Man must necessarily be at the center of our apostolate. Today, if we truly want to love, we must work for justice among all.

All our endeavors in helping man ought to be oriented towards his Essence (What He Is) not towards his accidental qualities or his possessions (What He Has). The only time an exception is in order is in case of emergency; when he is in great material need; even then, respect for his dignity as a person is indispensable. If we truly want to help man, we must form and educate him.

The Church's mission is to serve the total man: What He Is and What He Has. Through us man must begin to know Christ in whose life he participates; it is our obligation and responsibility to form him in the Faith so that he may be capable of accepting it—that Faith which is based in the Person of Christ. Man must be evangelized in his Being so that he may be able to dwell deeply in the mystery of Christ, to participate in that mystery and finally to celebrate Christ's life in the Liturgy.

All our undertakings should be community oriented—nothing should be done in isolation; the Church shall work in community, as a community and through the community—otherwise, all efforts shall be in vain.

Working Groups Plenary Session: Conclusions

Love means being able to give ourselves to others in a concrete manner, it means we must make a personal commitment:

—by searching very deeply for true values—those which give meaning to the very essence of man. The closer a man comes to an understanding of his essence, and the more he accepts that essence and acts according to it, the easier it is for him to live Christ's life and Christ to act through him.

—by searching for new ways of evaluating man—by placing him in his rightful place exempt from paternalistic attitudes, lack of interest, superficiality.

—by opening ourselves to an ongoing process of study and reflection.

—by making available to man that which is necessary to develop his potential and form him as a person and as a Christian.

The New York Church is very paternalistic; it gives to man, it allows him certain things—it makes no effort to help man help himself. It can be said that our Church, lacking the development called for in the [Vatican] Council's guidelines, remains dormant. The laity still need to receive adequate formation. One way to achieve this would be through seminars, not for the priests and religious, but for the laity. There is a great need for formation programs at the diocesan level for both young adults and adults. Man, in his essence, is not being taken into consideration. At present, all our efforts are wasted in trying to get great numbers of people to join our organizations instead of employing these efforts to bring about a change in our society. Since we lack priests of Latin American origin (although the Spanish Church here is mostly Latin American and constitutes more than 50% of the Catholic population in origin), better and greater lay participation is vitally necessary. Our leaders should be equipped to form more leaders; complementary help from the priests should be welcomed.

Our movements need to be evaluated: Are we engaged in the formation of man as a person? Are our efforts directed to man in his essence?

The Church and the diverse institutions are in need of change, but the world is in greater need. The Church, and its members, by themselves, constitute a part of the world and are at its service.

Historically, the parish structure was intended for a community or rural area; therefore, it is not convenient in our modern cities. We must come up with a new "parish" style. One that would really reach out into the community.

In the beginning, the law was not the unifying factor within the Church;

they were united by an understanding and acceptance of the living presence of the same Spirit among them; there was peace and harmony among all churches and the Church in Rome.

The Institutions in their present form will soon cease to exist, making way for new modes of expression. We are in a transition period where new communities are being created and old ones are left behind. We need to have faith in man . . . faith that he is capable of change, even though he may be a bishop.

SUNDAY, SEPTEMBER 26, 1971

Theme: "Church-Community"

The Church and the world have to be liberated at one and the same time. In the measure that the Church is liberated, so is the world. Man achieves his maturity in community with others; that is to say, the day-in day-out living experience with others, *convivencia,* tends to mature man. When we talk about *convivencia* we are not referring to a mere state of "being" together, since every group by the mere fact of coming together does not constitute a community. The best example of perfect community and communication is the Trinity. God wants us to share in that perfect community. For this reason He created us in his Image and Likeness and made us social beings. That is why our Being tends to define itself in community with others; in our daily contact. From this follows that if I do not struggle to become an integral part of the community, I act contrary to my very nature and obstruct my normal development.

Working Groups—Theme: Pastoral-Based Communities (Comunidades de base)

What is community? Community is based on an interpersonal relationship. It can begin by reason of a function or a particular common interest. At the beginning it shall only be a mere juxtaposition; through mutual efforts it will culminate in interpersonal relationship, in *convivencia* in community. This *convivencia* will some day lead to love and, thus, to justice. We shall begin by finding a common value (even though transitory) to achieve something more concrete—a reunion. Then, as our values grow we shall begin to form a group, an *equipo,* where mutual responsibilities shall be shared; and finally, we shall reach a community based on the ONE VALUE which will integrate us in one vision and common interest. The community is thus reached by a process during which the values which constitute us as a group are developed. Until we reach THE VALUE PAR EXCELLENCE, we have to undergo a continuous evaluation and revision of the principles governing us as a group. The aims that we have proposed for ourselves and the challenges we shall meet in our development as a community need also to be revised. All this shall be done taking into consideration the historical and concrete reality. This way, and only this way, shall we be able to create something new, something useful, and something of great value to all.

Plenary Session: Conclusions

If love is the impelling force in this world and what keeps our existence (as beings, as persons, as Christians), a community of love expressed in various forms is vital to us.

—The beginning of our community may be expressed as a group; but necessarily it will have to reach a certain level of unity if it is going to be community.

—We have not been able to reach a community level yet because we are lacking real interest, and because we do not want to be responsible to anyone, or for anything. There is no doubt that greater effort is needed to overcome this situation.

—Injustice, the root of all violence, must be fought.

—We must give man his rightful place—at the center of the universe—in community with beings like himself capable of loving and responding. Since man is capable of expressing himself through love, and the object of that love is God in whose image he was made, and his fellowman, whose likeness he shares, he must live in community.

—It is understood, however, that man does not cease to be a person when he becomes an integral part of the community. He should be treated with respect and admiration that his dignity as a person requires. It can be concluded that man receives the best possible aid from his fellowmen when he is made capable of developing as a responsible human being with all the consequences this implies. In our concrete reality in New York a means to achieve this would be through the availability of human and Christian formation imparted to the laity through seminars directed specifically to them. Man must be adequately formed if he is to become a living ferment.

—The Church has forgotten how to be a community of love; it has forgotten man and permitted itself the luxury of expending millions of dollars in buildings while our brethren go naked and hungry. There is a small number of people who are engaged in the struggle for man's sake, for his formation and development as a person. The present situation calls for revolutionaries, "communist," in the manner of Christ, to provoke a change and a conversion of all people to truly human and Christian values. But this must be done within the hierarchy, as well as within our movements. Only in this way, will man be able to reach Christ, and Christ become known to all man.

SATURDAY, OCTOBER 9, 1971

Points Agreed Upon

It was agreed:

1. To set apart a weekend every six months to conduct seminars for lay leaders and priests. During these seminars, among other things, a complete evaluation and revision of all movements shall be carried out.
2. To have joint meetings of members of the Cursillo movement and their leaders.
3. To make available documents and books to participants in these seminars.
4. That the Coordinating Committee invite new members to join and that the meetings should take place every month.
5. That a commission be formed to meet with the Cardinal. This commission should have members from all existing groups but it will not be representative of any one movement.

That membership of this commission be between fifteen and twenty.

Members elected to this commission were:

1. Luis Acosta
2. Haydée Borges
3. José A. Carrero
4. Octavio Fermín
5. Freddy Gil
6. Enrique Ilundáin
7. Jorgé Ithier
8. Eddie Kalbfleish
9. Tomás Liriano
10. Claudio Peña
11. Biviano Pizarro
12. Ismael Quiñones
13. Fr. Luis Ríos
14. Gloria Román
15. Pedro Santiago
16. Cristiana Santos
17. Candy Solá
18. José Sosa

This commission shall study urgent needs of the Spanish-speaking Community and will present petitions based on this study to the Cardinal either in a personal interview with him or by written statement, as judged convenient.

Piri Thomas is a black Puerto Rican who grew up in the streets of New York's Spanish Harlem. His autobiography, *Down These Mean Streets,* describes his personal odyssey through delinquency, dope, and prison. It is required reading in some high schools in New York City. His second book continues the story of his religious conversion to Pentecostalism and concludes with a description of his present commitment to people rather than institutionalized forms of religion. This is the first in a series of selections from Thomas's *Savior, Savior, Hold My Hand* interspersed throughout this book.

44. The Pentecostals

Piri Thomas

From *Thomas,* Savior, Savior, Hold My Hand *(Garden City, N.Y.: Doubleday and Co., 1972), pp. 19–21. Used by permission.*

Tía's fingers were busy fishing out long needles and some kinda thick thread, and her fingers were soon like with a mind of their own, taking care of creative business, knitting out some delicate doilies to decorate the backs of living room chairs.

"It is not too much to ask for you to visit my iglesia, is eet?" Her voice was madre warm.

I didn't answer. I just smiled, thinking about Tía's Pentecostal church and the visits I had made to it when I was a hundred years younger.

The most beautiful thing about the Pentecostals was their ability to pour themselves into the power of the Holy Spirit. They could blend—like nobody's business—into the words of the Holy Scriptures and do their best to uphold their conception of Christianity. It was a miracle how they could shut out the hot and cold running cockroaches and king-size rats and all the added horrors of decaying rotten tenement houses and garbage-littered streets, with drugs running through the veins of our ghetto kids. It was a miracle that they could endure the indignities poured upon our Barrios. I knew that every one of them didn't get weaker. They got stronger. Their prayers didn't get shorter. They got longer. Those who looked for God to come closer were blessed with El Bautismo del Espírito Santo, and they spoke a language that I could not understand. Tía had said it was the tongue of the angels, and only a few could interpret it.

Wow, I thought to myself. *If ever there were an escape this has got to be it. Is God gonna make it up to us in heaven?*

Caramba, I smiled, *maybe it ain't an escape, maybe like a sombre Pentecostal guy had once told me. Maybe, like he had said, they aren't interested in material wealth.*

God's Kingdom will provide enough for all in the sweet bye and bye. God's work and God's will be done. But shit. "How about starting here on earth, brother, with the nitty-gritty reality?" I had asked this Pentecostal guy. He had looked at me funny and had said, "God's Kingdom is not of this earth." "But we are," I had insisted. He just shook his head and walked away.

"Tía?"

"Sí, hijo." Her fingers never stopped knitting. But her eyes reached out to me.

"What does being a Pentecostal mean to you? I mean, like I'm asking without disrespect."

Tía smiled like always, sure and secure in her iglesia.

"It's what binds much of us poor Puertorriqueños together. It gives us strength to live in these conditions. It's like being part of a familia that is together in Cristo and we help each other with the little materials we may possess." She talked on about us not having silver and gold but having instead peace in our corazón and salvation as our goal.

Wouldn't it be better to have all four, I thought, not quite able to accept her religious jive. But for some strange reason I wanted to hear more.

I smiled gently, "Okay, Tía, I'll go to your iglesia and, Tía . . ." She looked straight into my eyes. "God's gotta know I'm trying, and trying beats a blank."

Tía kissed my hands and whispered in the most tender way, "Dios es amor."

God is Love, I thought. *Wonder why the hell we're such bad learners.*

"Piri, I will take these clothes down to the cellar in the morning and burn them to ashes in the boiler."

"Sí, Tía, buenas noches."

I went to my room, lay down, and spent what seemed like a week just falling asleep, thinking about things like God is love and hate is garbage and a first night in Sing Sing.

Caramba, I thought, *I hope when I wake up in the morning I'm in Tía's house.* Soon I fell asleep, sadly dreaming of Sing Sing.

CHAPTER SEVEN

THE PROBLEM

In the preparations for the national meeting scheduled for June 1972, there was an effort made to frame theologically the question of Hispano identity. The violence and abruptness of the demonstration by Catolicos por La Raza as well as the activism produced by the Delano strike and the grape boycott, demanded a theological, or at least an ecclesiastical, explanation.

One of the first articulations of the concept of a "Hispano National Church" came from the pen of Alberto Carrillo, a California Chicano who at that time was a Redemptorist priest. The canonical implication of his conclusion was a separation of Chicano Catholics from the direct control of the United States episcopate, as had been the case when Puerto Rico was placed under the Office of Propaganda Fidei in Rome. This was not to be. Nonetheless, Carrillo's argumentation has generally been incorporated into the meaning of Hispano church.

The encounters with the institution for most Hispanos, however, took on the dimensions described by Puerto Rican street-fighter-turned-poet, Piri Thomas. How can our religious needs be met by a middle class and white church institution? What is the meaning of celibacy? How can we confront Anglo clergy with the arrogance of their paternalism toward Hispanos? Answers were given in modest studies such as those conducted by priests like Roger Luna, a Salesian from Los Angeles, and Romeo Saldigloria, an Argentine Jesuit in New York. These research papers recalled history and insisted upon native leadership at decision-making levels. They highlighted the size of the Hispano community in comparison with their homelands and argued that pastoral care required native Hispano leadership at all levels.

45. Toward a National Hispano Church

Padre Alberto Carrillo

A paper presented at the October 1971 PADRES Congress. Used by permission.

As everyone at this congress well knows, the Chicano and Spanish-surnamed Catholic is by far the largest Catholic minority. We constitute 25 percent of the Catholic population. Yet it is interesting to note that of the 25 percent of the Catholic population that is Spanish-surnamed, the Chicano is the most uneducated person in the United States. He becomes "illiterate in two languages." Economically, he is disadvantaged, averaging less than $5,000 a year income. Politically, he is legally disfranchised. In the courts, he faces a system of double-standard justice. Being less than 5 percent of the national population, he is nevertheless representative of 21 percent of the casualties in Vietnam. Yet when he returns, he lives in the worst housing; he lives under a system of educational abortion and economic atrocity. He is more welcome in jail than in a college classroom. He has been programmed to poverty—because indeed opportunity and poverty in this country are ethnic.

All these things are made possible because institutions demand cultural suicide and self-negation as a ransom for acceptance and success. This is made possible with stereotype images of the Chicano as lazy, cruel, indifferent, violent, fatalistic by the image-makers, so that the country might salve its conscience in the perpetuation of the Chicano as its cheap labor force.

We know the problems. Let us ask why, why do they exist? It is not a matter of rights, and we should not get into a rhetoric of rights. No one denies that Chicanos have rights. It is a matter of opportunity for self-determination. We do not need a Civil Rights Act—we need an Opportunity of Self-determination Act, educationally, economically, politically, and yes, ecclesiastically. Why? Because of discrimination.

Again, let us make a distinction in rhetoric. We do not feel that it is the discrimination of hatred, of a KKK, of an overt nature that is dangerous. It is recognizable and consequently easy to fight. However, the discrimination the Chicano feels is the systematic, the inadvertent, one that is not based on hatred or malice, but on a system, a systematic discrimination.

It is important to recognize this, so one cannot say, "Because I can go into any motel or restaurant, there is no problem." It is important because the church has discriminated in this way against our people, and we cannot accuse the church of hatred or malice, because that is just simply not true.

Inadvertently, discrimination is based on four reasons—human reasons, if you like—or four principles. This has happened in every conquest in the history of the world, or any clash of cultural values: man/woman, youth/adult, Norman/Saxon, Spaniard/Aztec, Anglo/Chicano. Here's what happens:

1. The majority culture makes the policies that affect the minority; also, they establish the qualifications for those who shall make policy.

2. The majority culture assumes that the problems are the fault of the minority.

3. The majority culture assumes that there is no problem until it affects the majority peoples.

4. The majority culture assumes that their way is the superior and only way because it is the majority way.

Politically, economically, and educationally these are the reasons that have excluded minority peoples from opportunity. We could spell these out at another time. Let us just apply these things to the church. The church is no different from a political system, an educational system; it is sociologically human, and capable of reflecting the same failings of other human institutions that have failed Chicanos for the same reasons. There is no need to prove the church's failure to meet the needs of the Chicano, but let us try to understand why this has happened.

1. The majority culture makes the policies: In the United States 81 percent of the hierarchy is of either Irish or Germanic descent, and so come from a different value system; they make the policy for our people. How many provincials, mothers superior, representatives in priest senates and chanceries are Chicano? There are reasons why there are none, but the point is that people who do not even know the problems cannot be expected to find their solutions. Bishops who do not know the educational problem of the Chicano cannot be expected to put bilingual education into his schools.

2. The majority culture assumes that the problems are the fault of the minority: How many times have you been asked, "Why don't the Mexicans give more money?" "Why are they lazy?" "Why don't they have the initiative to go to college?" "Why are there no more Mexican priests?" When only 1 percent of our kids get to college, how can they possibly survive the academic and cultural shock of a seminary? How can people be blamed for being poor? How can people be blamed for being deprived of education, religious as well as secular? How can a person be blamed for not wanting to become "Irish" and prefer to celebrate Guadalupe rather than St. Patrick's day? Our people are not in the mainstream of Catholicism in this country because the church has not been relevant to them; they have not been given the dignity of being accepted for what they are, what they wish to be, why God made them. So it is not a Chicano problem; it is an Anglo problem, it is with education, etc.

3. *The majority culture assumes that there is no problem until it affects the majority culture:* Let us be honest even though it is painful. What would the official church attitude be if the grape pickers had been Irish? What would the official attitude of the church be if 60 percent of the Catholic kids dropped out of school because they were Catholic? What if all the problems that Chicanos faced were faced by Anglo Catholics? This is natural. This is human. Drugs were not a problem as long as they were confined to the barrios and ghettos, but now that the drugs are hurting the middle-class youth, we have a drug problem.

4. *The majority culture assumes that there is only one way to do things—their way:* Humanly speaking again, the church has assumed with the rest of American society, that we are a melting pot. Ecclesiastically we are an Irish-church melting pot. In general, cultural differences in religious expression have not been allowed because it was assumed they did not exist. A "good" Catholic was one who accepted the Irish ecclesiastical value system.

Yet there is a vast cultural difference in expressing religious sentiments and practices. Vatican II spelled this out quite clearly. The Chicano has a different view and different insights into the interpretation of law, liturgy, and moral theology, and these have been suppressed. And when one's values are suppressed, a person has two choices: cultural suicide, or rejection of the institution. Both phenomena are normal for the Spanish-speaking person in the United States toward his church.

In conclusion, the Chicano finds himself with all the disadvantages of being in a foreign mission but none of the advantages. Ecclesiastically the Chicano again suffers an inadvertent but real bloodless persecution in this country.

HOW ABOUT SOLUTIONS?

Sociologically, solutions can be found by a complete reversal of the four causes or reasons for inadvertent discrimination in any institution. Witness the Civil Rights Commission demanding racial parity in policy-making, in cultural input, in obvious social injustice. Can the church come up with a voluntary plan of compliance? Here are some of the things that would be necessary now:
— equitable (25%) representation in the hierarchy, provincialates, seminaries, chanceries, councils, senates to allow a just sharing of policy-making that touches our people.
— a massive educational program to make a bicultural clergy
— Chicano studies in the seminaries
— lay leadership courses, lay diaconate among Spanish-speaking

— admission of cultural innovative programs from Chicano clergy without fear
— participation in the Chicano struggle for equal opportunity in every sphere where the struggle exists
— a drastic change in Catholic education to make it relevant to Chicano students
— opening of Catholic higher education to Chicanos in equitable numbers
— development of Chicano seminaries
— development of Chicano liturgy, moral theology, cannon law interpretation

ALTERNATIVES

These general solutions mentioned are not luxuries, but necessities for the religious survival of our people in this country. Patience and time in this case are vices and real obstacles to the message of Christ and must be treated so. If the redemptive act of Christ is a value that must reach our people, we must then heed the words of Pope Paul: "to take up a double task of inspiring and of innovating in order to make structures evolve, so as to adapt them to the real needs of today."

Solutions can be found only with the admission of two premises: (a) the Chicano in the church is at a missionary status (when the ratio is one bishop for 7 million people and less than 200 priests); (b) Catholicism encourages cultural difference and development.

If indeed, the Chicano church is in the state of a mission, it cannot survive with normal pastoral practice; it must be served by a mission concept as outlined very clearly in the distinction made in *Ad gentes*.

Historical precedent in the United States articulates that similar problems were solved by national churches which allowed the faithful the right to practice Catholicism in their own cultures and not make acculturation blackmail to receive the redemptive act of Christ.

The entire document "On the Care of Migrants" by Pope Paul, insists on episcopal vicars, personal parishes, special concern for youth in colleges, and all necessary innovative means to end cultural shock, economic atrocity, and educational abortion within society and the church.

If solutions are to be found before it is too late, there can be only one answer: A NATIONAL CHICANO CHURCH UNDER THE PROPAGATION OF THE FAITH IN ROME.

46. Lenny

Piri Thomas

From *Thomas*, Savior, Savior, Hold My Hand *(Garden City, N.Y.: Doubleday and Co., 1972), pp. 325-327. Used by permission. (See p. 150, above, for information about the author.)*

. . . Afterward I approached Lenny in the gym.

"I'd like to talk to you, man."

"Gladly," he said.

"First of all, if you ever got something on your mind that concerns me, check it out with me. Like it's kind of weak to run to John so he can deliver me your feelings." I did my best to speak without anger. "Secondly, I can introduce you to everybody I know in El Barrio. But that's only an introduction. You got to earn your own way into being accepted."

"I don't understand what you mean. *I've got to earn my way into being accepted.* I've come here to help these people. Nobody forced me to commit myself to the work that's to be done here."

"That's the trouble, Lenny, with muchos like you who come to El Barrio with their great, liberal willingness to help. They come here gung-ho as groovy soldiers of Christ, armed with mucho acceptance of us and popped-eyed with the burning zeal to spread God's word among us. Then like they totally forget that everybody—don't matter who you are—has to *earn* acceptance."

"For God sakes, Lenny," I continued. "The Bible and Christianity aren't nothing new here in El Barrio. We got more storefront churches than Carter has liver pills. They may be poor but they're beau-coup sincere. The trouble is with the outside people from nice well-to-do churches who sincerely send people to work among us armed with all the knowledge of the Bible and a complete lack of understanding about what makes us tick. Christ sakes, Lenny, if you come to spread God's words, then just come and let us teach you about our humanity, and don't look on us like something that lived in the Stone Age."

"I don't see how you can talk to me like that." I could tell he was getting up tight.

"I'm just running it to you straight, man to man. Cause like we're equal, ain't we?"

"Of course, but your tone of voice leaves much to be desired."

"Oh hell, feller." My voice was getting stronger. "You better learn that we talk pretty frank and pretty strong in these streets and if you're expecting everybody's gonna 'sir' you to death, forget it. If you're respected, it's because you've earned it. If you're for real, it'll come through, but if you're just trying to store up points in heaven, forget it. We know what life's all about, like from bigotry to balling." I dug Lenny's facial muscles tighten up. He was boiling inside, but I didn't let up.

"You're a Christian, right, Lenny?"

He just stared at me.

"Well, I'm gonna ask you a question. Being a believer, you know that God will dig it if you're lying. Uh . . . are you prejudiced against non-white people?"

Lenny's face flickered just a little bit. I stood and waited for his answer and he let it out a little slow, but clear.

"Ah do have my prejudices . . . but being a Christian, I seek to overcome them."

"Without you saying it, the kids notice it and, Lenny, our kids don't need nobody with bigoted hearts and minds to pile more weight on them. You've dug that I don't particularly like you, and you're mucho right. You say you're a Christian and I say you're nothing but a hypocrite. And there's a lot like you, man."

Lenny's face got more up tight.

"You dare say that to me? To cast aspersions on my sincerity as a Christian?"

"Yeah, feller. I dare that and more if need be."

"You're the one who's not a Christian."

"You could be right, man. You could be right."

I walked away. As I did, I wondered how long it would take the message to get to John.

I never heard about it from John, but Lenny, from that time on, happened only to be where I wasn't.

47. Why So Few Mexican-American Priests?

Roger B. Luna, S.D.B.

From PADRES Newsletter, *March 1973. This article is the text of a paper delivered to the Western Vocation Directors Association Convention. Used by permission.*

I will address myself to the four main reasons given by the Mexican-American priests surveyed as to why there are so few Mexican-American priests at present. The principal reasons given were:
1. The Spanish tradition of not creating a native clergy.
2. Open discrimination against Mexicans by priests.
3. Taking Mexicans for granted on the part of the church; no special effort to keep them Catholic.
4. The lack of education, especially higher education, among Mexican young people.

I will address myself briefly to each of these reasons. I would like to state that much of the material that I am presenting is based on experiential evidence, not on books. Therefore, it is very difficult to prove some assertions. Also, I do not intend to offend or insult anyone: the work of pioneer Spanish, French, German, and Irish priests among the Spanish-speaking has been outstanding in terms of dedicated personnel and devoted ministry. However, a completely accurate history of the church in the Southwest also has to include an account of the failings of the all-too-human priests and bishops in their ministry to the Mexican-Americans. We must have the *whole* truth now because, for one thing, the Spanish-speaking faithful constitute a majority in many Southwest dioceses. And, in many cases, very little has been publicly said about their difficulties and their sufferings in a church that abruptly changed from Hispanic to Anglo after 1848. . . .

What follows is my own summation. What Father Chávez relates about New Mexico can also be applied to California, Texas, and other Southwestern states, but with a major difference: outside of New Mexico there was no Archbishop Byrne.[1]

1. Father Angélico Chávez, speaking of Archbishop Byrne, who had been transferred from Puerto Rico to serve the Mexican Americans, said: "In 1933, Archbishop Gergen founded the

Point 1: Not creating a native clergy. When the number of Spanish and French priests in the Southwest dwindled, Irish and German priests took over. The German served especially in Texas. In California, Irish priests predominated. Sadly enough, these Irish and German priests, dedicated though they were, did not overcome the racist attitudes which the Spanish and French priests before them had adopted. They did not work to form a native clergy in the Southwest—a native *Spanish-speaking* clergy. Like the French before them, the Irish clergy dreamed of setting up Irish bishops throughout the Southwest: their dream came true.

Point 2: Open discrimination against Mexicans by priests. A series of incidents which happened to a very educated and deeply Catholic family in the Los Angeles area will give some evidence of this discrimination.

The Zúñigas had fled from Mexico during the revolution. Mr. Zúñiga was the administrator of a huge hacienda belonging to a very wealthy family residing in Mexico City.

He came here ready to do anything, anything at all, for a living. He settled in Los Nietos (near Los Angeles), and the entire family went out to pick walnuts. Later on, he settled in Highgrove, a very peaceful little town just north of Riverside, with a small barrio.

The Zúñigas were upper-class Mexicans, highly educated, and very Catholic. They thought that they would find peace and happiness in this country. They did on the whole—they passed for "Spanish" not Mexican—except in the church.

A few weeks ago, the Zúñiga family related to me their sufferings at the hands of priests. During the 1920s and early 1930s there was only one Catholic church in Riverside, St. Francis de Sales. Mexicans were allowed only at the 8:00 A.M. mass. They had to crowd outside the door of the church until the American Catholics had entered. Only after all the Americans had entered, were Mexicans allowed to enter and to sit in the back. The same situation prevailed in Colton at San Salvador Church, which Catholics from Highgrove could also conveniently attend. What made the situation worse at San Salvador, however, was that the pastor was a Spaniard and that San Salvador had been built by Mexicans in the last century (the first church building was built in the early 1840s).

One day the Zúñigas attended the 10:00 o'clock mass at St. Francis de Sales Church. The Irish pastor went down the aisles asking all Mexicans to leave because only the 8:00 o'clock mass was for Mexicans. The Zúñigas, who had

seminary. He recruited Mexican boys to ordain them so that 'they could go back to eat beans in the Pueblos.' Archbishop Byrne, who succeeded him in 1943, came to be known as the champion of native vocations throughout the Southwest. Everywhere he went, he talked about vocations, and he personally recruited many Mexican boys. The clergy in general, mostly Irish and Germans did not understand the people: they usually despised them and made their criticisms of the people the principal topic of conversation at clergy gatherings. It was through Archbishop Byrne's efforts that New Mexico now has about 25 percent of all native Spanish-surnamed priests in the country."

missed the 8:00 o'clock mass, stood up angrily—the whole twelve of
them—and started to leave. The pastor told them, "Oh, not you!" They
countered heatedly, "But we're Mexicans!" And they walked out with the
rest.

The climax came when the mass of Our Lady of Guadalupe one raw
December morning took too long and went into the American mass. The
pastor was furious. He came out and scolded the Mexicans and told them not
to come back. The Mexicans swore they would do just that and that they
would build their own church.

A delegation of Mexican leaders, organized by Mr. Zúñiga and his sons,
went to Los Angeles to see Bishop Cantwell. The committee had already
gotten land donated for a new church, had gotten an architect, etc., and the
people were willing to build their church with their own hands. After much
deliberation and several trips to Los Angeles (quite a distance in those days),
the bishop agreed to allow them to build their own church, provided it was
not called Guadalupe; there were already too many Guadalupe churches in
the Diocese of Los Angeles. Also, the Extension Society, which was going to
help finance the church, would refuse to help if the church was called
Guadalupe. The people were again furious at this act against their Virgin.

The church was built by the people, and had to be called St. Francis of
Assisi. The name was very confusing for visitors to Riverside because the
American church was St. Francis de Sales, making both churches in Riverside
"St. Francis." It was only thirty years later, when Mexicans started to assert
themselves, that the Mexican people of Riverside demanded to have their
church renamed Guadalupe, as originally intended. In the early 1960s the
church was renamed Santuario (Shrine) of Our Lady of Guadalupe.

These incidents relating only to one family could be repeated thousands of
times in different parishes, especially in the case of the poorer, more uneducated and less Spanish-looking Mexican. Many priests considered Mexicans
an embarrassment: they were too poor, uneducated, simple, childish, undis-
ciplined, overemotional, superstitious.

Point 3: Taking Mexicans for granted. Since almost all Mexicans who came
to the United States were Catholics, priests and bishops did not worry too
much about them. The bishop and priests were much more concerned about
making converts from the Protestant white community. At the same time,
however, that priests were busy convert-making, many Protestant ministers
were converting Mexicans to their faith. In the Protestant churches very
often Mexicans found what they didn't find in the Catholic church: acceptance, warmth, sometimes financial aid, and more often than not, a minister
who was Latin-American or who could speak Spanish well. Also, many
Protestant churches sent young people to be educated in Protestant schools
and gave them leadership training. As a consequence, what we have now, for
instance, in East Los Angeles is a good number of young, personable Chicano

Protestant ministers, who are proselytizing vigorously in the Mexican community. Also, some of the most educated and articulate Mexican-American leaders are Protestant (e.g., the late Ruben Salazar).

The black community, even though it experienced much more overt discrimination from priests and from white Catholics, had at least the advantage of having two religious orders (the Society of the Divine Word and the Josephites) specialize in serving them. It is, then, not too surprising to note that there are more black priests numerically than Mexican-American priests. On the other hand, many Irish and Spanish priests, who for the most part took care of the Spanish-speaking in California, very rarely had real feeling (*cariño*) for Mexicans, even though they did dispense the sacraments to them faithfully.

I belong to the Salesian Society, which has specialized for about forty years in working for Italian immigrants in Los Angeles, San Francisco, Oakland, and also in the New York–New Jersey area. In the San Francisco area they also worked for the Portuguese. The bishops of several United States sees asked the Salesians to come to this country to take care of Italian immigrants, but to my knowledge, no religious order was given the mandate to specialize in taking care of Mexicans.

Point 4: Lack of education. The educational deprivation of Mexican-Americans is notorious. To begin with, most Mexicans who came to the United States were from the poorest and most uneducated classes of Mexico. Then, to make matters worse, schools serving the Mexican-American community have traditionally been substandard. The result is that at present, of the Mexican-American population twenty-five years or older, only 2 percent ever started college, and only 1.6 percent ever graduated. Of this group, only 28 percent ever graduated from high school. While the situation has improved during the last two or three years, the effects of the depressed educational scene in the Mexican-American community are still being felt.

So it was not too surprising, then, that boys coming from this environment either were not accepted into seminaries, or even if they were, did not persevere. Not until very recently did seminaries institute special courses for Mexican-American students who had deficiencies or who needed tutoring. And still, these seminaries are in the minority.

The problem then is significant; its solution will require special attention on the part of the entire church.

48. The Art of Courting

Piri Thomas

From *Thomas*, Savior, Savior, Hold My Hand *(Garden City, N.Y.: Doubleday and Co., 1972), pp. 99-101. Used by permission. (See p. 150, above, for information about the author.)*

Something was missing both inside and outside of me.

It kept churning in my mind and in my heart. I needed a woman. Not just any woman. But my own woman. Being a Pentecostal Puerto Rican-style was a tough bit. God Almighty. I used to sit and hear them shout out fire and hell sermons, and always they would push in, "Thou Shalt Not Commit Adultery," or, in other words, "Thou Shalt Not Sock It to a Woman if You Ain't Married to Her."

I was getting up tight, like my head was telling me that was one of the prices you hadda pay for being a Christian, while my other head was telling me, dang hombre, this ain't natural, but like I didn't let on to nobody on how up tight I was getting. Like after all, if priests can make it without a woman's love, so could I. But forget it, man, none of me could ever buy that. Like it ain't natural.

There was a service one night and some young guy was giving testimony on how he had prayed for some years for the Lord to show him the woman that was to be his wife and that after six years the Lord provided the opportunity. They had met and now were happily married.

Myself, along with the rest of the congregation, strained my neck trying to check out who the Lord had laid on him. The happy bridegroom asked his wife to stand up and wow-ee . . . blow-ee . . . The most ugliest, homeliest woman next to sin got up and smiled her love at the young Christian.

I swear I didn't mean to think blasphemous, but I couldn't make up my mind if God had blessed him or socked him with a mucho curse for some deep dark unknown sin of his. I shuddered and settled on a blessing, cause I was in the midst of making my request and was hoping (after seeing this) with all my heart that the Lord would treat me right. Cause that cat was forty times better looking than me and look what he got.

As I walked home with Tía after the service, I felt kind of ashamed for my past thoughts. They loved each other and their love gave them a special dimension that belonged only to them.

"Tía?" I said when we got to the stoop.

"Sí, hijo."

"I'm going to sit here for a while, it is okay?"

"It's okay, but not too late. You have to work tomorrow."

I listened as she slowly made her way up to the fifth floor. I kept watching people walking east and west on 117th Street, between Park and Lexington Avenue. My loneliness for a woman's love softly stole my thoughts.

I kept scrambling my brains trying to remember all the past stuff I'd heard from Moms and the rest of the olders on how to court a girl in the best tradition of Puerto Rican style.

Later I even got the help of Brother Rivera, but he laid it on me thick and full of ceremony. He sure was a romantic, cause by the time he got through trying to put me wise as to the art of courting, anybody would think I was trying to woo Nita in a palace in Spain.

"Uh, are you sure, Brother Rivera?"

"Sí, it's a very serious business when you are courting a girl with Spanish blood."

"What do you mean, Spanish blood, Brother Rivera. Nita was born in Puerto Rico. She ain't got nothing to do with Spain and fandangos."

I thought of myself underneath her fire escape in the backyard plucking some guitar and howling a love song while trying to keep my balance on top of a ton and a half of garbage.

Brother Rivera looked puzzled. "Er . . . don't you know that practically every Puerto Rican has the blood of Spaniards in one percentage or another?" he said.

Great shades, my mind went back to mucho time ago, when I was a kid and tried to find out from Moms if we had any noble blood in us. I let go of the flashback, thinking that my percentage was under lock and key.

I checked Brother Rivera's face to see if I could estimate how much of a percentage he had of Spanish sangre. He was copper-colored with Indian features, broad and strong. If his hair had been a little longer, he could have passed for a Geronimo. I smiled at Brother Rivera as he shifted his thin frame as if he were going to show me how to bow a la Spanish Court. He looked at me deeply and said softly, "Anyway, it's a beautiful ceremony. The art of courting." Obviously he must have been reminiscing on his own days of courtship.

49. Religious Problems of the Hispanos in the City of New York

Romeo F. Saldigloria, S.J.

From a paper prepared for the Spanish Apostolate Office, Archdiocese of New York, January 1972. Used by permission. Trans. A.M.S.A.

. . . How many Hispanos in the city of New York are Catholics? This is a difficult question to answer, especially for Americans who think about statistics and some religious tendencies differently. But the question can be posed pastorally: "To how many Hispanos who live in the city of New York does the church have the obligation of offering its pastoral care, since they are baptized in the Catholic church and want to belong to the church?"

According to the official *Catholic Directory* of 1967, the Archdiocese of New York has 1,848,000 Catholics and the Diocese of Brooklyn has 1,575,306 Catholics. But the same source tells us in 1971 that the Archdioceses suffered a loss of 11,700 Catholics (total: 1,836,000), and that the Diocese of Brooklyn has had a loss of 84,033 Catholics (total: 1,491,273), with a reduction in the city of New York of 95,733 Catholics in four years.

If these statistics are exact, the fear of the Hispano people is understandable. Are they counted among the children of the church? Or is there another way to describe or think about them? Plans for the future will be made according to the response to this question. . . .

We do not have rigorous statistics of how many Hispano Catholics are in the city of New York, but an approximate number, according to a census taken by certain religious women, the Legion of Mary, and priests, would give us a sum total that would reach some 55 percent of the Catholic population of the city. According to a letter of January 24, 1972, the Diocese of Brooklyn states that there are 53 percent. Some people, especially many Americans, do not accept this percentage and admit only 45 to 50 percent as the share of the Hispano Catholic population in the city of New York. For these people we posed above the clear question: "To how many Hispanos who live in the city of New York does the church have the obligation of offering its pastoral care, since they are baptized in the Catholic church and want to belong to the church?" . . .

Every Hispano priest, every American priest and every lay person is worried about the ever increasing numbers of Hispanos who go over to another religion or to a Protestant sect. Why?

The National Council of Churches assures us (January 20, 1972) that today 20 percent of the Hispanos belong to one of their denominations (not including the Jehovah's Witnesses). These thousands of Hispanos have gone over to a Protestant sect because in the city of New York they have more than 1,000 worship centers in their own language run by persons of their own race and mentality. The Jehovah's Witnesses' *Watchtower* (June 24, 1972) affirms that 5,301 Hispanos are Jehovah's Witnesses and that they have 52 prayer centers in the Spanish language, directed by Hispanos.

The Archdioceses of New York has 407 parishes (*The Catholic News*, 1971). Mass is said in Spanish in 97 parishes (statistic from the New York Spanish-speaking Apostolate Office). The Diocese of Brooklyn has 235 parishes, and mass is said in Spanish in 30 parishes (statistic from the Brooklyn Spanish-speaking Apostolate Office).

Total: In the 642 parishes of the city of New York, mass is said in Spanish in 107 churches (but sermons in Spanish are not given at all of them). This is 16.6 percent of all the Catholic churches in New York. But there are many Hispanos who do not think about the church. For them, the church of the city of New York is not a "Sign of Christ" living among its poorest children, but an "antisign." Among Hispanos who came to live in New York some time ago, the common cry is for integration into the American church, just as they want to be integrated to civic and political life by civil law and government.

The Declaration of Independence of the United States of America gives rights and imposes obligations which the Hispanos are disposed to obey; but there is another document that exists for them, the baptismal document, that gives them an irrenounceable right to worship God according to their ability, their understanding, and their uniqueness. It also gives them the right to be attended to and taught the gospel in a language that they can understand. In different meetings with Hispano leaders, this point was touched upon. They responded that there must be a return to Vatican Council II and not to the age of the colonization. . . .

What must be taken into account is that the Hispanos of the city of New York are more numerous than in some independent nations of Latin America, such as Costa Rica, Panama, Honduras—each of which has its own universities, radio and television stations, and various dioceses with numerous bishops. It must also be admitted that the Puerto Rican community, like the Dominican and the Cuban, is more numerous than some of the dioceses of their respective countries. And as an illustrative statistic, according to the official *Catholic Directory* of 1971, in the United States there are 31 archdioceses and 130 dioceses.

That is a total of 161 episcopal sees. Of the 161 sees: 19 have less than

50,000 Catholics; 42 have less than 100,000 Catholics; 43 have less than 200,000 Catholics; 18 have less than 300,000 Catholics; 23 have less than 400,000 Catholics; and one, Belmont Abbey, North Carolina, has only 562 Catholics.

Of the total of 161 dioceses of the United States there are 145 dioceses which do not reach 400,000 Catholics. The city of New York has enough Catholics to fill several dioceses.

We have mentioned a recent letter received from the Chancery of Brooklyn and signed on the 24th of January by the coordinator, Father John H. O'Brien, which affirms that the Hispanic population of the Diocese is between 600,000 and 800,000. This number is moderate: "This is a conservative figure . . .," he says, and he believes that 90 percent of the Hispanos of the diocese are Catholic. . . .

This population of Hispano Catholics is enough to make one or two or three dioceses in the United States with people of the same origin, the same language, and the same culture. Here then, are some of the solutions which are proposed. Underlying all of them is the urgent need for more persons (bishops, clergy, lay persons) to work with the Hispanos and their problems:

1. Better communication between the American Catholic people and the Hispanos.

2. More dialogue among the hierarchy, the American pastors, and the priests with Hispano lay persons.

3. Pastoral care that is planned for the family of God, and especially for the Hispanos, to be in collaboration with those who can help them.

4. A greater publicity of the problems of those who migrate to New York so that religious and civic leaders of the different Hispano countries can know them and help seek some concrete solution.

5. Greater dialogue in search of pastoral solutions with the different Hispano hierarchies of the countries of origin of the Hispano population of New York.

6. Securing a true Hispano hierarchy for the Hispanos of New York. The following is proposed:

    a. that there be three bishops, principally for the Puerto Ricans, the Cubans, and the Dominicans, who work together with an eye to the pastoral interest of all the Hispanos of New York and including the area surrounding the city.

    b. that this would be a hierarchy created out of necessity, not a replacement of the present hierarchy.

    c. that they would continue using all the means that until now have given good service, such as schools, Catholic Charities, churches, etc.

    d. that the bishops be native Hispanos, from religious orders or the diocesan clergy.

   e. that they know very well the pastoral, social, and labor problems of the Hispano people who live in New York, and that
they have a real interest in seeking to solve them, as best they
can.

   f. that the Hispano religious leaders have a voice of consultation
in the election of bishops.

7. More parishes with Hispano priests, above all in areas where the Hispano population is greatest.

8. Not to allow, inasmuch as is possible, the Hispano assistants to be alone
in the parishes, with all of the pastoral work of the Hispano people, greatest
when the community is very large.

9. To see to it that more American and Italian priests, and religious women
as well, learn the language and dedicate themselves to it completely: that is,
with 100 percent of their pastoral work for the Hispanos. To insist that
among these priests and religious—and even lay people—they take this work
as true missionary labor.

10. To see that American pastors of another nationality know how to speak
Spanish; and in case there is a choice between naming a pastor who knows the
language and one who does not, to see that the one who knows the language
should be chosen above all in areas where Hispanos form the majority.

11. To form a true Senate of Priests among those who work with Hispanos.

12. To form an efficient Ecumenical Commission in order to work among
the Spanish-speaking.

13. To direct from chanceries in New York . . . immediate steps for leadership on behalf of the poorest Hispanos in matters of educational development.

14. To seek help in an efficient and rapid way for the thousands of immigrants who illegally reside in the city. This would be a true work of charity.

We feel we have finished the task set us in this study. By writing it up, we
think that it can help all parties. We do not believe in confrontation, but in
true dialogue among the parties, above all with the pastors of the church. This
will lead to peace and unity among Christians and understanding in the Holy
Spirit.

50. In the White Church

Piri Thomas

From Thomas, Savior, Savior, Hold My Hand *(Garden City, N.Y.: Doubleday and Co., 1972) pp. 257-260. Used by permission. (See p. 150, above, for information about the author.)*

Things began to change between me and a certain brand of Christianity. That pink cloud of togetherness was beginning to dissolve. I had noticed things I hadn't dug before or perhaps hadn't wanted to dig in the white Christian/ghetto relationship. It was like we weren't equals. It was as if they were the chosen ones—despite the teachings in their Bibles—like they were sent to save us by getting us a hearing with Christ. But like it had to be on their own terms.

I let my eyes do a 360 degree turn around the inside of the church. It looked like the inside of a saved Madison Square Garden. The pews, the carved woodwork, the pulpit were like the kind found only at Tiffany's. I dug the people were really inhibited. Like they were afraid to bend and put a wrinkle in their elegant clothes. I overheard someone saying that one of the newly appointed deacons was a Wall Street broker. I soon spotted a nervous, middle-aged man up on the pulpit. I dug his fingers playing with gold cuff links that let out sparkling flashes of lights to attest to the fact that diamonds were inlaid on his cuff links. I dug people staring at us. Some smiled. Some whispered. Most ignored us. I dug their voices in prayer. I dug their voices lifted in song to God, and like I realized that what a difference there was between our storefront churches in El Barrio and this one.

Like ours are poor in bread, but really rich in spirit, and this was just rich in pesos. Maybe I'm wrong, I thought, but they're here in God's house acting like it was some kind of business appointment.

They looked at each other in a kind of "Who's Who" attitude, and regarded us with a *Suffer the Little Children to Come unto Me,* that is, if they ain't dirty little ghetto kids. Caramba, I knew inside me that all Christians weren't tied up in this kind of hypocritical bag, but those that were sure were muffing it for the nitty-gritty ones.

Man, I said to myself, *they even say Amen like they're counting money.*

After one particular service, I approached John. I tried to remain calm as I explained that we all felt out of place in this church.

"It's nothing they say, John," I explained. "It's in their looks. The kids aren't stupid, John. Lil Man and a lot of the kids got to me with their feelings. Like if we're suppose to be part of their Sunday School, how come we gotta be in a room all by ourselves?" I fought to keep my voice non-angry—but blew it. "Dammit to hell, ain't we good enough to sit with their young white sons and daughters. We ain't stupid. Their smiles and attitudes are so damn condescending. We're tired of feeling hung up in a hypocritical bag by those who hide themselves under the heading of Christian Fellowship. They can lie to themselves and try to lie to us, but dammit to hell, if God's so powerful as they make Him out to be, how can they be so stupid as to think they are pulling this bullshit over His eyes?"

John was quiet for a while, minutes. Then he said softly, "You mustn't let the devil come into your mind with false words."

"Oh God, damn it, John. Don't come on so weak."

"Well, you are young in the Lord, Piri, and there are many things you still don't understand. You must . . ."

"Yeah, John, I know. It's like we always must give in, must do right, must follow, must bow and scrape . . . smiling our behinds off and hanging on by our chins while the rest of the world lives on in some kind of glorified splendor. Bull Shit."

"You're not showing respect for the Lord, Piri, and you're certainly not showing it towards me."

"If talking nitty-gritty means no respect for the Lord and you . . . well . . . tough shit cookie."

"That's enough, Piri." John's expression was kind of stern and grim, but he smiled and added, "We'll just have to take all these feelings to the Lord in prayer."

"Or some place else, John, maybe some place higher."

"Maybe some place higher?" His voice didn't believe what he was hearing. "Like who?"

I smiled. "Maybe like to the Lord's grandfather. I'll see you later, John." I walked away but stopped at his voice.

"You ought to pray more often, Piri."

"Prayers gotta be strengthened with some kind of action, John. Without disrespect, amigo, if you've read history, too, you'd know many people have been taught to pray and when they finished praying and looked around, their land and respect was gone—taken away by the ones who had taught them to pray."

"Piri, don't let the devils use you."

"Don't worry, John, none of them will use me—or any of us if we can help it."

After the talk with John, I was up tight for a while but soon calmed down. I put myself to thinking about our own lil church across the street from the Great Church. If those people were for real, I knew, we might just see some kind of heaven together between the two churches. My God, some humans name this world Earth and some animals make it HELL.

The South Bronx, New York City (courtesy Bomexi)

Above: Virgilio Elizondo of MACC and Mary Mahoney and Edgar Beltrán of the Spanish-speaking Secretariat. Below: Pablo Sedillo of the Spanish-speaking Secretariat (courtesy Visitante Dominical)

Archbishop Patricio Flores
(courtesy Visitante Dominical)

Fr. Robert Stern,
Archdiocese of New York

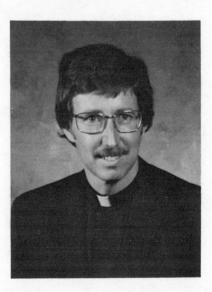

PART III

THE FORGE OF UNITY

Detrás de esa frase, "Puente entre dos culturas" y de algunas buenas volun-
tades que pudieron prohijarla, nos acecha el peligro de eternizarnos en un
cocktail de mediocridades, en un mosáico de fósiles desportillados y deslum-
brantes baratijas ultramodernas, en una burundanga estridente. No re-
neguemos de nada, y menos de las lecciones provechosas que nos haya
podido dar el yanqui; pero procuremos depurar los elementos dispares,
inarmónicos, que conviven en la olla podrida de nuestro ambiente.

Behind that phrase "bridge between two cultures" and some well-
intentioned souls who could have adopted it, lies in wait for us the danger of
becoming immortalized in a cocktail of mediocrities, in a mosaic of broken
fossils and flashy ultramodern trinkets, in a strident hodge-podge stew. We
do not deny any reality: much less the profitable lessons that the Yankee has
been able to give us, but we seek to purge the unequal and discordant
elements which cohabit the boiling stewpot of our situation.

—Tomás Blanco, Puerto Rico, 1935
(Trans. A.M.S.A.)

What are the theological models in the Hispano church? Following the text
of Avery Dulles's *Models of the Church* and combining his models with the
typology of Ivan Vallier in his essay on the religious elites of Latin America
(1967, pp. 203–210) should provide an answer. Dulles stresses theological
developments in the United States, while Vallier is more interested in social
interactions among Latin Americans. According to the latter, there is a connection between one's vision of the world and of the church. These fall in two basic
divisions: first, a view where class divisions make the world and the church
hierarchical in nature; and second, a view of equality among persons, projecting a church wherein salvation comes from cooperation. Each of these
views, the hierarchical and the cooperative, can be subdivided further, according to the focus. One thinks that either the church or the world is primary for

influencing humanity. A chart of these types can be drawn by slightly modifying the terms of Vallier (1967, p. 206). See Table 1.

Table 1 Typology of Hispano Catholic Leadership		Structural principle of Catholic activity	
		HIERARCHICAL	*COOPERATIVE*
Sphere from which church influence drawn	*INTERNAL to the church*	Cursillistas	Pastoralists
	EXTERNAL to the church	Politicians	Liberationists

THE *CURSILLISTAS*

The church as a perfect society, completely contained within itself, and offering distinctions between governors and governed according to an established divine plan is the traditional hierarchical concept. According to Dulles, this model has been somewhat softened by the inclusion of the model of "Mystical Body." While maintaining the hierarchical nature of the church, the theology of the Mystical Body stresses the harmony in the differentiated functions of bishops, clergy, religious, and laity. It might be said that these "states of life" operate as social classes, subordinating some Catholics to others in qualitative importance.

Among Hispanos in the United States church, this understanding of a hierarchical structure has been maintained by the Cursillo movement. Since its introduction into the United States in 1959, it has been immensely successful in attracting large numbers of Hispanos to participate in the intensive three-day study session in order to learn the meaning of Christianity in an adult way. The antecedents of the Cursillo movement are in preconciliar Spain, where lay persons found a role in the past generation in Catholic Action, based on the teachings of Popes Pius XI and XII. Of course, this model of church is found in movements other than the Cursillo, but for those who have worked in the Spanish-speaking apostolate, the designation of *cursillista* (one who has made the Cursillo), aptly fits those Hispano Catholics, clerical and lay, who think of the world and the church as hierarchical societies. They focus their Christian life upon the internal elements of church mission and worship and generally view the world as subordinate to the demands of solidifying church authority.

THE POLITICIANS

There are others who share this vision of church and world as hierarchical societies, but who recognize them to be involved in the affairs of the outside world. They see the prestige and status of the church as a means of altering policies in the secular sphere. Because they accept the inequalities of power as part of God's will for the church and the world, they tend to flatter church leadership in the person of prelates in order to gain advantages with civil authority. They can also use their influence with government to press their advantages of accessibility with bishops and cardinals. The best name for these persons is the one given to them by Vallier, "the politicians." They are also present in the Hispano community, although in far fewer numbers than the *cursillistas*.

THE PASTORALISTS

Dulles describes the church as sacrament, citing the Council in its article on the Constitution of the Church: "The Church is a kind of sacrament of intimate union with God and of the unity of all mankind; that is, she is a sign and instrument of such union and unity" (*Ecclesia Dei*, 59).

The word for those who have adopted this view of church is "pastoralists." They do not place much emphasis upon the hierarchical nature of the church, except as a "sign." Searching for equality without implying conformity, they are open to cooperation with all the elements that work for justice and peace in society. Still, they reserve to the church, as "sign" or sacrament, the transformation in faith of Christian activity. Taking the theme of the *anawim* and the poor, the Hispano pastoralists insist that the concrete expression of commitment can be measured by the amount of presence to the poor within the Catholic church—as concretely found in the Hispanos themselves. In other words, they view the internal richness of church life as the sublime and valuable dimension of witness to the Hispano community. Everyone should work at building a better world, getting involved in the social issues of the day and identifying strongly with the oppressed, especially the Hispanos in their struggles against injustice. But, on the other hand, a Christian is not "just a social worker" or a "community organizer." The direction for this activity is the witness and sign of concern that the Christian adds to his or her labors alongside the humanitarian. Ecumenical cooperation among Christians and collaboration with secularists and political movements is urged. This is in contrast to the hierarchical concept of the self-contained perfect society or the Mystical Body, which preserves the concept of social stratification. Vallier analyzes the pastoralist concern as truly cooperative with the world but focused upon internal church structures.

THE LIBERATIONISTS

The last category is the liberationists (Vallier calls them pluralists), who are in agreement with the pastoralists about the cooperative reality of the church's activity, but who focus more upon the church's incorporation into social movements rather than on sign value. For them, in Dulles's terms, the church is servant. Clearly, the theology of liberation fosters this model of church. And the Hispano church has many liberationists because the Latin Americans who are the primary exponents of this theology have been present to the process of Hispano church almost from the beginning. At times there is little difference between what pastoralists and liberationists say, but the way they go about achieving their involvement is very different. The pastoralists look for a greater visibility—sign value—to the church's presence in social issues. The liberationists evaluate not in terms of presence but of effects. They find no satisfaction in the church's participation in a picket of a factory with discriminatory hiring practices, unless the discrimination is brought to an end. The pastoralists, on the other hand, are apt to say something like this: "Well, the picket was a failure because the people did not organize themselves correctly. But at least the church was present to them in their struggle—sharing, growing, failing, suffering, but always loving." The liberationists respond, "That's the trouble with you: you're always talking about feelings—what the people need is more jobs. You can't eat sentiments. Maybe if you had been more interested in the needs of the people and less in witness and sign value, they would have organized correctly and would have the jobs today, together with all that love." The pastoralists criticize the liberationists for having lost the faith dimension, and the liberationists rejoin that the pastoralists "subjectivize" social action in an effort to control the situation, instead of putting themselves at the service of humankind.

The purpose of the lengthy descriptions in this introduction is not to justify one model over another, although each believer will have a preference. The process of Hispano church, however, cannot be understood unless it is clear that all Hispano Catholics do not think and act alike.

The four types, *cursillistas*, politicians, pastoralists, and liberationists, were together in Washington for the First National Hispano Pastoral Encounter. Those who were delegates had been selected basically because they reflected a vision similar to their constituency. It would be impossible to make a retrospective sociological study of which delegates held to each model of church. Nor is such knowledge necessary to grasp what happened in 1972.

The principle uniting the participants was the issue of increased Hispano participation in the decision-making of the Roman Catholic Church in the United States. The Hispano leaders were seeking acceptance from each other in order to present a united front to the national leadership of the United States Catholic church. This is why the then president of the National Council of Catholic Bishops (NCCB), John Cardinal Krol, was invited. He was presented with a view of Catholics from all over the country who were no different from others in the church except for one thing: they were Hispanos. The message was communicated that Puerto Ricans, Mexican Americans, Cubans, and all other Latin Americans stood together in their request for greater participation in the Catholic church. They would not settle for the issues to be resolved one by one in the local dioceses where, as "minority" groups, they negotiated from the disadvantages of few clergy, low social standing, poor economic support, etc. The Puerto Ricans, Mexican Americans, and the rest recognized the similarity of their respective situation, accepted each other as leaders, and sought a uniform action by the national Catholic church to remedy injustices.

The Encounter borrowed upon the concepts and arguments of blacks and secular Hispanos in the country in a quest for power and influence commensurate with numbers. There was a presumption that unity was automatic for all Hispanos who were "minority groups." The concern of the church was measurable in terms of dollars spent, the number of bishops appointed, and the power of agencies and departments dealing with Hispanos. Some could see nothing in this approach but power-seeking demands expressed in pious terminology. But the people in Washington in 1972 were pioneers, breaking new historical ground. Rivalries among Hispanos were secondary to the focus upon being Hispano and the sense of righteousness in the crusade. The Encounter was affirming a principle that the basic characteristic of the Hispano reality was not found in what one said, or did, but in who one was. Inevitably, this emphasis led to the gradual marginalization in succeeding regional encounters of the non-Hispano clergy and religious. Since they could never "be" Hispanos, even if what they said and did was exactly the same as their counterparts, they were not integral parts of the Hispano church.

The only experience that could have demonstrated the importance of agreeing upon a theological model of church as well as upon the principle of being a minority-group Hispano, was that of the church of Puerto Rico. The organizers of the Encounter, however, made no special invitation to the island's Catholics to participate, nor did they include Puerto Rican prelates at the meeting, although the Latin American episcopate was present. Only Father William Loperena, O.P. (see Chaps. Four and Twelve) was there from the island of Puerto Rico. And his presence as delegate was in the capacity of organizer among the Puerto Rican farm workers in Hartford, Connecticut.

In hindsight, it is unlikely that many Puerto Ricans from the island's church would have felt comfortable at the First Encounter. The tone of Hispano unity that permeated Trinity College for those four days in 1972 was derived from an experience of being a minority group in the United States. The Puerto Ricans on the island, however, are an overwhelming majority in every sense (see Chap. Twelve). This radically alters their perception of the meaning or need for Hispano church. Nevertheless, "Blood calls out to blood," as the saying goes. Two years later, in 1974, when the Northeast held its regional encounter in Holyoke, Massachusetts, Cardinal Aponte Martínez from San Juan was not only invited but played an important and strategic role in the development of the Hispano church in that region where Puerto Ricans are the majority. Thus the National Encounter of 1972 must be understood not only in terms of what was decided in Washington, but in the impetus it gave to growth and development beyond its immediate focus. This is why it must be described as a forge of unity.

CHAPTER EIGHT

THE FIRST ENCOUNTER

The First Hispano Pastoral Encounter was held at Trinity College in Washington, D.C., June 19-22, 1972. The documents produced by this encounter are of superior quality and have served since their publication as a kind of Magna Carta of the Hispano church. The documents interwove themes of sociology, pedagogy, and theology. In addition, the practical details of pastoral practice such as the goals, priorities, and methods for developing the Hispano church are elaborated. The excellent description of the planning process is reprinted in this anthology.

After opening remarks by Bishop Joseph L. Bernardin, speaking for the NCCB and the USCC (United States Catholic Conference), his Eminence Raúl Zambrano of Facatitiva, Colombia, spoke for CELAM (Latin American Episcopal Conference). The principal addresses were reserved for Virgilio Elizondo of MACC and Bishop Patricio Flores of San Antonio. Elizondo's presentation elucidated the cultural method of developing Hispano identity within the church. The discourse of Bishop Flores took on the nature of a pastoral letter and is here reprinted in its entirety.

Born in Ganado, Texas, on July 26, 1929, Flores was the son of migrant farm workers. After his family's sacrifices had enabled him to go through the seminary, he was ordained a priest of the Diocese of Houston on May 26, 1956. In 1970 he became auxiliary of San Antonio, and in 1978 was named ordinary of the Diocese of El Paso, Texas.

His talk on the church at the Encounter sounds like one of St. Paul's epistles, weaving together similes, exhortations, pathos, and argumentativeness in a wholesome unity. He asserts that there is a new theological dimension to the United States Catholic church to be found in the cultural and faith experiences of the Hispano peoples in this country. He offers his own personal history as an example. In many ways this talk answered the writer Piri Thomas (see p. 196), who, in a different context, asked that Jesus Christ would "come down and walk with us, nitty-gritty."

51. Genesis and Statement
of Purpose of the Planning Committee
for the First National Hispano Pastoral Encounter

From Planning Committee records, 1971–1972. Used by permission.

In September 1971 Father Robert Stern, director of the Spanish-speaking Apostolate of the Archdiocese of New York invited local Spanish-speaking leaders, Father Edgard Beltrán of CELAM, and Spanish-speaking diocesan directors from New England to participate in a meeting in New York to continue the development of a Pastoral Plan for the Spanish-speaking in the Archdiocese of New York.

During one of the discussions related to the needs and concerns of the Spanish-speaking Ministry, Father Edgard Beltrán proposed the idea of a National Encounter for Spanish-speaking leaders of the United States. The group explored further the importance and timeliness of such a National Encounter and unanimously supported the idea. The recommendations of this meeting were then presented in November to the Inter-Diocesan Coordinating Committee for the Spanish-speaking of the New York Metropolitan Region. The committee accepted the recommendation and delegated Father Robert L. Stern of the Archdiocese of New York and Father John O'Brien, diocesan director of Brooklyn, to discuss the possibility with Paul Sedillo, national director of the Division for the Spanish-speaking, United States Catholic Conference.

In October 1971, at the conclusion of the National Congress of Religious Educators held in Miami, the more than one hundred Spanish-speaking national delegates presented a declaration to the leadership of the Congress and to the National Conference of Catholic Bishops for consideration at their semiannual meeting in November. The issues stressed the need for more representation in the hierarchy of the United States, for proper formation of personnel working in the Spanish-speaking Apostolate, and for the convocation of a National Congress of Catholic Leaders of the Spanish-speaking community.

These two significant meetings were indicative of a growing awareness among the Spanish-speaking leaders of the United States of the need for better pastoral planning in the Spanish-speaking apostolate.

The convergence of these trend-setting recommendations took place in December 1971 in Washington, D.C., when Fathers Robert Stern and John O'Brien presented the proposal from the Inter-Diocesan Coordinating Committee for the Spanish-speaking of the New York Metropolitan Region to Paul Sedillo.

The national director of the Division for the Spanish-speaking, United States Catholic Conference, enthusiastically supported the recommendations from the Northeast and Miami congresses and presented them to the general secretary of the United States Catholic Conference in January 1972. Bishop Bernardin readily endorsed the proposal.

On February 9-10, 1972, an expanded *Planning Committee* met at the Center for Continuing Education, University of Chicago, to develop the plan and details of this first National Spanish-speaking Conference to be held in the spring of 1972 in Chicago, Illinois. During this meeting the purpose and structure was reviewed, the goals were determined, and a title was given to the Conference: *Primer Encuentro Hispano de Pastoral* [First Hispano Pastoral Encounter].

Unforseen circumstances later led to the postponement of the Encounter to June 1972 and the relocation to Washington, D.C.

On April 17-18, 1972, the Planning Committee met at Assumption Seminary in San Antonio, Texas. Mrs. Encarnación P. Armas, chairman, reported on the physical and financial arrangements of the Encounter to be held from June 19-22, 1972, at Trinity College in Washington, D.C. The program and list of resource people were reviewed, the Statement of Purpose and Guidelines to be presented as points of study in the various workshops were developed, and the manner of formulating and presenting the conclusions was determined. It was agreed that the final proceedings of the Encounter would be published in both Spanish and English.

A final meeting of the Planning Committee took place on June 18, 1972, prior to the opening session of the First Hispano Pastoral Encounter.

STATEMENT OF PURPOSE

The purpose of this First Hispano Pastoral Encounter is to begin to develop a pastoral plan for the Hispanic American community which composes approximately one quarter of the Catholic church in the United States. The Encounter is sponsored by the Catholic Bishops of the United States through this Division for the Spanish-speaking, United States Catholic Conference. Participants will be bishops of dioceses, their official delegates and persons with special responsibility for the Spanish-speaking apostolate. The Encounter is not a conference, but an extended workshop; its style will be participatory. Its specific purpose is to analyze the present pastoral situation in the Hispanic American community and to discuss possible solutions to the many problems that exist. Out of the deliberations of the Encounter will come much information which, after the Encounter, will be correlated and made available to the National Conference of Catholic Bishops and local dioceses for their consideration and implementation.

The Encounter will be organized around seven workshops which cover the essential elements of a pastoral plan. Two general presentations will set the theological and structural foundations for such a plan. Each workshop will be initiated by the presentation of a working document by a qualified and experienced person in that field. The extended group discussions will be focused toward the formulation of the statements and conclusions of the Encounter.

---

52. Pastoral Planning for the Spanish-speaking in the United States of America

Virgilio Elizondo

From Address to the First National Hispano Pastoral Encounter, held at Trinity College, Washington, D.C., June 19-22, 1972. Used by permission.

I. THE PHENOMENA OF THE SPANISH-SPEAKING IN THE UNITED STATES

Many people see the Mexican Americans, the Puerto Ricans, the Cubans, or any other Spanish-speaking person in the United States as a problem to be solved. In a recent talk in Phoenix, Arizona, Bishop McCarthy stated that he refused to see the Mexican American in his diocese as a problem to be solved, but rather as a person to be known and loved. To understand the Spanish-speaking in the United States we must take the very same attitude. They are not a problem to be solved, but persons to be understood, appreciated, and loved.

There are in the United States around 12 million Spanish-speaking peoples. This represents approximately 5 percent of the total population of this country. It is interesting to note in the listing of countries with Spanish-speaking citizens, that the United States ranks fifth in the list. It is also said that Los Angeles has more Mexicans and Mexican Americans than any other city in the world with the exception of Mexico City.

Certain characteristics may easily be discovered in the Spanish-speaking minority of the United States:

1. A higher index of growth than other groups in this country. Several reasons could easily be found for this high growth index. We will list here only the most commonly accepted ones. *(a)* Because of our proximity to the borders of other Spanish-speaking countries, the number of immigrants will continue. Legally, or illegally, the Spanish-speaking come to the United States and they come to stay. The United States continues to be for people in the developing countries a "mecca" where gold, good fortune, and dreams of a good life will continue to attract them in days to come. *(b)* For the Spanish-speaking, *Humanae Vitae* has never presented a serious problem. Our people love their families, and even though the size of the Spanish-speaking family may not be as large as in former times, the Spanish-speaking will never accept the concept of "zero population," which seems to be becoming popular in the United States. The birthrate and the migrations indicate that the index of growth of the Spanish-speaking in the United States will continue to increase.

2. There is within the Spanish-speaking groups in the United States a growing awareness of our uniqueness. We are not merely transplanted Europeans, but truly a mestizo people (a mixture of European and Indian) and, as such, a beautifully unique people.

3. Recognizing our uniqueness, there is a growing determination to preserve, perpetuate, and share with our fellow citizens the substance of our culture and our language. It is true that, for practical reasons, we accept certain forms of acculturation and the language of this country; but, at the same time, we retain the essence of that which constitutes us as a bilingual and bicultural minority. We are not ashamed of what we are. On the contrary, we are proud of the heritage we have received from our parents and ancestors. We are proud to be descendants of our great Indian and European forebears. We are proud of the fact that we are truly a "new people" and as such we will serve as a prophetic people to our fellow North American citizens who, for the most part, are mostly transplanted Europeans and not truly a new people in the New World, as the mestizo indeed is! This growing consciousness is helping us to discover our self-identity. Rather than forgetting our past, there is a growing desire to preserve it and share with the rest of America the best of our cultural traditions and language. This phenomenon is of utmost importance when we are considering the integration of our people and our active participation in the social, religious, economic, and political structures of our country.

It is vitally important for the church to realize and give serious consideration to the fact that 85 percent of this Spanish-speaking minority is faithful to the preservation of the Catholic faith of our parents. The Spanish-speaking constitutes 25 percent of the total Catholic population of the United States. This poses for the church a series of important questions which demand adequate answers. We who are the church and who are responsible for the Pastoral Mission of the Church must ask ourselves the following:

1. Does there truly exist a specific ministry for the Spanish-speaking Catholics in the United States as directed in the Vatican documents and in the Pastoral Letter of Pope Paul VI *Pastoralis Migratorum* (August 15, 1969)?

2. If such a plan does exist, what are its specifying elements?

3. If there is such a plan, is it a unified pastoral plan for the "total action of the whole church" or are we simply carrying on diverse activities, without precise objectives, without methods that guide the process, without well-planned organization, and without a critical evaluation? Is it not true that too often our efforts are isolated, individualistic, and frequently very frustrating even after much dedicated work?

4. Is it possible for us to discover and formulate a unified pastoral plan for the Spanish-speaking in the United States? Can we devise a concrete plan of action? Will such a plan be realistically feasible and humanly possible?

II. SPECIFICS FOR DEFINING THE PHENOMENA

Previous to seeking a possible solution, it is urgent that we carefully grasp and define the phenomena we are speaking about. In order to have a clearer concept and so be capable of formulating an objective pastoral plan of action, it is important that we consider two fundamental poles. One is the very nature of the church and the other is the concrete human beings today for whom the church is intended. The church by its very nature is mission and its mission is intended for the real person of today. This is a fundamental point if we are going to formulate an authentic pastoral action and not one which will be quick, practical, and most probably superficial and simplistic.

We must seriously reexamine and recognize the true nature of the church as mission, not that the church has a mission, but rather, that by its very nature the church is mission. The church was called into existence and continues to exist so as to be sent to bring the Good News of the gospel to all people. On the other hand, we must see to whom and for what reasons the church has been sent to humankind. The church has been sent to continue the work of Christ on earth. As such, it strives to serve, to invite, and to help real people of the times, not an abstract timeless person, but people here and now as they exist today. If we do not know today's person, with all his or her specifying characteristics, we will fail both humanity and Christ.

To see the church as mission we must consider it not merely as a philanthropic group of do-gooders, nor as a mere organization dedicated to the social, economic, and political development of people. Neither is the church simply a religious group whose attitude is one of proselytizing, indoctrinating, or imposing ideologies.

We are, according to the documents of Vatican II *(Lumen Gentium* 8), the *community* of those called into being, through our faith in Jesus the Lord, through our fraternal love, universal and operative, and through our eschatological hope—the *sign,* the sacrament of the new humanity which is in the process of edification. We are co-creators with the Father in the building up of the new person begun by Jesus the Lord, and which is in the process of growing in the power of the Spirit. Our mission is to proclaim this Good News not only in words but in deeds, or better yet, in the words of Vatican II, with *signs*—signs which make people feel the active and powerful presence of the salvific love of the Father—WORDS AND DEEDS.

We are discovering that the gospel is proclaimed above all through the image which we all see—Jesus. Jesus, before speaking words, as a person was actively projecting an image of interest in people, solicitude, concern for those with whom he lived. His fraternal love for people was seen and felt. The church today, in fidelity to Christ, must concern itself not only with doctrine (*ortodoxia*) but even more so with practice (*ortopraxis*); that is, it must actually live as Jesus lived when he walked the face of the earth. Through our practice of fraternal love, the world and our people will be able to see Jesus as truly risen because it will know in us a community that is animated by the Risen Christ and lives his very life. In our lifestyle, the Risen Lord must be made visible and real to the world today. Through our practice of fraternal love, the world and our people will be able to see and experience the salvific love of God which is operative in the world today.

Christ was image, and because he was image he had a message to give. So the church must have for its first priority the living of the life of Christ as he lives it in proclaiming the living gospel. In this fashion the church will be sign and image made visible for those who look toward it and come to it seeking. Once this image is made visible, then the church may preach and explain what it is living. Deeds without words are ambiguous; but words without living deeds of the gospel are a hypocrisy—not a sign of Christ, but an antisign.

So, in fidelity to Christ, the gospel, and the church's teaching, we must place our first priority in an authentic living of the gospel so that we may then proclaim with our lips what we are truly living. As Christ made the blind see, so the church through the fostering of education must open the eyes of the intelligence of all the unlettered and illiterate of the world, for only in knowing the world in which they live can people truly become co-creators in the development of the world.

As Christ raised the paralyzed and enabled them to walk, we must, guided by the gospel, interest ourselves in social and economic progress. Today, numberless people are paralyzed by social and economic systems which do not allow them to walk like human beings, which crush them, oppress them, and keep them down.

Just as it is urgent that the poor see the gospel with their own eyes, so the church must also take an interest in television, the language of image, and the satellites. If humans have been able to go to the moon, why cannot they elevate the present image of the Spanish-speaking North American so that he or she may be known by fellow citizens as one who might be different, yet equal in every way? We must use the gifts of God and modern life to proclaim the gospel truly—to bring out the best in every cultural group in our country. We must make visible via the modern means of communication the salvific love of God which is operating in our society.

Who is this person to whom we must address ourselves? We must know the person; we cannot try to impose our theories, but rather we must go with open eyes and hearts to analyze and know the person we are sent to serve.

All too often we go to serve others as though we were a Messiah from a foreign country without incarnating ourselves, as the Son of God did, into the group we are going to work with. We cannot save a human group from the outside. We will accomplish our task only when we get within the group so that, from within, we may lead them beyond to a new level of human existence. . . .

---

53. The Church: Diocesan and National

Bishop Patricio Flores

Text of address to First National Hispano Pastoral Encounter, held at Trinity College, Washington, D.C., June 19-22, 1972. Used by permission.

To start these reflections which we have titled "The Church: Diocesan and National," I want to emphasize that I have a great love for the church of Christ. It is because of this love that I am in the church, that I work in the church, that I want to stay in the church and that I want to receive more life from the church as well as give it some of my life.

If it were not so, if I were not in love with it, I would not be working with it. I have had very good offers to work elsewhere and at a very good salary. However, I did not enter the active ministry of the church for financial gain, or because I thought it would make my life easier or better. I believe that with regard to material and monetary compensation, I would have done better elsewhere.

I love the church, and it is through the church that I want to serve. I want to serve in the church because I believe in the value of the gospel of Christ for humanity.

Second, I am convinced that it is under the umbrella of the gospel of Christ that the true and proper religious development of people can be achieved.

Development should be completely human. And is this not the development of the total person and of all people? A humanism that is closed and not open to all the inspirations of the Spirit of God, who is the source of all, would produce an apparent success; but without God, human beings would only achieve their own failure.

A humanism without God is inhuman and incomplete. True humanism is opened to the absolute.

I believe in the necessity of the full development of human beings, but I believe that this development is not complete if it leaves out God. "Not by bread alone does man live." Certainly a person needs bread to live, but with bread alone, one does not live a full life. "Full belly, happy heart" is a proverb which does not satisfy one who has had some experience.

Another proverb says: "As the mule said to the harness, while there is grain and water, all is well." But as humans we must say: "That is all right for the mule, but for us, it is absurd." By this I mean to say that human beings cannot live the fullness of life without God. But I also say that if religion is badly applied, it can do as much harm to a people as if they were made to live without religion.

I think that religion can be for us a medicine, a tonic which can give us the true value of life and which can strengthen and fortify us. But this medicine, good in itself, if badly administered can have negative effects completely opposite to its original purposes.

I wanted to make clear and to underline my great love and dedication to the church and my faith in the value which Christ in his gospel has for our development, because I am going to make some strong constructive criticisms of the North American Catholic church.

I want it understood that I do it with love for the church which I lovingly call "Mother." The physician tells the patient exactly what is wrong because he wants to help the person. What I wish to say can be better expressed by an experience of mine which could be applied to the problem of the church in relation to those who speak Spanish.

Once I received an urgent call to a psychiatric hospital in Houston, Texas. A Mexican American girl had attempted to take her own life. I arrived at the door of the hospital at the same time as her worried mother and stepfather, who came because they had also been called. Upon letting us in, the nurse said that the patient only wanted to see me and that she had given orders not to see anyone else, not even her parents. The mother, in tears, asked me to tell her daughter that they were there, and that they loved her and wanted to see her.

I went to her room—how horrible it was! The girl and her bed were bathed in blood. She had cut her wrists with glass from the lamp's light bulb and said she did not want to live. She kept saying that she would be better off dead because she had already lost all desire to live. I tried to calm her down—we talked for an hour—but when I mentioned that her parents were outside, she again became furious and hysterical. I insisted that she see her parents, that she give them another chance, that she pardon them, etc. She finally gave in, but insisted that I stay with her during the visit with her parents.

I went and invited the parents who were, of course, very happy. But their happiness was quickly changed into shame because as we entered her room the girl furiously pointed her finger at the mother and shouted: "It's your fault that I'm in the shape I'm in. It's your fault that I'm here. You married the man that killed my father; you knew that since you two married, your husband began to molest me sexually—I complained to you hoping to get help. But you, instead of defending me, acted hurt. You accused me of being responsible for it all because I was a flirt—and I—what did I know about that? I was only twelve years old. When he forced me to do whatever he wanted with me, I yelled desperately, but you, Mamá, acted as if you were asleep and did not defend me. That stepfather did what he wanted with me—and did it many times—when I threatened to report him to my uncles, he ran me out of the house into the street saying that I was wicked, that I was a prostitute, and didn't deserve to be there. . . . I left the house at fourteen; the world and men have done with me what they wanted—but nobody really loves me, because according to them I am worthless." The girl continued: "Mamá, it's your fault that I'm here. You are my mother, but you didn't defend me—you did not speak up for me. You let your husband deprive me of and steal my most sacred possession—my purity. The two of you threw me out of the house when I most needed protection and guidance. I am what I am . . . it is your fault. I don't want to see you again. It's too late now . . . you have destroyed my life."

The girl accused the mother of four things:

1. Her mother did not defend her.

2. Her mother permitted the stealing of that which was most sacred—her purity.

3. Her mother acted deaf.

4. Her mother and stepfather threw her into the street and did not shelter her when she most needed it.

Brothers and sisters, what would we hear if we stopped to listen to the echo of cries and desperation of the Spanish-speaking Catholics in the United States? What we hear these days is horrible! The Spanish-speaking say so many things in spiritual suicide and one has to ask, "Could they be right in what they are saying and in how they feel?"

In the first place, I realize that the situation of the Spanish-speaking is desperate. I describe the gravity and urgency of the problem like that of a coffeepot on a fire; it is already boiling and if it is not taken off the fire in time it will boil over and all will be lost—or at least almost all. The Spanish-speaking are seething and before we know it they will be lost to the church. Why?

What should the church be for the people? It could be one of three things: (1) its liquidation; (2) its pacification; (3) its liberation.

It really should be *liberation* because Christ who is its Head and fountain came to the world to liberate us not only from sin, but also from injustice, from racism, and all the rest. He came "so that we might have life and have it more abundantly." But in many cases the church has been guilty of our liquidation or pacification—or has permitted it.

We could apply here the words of the young girl who said, "Being my mother you did not defend me against the oppressor—that stepfather." She continued, "You permitted that man to steal what was most sacred in my life." From us who have always lived here and from the Hispanos who have immigrated here, has been stolen our most sacred possession—our land, our language, our culture, our customs, our history and our way of religious expression. We have also been victims of oppression, discrimination, semi-slavery. We have been poorly paid for our work; we have lived in housing worse than that of the monkeys in a zoo; we have not been admitted to some schools, universities, etc.

The migrant workers continue to live in the worst conditions in this country—and the church remains silent.

Let me enumerate some things we have been deprived of, and the means of such deprivation:

1. *Our land:* A friend of mine in Houston told me: "When the missionaries came to America, we had the land, they had the Bibles. Now we have the Bibles and the missionaries have the land"—California, New Mexico, Texas, Louisiana, etc.

2. *Human sacrifices* were forbidden us by those who did not try to understand the true value of these sacrifices—but at the same time permitted the sacrifice of thousands upon thousands of indigenous at the hands of Christian civilized Europeans in order to confiscate their goods, their wives, to satisfy the egotism of the conquerors and the colonizers.

3. We were forbidden to utilize our *ritual dances* in honor of the gods, and we were obliged to honor God in a manner totally foreign to our being. Gregorian chant for the Universal Church—what a horror! I spent last week in Milwaukee and saw and participated in a Mexican-Puerto Rican mass. What a beautiful experience it was, because it was an event of the people where they united to praise God according to their own mode of expression.

4. *Abortion:* Here the position of the church has been firm against deprivation of life. I appreciate this because it is the right of an individual to be born. If my parents had practiced abortion I would not be here, being number seven in a family of nine. You would have lost the first Mexican American bishop. Thanks to my parents, though poor, they allowed me to be. I believe in the right to be born, but also I believe in the right to life after birth.

5. *Ethnicide:* It deprives the person of pride, it "squashes" the person, it destroys. Again I shall quote from the young victimized girl. "They robbed

me of my most sacred possession, purity, and you became deaf. . . ." Purity, the beauty of our culture and our customs, the values of our *religiosidad popular* are taken from us and the church remains silent—"Qui tacit consentire videtur" (He who remains silent, seems to give consent).

The young girl said: "They threw me out in the streets and gave me no shelter when I needed it most." How many times Spanish-speaking persons wanted this shelter—the warmth of the church—and its institutions closed the doors to them when they needed it the most!

Not too long ago, it was common for churches to have signs saying "Mexicans not allowed" or "The last four benches reserved for Mexicans." Perhaps today there are no signs—they have been removed—but there are still unremoved attitudes that are very evident and easily sensed. In some parishes, even though the physical doors have been opened, the North American people have not opened the doors of their hearts.

In my many visits to the Spanish-speaking, how often the migrants tell me that the churches do not want to allow them masses in Spanish, nor the use of parish halls for meetings, or if they do loan the hall, someone comes to fumigate it even before the meeting is over in order to deodorize it of the Mexican and Puerto Rican odor.

Two weeks ago a pastor asked my friend Encarnación Armas why Puerto Ricans and Mexican Americans didn't take baths more often so that they could change their color and then there would be no problem in accepting them in the American parishes. It seems that this man had never heard the song "I started to bathe a black [. . . and the blacker he became]."

It would be wonderful if these were tales of the past, if these things had happened among the unbelieving or the uncivilized—but this happens even today, and it is being done by people who are recognized as good Christians.

But the church, in the face of all this, seems to continue saying: "These are political problems, and in this area we must remain neutral." *Can we be neutral? What must be done?* It is obvious that if the church wants to keep calling the Spanish-speaking "her children" then the church must change attitudes and structures.

ATTITUDES

The church cannot ignore the presence of fifteen million Spanish-speaking persons in the United States. They cannot be put into the same institution without taking into account their own particular background. The Mexican Americans who were here before the coming of the English-speaking, as well as the Spanish-speaking who have migrated here recently, have brought and have their own mentality, their language, their culture, their religion, and their own needs. All these elements are part of a beautiful spiritual heritage which will last in the Spanish-speaking outside of their Motherland. This heritage, so rich in values, should be highly esteemed.

The church cannot insist that in order to be first-class citizens and Christians we must "AMERICANIZE OURSELVES" . . . the mere statement disorients us. If we were born on this continent we are already "Americans." What do we have to be or do in order to "Americanize" ourselves? The true Americans are our brothers and sisters, the Indians on the reservations: "To Americanize ourselves" means to absorb a little of or all the different European cultures. This would be all right because it would enrich our own culture even more. But if to "Americanize ourselves" means to learn English well, we are really saying that if we learn English well, all will be well, we will be well accepted, etc. I don't know if the bishops and priests believe that—I don't! For one thing, the black North Americans spoke only English; they didn't speak Spanish at all, and I ask: "Were they treated as first-class citizens and Christians?" And for another, I think that I learned English well, and even when I had three years of college in the seminary some Catholics would still not employ me—simply because I am brown, my name is Flores, and I am a descendant of Mexicans.

I cannot convince myself that "to be Americanized" means to speak English well and that speaking it well will mean total acceptance.

STRUCTURE

If the Catholic church in North America has these attitudes but does not want to lose the Spanish-speaking, then, while the American hierarchy is taking care of 75 percent of the faithful, it should allow other structures for the other 25 percent.

I believe that the need for restructuring ourselves in favor of the needs of the Spanish-speaking is urgent. Pope Paul himself in his famous *Populorum Progressio* says in number 32: "The present situation must be confronted with courage. Development demands courageous .transformation, profound innovations. Urgent reforms must be introduced without delay."

Let me pinpoint a few situations urgently in need of attention:

1. Only 5 percent of American Catholic youth attends mass today, compared to 90 to 95 percent twenty-five years ago.
2. The city of New York, including the Diocese of Brooklyn, has approximately 160 parishes of Spanish-speaking, but there are at the same time 1000 Protestant chapels with native pastors in the Hispano areas.
3. In Phoenix, Arizona, in one area with many Hispanos there are four Catholic churches for Spanish-speaking persons compared to fifty-seven Protestant churches.
4. In Texas, the 1970 Catholic population of Mexican Americans (95%) had only 52 priests and the Protestants (5%) had 554 Protestant Mexican American ministers. They see in each convert a possible minister.

After having presented so many problems that do not have a solution in the present structures, we come to the heart of this presentation: What diocesan, regional, and national structures do we see as possible for the Spanish-speaking in the United States?

DIOCESAN STRUCTURES

You [priests at the Encounter] are the cell which gives and maintains life within the dioceses. You are useful and necessary in your communities. Your people need you very much. Do not quit! Hold on! Do not get married while it is not permitted.

In every diocese there ought to be a commission or pastoral team which would attend to all the needs of the Spanish-speaking on their way to complete fulfillment. The Spanish-speaking should be represented in all departments.

This commission should be interested in all of the needs of the Spanish-speaking within their jurisdiction, be these doctrinal, social, liturgical, economic, educational, political, or legislative.

This team would provide leadership in the renewal and formation of all, especially of priests and laity working among the Spanish-speaking. It would not permit anyone to work among the Spanish-speaking without first knowing who they are and what attitudes they have.

This diocesan commission should see to it that the formation of priests who would work among the Spanish-speaking include not only the language, but also cultures and customs, and that they be familiar with the needs of those whom they will serve and be disposed to commit themselves to their solution.

The diocesan commission or team should foster vocations to the priesthood and religious life among the Hispanic community. Moreover, it would decide which seminary the candidate would attend, depending upon his total cultural background. If none meets his needs, a new seminary should be established. The commission should have the authority of the ordinary to function according to the needs of the people it is to serve. Also, it ought to have from the bishop the authority to move those priests who are obstacles to the work of the commission which serves the Spanish-speaking peoples.

There should be a bishop for the Spanish-speaking. He himself must be Spanish-speaking, a member of that Spanish-speaking people he serves. For example, Detroit, Chicago, New York, Miami, Los Angeles, etc. Two bishops in one diocese? ... it is possible ... one serving the Spanish-speaking and the other serving the English-speaking. Let me reiterate: (1) I believe it has been established that 25 percent of the North American church, the Spanish-speaking, are not being served properly because all the effort goes to serve the North Americans. (2) The pope recommends: "The present situation must be confronted with courage. Development demands courageous transformation, profound innovations. Urgent reforms must be introduced without delay" (*Populorum Progressio* 32).

Where there exists a great number of Spanish-speaking, the bishop must share his authority and responsibility with another bishop . . . the one who takes care of the Spanish-speaking.

In actuality, the bishop who has not wanted to share his authority and responsibility with another Catholic bishop has already shared it with Protestant ministers and bishops who have taken away so many of his people. He will have to share more of his authority and responsibility with more Protestants if he does not share it with Spanish-speaking bishops, or if proper attention is not given to the Spanish-speaking.

In the last paragraph (23) of *Christus Dominus* we read: "Likewise in similar circumstances, there must be provided to the faithful of a distinct language, either by means of Priests or Parishes of the same language or by an Episcopal Vicar who must know the language in question, and also if the case requires it actually to be a Bishop, and finally in any other opportune way."

NATIONAL PARISHES WITHIN THE DIOCESE

Recommendations:
1. A church edifice for all with different functions, provided that all are well received.
2. A church only for Spanish-speaking peoples when they are not well received and where the people are entirely Spanish-speaking.

REGIONAL CHURCH

I believe that one must be very careful in talking about regions. It seems to me that to have an alliance among a series of dioceses would be great and very beneficial. If in a determined region all the Spanish-speaking would morally unite themselves, it would be a force in their struggle: Unity makes Power—Power gives us Victory.

But to attempt to serve all, located in a vast region, with the same "team" would be quite dangerous, because in a region there could be an immense variety of cultures, customs, necessities, etc.

Thus, for the regions, I would suggest a regional alliance of the Spanish-speaking. In that region, each diocese would be served according to its special needs.

REGIONAL ALLIANCE

1. A regional alliance could form centers, like the Mexican American Cultural Center in San Antonio, Texas, to carry out investigations; to develop educational programs, to develop Spanish-speaking leadership; to develop the language, art, and culture proper to the Spanish-speaking of that region.
2. There could be regional institutes for all the Spanish-speaking peoples in a region—with a pluralistic curriculum to include the various cultures, arts, and needs of the area.

THE CHURCH AT THE NATIONAL LEVEL

Structures: You have already read in the material given you here that PADRES, at its National Convention, passed a resolution that a study should be made of the possibility of forming a national church within the total structure of Catholicism, but separate from the American episcopate.

The delegates insisted that they wanted more complete representation in all departments of the North American church, in which we are 25 percent Spanish-speaking (18 percent Mexican Americans).

Problems: To form a national church would be impossible, or at least detrimental. We do not have enough Mexican American priests and bishops to serve properly the needs of the Mexican Americans. A great majority of Mexican Americans would follow us—but not all will do so, and this would result in another division. We do not wish, we should not, and it is not good for us, to be separated more than we already are. Christ wants us together. We will do everything within our power to strengthen the ties between us and with all other Christians.

I personally recommend that we work within the structure. I say that we should work *within* because as of now we are *not* within at all. To accomplish this we must:

a. Speak out—"He who does not speak out, not even God hears him." We have not spoken enough—not enough! There have been only a few isolated voices—individuals. It is necessary to speak out as a national group.

b. It is necessary to speak out so that we can be represented in all departments of the structure of the North American church of which we are 25 percent. It is not enough to have only a division within the Department of Social Development and World Peace, where we have only five people to serve the whole Spanish-speaking nation. We should have Spanish-speaking peoples in all the departments: Education, Catechetics, Rural Life, Family Life, Communications, Liturgy, Migration, etc.

c. It is necessary to speak out and insist that there be a proportionate group of bishops within the Episcopal Conference; but we are told that (1) we do not qualify, and (2) "There will be more bishops when we have more priests." This should be inverted. To have more priests, first it will be necessary to have more Spanish-speaking bishops.

d. We should have a national Seminary for Spanish-speaking, where we keep in mind the plurality of cultures, but where together Spanish-speaking religious leaders can be formed.

I would like to conclude by reminding all of you present here at this First Hispano Pastoral Encounter, that we are the responsible ones to see to it that something does happen. May it not be said of us: "You were my mother, but you remained silent." Thank you! God bless you!

54. Walk with Us Nitty-Gritty

Piri Thomas

From Thomas, Savior, Savior, Hold My Hand *(Garden City, N.Y.: Doubleday and Co., 1972), pp. 360-361. Used by permission. (For information about the author, see p. 150, above.)*

"Nita, you say that God is with us? That's what the hell is wrong with so many of us. We cover our eyes with God and become content to live in these damn conditions. I know Christ is great, honey. I just wish he'd come down and walk with us nitty-gritty. Baby, I'm not putting God down. I'm just wondering why the hell we've allowed certain people to put us down. How the hell can I listen to the words of Christ and how He carried the cross? I can't carry no cross and be nailed to it at the same damned time. Wow, honey, don't you dig that to us people of the Barrio the ghetto is our church, and the only way we're gonna make a heaven out of this hell is by getting together. Jesus, honey, ain't I right?"

Nita smiled. I could tell she knew where I was coming from.

"Nita, there ain't no such word as defeat. Diggit. Like them blind churches better get to see where it's really at."

"Por qué no, Piri?" Nita said gently. She held my arm tightly with mucho love and corazón. We looked out the window and dug our Barrio below and some kind of light caught Nita and me as we held each other mucho close. The light silhouetted us sharp and clear so that the world couldn't help but see love and dignity. We kissed. Nita moved away from me slowly.

"Where are you going?" I asked softly.

"To church, negrito. I'm late now."

I looked out at the streets below and heard the door quietly close behind me. "We're gonna walk tall or not at all, World," I told myself. Then I smiled and half aloud whispered, "Hey, Jesus Christ, I betcha' there must be a million ghetto crosses out there."

CHAPTER NINE

THE RESPONSE

The Hispano Pastoral Encounter of 1972 can be examined in terms of change in the pastoral practice with Spanish-speaking people within the dioceses in the United States. The effects were uneven. Like the seeds of the Gospel parable, some fell on rocky ground, some among the thorns, some were eaten by the birds of the air, and some fell upon good ground and bore fruit a hundredfold.

Obviously the conclusions would have different effects in a huge city like New York as contrasted with a town like Highgrove, California. However there are more discrete factors that influenced the progress of development of the Hispano church after the Encounter, and it requires what sociologists call a "typology" to analyze them. The following five questions suggest the way the analysis must proceed.

RATIO

The first question must be: "What is the Hispano Community's ratio to the total population?" Simple numbers are not enough, since only 8,000 Hispano inhabitants in a town like Crystal City, Texas, with a total population of about 10,000, have a much more influential role in society than the 24,000 Puerto Ricans living in Newark, New Jersey, with a total population of 381,930.

PERCENTAGE OF CATHOLICS

The second question asks: "What is the percentage of Hispano Catholics to the total Catholic population?" Once again, regardless of numbers, the higher percentages will have a more favorable influence for the Hispano leadership's implementation of the Encounter's conclusions. For instance, the whole state of Arizona in 1970 had some 264,000 Hispanos, which is less than the 289,000 Hispanos in New Jersey. But there are only 414,561 Catholics in Arizona so that Hispanos form a healthy majority of 64 percent, while, in New Jersey, the Hispanos are only 13.5 percent of the total Catholic population of some 2.1 million.

ETHNICITY AND HISPANOS

The third question relates to the ethnic composition of the city or region where the Hispanos are found: "Are there many ethnic groups besides the Hispanos in the diocese?" If the answer is Yes, concessions to Hispanos will probably provoke other nationality groups to ask for similiar attention. In other words, the positions that the Encounter assumed for cultural pluralism to benefit Hispanos can be used for Italians, Poles, Slovaks, Lebanese, blacks, etc. As a result, the more ethnically diverse sections of the country are less vulnerable to arguments for cultural pluralism. The Encounter did introduce a mathematical formula to forestall obvious complications; however, the presence of many different ethnic groups blunts the Encounter's contrast of Hispano and Anglo-Saxon.

MONO-HISPANO OR MULTI-HISPANO

The fourth question concerns the pluralism of the local Hispano community: "Is the community mono-Hispano (where one group constitutes 80 percent or more of all Hispanos) or is it multi-Hispano (with several Latin American groups)?" The mono-Hispano communities have less diversity; hence their cultural homogeneity is likely to produce unity on questions of Hispano identity. For example, it is easier to organize a mostly Mexican American community than one made up of large groups of Cubans, Peruvians, Costa Ricans, Puerto Ricans, and Mexicans. Each subgroup has its own needs and vision, which must be reconciled before the total community can be mobilized. The mono-Hispano situation is more cohesive and therefore lends greater strength to the Hispanos when they collectively address an institution like the church or the government.

VALIDATION OF THE CLERGY

The fifth question is: "What clergy in the Spanish-speaking apostolate are cross-validated?" (Cross-validation is a process definable as "the acceptance of leaders across institutional and nationality barriers." It has been described in Chap. Six, pp. 117-18). Just as the farm workers' cause provided cross-validation for Mexican American clergy at a national level, the Encounter was the occasion for cross-validation at a diocesan and regional level. However, not all availed themselves of this opportunity, since some of the clergy felt they were already cross-validated and had no need to attend the Encounter.

In much of the Southwest before the Encounter, pastoral care of Hispanos was frequently the responsibility of religious clergy from Spain or Mexico. Moreover, national chapels (often with inferior financial resources), instead of the secular clergy, were expected to care for the Hispanos (McNamara, in Grebler et al., 1970). The Archdiocese of New York, on the other hand, demonstrated concern for the waves of migration from Puerto Rico by establishing a special pastoral office that financed the extensive and successful intercultural institute directed by Monsignor Ivan Illich (see Chap. Five). In some years, the majority of the ordination class of the archdiocese journeyed to Puerto Rico in order to study how to minister to Puerto Ricans. Thus many of the archdiocesan clergy in New York enjoyed the acceptance of the official church and of the people they had learned to serve. In a word, they were cross-validated.

The Midwest and parts of the Northeast had non-Hispano clergy who were likewise strongly identified with Hispano people. Chicago's famous and indefatigable Father Leo Mahon comes to mind. However, all too often these self-sacrificing priests were marginated from official chancery structures. They were generally not cross-validated, since the acceptance given them by the Hispano people was not matched by their own diocese. They simply lacked clout with the church. They resembled many of the Spaniards who were classified as "externs"; they were often treated as mercenaries and had little influence in church decisions, despite the fact that they carried the burden of work with the Spanish-speaking in many parishes and in movements such as the Cursillo.

It seems that the Encounter would help those clergy without cross-validation to gain great influence with the diocese, while those who were already cross-validated would not see any immediate advantage in adopting the suggestions of the Encounter. There is at times a kind of law of inertia within the policy-making circles of the church; an attitude prevails which can best by summed up with the maxim: "You don't change a game plan as long as you are scoring points."

Thus it is probably fair to say that the success of the New York Archdiocese with its Spanish Catholic Action Office was a major obstacle to the policy changes suggested by the 1972 Washington Encounter. On the other hand, there is little doubt that the conflicts between Hispanos and chancery during the dispute of 1969 with Católicos por La Raza (see pp. 123-33) when Cardinal McIntyre was ordinary made his successor, Timothy Manning, more likely to bring changes into the Los Angeles Archdiocese.

THE IMPLEMENTATION

When all of these factors are put into perspective, it can be seen why the implementation of the Encounter's conclusions would be an uneven process. The different Hispano communities across the country would enter into important posts at different times and in different ways according to the constellation of social and ecclesiastical conditions. The growth of the nascent Hispano church had to be nonorganic.

A quick review of the conditions described above indicates that the most favorable soil for quick maturation of the Hispano church was in a part of the country where (1) Hispanos were a high percentage of the total population, (2) Hispanos were a majority of the Catholics, (3) other Catholic ethnic groups were not large, (4) more than 80 percent of the Hispanos were of the same nationality, and (5) the idea of special diocesan attention to the Hispanos was necessary because the non-Hispano secular clergy were not cross-validated.

The region that best fits all these conditions is the Southwest of the United

States, stretching from Brownsville, Texas, passing north of San Antonio and sweeping across New Mexico and Arizona into Southern California. Indeed, since the Encounter the greatest visibility in terms of native Hispano bishops, Hispano clerical and religious associations, etc., has come from the Southwest. This progress has had less to do with some sort of superiority of Mexican Americans over Puerto Ricans than with the historical and sociological realities that have just been described.

A second and more subtle effect of the Encounter upon the United States Catholic church is found in the written response of the National Council of Catholic Bishops (NCCB) to the recommendations offered by the Conclusions Committee of the Encounter. The non-Hispano episcopal leadership in the United States tended to prefer the pastoralist model of church that was taking shape in San Antonio. A review of the bishops' response reveals a frequent use of MACC as an example of general development for all Hispanos. The Hispano pastoralist became the paradigm as the term is used by Avery Dulles (1974, p. 23).

> At various times in the history of the Church it has seemed possible to construct a total theology, or at least a total ecclesiology, on the basis of a single model. Such a dominant model is . . . a paradigm. A model rises to the status of a paradigm when it has proved successful in solving a great variety of problems and is expected to be an appropriate tool for unraveling anomalies as yet unsolved.

The approval given in 1973 by the NCCB's ad hoc committee to MACC enhanced the prestige of the San Antonio center and enabled it to continue attracting excellent theologians from Europe and Latin America. The students from MACC communicated and deepened the awareness of grassroots people of a new model of church in which Hispanos had an important role. Through PADRES and Hermanas, cross-validation was extended across barriers within the Hispano community to young and militant clergy and religious everywhere. This was eventually to prove important to the New York City Puerto Rican community. In 1973 PADRES invited Father Antonio M. Stevens Arroyo, the writer of this book, to become their regional representative. Shortly before, Hermanas had begun the same process with Sister Rosamaría Elías, a Trinitarian who worked in Brooklyn. Eventually, Sister María Iglesias, a Sister of Charity, was elected to the governance team of Hermanas. In these cases, the model of church emanating from the Southwest cross-validated the leadership of these Puerto Ricans, giving to all three a prominence at a national level that none had enjoyed in 1972. This force of diffusion became all the more powerful when Father Robert Stern's pastoral planning team in the Archdiocese of New York was dismembered. Ana María Díaz Ramírez details this process in the excerpt provided in this chapter.

Finally, the Washington Office of the Spanish-speaking was raised to the level of a secretariat, giving it more prestige. Unfortunately, it sometimes projected the image of a public relations center for the Hispano church of the Southwest rather than a coordinating agency for the whole country. This was most definitely not the intention of the talented director, Pablo Sedillo, and as will be seen in subsequent chapters, overcoming this regionalism became a principal focus of the secretariat. But in those first years, the secretariat was not in a position to interfere in the internal affairs of a diocese in order to create something that was not there. Hence attention had to be given to the successes of the pastoralist model of the Southwest as an argument at a national level for the viability of the Hispano church. All these factors combined to give a decidedly southwestern and pastoralist flavor to what the secretariat promoted as a model for national development of a Hispano church.

The original members of this committee were Archbishop Joseph L. Bernadin, chairman; Archbishop Thomas A. Donnellan; Bishop Juan A. Arzube; Bishop John J. Fitzpatrick; Bishop Patricio F. Flores; Bishop Raymond J. Gallagher; and Bishop Edward D. Head.

55. Report (May 1973) of the Ad Hoc Committee for the Spanish-speaking, National Conference of Catholic Bishops (NCCB), on the Conclusions of the First Hispano Pastoral Encounter, held June 1972 (excerpts).

The First Encounter, held June 1972 in Washington, D.C., was an important occasion for American Catholics of Spanish-speaking origin. Therefore, we are happy to serve on this Ad Hoc Committee set up to study the Encounter conclusions. The preface of the conclusions points out the need for greater participation of the Spanish-speaking in the leadership and decision-making roles of the Church in the United States. The Committee is aware that a large percentage of the Church in the United States is of Spanish-speaking origin. We will be doing everything we can, within the limitations placed on us, to assist in the emergence of leadership among the Spanish-speaking. Because of the high priority which the Conference places on the Apostolate for the Spanish-speaking, Cardinal Krol has asked us to give careful consideration to the conclusions and recommendations emanating from the Encounter. Following the meeting on October 31, 1972, of the Committee, with a number of those who prepared the Encounter conclusions, the members circulated this report. We will treat each of the conclusions in the order in which they were presented to us.

1. The first recommendation is that the USCC Division for the Spanish-speaking become a special office directly under the General Secretary. The Committee believes that the important matter here is not where the division is located on the organizational chart. It does not feel that any significant benefit would come from this change. The important point is that there be easy access to the General Secretary's office. The recent organization of USCC provides for more direct access to the General Secretary than previously. We admit that more needs to be done internally to relate the concerns of the division to the other departments, divisions, and offices of the Conference and suggest that the director of the Division for the Spanish-speaking and the General Secretary work together to accomplish this goal.

2. We agree that more Spanish-speaking people should be hired for the work of the USCC, and we urge the hiring of people of Spanish-speaking background whenever possible. Mindful of the fact that job opportunities may not always be available, names of such available personnel should be made known to the Conference, giving a brief resume of their qualifications and backgrounds.

3. By establishing this NCCB Ad Hoc Committee for the Spanish-speaking, Cardinal Krol has attempted to answer affirmatively this third recommendation. It is felt that this Ad Hoc Committee can adequately address itself to the needs of the Spanish-speaking people presently. Should it become necessary, the Ad Hoc Committee could become a standing committee in the future after more experience has been gained. In the meantime, the division is permitted and encouraged to avail itself of consultants beyond the Ad Hoc Committee.

4. We agree with the intent of this conclusion, but it is not practical since there are not enough members of NCCB of Hispanic origins to cover each of the many NCCB committees.

5. We agree that it would be advantageous to have more Spanish-speaking bishops in the Church in the United States. However, this is a very complex matter and beyond our competence as a committee. Recommendations for candidates to the episcopacy come from the ecclesiastical provinces and go to the Holy See. However, we would be willing to ask the bishops in the provinces and the NCCB Committee on the Selection of Bishops to consider carefully the question of a greater number of bishops from among the Spanish-speaking. In their private consultations, the bishops could specifically ask for the names of priests of Hispanic origin. It should be pointed out, however, that use of any quota system to determine how many Spanish-speaking bishops there should be is not feasible, since the matter depends on the availability of qualified candidates and other factors.

6. The Committee is keenly aware of the need for priority to be given to this apostolate and that means should be found for providing the needed

funding. The Committee is also aware of the financial assistance presently being given to the Spanish-speaking from the national level. For example, almost half of the 1971 disbursements of the Campaign for Human Development went towards projects for the Spanish-speaking. In 1972, the amount was again quite large. Approximately one-half of the budget of the USCC Division for Migration and Refugee Services goes to help Spanish-speaking people. The USCC, through the help of ABCM [American Board of Catholic Missions], provides $250,000 to the Division for the Spanish-speaking.

7. We agree that a national pastoral institute for the Spanish-speaking would be worthwhile. We recommend that the Mexican American Cultural Center of San Antonio, Texas, become a pilot project and that the pertinent NCCB/USCC offices work closely with the Center. With regard to funding, the Conference is not a funding agency and has no money available for this purpose. However, if USCC responsibility for the regional offices for the Spanish-speaking ceases according to the present plan, we recommend that some of the funds from the ABCM designated for the regional offices be made available to the Center for its work.

8. Regarding a national seminary for the Spanish-speaking, further study is being done by the NCCB Committee on Priestly Formation. A special subcommittee has been set up for this purpose. The subcommittee will be making recommendations regarding the training of Spanish-speaking priests and the points raised in this recommendation.

9. In keeping with the principle of subsidiarity, the Committee believes that the regional offices should be administered and supported by the regions themselves. Attempts to administer the regional offices from Washington have proven to be less than successful. The NCCB/USCC Committee on Research, Plans and Programs has declined to phase out USCC responsibility for the regional offices by December 31, 1973. This Committee recommends to the dioceses that consideration be given to the need for regional offices administered locally or regionally. In order to help with the establishment and operation of these offices, we recommend that the American Board of Catholic Missions consider assisting with the funding where the dioceses of a region want such an office and where the dioceses involved may have difficulty providing all the necessary funds.

This Committee is aware that the Committee on Social Development and World Peace intends to resubmit the question of regional offices for the Spanish-speaking to the Administrative Board for inclusion on the agenda of the November 1973 meeting of the general body of bishops.

10. Regional Pastoral Encounters are valuable expressions of concern and they provide concrete plans for pastoral life in the regions. Again, the Committee sees the principal organizational thrust for these regional meetings as originating from the regions themselves. The Spanish-speaking division should continue to be a catalyst in helping the dioceses or the regions

regarding these Encounters. It is hoped that, in the future, more bishops will be able to attend.

11. Pastoral institutes for the Spanish-speaking could develop according to need. We consider the Mexican American Cultural Center as a pilot project which we support. However, we advise watching and learning from its success at this point. The Committee feels that the establishment of other institutes at this time would be premature.

12-18. The Committee has no competence in matters pertaining to the individual dioceses since the local churches must make their own decisions about such matters. However, we are willing to make recommendations to the ordinaries regarding the points raised by the Encounter.

In dioceses with a significant number of Spanish-speaking Catholics, it is the judgment of the Committee that there should be a diocesan director for the Spanish-speaking Apostolate, along the lines suggested in recommendation 12. Adequate consultation among the Spanish-speaking should take place so that the persons chosen for this important work will have the support of those whom they are to serve. The particular circumstances of the diocese must always be considered since variations will call for different solutions to problems. The Committee also recommends to the ordinaries of dioceses with large numbers of Spanish-speaking Catholics the consideration of the possibility of an episcopal vicar for the Spanish-speaking so that special care can be given to this apostolate. It is understood that such vicars would function within the limits outlined in *Christus Dominus,* p. 17, and *Ecclesiae Sanctae,* p. 14, no. 4. With regard to auxiliary bishops, the Committee refers to what was said above regarding recommendation 5.

Number 16 recommends a collegial group to collaborate with the diocesan director of the Spanish-speaking Apostolate. While a board of this type would be helpful, it would be either a part of the diocesan pastoral council or closely related to it so that the pastoral mission of the Church will be unified in the diocese.

The Committee agrees completely with the recommendation that sufficient personnel who are fluent in Spanish language and culture be available in church agencies. Much has already been accomplished in this regard since many priests, religious, and laity who are working with the Spanish-speaking have received adequate training in the Spanish language and culture. But we urge a careful reconsideration of the matter on the diocesan level to ensure that the Spanish-speaking are given necessary pastoral care. Language institutes such as that located at the Mexican American Cultural Center in San Antonio offer the type of training needed in this regard. A number of diocesan newspapers have sections in the Spanish language when there is a notable proportion of Spanish-speaking Catholics in the diocese. The Committee thinks that other dioceses with large numbers of Spanish-speaking should give consideration to adopting a similar policy so that all the diocesan communications media, including radio and television, will become more sensitive to the needs of the Spanish-speaking. If within a diocese or region where there are many Spanish-speaking, there could be all-Spanish newspapers, this would be an even more effective solution to the problem of communications.

19-22. Small groups of Christians who gather to discuss their faith, to pray together, to perform charitable works, and to relate to each other socially have always been a part of the fabric of the Church. We encourage the development of such groups with the understanding that they continue to relate to parish and diocesan life. *Comunidades de base* may be an excellent way for the Spanish-speaking people to express their linguistic, cultural, and religious identity.

Number 20 speaks of church leaders for the local community. In addressing this question, we distinguish between lay and clerical leaders. The recruitment and formation of lay leaders may be done in a variety of ways to provide for the needs at the local level. There is much room for adaptation in this area. Regarding clerical leaders, more specific recommendations are needed. When made, they should be referred for study and evaluation to the NCCB Committee on Priestly Formation and Permanent Diaconate.

The Encounter recommended personal parishes as a form of local pastoral organizations for the Spanish-speaking. A personal parish is a worshiping community canonically established not on the basis of a certain territory, but rather on the basis of a certain group of people who have something in common. Personal parishes might be useful for the Spanish-speaking Apostolate. However, the matter of personal parishes is something that should be decided on the local level since circumstances vary widely from diocese to diocese. The Committee believes that *Comunidades de base* are able to flourish within the framework of national and territorial parishes and that personal parishes are not generally essential to this growth.

23. Our thought regarding more Spanish-speaking bishops was covered earlier under number 5.

24-25. Alternative patterns for formation of candidates to the priesthood would need study by the NCCB Committee on Priestly Formation. If more specific suggestions are made in this regard, they will be referred to that Committee. We agree that the formation of Spanish-speaking candidates, as well as candidates who will be serving the Spanish-speaking, should be bilingual and bicultural. The Mexican American Cultural Center has a capacity for providing for these needs. The Josephinum Seminary in Worthington, Ohio, has also developed a program for this purpose. . . .

41-46. The Committee is in general agreement with the suggestions made in this part of the Encounter. Clergy and religious who are not Spanish-speaking themselves, but who are working within Spanish-speaking communities, should have a missionary spirit and should attempt to familiarize themselves with the language and culture of the people among whom they are working. We urge all priests, young and old, to continue their formation and training so that they will be more effective in their ministry to the Spanish-speaking. The Mexican American Cultural Center in San Antonio provides for training programs which will be helpful in this process of continuing education.

We agree with the principal concern expressed in number 45 that adequate compensation and benefits should be given to all clergy working within the dioceses. Justice and fairness should be extended to every person in this ministry.

We are convinced that seminarians who will be working with the Spanish-speaking people should receive adequate training in the Spanish language and culture. Indeed all candidates for the priesthood in the United States must be made keenly aware of the problems confronting Spanish-speaking Americans.

47-48. The training of lay leaders who will assist in the development of apostolic programs is very important. We urge that the dioceses and regions involve the laity in existing training programs and urge the establishment of other training programs to respond to existing needs. The Committee again points to the value of the Mexican American Cultural Center as a place for the training of lay leaders.

49-54. The Committee believes that it would be counterproductive at this time to establish a national secretariat for the Spanish liturgy since such a secretariat would detract from the unity of the Church in this country. Another person has been added to the NCCB Secretariat for the Liturgy, however, and this development gives the secretariat a greater capacity for expanding its concern in the area of the Spanish-speaking. The secretariat, which is vitally interested in the matter, will work closely with the Mexican American Cultural Center's Institute of Religion and Culture in those areas in which liturgy is involved. The Committee agrees that the Secretariat should do all it can to be sensitized to the needs of the Spanish-speaking. The Ad Hoc Committee will discuss with the Bishops' Committee on the Liturgy and the secretariat how this can be accomplished. The recommendations found in this section are being referred to the Committee on the Liturgy for further study.

The Committee agrees with the concern raised in 4 regarding the right of all the faithful to access and use of Church buildings at convenient and appropriate times. Church facilities should be made available to Spanish-speaking groups for special liturgical celebrations.

55-59. The Committee agrees that greater attention needs to be given to the religious education of the Spanish-speaking community, both in terms of existing programs and possible new ones. We urge close cooperation between the Spanish-speaking religious educators and the USCC Division for Religious Education—CCD [Confraternity of Christian Doctrine]. The USCC Division has already responded to these recommendations and has agreed to the following:

1. In order to establish communication between the USCC Division and the Spanish-speaking community, Father Virgilio Elizondo, the President of the Mexican American Cultural Center in San Antonio, has been appointed to the editorial board of the *Living Light,* the journal of the Division for Religious Education.

2. Articles, research, and documentation reflecting catechesis within the Spanish-speaking communities consistent with the nature of the *Living Light* can be incorporated into this journal.

3. News program items can be included in the newsletter of the Division to the diocesan directors, *Nexus.*

4. The National Conference of Diocesan Directors for Religious Education–CCD can be asked to explore, with the diocesan directors of religious education–CCD in the 30 dioceses where Spanish-speaking Catholics form at least 35 percent of the Catholic population, what can be done to improve the catechetical effort toward Spanish-speaking Catholics in these dioceses.

5. Articles reflecting programs on the nature of adult catechesis within Spanish-speaking communities consistent with the nature of a new digest being published by the division, *Focus on Adults—A Digest,* can be included.

6. REX, the employment service of the division, may be expanded to accommodate religious educators within the Spanish-speaking communities.

The Committee urges the dioceses to make sufficient funds available for the religious education of all ages. . . .

The Report of the Ad Hoc Committee (above) was not the final word on Encounter requests. For instance, although the need of elevating the USCC Division for the Spanish-speaking to the status of a secretariat was discounted (see no. 1, p. 202), just such a change was forthcoming. The erection of regional centers proved to be a lasting contribution, while recommendations 12-18 regarding the local churches reflect the caution of the NCCB in accepting the new vision of the Encounter. In the same light, responses 19-22 on national and personal parishes are interesting. (The sections on the permanent diaconate and Catholic schools have been omitted.) As can be seen, MACC is cited repeatedly as the paradigm for future development.

In New York there were not a few complications in the attempts to make archdiocesan policy conform to these new guidelines. In the selection that follows, Ana María Díaz Ramírez, former administrative coordinator for Father Stern's Spanish-speaking Apostolate Office, details the conflicts that ensued, including the personal and political factors leading to Stern's resignation.

Ana María Díaz Ramírez was born in Moca, Puerto Rico, in 1942, and migrated with her family to the Upper West Side of Manhattan in 1953. She studied with the Maryknoll Sisters as a novice, but returned to Puerto Rico in 1965 to enter the Sisters of Fatima, a native Puerto Rican religious community. In 1969 she returned to New York and the lay state to work in the Spanish Apostolate Office under Father Stern. After her tenure at the archdiocese, she went to an executive post in Spanish-language catechetics and communications with the United Methodist Church. In 1977 she received a fellowship in Urban and Religious Sociology at Fordham University, where she is presently completing her doctoral studies.

56. The Life, Passion, and Death of the Spanish-speaking Apostolate of the Archdiocese of New York

Ana María Díaz Ramírez

Written in 1973 and first published here. Trans. A.M.S.A.

The archdiocesan office to attend to the needs of the Spanish-speaking people of the Archdiocese of New York was founded in 1953 as a response to a basic pastoral need of the city's Hispanic population, especially the Puerto Rican sector. In 1949 a study revealed that 50 percent of the resident Puerto Ricans in the city were married in Protestant churches and only 27 percent in the Catholic church; while on the island of Puerto Rico, 14 percent were married in Protestant churches and 61 percent in Catholic ceremonies. (Fitzpatrick, *Puerto Rican Americans,* Englewood Cliffs, N.J.: Prentice-Hall, 1971, pp. 87ff.). The office was created as a pastoral tool to deal with the Puerto Rican people and the Hispano in general, so that they would return to the Catholic community in which they had been reared. After approximately sixteen years of service from three coordinators—Monsignors Connolly, Wilson, and Fox—Father Robert L. Stern was named by Cardinal Cooke as director of the office. From the moment his appointment was known in the community, the Hispano people noted that this time it was not a monsignor who was named to the office, so that the appointment made by Cardinal Cooke downgraded the importance of the office.

For his part, Father Stern started to work with a great deal of enthusiasm at the restructuring of the office and in making new projections for the future. He had refused other posts, thinking that he could best fulfill his ministry by serving the Hispano people of the archdiocese. Certainly he was gifted enough to bring such a task to a happy conclusion if the proper ecclesiastical authorities had given him their support instead of opposing his efforts. Father Stern was a relatively young person for his post, full of vigor, with a clear vision and exceptional intellectual capability. Moreover, he was dedicated, hard-working, and, as far as the pastoral mission of the church was concerned, very human and progressive. From the beginning, he emphasized "apostolate," that is, the mission of the archdiocese among Hispanos. Thus the office changed its name from "Spanish Catholic Action" to the "Office of the Spanish-speaking Apostolate," signifying a change in mentality and a wider vision. The first effort of the office under Father Stern was focused on the training and formation of leaders within the community, who in turn would be able to relate effectively to the people. Hence he gave great emphasis to the lay apostolate. On the other hand, Father Stern proposed using the existing resources of the church institutions for the benefit of the Hispano people. Within his own office he secured the service of Puerto Rican persons and of Spanish-speaking lay persons, religious, and priests.

When Father Stern began his task at the Spanish Apostolate he had only one person from Monsignor Fox's staff. By April 1970 the office had its director (Father Stern), a Puerto Rican laywoman as secretary, a typist, an assistant director, a coordinator of communications, and a priest coordinator of the youth ministry. All of these persons worked fulltime. The office also counted on the volunteer services of another priest, who dedicated two days a week to planning and research, and a Puerto Rican priest in charge of the coordination of the summer language and Spanish culture program at the Institute of Intercultural Communications at Ponce's Catholic University of Puerto Rico and other centers in New York. In the first year, eleven new committees were formed: Liturgy Committee; Catechetical Committee; Lay Apostolate Committee; Family Apostolate Committee; Committee for the Cursillo Movement; Committee for Youth Ministry; Committee for Community Relations; Committee for Ecumenical Relations; Media and Communications Committee; Priests' Committee; and Committee for Religious Women.

One or more representatives of each committee, together with the director of the office and his secretary, formed the Coordinators Committee.

Moreover, the office had under its care (1) the Migrant Ministry, (2) the Spanish Center in Cornwall, New York, including the supervision of its personnel—the Oblate Sisters of the Most Holy Redeemer—who worked directly with the people in catechetics and social work, (3) St. Joseph's Cursillo Center, (4) a new branch of the Dunwoodie Seminary, projected in January 1970, which began that October to orient future priests regarding Hispano culture and language, (5) the Linguistic Institute during the summer in Ponce, (6) the well-known San Juan Fiesta, and (7) a new summer program that brought seminarians from the Dominican Republic for pastoral experience in New York. . . .

During Father Stern's term of office, the Cursillo was revised, and a new constitution was structured for the secretariat. In the field of family apostolate, the Christian Family Movement was formed with its secretariat. Also, a lay program of formation, Luz y Vida, was begun. The Legion of Mary and its secretariat was likewise reorganized. The School of Leaders in the Cursillo movement was continued and a Pastoral Institute was founded for lay persons, while the Linguistic Institute at Cardinal Hayes High School and its five regional centers continued. . . .

These programs were successfully managed after a lot of effort, work, meetings, and interviews with the vicar-general, to whom Father Stern was directly responsible. Notwithstanding, when Father Stern submitted his new budget for 1970, he met with various obstacles from his superiors and the administrators of the archdiocese. These were the same obstacles he had already encountered each time he proposed adding a new staff person to the office in order to accomplish and adequately satisfy the increasing volume of work that all these activities demanded. They were the same obstacles that he had to face when he asked for more office machines and materials for his work. There seemed to be no comprehension of the fact that the office kept growing rapidly only because it had to serve the pastoral and apostolic needs of the leadership of more than half (55%) of the New York Catholic population. . . .

For one reason or another, all Father Stern's efforts to expand the office and its service to Hispanos met with opposition from those "on high. . . ."

It is sad to accept the ugly truth that, even with our church, politics has a wide-open field; that it plays games with the best and most noble interests and aspirations of the Christian people; that the dignity of the person as child of God is downgraded, and more importance and priority are given to personal pettiness, to protocol, to appearances, and to little bits of money here and there. Is not the genuine mission of the church and its ministers to carry Christ and his gospel to humankind, cost what it may?

Certainly, the Office of the Spanish-speaking Apostolate of the Archdiocese of New York did not follow through with the expansion of services. Instead the office was devastated. All of the programs that Father Stern had begun and that had been successful in putting his office in direct contact with the people were taken away, little by little. Instead of bringing on staff persons from the community, as had been done up till then and was expected to continue, the office lost those which it had. Some left because they could no longer stand what was happening, others because they were dismissed. Thus the office began to lose prestige, power, force, and a good number of dedicated workers and leaders who had a lot to offer in the development of the office and the Spanish-speaking community. Meanwhile, programs were transferred to other Archdiocesan administrative offices.

The lay person in charge of Press, Radio and Television was fired.[1] In his place an extra-diocesan priest was hired, who had voluntarily come to the office a few hours two days each week.[2] Following the order of Monsignor Mahoney (the vicar-general), in December of 1971 after the rejection of the office budget, this priest and his secretary were assigned to the Office of Communications, under the direction of Monsignor Clark, ex-secretary of Cardinal Cooke. Also transferred from Father Stern's office was the translator (Ms. Díaz Ramírez), who had served until then as private secretary to the director, as translator, and as administrative coordinator of the office.

As far as the Liturgical Committee was concerned, it never was able to function well since the Diocesan Liturgical Commission interfered with its decisions and chose norms which only benefited the English-speaking people, oblivious of the logical conclusion that the Hispano people have special characteristics even in worship. No initiative was deemed licit or possible without first consulting and obtaining approbation from the Archdiocesan Liturgical Commission. . . .[3] Catechetics ran into the same luck, and at last was given over to the CCD Office. The Community Relations Committee was obliged to dissolve, due to lack of personnel in the office. When the lay person in charge of Press, Radio and Television was dismissed, the ecumenical relations he had established were also suspended, since the new coordinator of communications under Monsignor Clark did not wish to assume such responsibility. In this way the television and radio programs such as Face to Face in the World of Religion, the Religion News Commentary, the Ecumenical Supper, and the Midnight Mass[4] were lost. The group of priests and religious women lost interest. . . . Sometime later two associations were begun, one for Hispano priests and the other for Hispano religious women.[5] Nonetheless, the association for Hispano priests began outside the Spanish Apostolate and had nothing to do with the archdiocese; the association for Hispano religious women . . . is under the direction of the vicar for religious, not under the Spanish-speaking Apostolate.

To sum up: Father Stern wanted to expand the office; his budget was not approved. Father Stern wanted to expand services to the Hispano community; his staff was cut. Father Stern gave the services of his secretary, administrator, and translator to the Communications Office at the insistence of Monsignor Mahoney, and the Communications Office dismissed her without

1. The lay person in charge of Press, Radio and Television was Angel Pérez, a gifted Spaniard who had worked with Monsignor Fox in the office and in the Summer in the City program.

2. When Angel Pérez was dismissed, José L. Alvarez, a priest who had recently arrived from Spain, was hired. He later became the president of the Comité Pastoral del Noreste.

3. Hispano representation on the Liturgical Commission was achieved in 1973 after Stern had resigned his office.

4. The televised Puerto Rican Liturgy from New York, which gave members of different parishes an opportunity for direct participation every year, was replaced with the Spanish television production of the Pope's mass from Rome.

5. The association for Hispano priests begun at this time was ASH (Asociación de Sacerdotes Hispanos); the association for Hispano religious women was Las Hermanas of the East Coast.

consulting either her or Father Stern about the cause of the dismissal. Father Stern began a special program in Dunwoodie Seminary in language, culture, and pastoral ministry to Hispanos, and the seminary was put in charge of it even though nobody at the seminary was prepared for such a task. Father Stern tried to employ Puerto Rican priests, and he as well as they met with a lot of difficulties; as a result, neither Father Stern nor the four Puerto Rican priests presently work in the office. Father Stern tried to coordinate the Institute of Intercultural Communications more effectively; the cardinal insisted that the institute was not the responsibility of the office and passed it over to the supervision of the Catholic University of Puerto Rico. Father Stern tried to improve the Migrant Ministry, seeking the naming of a diocesan priest[6] to this post and a new religious congregation[7] to help him; but in the first months, the archdiocese irresponsibly did not pay either the priest or the religious, forcing them to beg for voluntary contributions.

Father Stern and the members of the Office of the Spanish-speaking Apostolate tried to reach the people through programs which were always oriented to the community. Now, however, Father Stern is openly accused in the official Catholic archdiocesan publication, *The Catholic News*, of having failed to have and maintain contact with the Spanish-speaking people—and this is the reason given for the new appointment of a vice-chancellor, who has lived out of the country for the past three years.

Father Stern is known to be responsible for the Pastoral Encounters celebrated in St. Joseph Seminary and at the Convent of Mary Reparatrix, where priests, religious, and lay people were invited. It is known that the conclusions of these Encounters[8] did not flatter the hierarchy of New York or its pastor, the cardinal. It is also known that the cardinal showed himself very upset with the result of these Encounters. When the commission to the cardinal—a group of lay persons which came as a direct result from these Encounters—went to see him with their requests, he accused Father Stern, in the presence of the group, of working against him and of being disloyal. According to the cardinal, Father Stern was using his money on Encounters to agitate against him. It is known that the cardinal ignored the requests. Likewise, Monsignor Mahoney declared that the request for a Spanish-speaking bishop to serve the Hispano people was impossible to grant because no appointment was likely at that time. Nonetheless, the same Monsignor

6. Father Neil Graham was named; previously a Spanish priest, Jesús Iriondo, had performed these duties.

7. As a result of friction in the Spanish-speaking Apostolate Office and within their own religious congregation, the Oblate Sisters of the Most Holy Redeemer ceased working for the office and the Migrant Ministry. They disbanded their religious community, although some continued to live together and work as lay persons in the community, and eventually in the office itself.

8. The conclusions from the First National Hispano Pastoral Encounter in Washington were similar to those of the New York-based Encounters. Neither was very flattering to the Archdiocese of New York.

Mahoney was named bishop just a little bit later, and not to serve the Spanish people. Finally, when Father Stern told the press, through the *Daily News*, the reason for his resignation, declaring that he could not count on the support or the confidence of his superiors, the Spanish-speaking director of the Office of Communications refused to give any information. Through fear of "those on high" he was satisfied to transfer the call from the newspaper to the Central Office under Monsignor Clark, knowing full well that it would serve to stifle the complaints of Father Stern and would offer the English-speaking hierarchy a chance to excuse itself for a lack of vision and true interest in the Spanish Office and the Hispano community.[9] Upon receiving the telephone call, Monsignor Clark responded: "We have no comment for now: at noon we will have a statement." Sure enough, at noon, without anyone knowing how they were able to move so quickly, they had named a vice-chancellor for Spanish-speaking affairs, and a press release was ready with the announcement. Nonetheless, even Father Stern, who was in his office, was not notified of the new appointment, either before or after. He had to find out over the radio. Five days later it was recommended that Father Stern leave the country and go to Rome to study a pastoral course. (From Rome to here it is difficult to hear the voice of a person who has little desire left for speaking out!)

At present, it seems that the only program of the Spanish-speaking Aposto-late which interests the cardinal is the Fiesta of San Juan. We ask, "Why?" Could it be that he wishes to speak again to the Puerto Rican and Hispano people about how much he loves them and what great appreciation he has for them? Actions speak more loudly than words. What do the Hispano people need? A San Juan Fiesta, one day a year and a few beautiful words pronounced with a perfect English accent? Or a little bit more—not of Charity—but of JUSTICE? The response ought to be given by the Hispano people of New York.

9. The person in charge of Spanish Communications was Father José Luis Alvarez.

CHAPTER TEN

THE PASTORALIST LEADERSHIP

The growth and development of the Hispano church after June 1972 was largely managed by those of a pastoralist orientation. The conceptual framework articulated by Elizondo gave new meaning to words like "pluralism" and "liberation." For his part, Bishop Flores enjoyed national prominence that enabled him to sail into new areas regarding ecumenism and questions of international justice. But in addition to these leading *pensadores* of the emerging Hispano church, new faces and new voices made their presence felt. Catechetics and political activism touched the consciousness of Hispano pastoralists from Los Angeles to New York.

The following is an excerpt from Chapter Seven of the book *Christianity and Culture,* written by Virgilio Elizondo. The explanation of oppression and colonization is described in theological as well as anthropological terms. Of particular importance is Elizondo's awareness of structures.

57. Conquered . . . Colonized . . . Oppressed

Virgilio P. Elizondo

From Elizondo, Christianity and Culture *(Huntington, Ind.: Our Sunday Visitor Press, 1975), pp. 129-130, 142-148. Used by permission.*

STRUCTURAL OPPRESSION

The oppression of the Spanish-speaking peoples of the United States is a historical fact. In Puerto Rico, Florida, California, Texas, and New Mexico, they have been abused and neglected; this treatment continues today. These lands have been conquered by the U.S., and colonized by people with customs and value systems from the eastern part of the country. . . .

214

. . . This chapter presents some of the factors in United States society that perpetuate this oppression. Because our economic, political, educational, social, and religious structures are organized for and directed by English-speaking citizens, these structures often cause suffering to bilingual citizens. I wish to make clear that not everyone who is a part of these structures is a conscious oppressor, nor does this work place conscious guilt on all of the English-speaking citizens. I hope to challenge people of good will to become aware of injustice and to struggle against it. . . .

CHARACTERISTICS OF THE DIALECTIC OF OPPRESSED AND OPPRESSOR

The developed-oppressed is forced to choose between being wholly himself and being divided; between ejecting the oppressor within and not ejecting him; between being a spectator and being where the action is; between speaking out his real feelings and remaining silent. He is powerless to transform the world. How can the oppressed, as a divided, unauthentic human being, participate in developing the pedagogy of his own liberation?

The Second Efforts: Liberation

Only as the oppressed begins to discover himself as the host of the inhuman oppressive society can he begin to contribute to the midwifery of his own liberating pedagogy. True liberation is a childbirth, and as with every childbirth, it will be a painful one. The man who emerges is a new man: not oppressor, not developed-oppressed, not oppressed, but truly a new man.

The liberation process begins when the oppressed becomes aware of his situation, and in this very awakening the world of the oppressor, with all its unjust structures, is unveiled. Mob violence never happens unless it has been preceded by a long history of institutionalized violence that has become respectable. When the oppressed begins to speak out and to disclose to the general public the continuing violence of many of the accepted institutions of society, the gestation process of liberation begins. As the oppressed awakens and commits himself to the task of transforming society, he begins to be the teacher, both of the oppressor and of the oppressed themselves. This is *the pedagogy of the oppressed.*

Characteristics of the Oppressed

Fatalism—*Hágase la voluntad de Dios*—is a characteristic of the oppressed and is often seen by the outsider as docility. The peasants have been domesticated. The only way for the oppressed to understand his lot of suffering is to convince himself that it is the will of God. As long as Christian missioners preach the "will of God" as a canonization of the status quo and fail to preach a strong denunciation of sin with all its oppressive circumstances, and do not announce the gospel of the new order, they will continue to be major contributors to oppression.

Hostility toward their own is often seen in the oppressed group. Suffering under the misery of the existing order and not being able to act against it without paying the price of their lives, they often manifest a type of horizontal violence, striking out at their closest relatives and friends for the pettiest of reasons. They will often take out their frustrations on those who are the closest to them. A man cannot kick out against the police or others who oppress him, so he takes it out on his own people. In San Antonio, Texas, 70% of the crimes committed in the poor Spanish-speaking areas take place among relatives and friends. This does not destroy the strong family unity, but rather is a contradiction, a forced reaction to the lived oppression. This hostility will also be apparent in efforts to keep comrades from advancement; it seems better to destroy one another than to help one another.

This hostility will also be taken out on those who have done the most for them; if someone wants to work with an oppressed group, he must learn very quickly to *depersonalize insults.* Anger and frustration will often be taken out on that person, not because the oppressed hates him, but precisely because that person is loved and thus is the only one the oppressed can take it out on. This sounds like a contradiction, *pero así es la vida.*

An irresistible attraction towards the oppressor also exists, a deep alienation coupled with the irresistible attraction to become like the oppressor at any cost. This is especially prevalent in the middle-class oppressed, who yearns to become like the oppressor and defend the ways of the oppressor at all cost. After all, it has cost him much to enter his world, even though he is still rejected by the dominant society.

Self-depreciation is another characteristic. Having become accustomed to hearing himself referred to as "good for nothing, lazy, unproductive," the person will say this of himself. Such a negative attitude is reinforced by movies, TV, and novels. When a person keeps hearing that he is good for nothing—*no sirve para nada*—this will be the only self he can know, for man knows himself only as reflected by others. This negative image of himself, which is forced on him by the oppressor, will lead to a deep self-depreciation.

The oppressed will live with a strong sense of inferiority. It seems to him that only the oppressor knows the right way of doing things and only the oppressor is smart enough to actually do them. In whatever project he begins, he starts with the great handicap of inferiority.

Characteristics of the Liberated-Oppressed

It may sound like a contradiction to speak about the "liberated-oppressed." In actuality the most oppressive societies always have a small group of authentically free people. They suffer the pains and abuses of the oppressor society; they, however, do not give in to the oppressor. They are sufficiently developed; at the same time these people remain somewhat poor (at least in the sense of material possessions); but they do not live in dehumanizing poverty and filth. In the southwestern United States are many of these people who, by U.S. standards, are considered middle-class or poor. They maintain their homes, jobs or small businesses, and educate their children. And they maintain their identity. They have a certain security and pride in who they are, knowing their past, appreciating their system of values, being happy and satisfied with what they have, and not joining the rat race of constantly trying to have more and to make more money.

Unlike the developed-oppressed, they do not lose their identity or cultural ties. On the contrary, they maintain their language, [and pass] on to their children a healthy pride in their history and in their identity through songs, poetry, art, and oral traditions. They accept many of the ways of the oppressor society as "working necessities" in order to subsist within the dominant society. But they neither aspire to become like the oppressor nor suffer the psychological problems of a dual existence. This is not to say that they do not suffer, for they do experience the insults and the stereotypes imposed by the dominant society.

In the most oppressive societies, a small group usually remains free; they are in the oppressed group, but they remain free in spite of all the oppressive structures. They maintain that inner freedom which no society, liberating or oppressive, can of itself give to an individual. This is the interior freedom of the spirit. They join the system sufficiently, but never completely sell out to it. They join it sufficiently to be identified with it (and therefore the system is willing to listen to them), but are never total members. They maintain their unique identity while entering into the structures of the other.

These free persons work quietly from within to bring change. They work gradually through the structures to destroy oppressive elements and bring about change. They become educated in the ways and vocabulary of the structures; thus they are able to speak about the oppression to those within the oppressive structures in ways that will be understood. When the "radical noisemakers" (who are always necessary to awaken the masses to the fact of oppression) have done their part, those awakened sincere members of the oppressor group will be able to work with the liberated oppressed to bring about a new society.

Qualities of the Oppressor-Liberator

A time comes when certain members of the oppressor group—normally good people who had never realized they were oppressors—awaken to the fact of oppression. To awaken and to stay uninvolved is a sin; to see evil and to allow it to continue is itself evil. Some of the awakened members of the oppressor group will *join* the oppressed in their struggle. Their role will be a fundamental one as it has been throughout history. As they cease to be exploiters or indifferent spectators or simply the heirs of exploitation and move to the side of the exploited, they almost always bring with them the marks of their origin: their prejudices and their deformations, which include a lack of confidence in the ability of the oppressed to think, to desire, and to know. The converts to the struggle for liberation truly want to transform the unjust order, but because of their background they believe that *they* must be the executors of the transformation. Conversion to the oppressed requires a profound rebirth. Those who authentically commit themselves to the people must re-examine themselves constantly. The qualities of a true oppressor-liberator, one who truly wants to enter into the struggle for liberation, are trust of the oppressed and the ability to learn from them.

Those who are committed to the oppressed must have a willingness to trust the people's power to think, to know what they want, to seek their own destiny. The oppressed must be trusted enough to allow them to make some mistakes and gradually to learn how to analyze their own situation. They will never learn as long as someone else tries to do it for them; they must be trusted even when human instincts push the missioner to "do it for them just once more." They must be trusted, even when they seem incapable, as the Lord trusted His followers.

The poor are the teachers, and one must be willing to learn from the needs and aspirations of the poor. Whoever wants to work with the oppressed and the poor must learn to be a good listener. To be willing to learn from the poor is already *the first proclamation of the Gospel,* because learning from someone is a very existential way of telling him that he is important and has something to offer. This affirmation of the fundamental dignity of the person is the beginning of rebirth unto liberation and salvation. To enter into true dialogue with those who have been rejected is to begin treating them as equals, and only from a position of equality can the liberation process make true progress.

The missioner must have a willingness to suffer with those he works with. The poor do not want pity from anyone, for it can be destructive. They do want compassion, someone to share their suffering and struggle so that from within the two may begin to work together for the liberation of both.

The poor are tired of having people want to do things for them; this can be dehumanizing. They are interested in having others do with them the things the poor themselves are convinced need to be done. As the new society begins to form, many persons are needed to help in its construction. Outsiders who want to join in the dialoguing process are most welcome, but outsiders who want to come in with their agendas, their answers, their way of doing things will turn out to be new oppressors; they are not welcome. The poor and the oppressed do not have a monopoly on the answers and the right way of doing things, but neither do the others; this is not a question of either/or, but one of true dialogue, an authentic search in which the oppressed and the oppressor-liberators join as equals in a true dialogue through which the correct way will gradually emerge.

A willingness to be patient is most important. Many times people are used to getting quick results. Often the poor do not know the many things that those in the establishment take for granted—the politics involved, the standard procedure to follow, the right person to see, the proper agency to deal with, and so forth. The learning process is not an easy one, and much patience and tolerance is needed. One of the constant temptations of the oppressor-liberator will be to do things for the oppressed.

As we have said, those who want to work with the oppressed must learn to depersonalize hurt. When there are frustrations and alienation, people tend to take it out on those closest to them: this also takes place in the apostolate. Often the many frustrations will be taken out on those who are the closest to the oppressed, doing the most for them. The oppressor-liberator must learn that this is actually a sign of love, and is not an insult. It is a sad human phenomenon that people often take out their frustrations on those they love the most. It is not right, but it is the way people react. Learning to depersonalize hurt will be an asset to all who are committed to the process of liberation.

The Role and the Need for the Oppressor-Liberator

The awakened oppressor's role is an essential one, for people are creative of one another. A man may tell himself that he is important and respectable, but until the other sees him as important and worthy of human dignity, he will not believe this. The main role of one who comes to work in the process of liberation is to bring out constantly and in diverse ways the beauty, greatness and dignity of the poor and oppressed. Through this activity, he will contribute to the creation of a new man through the image he helps to bring out and thus to the creation of a new society of truly equal but different human beings. . . .

The following is excerpted from a speech given by Bishop Patricio Flores before the Assembly of the National Council of Churches in Dallas in November 1972.

The bishop's talk shows the awareness of personal suffering and identification with Latin America that combine to create a truly militant and prophetic statement.

58. The Church Must Liberate

Bishop Patricio Flores

From Address to the Assembly of the National Council of Churches, Dallas, Texas, November 1972. Used by permission.

"He has sent me to bring the good news to the poor . . . to proclaim liberation to the prisoners . . . to set at liberty the oppressed" (Lk. 4:18).

Thus, at the outset, after baptism and sacrifice in the desert, Jesus took the words of Isaiah to define his public ministry—a ministry of liberation. At the end of his life, Jesus commissioned us, you and me, his church, to carry on his very work when he said: "As the Father has sent me, I also send you . . ." (Jn. 20:21).

In keeping with this ministry, in the definition of the ecumenical movement given by Dr. Philip Potter, the General Secretary of the World Council of Churches, in his *Christian Century* interviews of Aug. 30, "We cannot speak of the unity of the church without speaking of the unity of mankind. We cannot speak of the church's mission to proclaim the gospel of Jesus Christ without seeing that that gospel has political implications. We cannot speak about renewal of persons, groups and churches without facing the issues of power and authority, or of service without coming to terms with the struggle for justice—with the problem of violence and nonviolence."

I am of a migrant worker family. I worked in the fields with my family. With my family I suffered. My faith sustained me while my countrymen held me down. My faith sustained me while church people oppressed me. The way I look on the world, the insights I have, the service I give have undoubtedly been shaped by the fortune of my experience as a Mexican American migrant worker. The gospel of Jesus liberated me and requires me to accept Jesus' definition of the ministry as my own.

Have you read the text of the film strip we will be viewing? Did you read the issue paper on the United States and South Africa? No need to review it for you. How disgusting is the truth of our sin against mankind when it is laid so clearly before us. For how long will the people of the church permit this country, the interlocking forces of government and the economy, to imprison, to kill, to pillage and rape the resources of other lands and other peoples? For how long will the people of the church permit this country and permit themselves to pit white against black, Anglo against Mexican, white against Indian, affluent and comfortable against the imprisoned and the hungry, here in our own United States?

I do not mean to belittle the tiny prophetic voice of churchmanship when I point to the reality of sin among professing Christians. But I do mean to ask (as I must continually ask myself) what is wrong with churchmanship, what is wrong with the way we preach the gospel, that the liberating message does not get through? What is the responsibility of churchmanship for the sins of the members of the church?

The present condition of man must be unacceptable to the Christian. I do not refer simply to poverty or to bombs dropping in Vietnam. It is the very division of man into the affluent and the poor which is puzzling. It is the very way we permit our social systems to rob natural resources and labor from one part of the world to benefit a tiny proportion of the world's population which is questionable.

LIBERATION MINISTRY

We may shed tears at the murders at Southern University in Louisiana, at the sight of a child screaming from napalm burns, at the $80 annual income of a family in one of the nations of Latin America. Often we give thanks for our blessings and say: "All the rest is just too complex to deal with." We permit the injustice which imprisons both the affluent and the poor to go on and on.

Justice, liberation, self-development. The task of the Christian is all of these, but the unique task of the church is liberation. The task of the church is liberation whether it is from the imprisoning psychology of the affluent and acquisitive and the social systems by which they keep their dominance, or liberation from the debilitating hopelessness felt by those who at the beginning of a day cannot see a way to feed their children in the evening.

The ministry of Jesus was one of liberation! It is to the freeing of man from the prison of his own building—to his conversion—which the gospel speaks. The gospel demands a conversion which moves a man or a woman to do justice, to engage in their own task of self-development and the self-development of their own people. The task of the church is to make conversion possible, by trying to define what conversion means.

There is no conversion to Jesus which does not liberate man to do justice or to seek self-development. Conversion and dominance are incompatible. Conversion and war are incompatible. Conversion and imposed racial separation are incompatible.

It is not sufficient to weep for the priest who is martyred by the regime in Brazil, without acting to prevent the complicity of the United States of America in that act of murder. It is not sufficient to be shocked at the sight of that little girl screaming with napalm burns as she flees her village, without acting not merely to bring an end to the bombing, but to the very selfishness of our country which brought us to Indochina in this manner in the first place.

It is not sufficient to negotiate or to vote for peace without accepting back into the country those who through discipline and strength of conscience saw the Vietnam war for the evil it was. There is nothing to forgive; amnesty is required for it was the judgment of the majority of us (we now have the courage to say) that was faulty. Any man who says that he can think of nothing more immoral than to grant amnesty in this situation has a grossly distorted sense of values.

Five social systems or movements stand out among many which pose such serious problems of social injustice that the church cannot ignore their implications; to wit:

1. The ordering of the world's economy around the welfare of those who live in the corporate states.

2. The military–industrial complex.

3. The present governance and consequent unresponsiveness of the corporate economy.

4. Western-dominated systems of education.

5. The present governance of the major audio-visual media.

The use of capital and the development of a corporate economy has without doubt produced great benefits for mankind. But it has become increasingly evident that large corporations reaching across national boundaries drain natural resources and labor from poor countries primarily for the benefit of a small proportion of affluent people in the world. A select few may live in ease and comfort and 90 percent of some nations are starving. People are held in virtual bondage in nations of Latin America, Africa and Asia by an unholy alliance of large corporations and big-power governments, so that the selfish desires of the affluent continue to be fed.

Such an ordering of a world economy is immoral and must be rejected and fought by the church. The system as we know it holds in bondage not only those who are exploited to maintain the flow of wealth largely in one direction, but it also holds in the bondage of unslaked thirst for goods and power and sense of superiority those who reap the benefits.

MILITARY GROWTH AND JOBS

General Eisenhower proved more a prophet than the church when he singled out the unholy alliance of the military and the industrial complex. One would have imagined that a sharp curtailment of the $30 billion the United States was spending on destruction in Vietnam might have resulted in a decreased budget for the Pentagon. But no. We are told Vietnam spending has been cut back some $20-27 billion, but the new Pentagon budget is even larger than before.

The dependence of our economy here at home on jobs connected with the spiral of military growth is nearly so great that people in the United States may soon become afraid to end war on this basis alone.

Military spending generates the sharp inflation suffered most by those who are poor, while the resulting profits flow through the corporate economy into the pocketbooks of the middle class who share in the ownership of the large corporations producing the goods of war.

Yet it is still the poor who go off to fight the wars. It is the poor who die at war, and those who return are poorer than before—jobless.

The Christian must say that war must end; not just the war in Indochina, but all war. If anyone is justified in engaging in armed conflict it is the poor and the oppressed of the world, not the affluent. War is evil and the Christian cannot support it. A world order based on big-power dominance serves, as history has taught us, to enslave the poor that the affluent may feel secure. Such an order is wrong and must be changed. It is a barrier to the liberation and development of man.

Some corporations headquartered in the United States have more employees overseas than the U.S. State Department. Some corporations, sopping natural resources out of developing countries, plot to overthrow governments seeking justice for their people. Typically when we speak of modern corporate life, we are speaking of companies where ownership is so diversified that corporate managers are really responsible to no one.

Our government has proved unable to regulate corporate life to produce for the benefit of all; indeed if one looks at the large corporation and its alliance with the military, or its behavior overseas, it is apparent that government and corporate managers are hand in glove; there is little to distinguish the behavior of one from another; they prop each other up. It seems that government exists to protect and enlarge opportunity for corporate wealth to grow. Even at home it is representatives of capital management who most often sit on and control the very regulatory agencies which were once designed to see that the corporation served society.

Some say the system is not perfect, but that it is the best ever devised by man. Well, it is not perfect. Man must do better, or the large corporation, managed by men shielded from public control, will otherwise be the imperialism of the twenty-first century.

The present governance of corporate life has proved it perpetuates greed and injustice, has proved that it cannot be responsive to humane values. The governance must be changed, so that the corporate economy serves all men, not just here at home, but throughout the world. Representatives of the people chosen by the people must control the future and behavior of the modern corporation.

If the judgments of the prophets of old were harsh and not very palatable to those to whom they were addressed, they were judgments which were needed. Some dismiss Ivan Illich as a prophet. But prophets are sent by the

Lord to be listened to. With crystal clarity Illich has demonstrated that the Western-dominated educational process serves to extend and perpetuate the ascendance of the affluent and holds the simple and the poor in bondage.

I do not mean to belittle the contribution made to education in my own state of Texas by citing serious shortcomings in the significant Report of the Governor's Committee on Public School Education entitled "The Challenge and the Chance," made to Governor John Connally in 1968. But listen to some excerpts from the first section on "Perspectives and Goals":

> Most Texans recognize the role of the public schools in building socially acceptable behavior. . . . But it is clear that traditional forms and methods have failed to equip the disadvantaged for constructive citizenship in modern complex society. That failure has contributed heavily to such crucial problems as delinquency, unemployment and soaring welfare costs.

EDUCATION: ACQUISITION'S HANDMAIDEN

Examples like this abound throughout the United States. Education in the West has become a handmaiden of corporate production, of a bourgeois society, of a society bent on acquisition. Western-dominated education imprisons the affluent in a psychology of acquisitiveness and exclusivity of moral vision, and at the same time perpetuates the dominance of the affluent over the poor.

The Bolivian peasant may have a lifetime income expectancy of some $2,400, while the white college graduate in the United States has an income expectancy of $270,000. Many U.S. students can tell you how sterile the system has become; but it is pursued nonetheless, apart from life experience, because it leads to an income 100 times that of someone else. And it perpetuates that difference.

The recent suit filed by a high school graduate charging that he got his diploma though he was taught to read only to the fifth-grade level points to but one symptom of the sickness we tolerate.

Education is important, can bring important benefits to man; but it must be shared in ways which are relevant to the needs of all men.

To Plato, Aristotle, Thomas Aquinas as well as to Whitehead and Dewey, education, as in the words of Paulo Freire of Brazil, now with the World Council of Churches, was "the practice of liberty." How imprisoning is a liberty which leaves one dominating others! "The word of God," said Freire, "is inviting me to recreate the world, not for my brothers' domination but for their liberation."

In recent years the growth of technology in radio and television has offered a marvelous opportunity for men to help each other become free and to develop. The impact of these media and the advancing technology around them has, in our country at least, become a dominant force shaping human values, often even supplanting the historical role of the family. But, because the media have developed and are governed by the motivation of profit tied to our peculiar kind of corporate economy, they have become part of a system which so easily warps human values and appeals to the weakness rather than the best in man.

My thesis, here also, is that the present governance of these media must be changed from one which largely ties what is offered in the way of public entertainment and education to marketability and sales of products.

Countless examples demonstrate the pit into which we have fallen. Two will suffice: First of all the weak nature of governmental regulation of public airways is demonstrated by almost constant industry dominance of the regulatory mechanism, another example of the present alliance between large corporate dominance and the management of our government. Second, we are increasingly faced with the problem of media financial losses because of the need to withdraw harmful advertising. It is unfortunate, of course, that most of us consider the advertising as only possibly harmful. The educational potential is too significant to let things go on as they are. (In this area the one serious church effort of which I am aware is that led by Dr. Everett Parker of the United Church of Christ.)

We do admire the declaration of the Evangelical Methodist Church in Bolivia, published in March 1970. In this marvelous document the church cited its willingness to cooperate with others, and with the government, in the liberation and development of the Bolivian man. But not uncritically.

For, as the Methodists of Bolivia said:

> Before all else our loyalty is to Jesus Christ and to his gospel, a whole gospel which is "for all men and for all of man." . . . The God whom we know in the Bible is a liberating God, a God who destroys myths and alienations, a God who intervenes in history in order to point out the way of justice and mercy. He is the God who liberates slaves, who causes empires to fall and raises up the oppressed. . . . A well-understood evangelization—the proclamation of the good news and the confrontation of man with the liberating gospel of Jesus Christ— initiates man on the road to his full humanization.

That working for conversion, or that accepting the ministry of liberation, should place the church in the midst of conflict is only to recognize the reality of human life. This was a reality which Christ himself recognized. He appealed to his Father to deliver him from it, but it was not his Father's will. And so for fulfilling his ministry, a ministry of liberation, the unique ministry he left all of us in his church, Jesus was murdered.

One of the young, aggressive clerics who contributed substantially to the positive elements in the growth of the Hispano church is the Jesuit Edmundo Rodríguez. Born in El Paso, Texas, in 1935, "Mundo" entered the Society of Jesus after his Catholic school education and was ordained a Jesuit priest in June 1966. He came to San Antonio in 1968, and quickly became immersed in the process of forming PADRES and MACC. Named pastor of Our Lady of Guadalupe Parish in 1969, he worked quietly and patiently toward a six-parish coalition for the Mexican American population of San Antonio. His work was an indispensable preparation for the community organization described below. This 1974 white paper on catechetics explains most of the elements in the pastoralist approach.

59. Parish Catechetics

Edmundo Rodriguez, S. J.

This position paper, written in 1972, is used by permission.

Many parishes and groups of parishes have for some years now been struggling to discover "what works" today in a modern catechetical program. We no longer "teach catechism" but, rather, conduct classes in "religious education" and "adult basic theology"! We no longer use question-and-answer methods but discussion techniques, field trips, and group encounters. Still, most instruction is judged successful by the numbers involved more than by the qualitative results.

The real question, it seems to me, is whether the philosophy underpinning most catechetical programs is primarily one aimed at preserving the institutional church by ensuring large turnouts at Sunday mass and many contributors, or whether it is primarily one aimed at building an effective Christian community. Oftentimes, in our attempts to reach the many, we neglect the few and end by reaching everyone only in a very superficial way. Our efforts, then, if they are going to result in *qualitative* excellence, must be made with certain presuppositions in mind:

1. Religion is not something appended to life, but an integral part of it. Insofar as religious training becomes an appendage to rather than part of the fabric of an individual's, as a community's, life pattern, it becomes a game, or at best merely ritualization.

2. The gospel of Jesus Christ is a message with real relevance for *life as it is lived*. If it has no impact on our relationships across the board, then we have

not really understood its message of "justice, mercy, and good faith" (Mt. 9:13). The separation of Christianity from the rest of life is a throwback to paganism rather than a consequence of the Incarnation.

3. After the Incarnation, the development of community in its fullest human dimension and of true Christian community are one and the same thing. Theologians in this century have struggled valiantly to try to break the whole church away from the prejudice that the Christian sits on the shoulder of the human. Again, we are struggling with additions and appendages and the refined separation of natural and supernatural, which either violates nature or makes religion a game.

4. The message of Christ and Christian attitudes are passed on in the first place by the reality, life, and action of groups and individuals committed to the following of Christ and almost not at all by formal academic study. When we stress formalized instruction, we are practically saying that only the literate, the educated, and the cultured have the capacity to be Christians. This prejudices our approach to people in low-income areas because we tend to regard them as "unfit" for receiving the whole message of Jesus.

5. Religious instruction should then be more by incorporation into the life and work of a Christian community than by formalized teaching. Nevertheless, because there must be those who explain the traditions and try to elucidate the values of the community to others, these must try to gain a deep understanding of the human needs of the community. A priest, who is one called to form the community of Christians, has to know his community well and know both the obstacles to the growth of Christian faith and the riches within the community which can make that faith flourish. Without this, the priest and the people will almost certainly talk *past* each other.

6. The cultic aspects of liturgy and sacraments should be a rehearsal of the faith-in-life of the community and thus be a *fruition* of a process rather than a spiritual watering station which is approached with greater or lesser frequency. If the cultic (liturgy) is not understood as the culmination of a process of formation, a rehearsal and celebration of the love and friendship exchanged by members of a given community, it will probably stifle growth of that community by giving it a false sense of religiosity. Performing cultic actions, however well prescribed and approved by tradition and authorities, without the "heart" of what religion is supposed to be all about, is simply not a religious act, but *playing* at being religious. Young people are often quick to detect game playing in those who either have not understood the real nitty-gritty relevancy of the Gospels, or else are afraid to face real-life situations in depth.

The presuppositions outlined above are not conducive to work with the masses. Rather, they point toward the development of small groups of leaders, who, having discerned issues, clarified values, and planned sagaciously, can exert an influence far beyond their numbers. This is, of course, the key to any successful revolution. Jesus knew it and so his revolution took hold and had permanence. The discernment of real-life issues is the first step—it is the group equivalent of self-knowledge.

"Issue discernment" is a process whereby a group gathers information about the entire context of their lives, first in order to begin to make some sense of the multiplicity of things that happen; second, to try to act from more complete factual knowledge rather than hazy misconceptions; and third, to pass from spectatorhood to participation. Every group, especially those with a religious orientation, should spend time discerning together, knowing themselves and their own shared situation more deeply. The process of discernment is especially important for the instructor of religion because he or she needs to know not only the factual situation, but more especially the judgments made by one's pupils about their own situation. It is only thus that the instructor and the pupils will not talk past each other.

Christianity, however, will not be passed on by merely discerning a human situation together. Jesus taught a way of life, a pervasive philosophy that must be understood, lived, and passed on. Most of us experience his teachings in a very disjointed way, however, and pass them on much the same way. Say "religion" to almost anyone and it conjures up a series of disconnected images which make sense separately (sometimes) but not together.

A parish program, therefore, should have as one of its main objectives to present to the hearers a unified idea of the teachings and traditions. This means unifying everything around one central image-idea. The most productive one for some is that of the eucharistic community.

The church is the eucharistic community. The church unifies in itself the whole tradition dating back to the earliest biblical times as well as the present moving into the future. The concept of eucharistic community can unify the sacraments. For example:

Baptism is the initiation, the welcome of the child or the catechumen into the eucharistic community. The community opens its arms and commits itself to share its faith and traditions with the new member much as a human family shares itself with a newborn child. The initiation is the promise to incorporate the person fully into participation of the Table of the Lord.

Confirmation can be presented as ratification of baptism, as the response, at a mature level, of the person welcomed by the community in baptism. It is a public dedication to carry out the purposes of Christ in and through the eucharistic community and that community's reaffirmation to share its faith and its works, the understanding and practice of which is the work of the Holy Spirit.

The Eucharist is, of course, the center sacrament in this presentation. It is the coming together of the community to rehearse its foundations in the gospel of Jesus Christ, to celebrate its unity amid diversity, to set itself in motion toward the world in service, and to stand before God the Father with a great *Amen* to his creative purposes. The Eucharistic celebration has little meaning unless there is already a process of unification that is taking place within the community and a growing sense of mission. "Fun and games" liturgies, which have little to do with what is really happening between people in the community and what is happening in the world, are so much distraction from real religiosity.

Penance, or Confession, is the sign shared in rebuilding a disrupted or disunited community. The community, if it is going to follow the teachings of Christ, must be ready to forgive its members "seven times seventy times" in the faith that love reforms more than punishment.

Marriage is a more intensive personal and familial form of community, a cell within a cell, where individuals can in no way hide behind the collectivity to avoid facing their attitudes toward their "neighbor." The larger community may be a reflection of the interpersonal exchanges being carried on at the nuclear level.

Holy Orders is the sign by which some are called to direct the formation of the eucharistic community. They must not only bring the community together, but lead its members to uncover the "riches of Christ" and the attitudes of openness and service, which will alone make that community worthy of the name "Christian." A community is not "open" if its only concern is its own service, if it is detached from and uninvolved in the solution of human social problems; and it is not humble if it places itself first and thus becomes conscious or unconsciously "elite" in the uncatholic sense of the word.

The Sacrament of the Sick is the sign whereby the community, through its faith, calls upon the healing power of God for the sake of those ailing. It is the sign of the community's concern for its sick and dying.

Thus, the idea of eucharistic community can be used to unify all the sacraments. Not that the sacraments as signs of the community exhaust the meaning of the sacraments, but that this idea can help the person grasp them in their relationship to each other. This is not, of course, a new notion. Karl Rahner suggested seeing the church (community) as the fundamental sacrament from which all the rest flows. What needs to happen is that the notion become popularized and operative, just as the concept of the church as the whole People of God needs to become popularized and operative through catechetical and liturgical instruction.

It appears to me that if parishes become more conscious of encouraging strong cells in which eyeball-to-eyeball development can take place, and unify the operating concepts of the Gospels and relate them to the real issues, although it may not bring more people to church, it should give those who come a deeper sense of cohesiveness and purpose.

The political organizing of pastoralists like Edmundo Rodríguez in San Antonio has matured into the impressive organization called Communities

Organized for Public Services (COPS). This organization, which is predominantly Mexican American and Catholic in membership, has brought about
long-overdue changes in the life of San Antonians. Perhaps it iş not strange
that after some 130 years of Anglo political domination, the Mexican American
people of San Antonio should flex their political muscles. Indeed, Puerto
Ricans in New York, in a shorter time of twenty years, have probably achieved
more political representation. But the important question is not so much
"when" as "how" and "by whom." In San Antonio, the Hispano church deserves most of the credit. The following article by Rick Casey explains why.

60. Bishops Back Barrio Power

Rick Casey

From National Catholic Reporter, *December 3, 1976. Used by permission.*

SAN ANTONIO, Texas—Archbishop Francis Furey continued his liaison
with a controversial community organization here by telling 5,000 of its
members last week, "We are not looking for charity. We are looking for
justice."

In a talk frequently interrupted by applause, he added, "If we get that,
we're going to be good boys and girls. If not, well, we'll see about it."

The occasion was the third annual convention of Communities Organized
for Public Services (COPS), a middle-class but militant organization which
has used Saul Alinsky techniques to provide residents of San Antonio's huge
barrios with the first real power they have wielded in this city.

The convention was a showcase for probably the most direct and vigorous
involvement of the institutional church in reform politics in this country.

The ties between COPS and the Catholic church here were symbolized not
only by Furey's words, but also by the fact that of the eight persons seated on
stage for the convention, the only ones who were not COPS officials were
Furey, Auxiliary Bishop Patricio Flores and Auxiliary Bishop-elect Raymond
Peña.

In addition, 36 of the 39 neighborhood organizations which sent delegations to the convention were Catholic parishes.

While Furey has given COPS backing from the top (including helping it
secure about $150,000 in Campaign for Human Development grants), parish
priests and lay leaders have provided the local organization.

The new president elected by the convention, Beatrice Gallego, was a
Parent-teacher Association leader and a leading member of the St. James

parish ladies' council. The outgoing president, Andy Sarabia, was a leader in his parish council. He has not been named to replace Peña on the Campaign for Human Development's national board.

The organization showed its intention to move its coalition beyond Mexican-American Catholics, however, by electing Clara Williams, a black Protestant, as first vice president of COPS.

The convention theme, "Money vs. People," expresses the struggle which has developed between COPS and the political powers that have traditionally run San Antonio. As a result, both the group and Bishops Furey and Flores have become controversial.

During the past several years COPS has used confrontation techniques as well as the ballot box to halt tax subsidies to wealthy land developers and to redirect hundreds of millions of tax dollars into the inner city. By doing its homework and carefully monitoring various segments of city government, the group has put bureaucrats and politicians on notice that the barrios can no longer be ignored.

Political observers here say much of what COPS has accomplished has been made easier by the fact that the wealthy developers and other established powers did not take the organization seriously, expecting it to disintegrate like previous barrio movements. The COPS officials are aware those days are over.

Both Sarabia and Gallego spoke about the Business and Industrial Political Action Committee (BIPAC), an organization which is raising money to elect a mayor and a city council beyond COPS' reach next year.

"For every dollar they raise, we need to come up with voters," said Sarabia.

Flores put it another way: "You and I do not have green power, but neither did Jesus. You and I do not have military power, but neither did he. You and I have what Jesus had—people power. The confrontation rests on the beautiful power of the people."

Flores also spoke about the organization's growth, recalling that four years ago he and several others met to discuss the possibility of a community organization.

"The eight of us who met never dreamed that such a thing would happen in such a short span," he said. "From what we can see here this afternoon I can only say, baby, you're just beginning to walk. More power to you."

Both Flores and Furey were given enthusiastic standing ovations. In addition, Furey was given a plaque in gratitude for his support.

"He has taken a lot of flak from important and influential people, but he has stood with us," said Sarabia.

In a rousing speech following the presentation of the plaque, Furey called COPS "one of the best things that has ever happened to San Antonio," and concluded in Spanish, with a paraphrase of the Cursillo motto: "With COPS all. Without COPS nothing."

The Northeast became the last of the regions with significant numbers of Hispanos to have a regional Encounter to implement the conclusions from the national meeting held two years previously (1972) in Washington. Held in Holyoke, Massachusetts, it was the largest of the regional Encounters with almost 300 delegates, and it was the only Encounter where Puerto Ricans formed the majority of the Hispanos. The tardiness of the Northeast in celebrating the meeting reflected the difficulty found in adapting the Mexican American pastoralist model to the needs of the Northeast (see pp. 197-201; 208-13). Conflicts developed among the different planning committees, and the representative of the secretariat in Washington did not settle these difficulties with clear-cut effectiveness. The active leadership of the New York Archdiocese became decisive in the Encounter. Cardinal Cooke personally spent almost two days in Holyoke, pledging his moral and financial support to the participants. His sincerity helped dispel the residue of ill-will that lingered among those who had worked with the frustrated Father Robert L. Stern. Moreover, the presence of Cardinal Aponte Martínez from San Juan, Puerto Rico, gave the Northeast Encounter a strongly Puerto Rican identification. The process of forming the Hispano church had attracted the bishops of the island into active support.

The Northeast Regional Encounter gave major importance to lay leadership, in contrast with other Encounters where the Hispano bishops, PADRES, and Hermanas had taken a central role. The major talks were delivered by two lay persons: Rosa Correa from Bridgeport, Connecticut, Diocese and Luis Fontánez of New York, whose presentation is cited below.

Fontánez was born in 1930 in Río Piedras, Puerto Rico, and came to New York City when he was sixteen years old. He did undergraduate and graduate studies at New York University, where he earned a master's degree in education in 1956. He worked among the Puerto Ricans of the city in his spare time, forming parish credit unions, and was eventually to become president of the St. Vincent de Paul Society in the archdiocese. His major apostolate, however, was in the Cursillo movement, in which he has held many important posts. After the Encounter, he was elected a member of the Northeast Pastoral Council, which became responsible for creating the regional pastoral center in New York that opened its doors in April 1976. That same year, Fontánez took orders as a deacon and in 1977 became the first chairman of the Hispanic Association of Deacons in the Northeast. His theology ties the pastoralist approach to the specific social issues most deeply felt by Puerto Rican *cursillistas*.

61. The Theology of Social Justice

Luis Fontánez

From Address to the Northeast Regional Encounter, November 29, 1974. Used by permission. Trans. A.M.S.A.

In the past few years there has been talk of conscientization, of liberation, of social justice, and I am not very sure if, sometimes, everything can be reduced to terms from a dictionary that serve to stir up illusions of a utopian idealism. I have not seen a great deal of activity on behalf of the intrinsic sense of these terms and, because of that, I risk challenging the participants of this Encounter to philosophize less and to work more for the well-being of our Hispano people in the Northeast region of the United States.

I have been asked to speak about the Theology of Social Justice, but I am not a theologian, nor a Scripture scholar, nor a sociologist: I am simply one more of the People of God, committed to the struggle of bringing this people to the "Promised Land." Hence, I do not intend to offer here a profound theological treatise, but rather, to treat of a biblical theological reflection, with intentions of steering this Encounter toward a work plan to benefit this Hispano sector of the People of God, especially in the Northeast region of the United States that has suffered so much, and still suffers from persecution, rejection, oppression, and so many other forms of injustice.

It is evident, then, that a study on social justice is based on a profound analysis of the development and liberation of each person, of each society, of each people. This is a development which has to root itself in all social activity directed toward the poor, resting on the fundamental requisite of love. Only on this plane can the messianic promise and the eschatological reality manifested in the gospel of Jesus Christ be interpreted.

All theology today tends toward the conscientization of people in their temporal reality because it is thus that they realize themselves in history as history, a realization that includes each individual's dimension, family, politics, society, and culture. That is to say, people realize themselves to the extent that they enter into historical existence. Thus human beings make themselves human by their development. . . .

The church, in its redemptive concern, has the responsibility of liberating the person from sin, but it also has to try to liberate those structures and institutions where sin originates and flourishes. Love of neighbor does not mean avoiding confrontations, but means trying to liberate the oppressed from the oppressor, and the oppressor from ambition for power and selfishness. The church thus exists for the complete liberation of humanity from all slavery, whether motivated by hardness of heart or by the injustice of the social environment. Every conversion is influenced by socioeconomic conditions, politics, and factors which are cultural and human, wherever they occur. If these structures are not changed, true conversion is impossible. Hunger, poverty, and misery are not acts of God, to whose will we must conform, but a consequence of the actions of human beings moved by indifference, dislike, and an enslaving attitude. Already in Jeremiah and Hosea we see that love of God consists in works of justice to the poor and the oppressed (Jer. 22; Hos. 4). The church, in its redemptive function of liberating humanity, has to consider new structures, new institutions and relations, as well as different attitudes which not only reach a conversion of hearts, but also bring about a social transformation.

It is, however, a painful reality that the doctrine of the church has been held on a basically theoretical plane rather than one of implementation and practice. If we look at the history of humankind, we can see and feel a God who has revealed himself to us in a progressive realization of his plan of liberation and salvation, a plan that is fulfilled and realized once and for all in the Paschal Mystery. In Christ the process of total freedom achieves its culmination (see *Gaudium et spes*). Thus all activity directed toward the transformation of our society results in a translation of the gospel, or, if you will, the progressive realization of the redemptive mission of the church for humankind and its liberation from every form of oppression. According to this gospel message, the relationship of person with neighbor is linked to one's relationship with God and one's response to the love of God, who redeems us, saves us, and frees us in Christ; and it is made evident in one's love and service of other people. Love of neighbor and justice, then, are inseparable, since love implies justice, a recognition of the dignity and the rights of people. Our commitment to the poor and exploited will be the sign of our love for God, because ". . . as long as you did it for one of these, the least of my brethren, you did it for me" (Mt. 25:40). To struggle for the liberation of the oppressed always has to be our greatest longing.

Justice assumes its fullness only in love, since each person is both a visible image of the invisible God and a brother or sister of Christ. The Christian has to find in each person the same God in his continuous demand for justice and love. We are not going to find this God except in our encounter with the poor, with the needy, with the oppressed, who constitute our neighbor. We have the actual presence of our neighbor around the corner: in those workers enslaved and oppressed by the power of ambition and selfishness, in those immigrants, called "illegal criminals," whose only crime has been the "exodus" from certain conditions of oppression in search of "bread" and the "staff of life, " and those others, farm workers who are reduced to kissing the feet of their bosses, in order that they be permitted to breathe; this is a neighbor stripped of every sense of dignity and reduced to the condition of a slave.

This present reality of our situation, by the light of faith, has to carry us to the core of the Bible message in order that a consciousness of the authenticity of the gospel and its demands be created. This gospel of Jesus Christ demands of us a commitment to the liberation of humankind, but if this message of love and justice is not crystallized in our activity, in our works on behalf of justice, this message will lose any semblance of credibility. It is not enough to say that the love of God and the love of neighbor are inseparable. This love has to show itself in works on behalf of the oppressed.

Christ gave to the church the great mission of bringing the Good News of salvation to everyone, the building up of the community of brotherhood, but this requires justice as base and foundation for its existence. For this reason, when the rights of its members and their salvation are violated, the church has the obligation to proclaim justice and denounce injustice. In this way, the church will be witness in the world of the message of love and justice proclaimed by the gospel. But where is the church? Why are the cries of denunciation on behalf of the helpless not heard? Our Hispano families are at the edge of despair; our children are being annihilated by those who make of youth a market place of personal profit; and our women are converted into guinea pigs in experiments to reduce and even eliminate the continuance of the Hispano family in the United States, most especially in this Northeast region. Denunciation, with all possible courage and with all our might, is indispensable against all injustice, never forgetting, however, our deepest sense of charity and our position as Christians.

On the other hand, the church cannot look only outside itself; it must also reflect upon and look within its most intimate being. Above all, the church has to recognize and respect the rights of its members. It has to end all forms of inequality, since all injustice is denounced by the gospel. As proof of this obligation, the church has to show a wider cooperation with different ethnic groups, and this cooperation has to translate itself into spiritual communion and a just division of human and material resources. This will make possible the planning and implementation of programs for human and spiritual formation, within one's own cultural realm. Only in this way will it be possible to form the necessary leaven for the development of the human being.

The church, as the presence of the liberating action of Christ, has to offer opposition to every practice of racial discrimination and discrimination against minorities. We know that great injustices have been committed against Hispanos, and that if it is to be the light and love of the world, the church has to respond to these injustices. Help for our Hispano community is imperative, as much in the spiritual order as in the material, if we are to acquire the dignity and the status that belong to us in the church. Thus we can enrich others with our rich and beautiful culture. Why do many want to de-Hispanicize and to Americanize us? What crime is there in being Hispano? We are Hispanos and we want to be Hispanos, with all the pride that it requires, because thus God the Father Almighty created us, and we love our parents and forebears.

The church in this Northeast region of the United States, if it is faithful to the mission of liberation and recognizes this polycultural condition, has to see the imperative necessity of a native Hispano ministry, of a native Hispano liturgy, and of some Hispano pastors who are able to maintain their identity and pride as Hispano people. This consideration does not exclude the active participation of those American continental brothers who have made efforts and are still striving to understand not only the language, but our culture as well, and thus to serve in the Hispano ministry. In this way, the church will make itself defender of the cultural values of its Hispano children, promoting the esteem and respect of our dignity and pride. People will be able to enjoy a brotherhood and a full life only through their culture or through the cultivation of natural values and resources. . . .

In December 1975, through the United States Catholic Conference Secretariat for the Spanish-speaking, the Hispanic Committee formed by Mr. Paul Sedillo for the Eucharistic Congress in Philadelphia published the first of a series of catechetical-liturgical programs. The following excerpt demonstrates the awareness of cultural diversity and utilizes the religious instincts of Hispano people in order to mobilize them to prayer, action, and good works. These programs were prepared largely by Mr. Francisco Diana, at that time the catechetical expert at the USCC for the Spanish-speaking.

62. A Program in Preparation for Christmas (excerpt)

USCC Hispanic Committee

Used by permission.

INTRODUCTION TO THE PROGRAM OF CHRISTMAS

This program is based on a cultural act and traditional logic that is partly rooted in the Hispano community of the United States. The celebration of

Christmas is preceded by religious practices, or by social practices that have had a religious origin and are still preserved in the countries where they originated. Among these practices the most important ones are three:

The construction of the *"Nativities"*: They are also referred to as "mangers," as "stables," and their location is in the family home.

The "Nativity" is the stage-set using figures and decorations that illustrate Baby Jesus lying in the manger (cradle of straw) surrounded by his Mother Mary and his father Joseph. One aggregates to these special figures, the shepherds, not forgetting to include the corral animals, especially the ass, or donkey, and the ox.

This scene is traditional to all Hispano countries—Central and South America, including the Caribbean, and Spain. The variant lies within the many countries of Hispano America. The major importance is placed on the "Nativity" rather than on the Christmas tree. In fact, the American Christmas tree is the infiltration of another culture. This scene in some parts is followed by the tradition that the cradle of the Child remains empty until the night of December 24, and the three Wise Men enter the scene by the night of January 6. In many places the "Nativity" is represented by live actors.

The "Posadas": Deeply rooted in Mexico, the traditional "Posadas" are practiced by nearly all of the Mexican Americans and Mexicans in the United States. Sometimes, beginning in a parish, the "Posadas" do not always follow the same format, due to the fact that usually someone is chosen to represent Mary and Joseph in their pilgrimage to Bethlehem where they have gone to seek lodging. The music of the "Posadas" reflects the traditional content and meaning, mixed with the character and happiness of the Hispano. In many places, the use of the donkey is essential to the celebration. The "Posada" is given in the form of a pilgrimage, where *posada,* or lodging, is asked for the pilgrims going from one place to another, and being greeted with song, music, and food. This is done in such a way that everyone in the "barrio" can participate. If the "Posada" is given as a pilgrimage, denoting a biblical meaning, then we should take advantage and profit from it. (*Somos pueblo en marcha.*)

The "Parrandas": Having many variations, they are very traditional in Puerto Rico but also in many other places in the Caribbean and Latin America. It is almost empty of religious meaning when it reaches us. But with a great similarity to the custom of the "Posada," its indigenous music, the act of exchanging presents then, the singing of Christmas carols, the *"Parrandas"* come with a religious content mixed with a very interesting cultural wealth. Even today, it is customary in the central parts of the "Enchanted Island" (Puerto Rico) to begin the "Parrandas" in the courtyard of the main church of the town in order from there to depart to the homes, sometimes taking children dressed as Mary, Joseph, and the Child; sometimes using the donkey; but always exchanging gifts with carols—the latter being full of religious and cultural meaning. Also, in the "Parrandas," as in the "Posadas," they ask:

"Abrame la puerta, que estoy en la calle," etc., and so they are welcomed into the homes. A Puerto Rican *aguinaldo* begins a chorus that says: "Más vale la Virgen que todas las flores," and in one of the lyrics to the same song, they intercalate the verse: "Si me dan pasteles, dénmelos calientes, que pasteles fríos, empachan la gente." Indicative of these songs and carols is the unity of life and the religious faith of the people.

Precisely the essence of this program is to profit from the celebrations of these customs as a basis to introduce the most profound Christian meaning. This meaning continues in the form of "Novenas" during the nine days that precede the vigil of Christmas; if you wish, "Novenas" can be called "Circles of Prayer," "Communal Meditations," etc. It depends on what title or expression has significance for your local community. We use "Novena" due to the fact that it is a term traditionally known throughout the Hispano community, although we understand that it may seem antiquated or outmoded. What is important is the content that is present, based on the episcopacy, on the theme of the American bicentennial (Liberty and Justice for All), on the universal theme of hunger, or on the theme of the Eucharistic Congress, which is, of course, the Eucharist. All of it in the form of prayer/meditation/prayer.

Archbishop Roberto F. Sánchez
(courtesy Visitante Dominical)

CHAPTER ELEVEN

SHOOTING FOR THE STARS

In the euphoria created by many of the early successes of the Hispano church's entry into the wider dimensions of national Catholic life, there was a tendency to expand horizons beyond the immediate concerns of the Spanish-speaking. This was echoed in magazines such as *Maryknoll,* which developed the meaning of the Hispano church in terms that could be understood by pious Catholics used to supporting "the missions." In April 1973, *Our Sunday Visitor* undertook a weekly edition in Spanish, *El Vistante Dominical,* providing a much-needed means of communication for the country's Hispanos. At international meetings of the Catholic Interamerican Cooperation Program (CICOP), sponsored by the Latin American Bureau of the USCC, Mexican Americans and Puerto Ricans challenged the attention given to problems in distant countries while the same type of problems in America were being ignored or brushed aside. Finally, the cry for Hispano bishops was raised again. In particular, Mexican American leaders, such as Archbishop Roberto Sánchez, were anxious to ensure a truly national character to Hispano leadership by urging that non-Mexican American Hispanos be named to the episcopate in areas where there were Puerto Ricans, Cubans, and other Latin Americans. Unfortunately, when the desire to be bishop is a personal rather than a community ambition, it can cause some ambiguity in the development of the Hispano church.

63. Preserve the Faith and Culture

An editorial from Maryknoll *magazine, March 1973. Used by permission.*

Some of our readers may ask why Maryknoll, whose mission work is overseas, devotes an entire issue of its magazine to the Spanish-speaking in the United States. There are many reasons. First of all, right now, about 25 percent of all Catholics in the United States are either Hispanos, Puerto

Ricans, Cubans or immigrants from the Latin American republics. This makes the United States the fifth largest Spanish-speaking country in the world after Mexico, Spain, Argentina and Colombia.

Maryknoll and other mission groups have worked in the apostolate for many years with people from this cultural background. It would be strange at this point if those who have gone overseas to preach the Gospel to Latin Americans were to be unconcerned with their situation in this country today. This is particularly urgent in view of the fact that the majority of the Spanish-speaking suffer from discrimination and a level of poverty that is a scandal in such a rich country. The Church should be in the forefront of those speaking out against such injustices as described in this issue. Together with this concern for justice, missioners understand the need for a people to adapt the Gospel to their own culture. This means that the Hispano American should not be forced to give up his culture and background to be an American Catholic. He should be encouraged to have his own forms of liturgy as well as a ministry adapted to his needs.

SPANISH-SPEAKING LEADERS

In turn this means that there must be more Spanish-speaking bishops, pastors, priests, religious and lay leaders. The reason for this is that no matter how competent and well intentioned others may be, ultimately it is the Spanish-speaking themselves who should do the adapting and have a presence and voice in all sectors of the Church. Right now there are not enough priests and trained laity among the Spanish-speaking to do this. So special programs of vocational recruitment for the religious life and training for laity to assume roles of leadership should be further encouraged and expanded.

Some may ask whether encouraging an ethnic group to preserve its own language and to have its own liturgies and forms of ministry might foster separatism in the U.S. Catholic community. There is always the danger of division.

CULTURAL DIVERSITY

Faith, however, is a personal response to God made by a believer within a certain cultural context. Just as in New Testament days St. Paul reminded St. Peter that to be a Christian a person need not follow Jewish ceremonial and hygienic practices, so to follow Christ today a person need not throw off the culture he was born with. Moreover, the preservation and support of the Hispano American culture is a necessity. A person learns his faith within a cultural framework and if he loses the cultural framework, he often loses that which came with it.

No matter how proficient a person becomes in another language, his own tongue is that which he can use best to express deepest emotional feelings of love of God and man. Moreover, no one culture can begin to exhaust the richness of the Gospel of Jesus. A variety of cultural expressions of faith tells us more, not less, about God.

When a culture is destroyed a beautiful expression of humanity is lost. It is a shame that in the past the unique cultural contribution of minority groups coming to the United States has been greatly lessened through a misplaced emphasis on uniformity. However, with the increasing number of Spanish-speaking Catholics in the United States through migration and normal birth rates, the opportunity increases for the U.S. Church to have a new aposto-late which can benefit both the Hispano Americans and the rest of the Church.

64. Statement of the Hispano Group at CICOP 1973, Dallas, Texas

Used by permission. Trans. A.M.S.A.

The group was composed of twenty-five persons from the United States and a single observer from Colombia. We discussed the topic of theology, and subtopics such as liberation from the theology of the Gringos/Yankees, foreign aid from Latin America, and the contributions of the Spanish-speaking in the United States.

We felt ourselves annoyed, frustrated and, most of all, just plain angry by the total indifference toward the Hispano people in this country of CICOP 1973 and the Latin American Bureau (LAB) which sponsors it. This led us to conclude that there is no sincerity in the effort to develop the peoples of Latin America as church. It is unbelieveable that the Latin American Bureau pretends to take seriously the problems of Latin America when it totally ignores the present-day problems of Latinos in the United States. Hence our reflection led us to challenge its theological integrity.

We recommend the following steps:

1. That there be a restructuring of the LAB so that it can deal with the interests of Hispanos, both within the United States and in Latin America. This would include: *(a)* financial support of programs for Hispanos of the United States; *(b)* the naming of a Hispano as director, or at least associate

242 THE FORGE OF UNITY

director, of the LAB; *(c)* cooperation with programs of pastoral and theological formation with the Hispanic Division of the USCC and other organizations of formation such as the Mexican American Cultural Center.

2. That there be no CICOP 1974 unless: *(a)* it be directed to a type of interamerican cooperation which focuses on the problems that the Hispano church of the Americas encounters; *(b)* that the format facilitate participation by local teams from the grassroots in workshops of reflection on the praxis that they are accomplishing.

---

65. Bishops for the Hispano Church

Jo-ann Price

From El Visitante Dominical, *April 27, 1975. Used by permission. Trans. A.M.S.A.*

ATLANTIC CITY, NEW JERSEY—In a meeting of the National Association of Catholic Educators before an audience of experts on Catholic vocations in this city, the Archbishop of Santa Fe, New Mexico, Roberto F. Sánchez, said that he was thinking of meeting on June 2nd with Pope Paul VI to inform him of the situation of Hispanos who have only five bishops for their ministry in the United States, although they constitute some 26 percent of the Catholics in North America.

The forty-one-year-old Archbishop Sánchez said that the most important areas where this matter requires study are New York, Chicago and Miami.

He said that the Apostolic Delegate to the United States, Archbishop Jean Jadot, was very concerned with the lack of bishops and clergy for Cuban Americans, Mexican Americans and other descendants of Latinos. Moreover, he predicted, "I believe that more bishops will be named in the future, especially for these very important cities."

The young Archbishop of New Mexico politely but strongly said that "we need these symbols"—Latino bishops—within the American hierarchy. He said that "the level of consciousness has risen" in this regard among the bishops of the North American Church who are predominantly of Irish ancestry. . . .

The Dominican friar William Loperena was born in Moca, Puerto Rico, on December 14, 1935. After some years, as a teenager, in New York City, he returned to Puerto Rico to enter the Dutch Province of the Dominican Order, which directs the Dominican foundations on the island. He returned to the States to study for his B.A. at Providence College in Rhode Island and was sent to the Albertinum at Neimegen in Holland for his theological training. He graduated *summa cum laude,* as Lector in Sacred Theology, and returned from Holland to Puerto Rico, where he was ordained on July 25, 1961. He was stationed in Comerío, Puerto Rico, where he was to experience the difficulties described in this book (see pp. 90-91, 262).

He wrote the following satiric essay in criticism of ecclesiastical social climbers who abandon the poor in order to become bishops. While it is undeniable that the same sort of personal ambition has affected some clerics in the Hispano church, one of the achievements of Hispanos has been to alter the image of bishop. The emphasis upon grassroots participation and pastoral concerns has made the role of the Hispano bishop one that is oriented toward the people. Padre Loperena uses irony in asserting that a bishop's place is with the grassroots.

66. Episcopitis

William Loperena, O.P.

Used by permission. Trans. A.M.S.A.

Episcopitis is a sickness that strikes priests and, on rare occasions, pious lay persons. Like cancer, its causes are unknown. There are various theories, but none has been proved correct.

Episcopitis is a sickness characterized by a neurotic desire to BE A BISHOP AT ALL COSTS. It affects the sick person completely: mind, emotions, behavior, attitude, appearance. Many present-day bishops have suffered from severe episcopitis and the present advanced stage of the disease is characterized by gross acts of authoritarianism in order to save the mitre (this is a sharp protrusion which juts out of the head of the patient) and by actions to make themselves into cardinals.

THE SYMPTOMS

The different known cases of episcopitis have registered the following symptoms:

1. Brown-nosing bishops (or a pope) to the extreme of making them right when they are not, or bringing them breakfast in bed.
2. Dressing with the Roman collar even for sleeping.
3. Learning canon law by heart and with the commentaries of those who have it "made" in the Vatican.
4. Attending all meetings and banquets of prominent ecclesiastics and rich persons and quoting from books that are to the liking of the guests.
5. Lobbying for key positions in dioceses and working in parishes of high social, economic, or political rank, where they can be spiritual directors to the top officials of the country.
6. Studiously avoiding any political thinking that might compromise their position.
7. Promoting bingos, parochial schools, novenas, bazaars, blessings of banks, etc.
8. Losing their patriotic values even to the point of speaking with the accent of a "curate" and losing their sensitivity toward the small pleasures of just plain folks.
9. With the clerical authoritarianism of an arrogant "I-know-it-all" attitude, obliging others to do their will and making things into issues of "divine necessity."
10. Living in a religious ghetto apart from the world, time, and people, divorced from simple occurrences and reality in general.

THE EFFECTS

This sickness is most dangerous for its effects on society. In church archives one finds terrible examples of the diabolical destructiveness of this sickness:

1. International wars, depending on the stage to which the sickness has advanced (even popes have been victims).
2. The priests have suffered from madness, schizophrenia, paranoia.
3. They have closed down schools, religious orders, and important undertakings.
4. They have divided groups, peoples, countries, and entire continents.

5. They have constructed expensive monuments, unserviceable and monstrous signs of contradiction and decadence.
6. They have corrupted imagination, creativity, sentiment, science, and youth.
7. They have squandered resources shamefully.
8. They have destroyed persons, talents, races, and lifestyles.
9. They have supported feudalism, monarchy, the bourgeoisie, capitalism, and imperialism.
10. They have institutionalized cruelty, the Inquisition, the Crusades, prisons, sadism, massacres, exploitation, and prolonged oppression.

THE TREATMENT

Episcopitis is incurable. Like leprosy, it has been possible only to isolate the victims. There have been several episcopitis asylums:

1. That of the *Pharisees* abandoned by Jesus and his disciples.
2. That of the *Judaizers* abandoned by the baptized of the primitive church.
3. That of the *Holy Roman Empire* set aside by the monks of the fourth century in order not to be contaminated with episcopitis.
4. That of the *Latin church* of the Roman pontiff abandoned by the Greek church for fear of being contaminated.
5. That of the *Roman church* abandoned by the Protestant Reformation.
6. That of the *politicking religion* abandoned by the French Revolution.
7. That of the *ecclesiastical institutions* abandoned by the masses of people in the nineteenth century.
8. That of the *religion as opium of the people* abandoned by the Socialist revolutions.
9. That of *sacralism* abandoned by all those who would not allow the abuse of the name of God for profane interests masked as "transcendence."
10. That of *faith as ideology* abandoned by Father Camilo Torres, the Berrigan brothers, and millions of Christians committed to the oppressed.

All of these episcopitis asylums have been ineffective. They have reduced the sickness to merely psychological problems. Some have tried to deal with the sick persons as if they were normal and sane, but that has only worsened the symptoms. They have left the sick persons unimproved and the sick have destroyed them ferociously. And they can destroy us all.

Let us then seek out the sufferers of episcopitis of Puerto Rico. Let us analyze their symptoms, effects, and remedies. Let us seek a cure.

Above (left to right): Ana Maria Diaz Ramirez (see pp. 208ff. and 336ff.), Maria Iglesias of Hermanas, and Gregoria Ortega of Hermanas

Below: César Chávez, Roberto Peña, Archbishop Patricio Flores (courtesy PADRES)

PART IV

THE RAINBOW OF PLURALISM

We need our own thing. If we are given a machine that is already built, it defeats part of the purpose, which is development. If we invent our own thing, the development may be slower, but it is more profound.

—Bishop Patricio Flores, 1973

For almost one hundred years, millions of Spanish-speaking people had been unorganized within the United States Catholic church. But in five years the leadership of the national Hispano church converted this mass presence into articulate influence with recognizable clout. This swift development of consensus and cohesion involved considerable skill. In previous essays, the genesis of this remarkably effective Hispano leadership has been described. First, it was shown how the *pensadores* provided style and symbols of identity as Hispanos and as Catholics. Second, Hispano leadership gained legitimization within a national Catholic church context; third, the Mexican American pastoralists from the Southwest assumed the role of primacy among the Hispano leaders after the First National Hispano Pastoral Encounter. In this fourth integrating essay, it will be necessary to examine how influence was so swiftly enlarged and how a new richness and a consciousness of intra-Hispano diversity began to emerge. This led to the Second National Hispano Pastoral Encounter in Washington, D.C., during August 1977.

According to Aristotle, the knack of getting things done, or the art of the possible, is politics. Certainly the orchestration of influence in church structures and the mobilization of resources from within the Hispano community for such a maximum effect could only have been accomplished because the national Hispano leaders were good politicians. Sometimes leaders in the church are uncomfortable with this thought. There is a tendency to feel that the use of political terminology is unbecoming and profane within the context of moral aspiration that is religion. That is not to say that these persons are unaware that such "politics" is necessary; they prefer, I presume, only to avoid labeling it as such.

The sensitivities can be assuaged with the honest admission that "politics" has been present in the church from the time that Jesus used personal charism and fisherman language to entice the apostles to follow him (Jn. 1:38ff.; Mt. 4:18-22; Mk. 1:16-20; Lk. 5:1-11, et passim). There is nothing "dirty" in politics unless it be the motives or the goals that vitiate the leadership.

Good leaders know how to use their influence to convince groups of effective courses of action. The persuasion goes beyond mere education, since if the courses of action were self-explanatory, the group would not need the leader to mobilize it toward action.

Influence involves the movement by a group of persons on the word of a leader toward goals and objectives either not fully understood or imperfectly accepted. This means that there is always manipulation of a sort in politics: moving people where they don't want to go because either they do not yet understand what is at stake or they are not fully convinced intellectually or emotionally as to the best course of action. The leader uses influence to make his or her opinion the basis for the total group's decision. This persuasion and mobilization of others, this "knack for getting things done with people," is the stuff of politics. F. G. Bailey, a British anthropologist, suggests that this manipulation can best be understood in the context of a "game" (Bailey, 1969, pp. 1ff.). The people in a group, he argues, exchange some of their present equilibrium in order to gain the advantages offered by the leader. They will promise action to gain knowledge of the purposes and insights of the leader. The leader, on the other hand, acts as a salesperson, describing the attractive benefits and hiding the unpleasant risks as much as possible. The leader knows he or she is manipulating; the people know they are being manipulated; but it is done in the atmosphere of a game. Politics resembles people in a market place haggling over oranges at the fruitstand: touching, squeezing, complaining, threatening, questioning, exhorting, and sermonizing, with every intention of arriving at mutual satisfaction. Unwritten rules permit this kind of push and pull as long as mutual respect is not lost.

The lone Mexican American bishop of 1972, the fledgling MACC, and the USCC Spanish-speaking Office had to "increase and multiply" if they were to follow the directives of the First National Hispano Pastoral Encounter. This meant more Hispano bishops in the Southwest and in other sections of the country. It implied that MACC initiate other pastoral centers, or "mini-MACCs," that would utilize the prestige, faculty, programs, and model of the San Antonio center. It argued that the USCC Office for the Spanish-speaking take on a national mission to represent not just Mexican American farm workers, but all Hispanos and all areas of apostolate from catechetics and liturgy to theology and the media. These expansion efforts required new personnel in order to fill the new posts, and the pastoralist leadership from the Southwest that had created the posts also suggested who should fill them. The Mexican American leadership had not suddenly created new sources of power; rather, they adopted a role of maintaining a position of brokerage between the official Catholic church and the Hispano people, in the hope of multiplying fundamental changes. To be fair, the Mexican American leadership was also involved in a "game" with the official Catholic church represented by the NCCB and the USCC. They had to be careful not to squander their influence on causes that would not build greater Hispano participation. They were forced, therefore, to eliminate from their priorities highly controversial issues or complex questions that would be counterproductive to the momentum that had been generated by Hispano successes. At the same time, they had to avoid rifts and division in the ranks, since such divisions would erode their credibility as representatives and spokespersons for 25 percent of the Catholics in the United States.

In their task, the emerging native Hispano hierarchy and the Mexican American leadership in Washington and at MACC were faced with two options. They could have allowed themselves to become "tokens" as they moved upward in national church politics, and thus surrender the values of the Hispano communities they represented. Their other option was to attempt to develop native Hispano leadership. Happily this latter was their choice. They extended the visibility that the Encounter had given Hispanos to an ever-widening circle of capable leaders.

Efforts were directed toward what can best be described as a "Trojan Horse strategy." The idea was to place large numbers of Hispanos in important posts within local and national structures as quickly as possible on the premise that once inside, these Hispanos would "open the gates" for other Hispanos. This was seen as the way to begin transforming the church into a new pluralistic Catholic community in the United States. But there was a problem. The number of qualified Hispano leaders was greater than the number of opportunities available. In making the selection of a candidate for advancement, the Mexican American pastoralists had to choose among different personalities, representing different regions and models of church. Thus the Hispano church, which had unanimously recommended pluralism to the entire United States Catholic church in 1972, was forced to discover its own forms of pluralism. This discovery centered upon the different concepts of "culture" and the various meanings of "liberation."

Bishop Juan Arzube of Los Angeles (courtesy PADRES)

CHAPTER TWELVE

DIFFERING CONCEPTS OF CULTURE

Culture can be defined in terms of folklore or as ideology. In the first sense, culture searches for stability by a reinterpretation of the past. It is a conscious repetition of accepted and traditional values, so that "cultural sensitivity" is a form of historical recall. But culture can also be seen as an evolving values system, a philosophy and political ideology. Culture understood in this second way becomes a symbolic anticipation of a new form of society (see Table 2).

Table 2

Stable Forms of Cultural Leadership	Evolving Forms of Cultural Leadership
People are "trained" in culture	Culture is a reflective and questioning process which is intimately personal and nontransferable
Cultural sensitivity depends upon the repetition of knowledge as given by "leaders"	Cultural sensitivity is present in individual creativity of cultural values applied to new circumstances
Culture is a collection of traditions involving "safe" modes of living tried and tested by history	Culture is a set of attitudes attempting to recreate the world according to the values of people; it is revolutionary and liberating of all old structures that have no human dimension

---

In the Hispano church a rift eventually developed between Mexican Americans, who thought of culture as folklore stabilizing identity, and the Chicanos, who thought of it as ideology evolving new values. A similar tension among Puerto Ricans produced the term "Neorican" to describe the children born in New York to Puerto Rican migrants. In the selections of this chapter, the consensus of Puerto Ricans is reflected in the preference for an evolving sense of values as definition of "Puerto Rican." Mexican Americans have not yet resolved the issue, although recently militants have insisted on the term "Mexican" in order to avoid ambiguity. Such militants gathered at the National Chicano Forum in Salt Lake City in May 1976 and produced resolutions (see p. 256) similar to the Puerto Rican consensus.

The self-examination of Chicano and Mexican American identity is important to church leaders who have to deal pastorally with both segments. For instance, the Mexican American Cultural Center has suggested that its acronym MACC can also mean "Movement for Christian Cultural Activities." This apparently is an attempt to avoid categorization as "Mexican American" in exclusion of a Chicano reality. Two important studies on the question of church and Chicanos/Mexican Americans were made on the West Coast by Antonio R. Soto *(Chicano and the Church,* Denver: Marfel, 1975), and by Padre Juan Hurtado *(An Attitudinal Study of Social Distance between the Mexican American and the Church,* San Antonio: MACC, 1975).

Hurtado was born December 13, 1930, in Anaheim, California, the son of migrant Mexican fruit pickers. At the age of twenty he joined the Augustinian Recollects and began his priestly studies in Kansas and New York. Ordained in 1958, he was seminary professor, vocation director in New England, and director of the Augustinian seminary. In 1969 he returned to his native California and, after resigning from his religious order, began working in 1972 as a priest of the San Diego Diocese at the Padre Hidalgo Center. He received his doctorate from International University in San Diego in 1975 and has since become coordinator at the Institute for Cultural Pluralism at San Diego State University. In the selection which follows, taken from his doctoral dissertation, Hurtado sees Chicanos as further from the church than Mexican Americans and suggests some solutions for this state of affairs.

67. An Attitudinal Study of Social Distance between the Mexican American and the Church

Juan Hurtado

From Hurtado, An Attitudinal Study . . . *(San Antonio: MACC, 1975), pp. 203-211. Used by permission.*

IMPLICATIONS OF THE FINDINGS

Sex of the respondent is an important variable in determining social-distance attitudes of the Spanish-speaking toward the Catholic church. Although women may, in particular instances, be just as distant and hostile to the church as men, the study shows clearly that the overall average of women, generally speaking, is closer and more favorable to the church than men.

According to the findings, age is not a significant factor in determining differences of social distance among the Spanish-speaking. Surprisingly, the majority of the youth of this study were not as distant or unfavorable toward the church as public opinion would influence one to expect. Also, the older and retired Spanish-speaking were not as close and favorable toward the church as is often thought. It is a significant finding that hypothesis two was not rejected. This is to say that social distance toward the church cuts proportionally across all age levels of the Spanish-speaking. Based on the data obtained from the study, expressions such as "youths are alienated from the Church" and "the elderly are 'turned on' to the Church" may have to be reexamined.

Ethnic identity among the Spanish-speaking of San Diego County is a most significant social-distance factor. How one identifies oneself or wishes to be referred to by others, such as Mexican American, Chicano, or Mexican, is an important variable in determining the relationship between the church and the Spanish-speaking. Chicanos stand out as being the more distant, hostile, and unfavorable toward the Catholic church, while Mexicans reflect a closer, less critical, and more favorable attitude. In determining social-distance attitudes of the Spanish-speaking toward the institutional church, it becomes vitally important to know how the Spanish-speaking identify themselves or wish to be referred to culturally, socially, historically, and ideologically. The implication of this finding is that, of all the Spanish-speaking groups, Chicanos are being reached the least by the institutional Catholic church.

The educational level among the Spanish-speaking of San Diego County is another significant factor in determining the social-distance attitudes toward the church. According to the data obtained and presented in the study, the higher the educational level of the individual, the greater the social distance from the church, while the lower the educational level of the person, the closer the relationship toward the church. The implications suggest a number of questions: Why is the Catholic church attracting a proportionately higher number of lower-educated persons of the Spanish-speaking community? Why is it failing to attract the more sophisticated and educated professional Mexican American? What needs are not being met by the Catholic church toward the more educated and professional Chicano/Mexican American? Or is the church, as it is now structured, meaningful only to the less educated?

The income factor of the Spanish-speaking of San Diego County proves to be another significant variable in the upper-income level, i.e., $13,001 and more. The study reveals that once the upper-income level is reached, persons tend to be significantly distant from the Catholic church. This implication raises a number of unanswered questions. Once a person has found financial security, is he less inclined toward the church? Why is the church less attractive to persons of upper-income levels? Why is it that the church attracts proportionately more lower- and middle-income types of Spanish-speaking people than upper- and higher-income levels?

The religious/civic type of organization to which the Spanish-speaking members belong is an important factor in the study of social-distance attitudes toward the Catholic church. The study indicates that those who belong to civic organizations are not as close to the church as those who belong to religious organizations. The type of organization to which the person belongs seems to be closely related to the variables of ethnic identity, education, and income. This can be stated in the following words: The Chicano/Mexican American, frequently more educated than the Mexican, with a higher income, and more inclined to join a civic rather than a religious organization, is more distant from the Church than the Mexican, who on the other hand is often less educated, has a lower income, is more inclined to join a religious rather than a civic organization, and is closer to the church than the Chicano/Mexican American.

The views expressed by the participants on the selected church issues make clear the following implications:

1. Many Anglo priests do not understand the language and culture of the Spanish-speaking. There is a shortage of Hispano priests serving the Spanish-speaking.

2. The church is failing to reach the Spanish-speaking, especially in its use of spiritual and financial resources to combat the social problems of the Spanish-speaking.

3. The church in the United States reflects the cultural values of the Anglo society. Consequently, many Anglo priests treat the Spanish-speaking as foreigners and aliens.

4. The Spanish-speaking lack an adequate voice in the decision-making policy of the church. Thus, there is need for more Mexican American bishops as ordinaries, i.e., with the power of jurisdiction in the dioceses they serve, to foster a better relationship between the Spanish-speaking and the church.

Although a large percentage of the Spanish-speaking feel close to the church, at the same time a significant number of them indicate they have personal reasons to criticize the institutional church. A large number of the participants reflect an evident dissatisfaction with certain church issues, such as not having voice and participation in the decision-making policy of the church in matters that pertain to the Spanish-speaking. It is the opinion of the author that a study of this nature ten years ago would not have been possible, for the simple reason that the people would not have been ready to analyze and criticize the church. Only within the last ten years, thanks to Vatican Council II which provided a spirit of openness and frankness within the church, many Spanish-speaking people have developed a deeper awareness and a more critical analysis of the church.

More and more people are beginning to grasp fully the meaning and significance of the two elements that constitute the church: the divine and the human. The divine element, Jesus the Lord, is not subject to criticism, but the human element of the church is. In this study, when references are made to criticisms against the church, they are not directed against the divine doctrine or sacred message of Jesus, the Lord, but against the ideas and actions of human beings who seek to express that message in a human and social dimension. The church is a divine institution entrusted by its Founder, Jesus the Lord, to express the Christian message to the world. But the institutional church is governed and administered by men, who are human beings. Thus, when the institutional church fails in the human social expression of the divine message, it must be subject to criticism. "It is this human expression of the Christian message, not the message, which has failed the Mexican American of the Southwest" (Carillo, 1971, p. 75). When the Spanish-speaking people criticize the church, it must be seen in this context.

The higher the educational and economic level of the participants, the more distant they are from the church. This finding may well be explained in that the conduct and expected leadership of church leaders are more keenly subject to critical analysis and scrutinizing evaluation by the highly educated than the less educationally prepared individual. Furthermore, a high level of education and a good-paying salary are often correlated. For example, a family in a higher-income level is financially in a better position to send the children to a college or university of their choice than a middle- or lower-income family. And usually those with a higher education obtain a better-paying job. Thus it often happens that those individuals in a high-income bracket are educationally well prepared and possess the evaluative skills to make a more critical analysis of the institutional church and of its leaders than those individuals with lower incomes, who often, but not necessarily, are less educationally prepared to make that critical analysis.

The study shows that among the participants who identified themselves as Mexican Americans, Mexicans, and Chicanos, the Chicanos were the more distant from the church. When one attempts to explain why Chicanos are more distant from the church, there is danger of simplistic analysis and stereotyping. There is need for more information to provide insights to this social phenomenon. Suffice it to say that not all Chicanos feel or think the same toward the church. Chicanos, as well as Mexicans and Mexican Americans, are not homogeneous, but heterogeneous. They cannot be boxed into one type of thinking, one kind of behavior, one class of people. Not all Chicanos can be considered as alienated from, or angry or hostile toward, the church. In the same way, not all Mexicans can be considered as being close to the institutional church. Some Chicanos recognize the faults of the church, but nevertheless remain faithful to her practices. They attempt to work within the institutional church for reforms and relevancy to the Spanish-speaking people. In the final analysis, perhaps Chicanos, Mexicans, and Mexican Americans, who indicated they were distant from the institutional church in the United States, are searching for relevant cultural forms of personal religious expression that are not presently found in the traditional forms of institutional worship.

The study further reveals that there are no significant differences of social-distance attitudes toward the church among the various age levels of the participants. This finding does not support the customary thinking that most of the young people are alienated from the church and that retired and elderly persons are all close to the church. The data gathered from the study indicate that social distance from the church cuts proportionately across the various age levels of the participants. Thus there are proportionate numbers of young people close to the church as well as distant from the church. In the same way there are proportionate numbers of retired and elderly people distant from the church as well as close to the church. The same can be said for the rest of the age levels.

More information is needed to explain the finding of social distance from the church in regard to the age variable. One explanation may be that people of the various ages of this study now have a greater awareness of what the church is and should be than they did ten years ago. Vatican Council II encouraged a greater openness and frankness within the church. More and more people are realizing that positive and constructive criticism against the institutional church does not make them "unfaithful" or "disloyal" Catholics, or that God will punish them for speaking out against the church. Nevertheless, a number of the participants of this study seemed to reflect a certain hesitancy to make known their honest and sincere feelings on certain issues that dealt with an analysis and evaluation of the church's relationship to the Spanish-speaking. For example, participants were asked if they have personal criticisms against the church, and a number hesitated to respond. This is quite understandable in view of the cultural and traditional training and background of the Spanish-speaking to have great respect and reverence for the church and its priests. But as the Spanish-speaking people gain a greater awareness and insight into the responsibility of their Christian vocation as it relates to the church and contemporary society, honest and constructive criticism against the institutional church will not be seen as disrespectful or irreverent. On the contrary, it will be interpreted by the Spanish-speaking as a challenge for the future growth and true liberating spirit of the church.

As a final note on this section of the study, it should be emphasized that there are serious problems within the institutional church in the United States which impede the full integration and active participation of the Spanish-speaking people. Based on seventeen years of experience in working within the institutional church, the author feels that the prospect for positive change within the church to alleviate these problems is, at best, dubious. This observation is founded on the past intransigent behavior of the dominant church leadership (i.e., bishops) in regard to the efforts of the Spanish-speaking people and clergy to make changes within the Catholic church in the United States. . . .

68. Resolutions of the National Chicano Forum, Salt Lake City, Utah, May 27-30, 1976 (excerpt)

How to deal with our own country presents the biggest challenge to us as Chicanos. It is historically evident that we, along with other minorities, continue to be deprived of full participation, benefits and protection under the law. We see more brotherhood with the oppressed from throughout the world, the exploited, the colonized, than the affluent society with which we live side by side in this country. Powerless, needy and desperate, we have few alternatives within the systems that keep us so. The strength we seek is bound to be found in our own unity. So is the answer to the question at hand: how do we deal with our own country?

The purpose of the National Chicano Forum was to (a) foment discussion on the major ideological problems facing our communities, (b) evaluate strategies for change, (c) exchange concrete ideas, information and perspectives.

On ideology, it was resolved that these recommendations be taken back to our people and communicated for reflection and praxis.

1. We massively educate *la gente* that there are no distinctions between *el Mexicano/Chicano*.
2. Historically speaking, there is a Chicano nation.
3. We recognize our real enemy as the ruling class.
4. We have a definite political/economic ideology and our leadership should promote it.
5. We believe this political/economic ideology to be a Marxist-Leninist socialism.
6. We do not support the imposition of any particular political/economic ideology on our communities.
7. Our unity comes from the awareness that we are in a class struggle.
8. Cultural Nationalism is intrinsic to the development of liberation.
9. *Lucha es parte del movimiento.* [Struggle is part of the movement.]
10. Our struggle for liberation is in solidarity with the struggle for liberation of all peoples.

69. *Corrido*

Juanita Domínguez

From Rendón, Chicano Manifesto *(New York: Collier Books, 1971), pp. 182-183. Trans. Armando B. Rendón.*

When the Poor People's march advanced to Washington, D.C., Juanita Domínguez, of the Crusade, wrote new words to a corrido called "La Rielera," composed during the 1910 revolution. It is in the spirit of a new people with a new awareness of themselves. It says as much of what nationalism and what the Chicano revolt are about as anything else that can be written or said:

Chorus I:
　　Yo soy Chicano, tengo color
　　Americano pero con honor
　　Cuando me dicen que hay revolución
　　Defiendo mi raza con mucho valor.

1. Tengo todita mi gente
　　Para la revolución
　　Voy a luchar con los pobres
　　Pa que se acabe el bolón.　　　　　　　　　　*Chorus I.*

2. Tengo mi par de caballos
　　Para la revolución
　　Uno se llama El Canario
　　El otro se llama El Gorrión.　　　　　　　　*Chorus I.*

3. Tengo mi orgullo y machismo
　　Mi cultura y corazón
　　Tengo mi fe y diferencias y
　　Lucho con gran razón.

Chorus II:
　　Tengo mi orgullo, tengo mi fe
　　Soy diferente, soy color café

Tengo cultura, tengo corazón
Y no me los quita, a mi ni un cabrón.

*   *   *

Chorus I:
  I am Chicano, brownskinned,
  an American but with honor.
  When they tell me the revolution has started,
  I will defend my people with all my courage.

1. My people are all united,
   for the revolution.
   I will fight with the poor
   to end oppression.   *Chorus I.*

2. I have my pair of horses
   for the revolution,
   one is called the Canary,
   the other, the Sparrow.   *Chorus I.*

3. I have my pride and manliness,
   my culture and love,
   I have my faith, I'm different,
   and I fight with great reason.

Chorus II:
  I have my pride, I have my faith.
  I'm different, my skin is brown.
  I have a culture, I have a heart.
  And no one can take them from me, no, not any bastard.

Hispano identity is more difficult to achieve in the big cities of the United States than in the migrant farm camps. The agricultural worker maintains the patterns and rhythms of a traditional Hispano society, but the city dweller, especially when outside the Southwest and Puerto Rico, is forced into alienation. The questions raised by the contrast in lifestyles, even when the Hispano is politically aware, are disturbing ones. In New York City, "Neorican," or just plain "Rican," was used for a time to designate a person of Puerto Rican ancestry born and raised in New York. Ideological meanings were attached to this description, although serious debate among militants reached the conclusion that "Puerto Rican" is a proper term for all the Puerto Rican people. The following selections reflect a debate between the stateside-born editors of

The Rican, published out of Chicago, and the island-born and based Manuel Maldonado Denis, writing for Claridad, newspaper of the Puerto Rican Socialist Party (PSP) in Puerto Rico.

70. Editorial

From The Rican, *no. 3 (Spring 1973), p. 3.*

We were disheartened to read a recent article in *Claridad*, "Rican or Puerto Rican?" Its content clearly indicated the author did not fully comprehend the meaning of "Rican," nor was he sufficiently acquainted with *The Rican Journal* to which he addressed his criticism.

A Puerto Rican either born or raised to a significant extent in the United States mainland operates from a particular social/historical context not often encountered by the Islander. To question, as the author did, a Rican's puertorriqueñismo approaches racism, but to deny his or her unique and different historical/cultural experience is to be out of touch with what is happening in the States. It can be argued that a Rican is as boricua or puertorriqueño as every brother and sister born and raised on the Island. Equating Rican with non-Puerto Rican is a gross misunderstanding. This reasoning can lead to geographical ethnocentrism and, as a consequence, rationalize a type of discrimination against our very own people.

We are a people of all three races, speaking several languages, with differing economic and environmental circumstances. We reside in all fifty states of the Union, in Hispanic America, and abroad. This is not to say, however, that one cultural experience is better than another. As a colonized and divided people, we have all suffered through differing external constraints imposed on us by varying social realities. The process of colonization enhances these differences, maximizing them when seemingly advantageous. *The Rican* journal is directed toward a specific reality facing one-third of all Puerto Rican people, namely those not living in the Island; a group, up to now, much abused and manipulated by tightly controlled institutions and repressive social forces.

A Rican is unique in that he or she is subject to a different type of oppression from that found in the Island. Denoting this experience by the word "Rican" by no means implies elements of non-identity or separateness from Puerto Rico. Our journal attempts to expose this reality which we in the mainland must vocally present and bring to the fore. The word "Rican," therefore, expresses a different life experience among our people.

Certain critics become overly concerned with labels and titles rather than the substance and meaning which these verbal designations represent. Critics will always exist, but let us aim to minimize petty differences and work toward the larger goal of human liberation. ¡Juntos!

---

71. Neo-Ricans? No! Puerto Ricans!

Manuel Maldonaldo Denis

From "In the Struggle," column in Claridad, *April 15, 1973. Used by permission.*

In one of his apparent efforts to leave behind hothouse politics, the Honorable Juan Manuel García Passalacqua has written a book where he dedicates a chapter to what he calls "the Neo-Ricans." This is not something new. Thus, for example, we have a literary review created by Samuel Betances with its headquarters in the United States and which is entitled *The Rican*. The author of this column himself once had occasion to use, mistakenly, the term "Newyoricans" in order to refer to those Puerto Ricans born in New York. Accordingly I have come to understand after almost a year of living in New York, that the classification of Puerto Ricans of the great city in a category apart from the ones born in Puerto Rico is not only an error from a cultural standpoint, but also a political error of the first magnitude. I believe moreover that the category itself involves, consciously or unconsciously, a prejudice—that can be traced to the social class situation of those who use it—and has profound consequences for the struggle for the liberation of Puerto Rico. It is necessary to eradicate this misuse as soon as possible.

No one can deny any more that the Puerto Ricans who have migrated to the United States live in a world which is, in some aspects, different from the one we know on the island. (It is enough to single out, at any rate, one question of great importance: the Puerto Rican who lives on the island finds himself in a numerical majority in respect to other groups—North Americans, Cubans, etc.—while the contrary is true when he goes to live in New York. Another example of what has been said is the language, the customs, etc.) The important thing is the fact that the Puerto Ricans who live on the island just as those who have migrated are faced with an analogous situation: both are objects of a continuous cultural aggression directed toward the dissolution of the historical and cultural ties that link them to our people, both suffer from this collective impotence that is congenital with every colonial situation. Nevertheless, in the case of the Puerto Ricans in the United States, the character of the cultural aggression and of the collective impotence is more brutal, more evident, more blatant.

Despite the dismantled ideology of the "Melting Pot" and its variants—including that which sees the United States as a multinational reality (Glazer and Moynihan, for example)—it is certain that in a society like the North American one, there is no room for cultural pluralism. The point of reference of each migrant group has been—as the aforementioned Glazer and Moynihan point out—that of "approximating the Anglo-Saxon center." Given these circumstances, the mood of the process of cultural assimilation in the North American society is impervious to any autonomous expression—to all cultural manifestation that goes against the grain of the predominant cosmovision in the cultural world just described. This is what explains the problem of the use of English as a vehicle of communication. The child born in New York or Hartford has been robbed of his language, has had his name changed (if he is Ricardo, he becomes Richard; if Roberto, Robert). In addition, to speak Spanish to another Puerto Rican is a mortal sin, better yet, it is original sin.

Well then, the cultural assimilation in Puerto Rico takes other channels. The process is less direct, less brutal, but no less insidious. In Borinquen they pretend to have assimilated us in Spanish. What is important is not that we speak in English—as happens with our countrymen to the North—but that we adopt the values, the cosmovision that the dominant class wishes that we adopt. The question is not if we speak in English, rather if we think like North Americans. In this sense the criterion of who is Puerto Rican is not based on one's capacity to speak Spanish correctly—Ferré is so *cursi*[1] that he speaks with the *ceceo*—but is based on identification with the values representative of the struggle for the national liberation of Puerto Rico.

There do not exist, therefore, Neo-Ricans and Puerto Ricans. Puerto Ricanness is not rooted in a merely cultural criterion, but in a political identification with the destiny of Puerto Rico. Such a thing as the Neo-Rican does not exist, we are all of us Puerto Ricans to the extent that we are identified with the struggle of our people to achieve the liberation of our country and to put an end to this colonialism which impedes our full experience of peoplehood.

1. *Cursi*=false elegance; a Mexican American might say *gachupin* or *malinche*; the terms are pejorative for one who affects cultural ties to Spain as a sign of superiority over the Creole population. The *ceceo* refers to the use of the *theta*, or North and Central Spanish pronunciation of the z and soft c as a *th*. Ferré is an ex-governor of the island.—Ed.

Padre William Loperena (see p. 243) has exceptional musical talents. He composed and recorded the *Misa jíbara,* or Puerto Rican folk mass, even before the liturgical reforms of Vatican Council II had taken full effect. His compositions are well known and sung wherever there are Puerto Rican Catholics.

After the suspension of the Comerío experiment in 1971 (see pp. 90-91), Loperena left Puerto Rico and traveled to the West Coast of the United States to study the organizing efforts of the United Farm Workers (UFW). He launched a similar effort later with the cooperation of others. The Puerto Rican church-affiliated agency took the name Ecumenical Farm Workers Ministry (META). During the years 1972–1974, Padre William worked in the Hartford valley of Connecticut and helped in the creation of a Puerto Rican Agricultural Workers Association (ATA), which has since merged with the UFW of César Chávez.

The following paper, reprinted in its entirety, was prepared for the Northeast Regional Pastoral Encounter, November 1974, to which Loperena was a delegate. In this presentation, he describes the centrality of migration to the cultural and economic experience of alienation.

72. The Phenomenon of Migration as a Central Religious Experience

Padre William Loperena, O.P.

Text of a paper presented at the Northeast Regional Pastoral Encounter, Holyoke, Massachusetts, November 1974. Used by permission. Trans. A.M.S.A.

It is not a mere coincidence that Abraham is, as the Father of the Hebrew People, a migrant. It was precisely that *migratory* experience that made the unveiling of the Living God possible for him. Theology is therefore full of the vocabulary of the migrant: exodus, pilgrims, way of the cross, sent from heaven, the flight from Egypt, the flight to Egypt, etc. The whole history of both the People of Israel and the church is the history of migratory people. The very word "pastoral" is the image of a moving flock under a loving keeper.

Those who undergo that specific experience of migrating somehow become more sensitive to religious experience. First of all, they easily discover that only God is the owner of this world, that he is the Creator. They know intensely that the earth is only part of a bigger cosmos. And they realize that quantitative reality is only a part of deeper dimensions of human life. By their suffering and sacrifice, migrants can, better than anybody else, appreciate the value of human life. By being victims of rejection by those they meet in the way, they hold fast to virtue and morality. And because they find it very difficult to subsist, they know the importance of work, food, economy. Their lives being in constant struggle, they understand justice. The migrant is not a hypocrite.

The history of the North American church has been the history of migrants: Puritans moving to the West, Irish, Polish, Germans, Italians, Greek, Puerto Ricans, Latin Americans, etc. It has been the history of these migrants defending themselves against the established peoples and creating newer forms of religious expressions. But sadly, it has been also the destruction of the myths of the Indians and of the Chicanos, and the adulterous relations with the powerful, forgetting the old days when we all were migrants in a foreign country.

The most profoundly theological and historical accomplishment of this Encounter, it seems to me, therefore, would be to *restore migration to its proper pastoral place: the center.* As Vatican II was able to reshape the Christian church, as Medellín was able to re-create Latin American Catholics, so can this Encounter relevantly organize our ecclesiastical institutions, if just we would dare to put the migrants in the place that religiously befits them: the center. This means in reality: ordain migrants as bishops, priests, and deacons; admit sisters from migrant women, organize parishes of migrants, get deeply involved in the issues of the migrants, keep an eye on migratory policies, and forget about the comforts of the settled. Guided by the Holy Spirit, Vatican Council II dared to center the problem of evangelizing in the problem of today's human being, the bishops at Medellín dared to centralize pastoral work on the underdevelopment and dependency of the faithful. Why can't this Encounter centralize the problem of the North American church on the experience of *migration?*

Migration is not a local experience. The Council of Churches has called attention to European migration. The United Nations has also documented the problem of international migration. In practically every nation, migration has been dealt with somehow. Through the issue of migration, many people have become aware of the realities of their own situation in this world. But the church in the United States is the one that could deal much more richly with migration, because it is here that the most dramatic types of migratory problematic occur. Just to give three dramatic experiences: the farm workers movement, the issue of "illegals," the massive Puerto Rican migration from the Caribbean. It is interesting that these three are Roman Catholic.

THE FARM WORKERS MOVEMENT

The situation of all farm workers in the United States dramatizes all thinkable socially decrepit conditions: health, education, low income, unemployment, etc. It also dramatizes the whole economic setup of this country, from simple small-farming to the most complex multinational corporations. In fact, a whole graduate course on economics could be taught taking farm work as constant. And a real political participation of farm workers is simply unthinkable in the modern United States. And still it is the production of farm workers that is maintaining the social, economic, and political institutions of this country, not to say the culture.

Farm workers are migrants, not by definition, but because of a particular condition in this country: *they do not have any property.* The lack of property is what makes them migrants. Any effort to help the migrant farm workers in this country has to be in terms of acquisition of competitive property. History shows us that farm workers became migrants when they lost their *tierra,* here, or in Africa, or in Puerto Rico.

Part of the farm workers' struggle, *and only part,* is the United Farm Workers. This is a merely unionizing aspect of the total problem of farm workers' migratory reality. The history of Puerto Rico demonstrates that unionizing farm workers, without a profound land reform, is in the long run a lost battle. The unionization of farm workers in Puerto Rico brought higher salaries and fewer jobs, the eventual need for migration to the United States in the 1940s, and the elimination of agriculture in the 1960s.

Another part, and only a part, of the farm workers' struggle is the Puerto Rican Farm Workers Association (ATA). Confronting the migratory policies of the government alone, without the positive reconstruction of the agriculture of Puerto Rico, and without the strong resistance to other industrial and mineral policies, would leave the migrants without property.

How about the black farm workers from the South? How about the "day hauls" from the cities? How about the students? How about the illegals who come to work in the farms throughout the United States? How about the farm workers where the United Fruit Co. and other multinational corporations have shunted farm workers to the slum areas of the big cities? Millions of human beings directly affected by their migratory reality! Indeed, this *is* a central theological question.

THE "ILLEGALS"

We all have had the experience of trying to help Latin American persons who do not have their "papers" in order. And we do not know what to do with them. If we help them through "legal" channels, we become guilty of getting them deported eventually, and they will blame us. Or labor unions would accuse us of helping wetbacks. If we do not help them, then they will blame us for not helping brothers of the Catholic religion. If we protest against the authorities, then we are accused of mixing in politics. If we denounce the real causes of their migration, then we are accused of being anti-American communists. If we care for them in our parishes, the other ethnic groups accuse us of partiality. If we do not care openly for them, we are accused of lack of commitment. If we join other church groups involved in the problem, we are accused of Protestantism. It is a mess!

Still there are millions of those "spiks," of those "foreigners." And they are Catholics, and they "have a soul to be saved." Nothing will stop them from coming to the rectories, to the Spanish apostolates, to any place where the good "padre" might find himself. And they expect us to be effective with their problems.

The worst mistake we can make against them is to treat them as if they came to the United States because this is paradise, looking for a "democratic" Nixonian national ideal of ultimate Christianity where economic possibilities are the result of science and virtue. Nonsense. They are forced to come to the United States because they are either (1) escaping from political repression, or (2) moved by the economies of their countries which have been invaded by multinational "joint-venture" corporations of agri-business that have absolutely no room for unskilled labor, and by a parasitic industrial development that has room only for an elitist type of urban worker. They are in the United States because the United States has sponsored in the State Department economic invasion to their homelands. They have no guilt, and they do nothing "illegal" by coming to the only possible alternative: the origin of their misery. What is immoral is that the corporations changed the economy of the Latin American countries *without taking responsibility for dealing properly with the horrible effects of their economic new policies in the mass of Latin American workers,* such as unemployment, disregard for other sectors of the economy, urbanization, and anarchic migration.

THE PUERTO RICAN MIGRATION

In order to avoid the possibility that somebody might accuse me of being a biased, one-sided Marxist *independentista,* and therefore miss the tremendous importance of the incredible phenomenon of the Puerto Rican exodus, I am going to limit my reflections exclusively to the official document of the Commonwealth [of Puerto Rico] entitled: *Report on Unemployment, Training, and Educational Opportunities,* by the secretary of labor, the director of Fomento, the secretary of instruction, and the ex-president of the Board of Higher Education of Puerto Rico.

It took from 1951 to 1969, a period of rapid and successful economic development and an enormous volume of migration, to reduce unemployment in a gradual, although uniform way, from 15.4% to 10.7% [p. 2]. . . . Emigration reduced the growth of the population of Puerto Rico by almost 800,000 persons in a direct or indirect way, and by another 600,000 corresponding to the children born outside the island to the emigrants [p.2]. . . . We can conclude that the reduction of unemployment was due as much or more to the continuous emigration and the reduction in the participation average than to the creation of new jobs [p. 3]. . . . Emigration of the unemployed that voluntarily have decided to leave has constituted the escape valve that has kept unemployment from reaching catastrophic proportions [p. 4]. . . .

We recommend, therefore, that even if the factor migration is highly unpredictable, the efforts to help migrants to adapt to the new environment be intensified so that the option to stay outside of Puerto Rico could be easier for them [p. 14]. . . . Emigration still constitutes a resting spot in the up-hill struggle to provide employment to the whole labor force of Puerto Rico, even if the North American economy in the last years has suffered substantial reduction in its receptivity to unskilled labor [p. 19]. . . . The Government of Puerto Rico should give funds to start an active program to guarantee that the governments of the communities where there are Puerto Ricans, as well as the Federal Government, take responsibility toward those migrant groups [p. 21]. . . . General orientation could be offered to the migrant who thinks of leaving Puerto Rico with respect to employment opportunities, housing possibilities, education and other services in different communities of the United States [p. 22]. . . . We should try to get Puerto Ricans to settle in these communities where they can find better opportunities, not only of work, but also of living, and that the greater number of Puerto Ricans that presently are crowded in the metropolitan areas of New York and other big cities, could move to other areas less inhabited by Puerto Rican migrants [p. 22]. . . . to develop a Program of Contracts of Labor in Non-Agricultural Jobs, following a pattern similar to agricultural contracts. . . [p. 22]. This could be called "organized emigration.". . . Relations with large corporations could be developed . . . [p. 23].

. . . The Government will have to design a plan of action that results in the reduction of the job demand through a series of measures related to (1) a migratory policy redounding in a minor influx of people towards Puerto Rico and possibly in a greater flux of Puerto Ricans to the exterior; (2) an active policy to retain the greatest number possible of young people in the school system. The policy of birth control, which is also urgent and necessary, would come to have effect on the working class in a date posterior to 1985 [p. 66]. . . . According to the studies done on sterilization, nearly 33% of the female population in reproductive age has been sterilized. In other words, of the 485,948 women of reproductive age resident in Puerto Rico, excepting those in San Juan, 160,363 are sterilized. This leaves a potential clientele of 325,363 women, of whom there are nearly 75,000 who now are making use of the medical services and contraceptives offered by the Department of

Health and the Puerto Rican Association for Family Welfare, and a population of 250,585 women remaining [p. 15]. . . .

There is agreement on the methods to be used to reduce fertility which are (1) sterilization, (2) anticontraceptive methods, and (3) education, widely defined [p. 15].

. . . Family planning is basically a problem of health, now that the use of contraceptive methods can create health problems and have an intimate relation with the health of the mother, the children, and the family. The Program for Mothers and Children in the Department is the natural means of attracting possible clients. Ninety-eight percent of mothers give birth in hospitals and 60% of these in public hospitals. As a result, the potential clients are within the reach of the Department of Health [p. 16]. . . . This [plan] can be realized through doctors and obstetrical nurses who attend pregnant women [p. 16].

According to the plan of the Department of Health, the Department of Social Services limits itself to orienting women recipients of Public Welfare and to referring them to the facilities of the Department of Health [p. 16].

This *Report,* which has been approved and which is already being implemented both here and in Puerto Rico, speaks for itself. The idea is that Puerto Rico should become a $10 billion copper center in the Caribbean, a place of superports for supertankers, and a living place for technicians, by 1985. To attain that, all unnecessary population has to be evacuated or unborn. This plan gives to the Puerto Rican migrant in the United States a unique theological position historically different from all other migrations. And 1985 marks a concrete goal and a concrete challenge for the Catholic church: whether to go along with that plan, or to oppose it, resist it, destroy it, present a better alternative. If the Catholic church decides to go along with the plan, then we would have to get ready to receive in 12 years about1,000,000 more Puerto Ricans in the Northeast region.

This *Report* is a macabre plan to create an island country where the native population is encouraged to leave for the slums of the United States, where tourism is encouraged for all except the people of that country, where the poor are sterilized through an immoral attack upon their rights through all the government-controlled agencies and hospitals, and the land is sold to business interests which destroy the topsoil, poison the atmosphere, import technical workers from other countries, and cover over with cement what the *jíbaros* call "Puerto Rico—Garden of Flowers."

Please do not think that this is only a problem of Puerto Ricans; all eyes are on this project. If it succeeds in its purposes of so-called industrial development, forced migration of the poor, and sterilization of women—and now of men—the same plan will be copied in the Dominican Republic, Costa

Rica, Colombia, Guatemala, and many other Latin American countries. In fact, no one who has studied economics can doubt for a minute that such plans are already underway. Our concept of social justice here in this Northeast region goes beyond our personal convenience and returns to the lands of our birth.

But if Catholics decide to oppose, resist, destroy the plan, and present a better alternative, then the church of the United States will have to coordinate with the Latin American church in a very well-defined strategy, and will have to concentrate efforts and resources on a national scale.

An effective commitment of the Catholic church in the pastoral question of migration necessarily means concrete commitment to both the farm workers movement and the Latin American illegal immigrants. Farm workers and illegals, like Puerto Rican migrants, are the direct consequence of the industrial policies of copper, energy, and similar corporate interests which care more for their technological goals than for the real situation of human beings on God's created earth.

CONCLUSION

The migratory experience of farm workers, illegals, and Puerto Ricans makes possible for all Catholics and people of good will the unveiling, the revelation, of the Living God. North American theology should be full of the Word of God in the vocabulary of the migrants. Today's history of the church is the history of the Hispano migrants, claiming to be "justified" from their opprobrium. The "pastoral" mission of the church then has to take care of this flock of migrants.

The Puerto Rican migration is a unique type of migration, and could become the redeeming element of other migrants. But the church has to decide between going along with the famous *Report,* or destroying it. We only have 12 years, until 1985. As we read in Matthew's Gospel, "Don't fear those who kill the body, for they cannot kill the soul."

CHAPTER THIRTEEN

TOWARD A DEFINITION OF LIBERATION

In addition to an ideological difference about the meaning of culture, there were misunderstandings in the Hispano church about the definition of liberation. In the early seventies, conscientization, as heralded by the Brazilian educator Paulo Freire, had been an important focus of MACC and the emerging Mexican American leadership. This understanding of liberation blended well with the concept of cultural pluralism or dialectical idealism in the tradition of Vasconcelos. For those who thought this way, to be aware of the need for liberation was itself liberation at a psychological level and would lead to praxis. However, the undeniable Marxist orientation of the theologians from Latin America provoked questions from non-Hispano church quarters (e.g., Robert McAfee Brown in Eagleson and Torres, 1975, pp. xvii, 94). Was "liberation" to be understood as "a socialist state"? On this point, the Mexican American pastoralists, whose understanding of liberation was "conscientization," were bound to be in conflict with liberationists whose definition required a new political order.

The Chicano liberationists, principally through the leadership of PADRES president Roberto Peña, O.M.I., reached out to liberationists in other regions and of other national backgrounds. This reflected a tendency of Chicano militancy in the Southwest that was moving toward solidarity with Latin America, the Third World, and especially with the Puerto Rican independence movement. Similar contacts were continued, reaching out to Christians for Socialism in Puerto Rico and like movements in Mexico. Peña met in 1976 with the university students of the New York Puerto Rican Naborí, a *comunidad de base* that was moving toward these goals in a Hispano youth movement called the Concilio Pastoral Juvenil (CPJ). Within the year, this proved the basis for the first coordinated national Hispano youth activity within the Catholic church, Operation Understanding, which took place during the 41st Eucharistic Congress in Philadelphia in 1976. The similarity between Peña's vision and the platform of groups like the National Chicano Forum proved disturbing to pastoralists everywhere.

The pastoralist leadership, to use a military phrase, "defended their flank" and encouraged Puerto Rican leadership in the Northeast to imitate programs of liberation-by-conscientization which came from MACC and the USCC Secretariat. Edgard Beltrán revisited the Northeast on several occasions in 1975 through 1976, bolstering the leadership role of those Puerto Ricans who reflected the pastoralist mentality—most of whom had never been identified in a political way with Puerto Rican independence. An important figure in this process was María Iglesias, a Sister of Charity who had been elected to the team government of Hermanas.

Among the *cursillista* leadership across the country, there was a questioning of the Trojan Horse strategy. They had anticipated more lay leadership and were disappointed to see that the emphasis at MACC and at the Northeast Regional Center, which had opened in April 1975, was on the training of clerical groups and religious women. Perhaps some *cursillistas* felt that the clerical emphasis was a betrayal of the original goals of leadership development for the grass roots. At other times, there was a nationalistic biting edge to the criticism, as for instance with the Northeast Regional Center, which did not have any Puerto Rican on the executive staff.

Many of the European-born Spanish priests in the Northeast and some Cuban priests in Miami felt the need to form new organizations. Their conceptions of church were not being defended by either the pastoralists or the liberationists in PADRES. Many preferred a church with the traditional hierarchical order, but at the same time were militant against a second-class status for Hispanos in their dioceses. Uncertain of the advantages of assimilating to PADRES, two priest associations with the same name were formed in New York and Miami. These were both called Asociación de Sacerdotes Hispanos (ASH), although they were not affiliated.

The diversity within the Hispano church had not only developed into components of different nationality and region, but had been divided and subdivided according to concepts of culture, liberation, and model of church. The fragmentation of the Hispano church, however, never lost a center of gravity. Realignments of loyalties and new constellations of alliance were in the making. This process of conflict over the meaning of liberation gradually stabilized through certain events beginning in 1975 with the Theology in the Americas Conference and continuing into 1976 with the National Encounter of PADRES, the 41st Eucharistic Congress, and the Call to Action Conference. The value in maintaining a strong liberationist model within the Hispano church was dramatized by several events: the fiscal crisis in New York, the arrest of the Hispano bishops in Riobamba, and the excommunication of Christians for Socialism in Puerto Rico.

The Theology in the Americas Conference in Detroit, 1975, was an attempt to bring the leading theologians of liberation from Latin America into dialogue with North American scholars and activists. Some of the invited speakers, Gustavo Gutiérrez, Enrique Dussel, and José Miranda, were not strangers at MACC. Yet the meeting generated certain judgments that it was "radical" on the part of the Catholic press (*National Catholic Reporter* editorial, Sept. 5, 1975). The nonappearance of Virgilio Elizondo and the nonparticipation of Hispano bishops and the official staff of the Secretariat of the USCC was interpreted as a rejection of the conference (Sandoval, *El Visitante Dominical,* September 21, 1975). It is impossible here to ascertain motivations, but it is certain that the ensuing statement of the combined Puerto Rican-Chicano group favored the liberationist model of church, making it difficult for the pastoralist to concur in the formulation.

The Chicano working paper has been published by Orbis Books (Eagleson and Torres, 1975, pp. 207-212). The following is the complete text of the Puerto Rican paper prepared for the conference, first made available through CEMI.

73. Puerto Rico Is Not an Island: Outlines of a Puerto Rican Liberation Theology

William Loperena, O.P. (the Island) and Antonio M. Stevens Arroyo, C.P. (United States)

Text of a statement prepared for the Theology in the Americas Conference, held in Detroit, Michigan, in 1975.

The basic consideration for any theology of liberation for Puerto Ricans, whether they live on the island or on the mainland, is the question of identity. In the normal psychological development all human persons undergo, insecurity and self-questioning are necessary phases: the case of Puerto Rico provides an occasion to examine this process in a whole nation.

Puerto Ricans are presented with an ambiguous birthright, being completely accepted neither as Latin Americans of a distinct nationality, nor as United States citizens participating in mainstream America. Some say that because they live under two flags, those of the United States and of Puerto Rico, Puerto Ricans have the best of both worlds. Others say that the Boricuas have the worst half of each. No matter how one tries to minimize its effects, this highly political question creates unique psycho-social effects.

In order to accommodate themselves to the serious contradictions of their collective existence, Puerto Ricans often have recourse to rationalizations. And these, in turn, create "myths" such as the vision of Puerto Rico, as "the tiny island in the Caribbean" that can expect only "insularism" (the title of a famous book of the 1930s by Antonio S. Pedeira). Historically, island and port cities are centers not of insularism, but of cosmopolitanism. Far from being isolated, they are crossroads of commerce and culture, frequently crucibles of empires and invention. Crete, Malta, Sicily, and England are some examples of islands which have cosmopolitan meaning. Puerto Rico's history is proof that it is closer to the cosmopolitan ideal than to that of insularism. But because it is a colony—the result rather than the cause of an empire—Puerto Rico finds itself with the myth of insularism, which restrains the development of an indigenous identity. The corresponding stereotype of Puerto Ricans as an impotent and pacific people with quaint customs is therefore a false one.

Puerto Rico is a *pueblo,* a people with concrete historical heritage derived from tribes of Indians, slaves from Africa, conquerors from Spain, and immigrants from Europe, joined together through a dialectical process. Two powers have denied the reality of Puerto Rico as a people: the Spanish Crown and the Congress of the United States. They have utilized much of in-stitutionalized religion to extend and continue the condition of oppression of the Puerto Rican powers. Since the internalization of the myth of Puerto Rico's insularism is an essential part of colonial domination, the churches—Catholic and Protestant—have repeated the theme. They have founded and guided their ministries in the pattern of territorial and institutional jurisdic-tions. With rare exception, the mainline churches organize by territories, by dioceses, by parishes. The Protestant missionaries who met in New York at the turn of the century to consider their task in the newly conquered Puerto Rico have left a unique testimony to this concept of Puerto Rico as a territory:

> At this remarkable prayer meeting they knelt around the map . . . upon the table and prayed God might help us to enter Porto Rico in such a way that there might never be a missionary hostility of any kind in that island. Then they divided the island into four sections, each board assuming responsibility for one of these sections. Through this Comity Agreement they hoped to eliminate the waste of power caused by friction and competition, to seek the best economy and cooperation, and, above all, to impress upon the people of Porto Rico the essential harmony and unity of our common Christianity.[1]

In the tradition of the *Arielistas,* the Puerto Rican free-thinkers who had opposed Spanish rule in the 1890s were sympathetic to United States politi-cal institutions and economic capitalism in the 1900s. Opposition to United States, domination was voiced by an elite class that romanticized the Catholi-cism and culture of Spain, but promised little social reform. As a result, the masses of people found little sympathy as a nation in the Protestant churches, which fostered assimilation to the United States, or in the Catholic church, which championed a return to retrograde feudalistic structures of a tradi-tional agricultural society. Gradually, the majority of Puerto Ricans began to look for religious meaning, not in institutionalized and territorial churches, but in movements, in Pentecostal and millenarian cults which were anti-

1. Emilio Pantojas García, "La Iglesia Protestante y la Americanización de Puerto Rico, 1898–1917" (Río Piedras: UPR, Ciencias Sociales, 1974), p. 6.

institutional in spirit. Puerto Rico has been a veritable cradle of Latin American Pentecostalism, Spiritism, and even syncretistic cults like the one of *"la Diosa Mita"* (Stevens Arroyo, in Mapp, ed., 1974, pp. 119–131). René Marqués, playwright and commentator on culture, has been prompted to say that "Puerto Ricans are not so much a religious people as a people in search of religion."

The theology of liberation in Puerto Rico, then, must be a dialectical criticism between established churches which all too often mirror the political structures of colonialism and the struggle of the masses to find meaning in their historical identity as a people. This coincides with contemporary social science. As Dr. Manuel Maldonado Denis (1972, p. 2) writes:

> I will therefore interpret our history as the scene of a struggle between these two forces: those who are in agreement with the demise of colonialism as a world historical trend, and those who are anti-historical and retrogressive in their support of colonialism.

In Puerto Rico, Pedro Albizu Campos, president of the Nationalist Party, was the first to unite Puerto Rican patriotism and radical change of the island's economic dependence on the United States as themes of nationhood. Albizu saw in Catholicism the value system to combat the disintegration of Puerto Rico's traditions, upon which was founded the consciousness of peoplehood. His efforts during the 1930s, crystallized as they were in Puerto Rico as a people and not as a territory, followed the waves of migration to the mainland United States. As large numbers of Puerto Ricans migrated to New York City, many became active members of Albizu's Nationalist Party. This was due in no small measure to their daily confrontation with racial discrimination. Welded into a political force with the emerging CIO and the Socialism of Harlem Congressman Vito Marcantonio, Puerto Rican Nationalists played a significant role in the forming of a Puerto Rican identity. Persons such as Luisa A. Quintero, journalist; Angel Arroyo, poet and author; Julia Burgos, poetess and activist; Gerena Valentín, community organizer; and especially Lolita Lebrón, patriot, all formed part of this early community. These persons generally were supporters of a Pan-Americanism which defended the cause of Sandino in Nicaragua and protested the dictatorships of Cuba and the Dominican Republic. Importantly, most of them were also strongly identified with Catholicism. But with the imprisonment of Albizu in 1937, the pulverizing propaganda of Muñoz Marín's Popular Democratic Party, the McCarthy purges, and ill-fated attacks on Blair House, on Congress, and the town of Jayuya in Puerto Rico, the effectiveness of this vanguard was blunted.

The great migration of Puerto Ricans to the United States (1946–1964) altered the relationship of continuity between those on the island and those on the mainland. No longer was it the more ambitious and the professionals who migrated; now hundreds of thousands of mountain people, or *jíbaros,* streamed into New York City. Never before has such a high percentage of one nation left their homeland behind. Only the Irish migration, at the time of the potato famines, can be used for comparison. Yet the Puerto Rican migration took place not during a natural disaster, but rather, during those years of economic modernization called "Operation Bootstrap." The encouragement of migration spawned a new series of myths. The travelers to New York were told that their North American citizenship entitled them to entry into a new world of promises, while behind their backs, so to speak, those who remained were told the migrants had left Puerto Rico in search of welfare, prostitution, drugs, and crime. These contradictions, coupled with an almost equal population division of the people between the island and the mainland, caused a great deal of self-searching. In the face of mass migration, the inadequacy of traditional religious movements on the island, such as the Holy Name and the Cursillo and the various Pentecostal and Evangelical crusades, became apparent. Social disintegration and immorality on the island became traits inseparable from the socioeconomic system that had been launched with so much enthusiasm as the "Commonwealth Status." Thus, in the 1960s, many young Puerto Ricans who had chosen church careers in the idealistic 1950s began to question their commitments to the church and reexamined their identity as Puerto Ricans.

Some of these, priests, sisters, ministers, or groups involved in pastoral work in concrete social conditions, tried to change the perspective of their institutions. They stopped considering Puerto Rico as an island, and began to strategize and organize the people for clear goals. Many had been compelled to seek professional and ministerial training in mainland seminaries and convents. They already had rejected, or were in the process of rejecting, an imposed professional role of Americanizer and were on the way to becoming authentically Puerto Rican. The more they studied the anthropological, social, political, economic, and cultural realities of the communities they knew, the more they realized that the original sin of institutions which caused their religious impotence was precisely that these never dared to recognize the collective reality of Puerto Rico. In the secular sphere the MPI (Movement for Independence) was reconsidering the struggle of the Puerto Rican people, and adopting a political stance toward socialism. Inasmuch as this MPI was not yet a political party (later it would be the basis for the PSP, or Puerto Rican Socialist Party), some church persons were drawn into these circles of reflection and action. Hence, as the involvement of the religious personnel became more concrete and specific, it was more and more closely identified as a part of "an underground conspiracy," and more and more church people were branded as "communists." This resulted in the marginalization of these activist elements from the institutionalized church bodies. Everything they did, everything they said was vitiated because of its contact with the specific issues of liberation: worker's movements, socialist economy, liturgical and educational trends, and issues such as mines, the superport for petroleum refining, the test bombing on Culebra Island, migration of farm workers to the United States, etc. The process of marginalization from church crossed the line into overt repression with the famous case of the expulsion of four Dominican priests from their parishes in 1971. As a newspaper reported it:

> The suspension of the priests of the parishes of Yauco and Comerío is the first step in a plan prepared by our bishops to remove all communist elements and instruments which operate freely, taking as their base the official agencies of the Holy Church. . . . There are communist priests who are committed to an international conspiracy which has as its target the underprivileged classes of Latin America.[2]

Fortunately, most of the "rebel" religious groups were able to subsist in their battle:

1. *Centro Juan XXIII,* lead by the Puerto Rican Monsignor Antulio Parrilla Bonilla, S.J., dedicates its efforts to research of very concrete Puerto Rican realities in the light of the documents of the Vatican Council and the conclusions of Medellín.

2. *Fundación Santo Domingo,* led by four Dominican priests in the rural area, tries to create models of action in the psychological, social, political, and cultural realities of the Puerto Ricans in conjunction with national and international movements.

3. *Misión Industrial,* tries to empower the workers movement in the light of scientific analysis of concrete plans of the industrial setup and governmental policies, especially in regard to environmental protection.

4. *PRISA (Center for Social Research and Communication),* ecumenical effort of twenty-four projects dealing with four basic issues: increased rates of specific pathologies, progressive reduction of agricultural and fishery capabilities, overall problems resulting from investment which do not correspond to the needs of the people, problems of distributive justice concerning economic expansion.

5. *JOC (Christian Youth),* communicates to the Puerto Rican Youth the expectations of the workers throughout the world from a Christian perspective in the famous methodology of see, judge, act.

6. *Asociación de Sacerdotes de Puerto Rico,* tries to cope with the gap between the hierarchy and the priests.

7. *Center for Conscientization,* a staff of experts in the method of Paulo Freire, which provides professional help to projects, agencies, etc., working at the basic problems of Puerto Ricans.

8. *Spanish Commission of the Episcopal Church,* gives resources to liberating models throughout the United States and Puerto Rico.

2. Trans. from "Barren infiltración comunista en iglesia," *Decisión,* September 10–23, 1972.

These groups have not separated themselves from their original institutions, except ideologically: while institutions keep looking at Puerto Rico as a territory, these groups look at Puerto Rico as a defined nation. These groups do not compete with the institutions, but operate in an independent new way. They do not have a centralized organization, but in general they coordinate with each other. They also work with "secular" institutions and groups, such as: the Puerto Rican Socialist Party, *El Comité* of the United States, the World Peace Commission, the Solidarity Committee, etc.

Their experience has led them to consensus principles, which still need more careful articulation in verbal form; tragically, they are forced to work in an atmosphere of suspicion, mistrust, hostility, and even religious persecution. This explains the stridency of Puerto Rican liberation theology and its great clarity: stridency, because it is realized at great personal sacrifice; clarity, because it is a concrete and daily experience.

THE NEW YORK PUERTO RICANS

The history of the Puerto Rican community development in the city of New York can be roughly summarized in four major periods, each with its own religious and economic characteristics.[3]

1946–1955: In this period, which roughly coincides with the post-World War II migration and the similar phenomenon after the Korean War, large numbers of Puerto Ricans entered the United States by arriving in New York City. At that time the postwar boom made American products, particularly in the garment trade, in great demand all over the world. The returning veterans of white and ethnic background were gravitating to the suburbs of Long Island, New Jersey, and Westchester counties, and vacating large areas of employment and residence in the city. The Puerto Rican people entered easily into these vacant positions in the New York society and some began to assimilate to the fabric of North American life in patterns similar to previous ethnic groups. The church response, particularly that of Catholics, was to continue the national language chapels that had served previous Puerto Rican and Latin American peoples.

1955–1965: In this period scores of key industries began to surrender to technological trends and relocated to new industrial parks in the suburbs and frequently overseas. The presence of urban poor and unemployed became more visible and, in the prosperity of the era, sparked the introduction of paternalistic welfare programs. These efforts were directed by a North American liberalism which presumed poverty was caused by lack of opportunity. All social work was aimed at helping the poor to adjust, explaining their plight as due to lack of either education or knowledge of English, or to racism.

3. *Taller sobre migración* (New York: CUNY Center for Puerto Rican Studies, 1974).

The churches were oriented to self-help programs that stressed the aspects of human dignity, demanded civil rights, and pictured those with socially unacceptable behavior as victims who could learn better ways if they were accepted into society. The musical *West Side Story* graphically portrayed these struggles by showing the inability of anything less than love to overcome gang warfare, juvenile delinquency, and drugs.

1965–1973: These were the years of the administration of Mayor John V. Lindsay in New York City. It witnessed a new assertiveness of the Puerto Rican people as a minority group in the mainland's politics, and the exodus of industry from the city in the economic order. The two phenomena were interrelated inasmuch as the increasing impoverishment of large sectors of the city population created social unrest that could be resolved only by a smokescreen of "political participation." This was a convenient route to follow because the War on Poverty of President Johnson sent large sums of federal money into the hands of minority-community organizers.

This extension of liberalism's political structures to blacks and Puerto Ricans introduced competitiveness as a measure of success, no longer among individuals but among ethnic and racial groups. For example, now housing projects were not built as temporary lodging for the poor until they got "good" jobs. Instead they were to be model communities, "urban villages" that reflected the American dream of an "integrated neighborhood." In this system liberal-type Puerto Rican agencies gained visibility as power brokers for the collective Puerto Rican interests. ASPIRA (a Puerto Rican educational agency), the Puerto Rican Forum, the Puerto Rican Community Development Project, and others became involved in power struggles against blacks, working-class whites and, ultimately, against each other.

The seeds of contradiction were present in opening up so much of an area of social and political awareness. In the Catholic church, for instance, Summer in the City, an imaginative program of Monsignor Bob Fox, stressed the creation of community in the face of material poverty by a creative humanity. Many of those who began protests to secure more funds from the liberal establishment would eventually come to protest the establishment. Catholic activists of the right, like Father Louis Gigante, advocated a return to "machine politics": other church leaders, however, chose to "drop out" and began promoting the charismatic renewal of the Pentecostals.

Toward the end of the Lindsay administration, the tokenism of some professional Puerto Rican agencies was discredited and a rupture appeared between local grass-roots poverty agencies, local school boards, and drug rehabilitation projects, on the one hand, and the professional institutions that had designed them, on the other. The grass-roots organizations used slogans about "the poor people deciding" in order to reject control from above, and, with their ability to deliver votes, became the principal targets for political favors. A similar phenomenon occurred within the Catholic church as the

Puerto Rican people began to reject—at least theoretically—the foreign clergy. This resurgence of a nationalistic feeling reflected the country's swing toward ethnic politics. The cause of a "Hispano church" became an identity crisis for most traditional Puerto Rican Catholics. Drawn neither to politics nor toward the Charismatic Renewal, most of these Cursillo-trained people began parroting a call for quantitative representation within the church, e.g., a Puerto Rican bishop, etc. This was the background and mentality of most of those who participated in the press conference of March 28, 1973, which was organized by a group called CHAPJ (Cristianos Hispano–Americanos por Justicia).

1974 to the Present: The present period of Puerto Rican development in New York is one of disintegration. In the period 1960–1975, the city lost 420,000 jobs, so that employment is below what it was in 1950, although the total of jobs in the United States has grown 80 percent. More importantly, the industrial jobs, those in which Puerto Ricans are concentrated, fell to about one-half the 1955 total. When the banks refused to extend credit, the city was forced to pay the bill for a disproportionate political development at the expense of economic health. In the interest of economies, the city is eliminating services, schools, departments, parks, museums, etc., and the workers who made these benefits possible to the city inhabitants. In the face of such massive retrenchment, the whole meaning of "city" changes. Since political favors also are too costly, the shrinking economic base cannot be covered up. The only way to maintain a semblance of social order is to avoid offending those who can protest effectively, and instead afflict most heavily those who lack clout. The end of the old-style liberal formula for city government required a "caretaker" whose principal roots were with the working-class constituencies of white ethnics, the city workers and teachers, who would be most directly affected. This meant Abraham Beame, a political war-horse, for mayor to succeed Lindsay. The opposition to Beame's triumphal entry into Gracie Mansion came from what was left of the Reform Liberals and the Puerto Rican community, which made this strange alliance because Herman Badillo was the standard-bearer of a continuation of the Lindsay policies.

The churches have been faced with similar economic problems. They have not demonstrated a significantly more noble approach. Every day a Catholic school closes or a program is cut back. More often than not this is done on a purely economic basis: saving money and serving "our" Catholic people. The curtailments inevitably fall heavily upon Puerto Ricans.

In sum, the malaise in New York City is not worse than the problems in Puerto Rico. In both instances, the cause of oppression is neo-colonial structures which deny the nature and rights of a Puerto Rican people. The oppression frequently becomes repression, adopting fascist-type characteristics which use forced sterilization and police brutality as forms of control. In

New York City the particular dialectics of this neo-colonialism are different in form from those in Puerto Rico, but their effects are essentially the same. Moreover, any theology of liberation must take into account the internalization by the majority of Puerto Ricans of the colonial mentality that has created all-too-familiar myths.

MYTHS AGAINST PEOPLEHOOD

Two important aspects of liberation must center, first, around the stigma attached to Puerto Ricans, and second, on the vitiation or "lumpenization" of the masses of people. The first is an external adscription of nonpersonhood; the second is the internal acceptance of the same. The use of the word "stigma" is derived from Erving Goffman (1963). He describes stigma within a socio-psychological background. The concept is more useful than just "racism" because liberalism has co-opted racism by making it quantitative. In New York City today, if we read the law books, racism is *structurally* inoperative. There are few if any public policies that do not operate on some sort of quota system or are not scrutinized by "affirmative action." Yet the polarization of the races is escalating. This is because the dynamics around the stigma of race are not diffused by a quantitative approach. North American liberalism asserts that racism has created the poverty and ignorance of the Puerto Ricans: racists excluded these people from jobs, housing, schooling, etc. Hence, the argument runs, the racists must now be forced to give a proportionate share of these opportunities to the victims of racism. Since the class structure is not attacked, this implies that those who will do the most "sharing" are those at the bottom of the social strata. Obviously, more Puerto Ricans will be poor than rich, just as in society there are more poor than rich. The worse the effects of racism, the more needed are the quotas. In order to gain the advantages of state intervention in the name of civil rights, Puerto Ricans are encouraged to prove themselves more victimized by crime, vice, unemployment, and poverty than the blacks or other groups. In this system, the leaders who most clearly demonstrate the impotence of Puerto Ricans are the most likely to be rewarded with political benefits and favors. Naturally, this encourages talented people to disguise their talents, productive Puerto Ricans to become unproductive. Moreover, it creates a "backlash" on the part of working-class whites and blacks who are penalized for their productiveness and forced to share scarce opportunities with the least-qualified Puerto Ricans. It is, in plain terms, discrimination in reverse—but has proved to be an effective tool of the bourgeoisie to divide the working-class.

The public image of the stigma of being Puerto Rican generates a dynamism that makes it a self-fulfilling prophecy. The Puerto Rican internalizes these negative images: this is the process of "lumpenization" whereby the whole community becomes corrupt. According to the Latin American economist Gunder Frank, a managerial class (*lumpen-bourgeoisie*) controls the unfolding of a false or lumpen-development. All progress is based on an economic and cultural dependence of the most gross and overt form. In New York City, such Puerto Rican leaders are called "poverty pimps." Their grotesque ambition contrasts with the establishment type, who is petty bourgeois. This is why Ramón Vélez was always pitted against Herman Badillo: it was a question of class.

Today the New York government promotes gambling (the New York State Lottery and Off-Track Betting), subsidizes unemployment by food stamps and the welfare system, and because of inadequate police action, allows widespread sale of drugs, street crime, rapes, and intentional destruction of property by vandalism and fires. *Baile, baraja y botella* (translated as "Dancing, dice and drink") was the nineteenth-century device of internalizing colonialism in Puerto Rico. Today there is heroin for the drinking, OTB for the dice, and Salsa for dancing. The stereotype produced by stigma is internalized. Puerto Ricans become lumpen—not lumpen-proletariat—simply lumpen. The description by Oscar Lewis in *La Vida*, although it was inaccurate on many scores, seems to have captured the personal dynamics of this situation in his "culture of poverty." He asserts that while the character of the individuals concerned and their lust for life were not dimmed by this process, their basic human and communitarian responses were perverted.

Of great importance is the situation of the secondary migrants, or those who were brought to this country by their parents. (Likewise we ought to include in this category those born in the United States of Puerto Rican parents.) They have been collectively referred to as the "Neorican," denoting a fusing of two identities. With some exceptions (and ones not to be lightly dismissed), it is this Puerto Rican who lives by the culture of poverty, never having known anything else. For him lumpen is lifestyle: Alfredo López, in *The Puerto Rican Papers*, calls it "slick." Even for those with family backgrounds that are "proper" or petit bourgeois, it seems impossible to exercise visible leadership without some appeal to this image that has been nurtured on "slick." The examples of media Puerto Ricans come to mind: Geraldo Rivera, Freddie Prinz, Felipe Luciano. One can even ask if there are "lumpen-radicals." Some of the militancy of this generation as well as its adoption of radical language would seem to answer this question affirmatively.

Not all Puerto Ricans suffer in the same way, of course. With the establishment of many Puerto Rican Studies departments during the militancy of the late 1960s, larger and larger numbers of young Puerto Ricans destined for professional jobs became radicalized. They began entering the job market in the middle seventies just as the budget cuts affected the city. Their collective response to the crisis of New York will no doubt be aided by a developed class-consciousness.

Perhaps of even greater importance is the return migrant. The myths created by stigma and lumpenization are strangely echoed in the cry for *estadidad jíbara*, that is, for total annexation of Puerto Rico by the United States on the premise that Puerto Ricans could "get more" and have little or no taxes to pay if Puerto Rico were a state of the Union. Notice that the political rhetoric insists on being a "first-class" citizen, but the purpose is to be a beggar rewarded for his need. This mentality presents a danger to Puerto Rico's status quo, both because of an increasing number of return migrants (some 16 percent of the island population) and because of the ideological sterility of the commonwealth status.

THE ROLE OF THE CHURCH

Today the backbone of Puerto Rican Catholicism in the United States is the Cursillo movement. The Cursillo is a protest against the process of lumpenization. Much of the clannishness and sectarian attitudes generated over the years by the movement can be understood in terms of working-class reaction to the process of alienation. Unfortunately, the focus is usually the institutional church and not the real world.

For the most part, the clergy trained to speak Spanish during the sixties are aware of their limitation. However, even if they are anxious to participate in an indigenization of the church and an end to its paternalism, they tend to view the struggle outside the question of nationalism. They prefer to analyze conflict in ideological terms such as "conservative vs. liberal" or even in administrative ones, "parish priest vs. chancery official." Moreover, many are simply "tired out" from activism. Some have entered into the Charismatic Renewal. The imported clergy from Spain, on the other hand, scarcely if ever escape the claims of anti-Nationalism, always pitting "gringo vs. Hispano" and frequently denying any value to Puerto Rican reality in the fabrication of a grand "Hispanidad" loyal to *La madre patria*.

There is hope, however, that serious reflection upon the dimension of the social oppression in the city will find good earth for sowing. One group committed to praxis and capable of class-conscious activity is Naborí. Comprised of City University students, this is a *comunidad de base* that seems to have been able to achieve some modest goals within the limitations of student life and youth ministry. Of particular importance was a two-month-long institute that engaged Hispano youth from many states in a work-learn situation among the migrant agricultural workers in Connecticut in the summer of 1975.

The Protestants of Acción Cívica Evangélica began in 1974 to move the largely pietistic Pentecostal churches into social organization. They now sponsor nutrition programs, youth-employment offices, minicenters for the elderly, and political-education classes. At least some of the younger elements within this group are keenly aware of the theology of liberation and consciously attempt to use it toward deepening the awareness of the participants in the organization.

Much smaller Catholic groups such as The Alternative Coalition (TAC) and local parish *comunidad de base* organization provide potential, but have little visibility at present.

THEOLOGICAL THEMES

Some personal reflections suggest theological themes to cast some light upon the Puerto Rican situation in the United States. Christians know the fecundity of faith in being a migrant people. Abraham went to a new country, Moses led the Hebrew people back to the Promised Land. Both of them brought back new sophistication owing to contact with foreign cultures. Jesus himself had to satisfy a midrash concept of return from Egypt in order to fulfill the Scriptures.

Foreigners were the catalyst of greater faith. The encounter with the Samaritan woman at the well surprised the disciples, as did the great faith of the Roman centurion. The "Good Samaritan" was the model for love of neighbor in need, and the gratitude of the cured leper caused Jesus consternation with his own kind.

Jesus worked with lumpen. He said that the kingdom would be filled with the sinners, prostitutes and publicans before the hypocritical men of the religious establishment.

The social education begun by such programs as Summer in the City, must go to the roots of class-consciousness. The reactionary church of the chancery can be ignored, but there is real danger from the clergy who seek federal and state and city monies to finance programs "to help our people." These clergy, like the "poverty-pimps" they denounce, are part of the lumpen-bourgeoisie.

In terms of the Puerto Rican working-class, the work of the church must be seen in terms of cross-racial class solidarity. The middle-class white church clergy must learn to deal successfully with Puerto Rican lumpen. In so doing, there cannot remain vestiges of paternalism or "do-goodism." This calls for careful screening of those at work in the ministry, and a thoroughgoing radicalism before beginning.

Finally, the Cursillo concept of an all-healing divine grace must be avoided. There is no such thing as "cheap grace." It if is true that the Lord of History is capable of more than individual people, it is nonetheless true that his role as Lord came from suffering and death. Jesus gave his life in an effort to hand over his spirit in a struggle against the prince of this world. And in his victory over death, however it is understood, he proclaims to those with faith: "Have no fear: I have overcome the world."

The National Encounter of PADRES, held in New York City in April 1976, reduced tensions between liberationists and pastoralists in the Hispano church. The president of PADRES, Roberto Peña, desired a multi-Hispano dimension for this first PADRES Encounter outside California or the Southwest. Bishop Juan Arzube of Los Angeles was invited to give the keynote address, and bishops Antulio Parrilla Bonilla from Puerto Rico (see pp. 90-91) and Roque Adames from Santiago de los Caballeros in the Dominican Republic provided a Caribbean presence at the proceedings.

During the Encounter, some of the members of ASH in New York (see p. 270) spoke of joining together with non-Hispano clergy of the area instead of individually becoming members of PADRES. This eventually led to the foundation of Padres of the Apostolate of the Northeast (PAN). PAN placed priority on the goals of fraternity and the legal rights of priests in the Northeast. Moreover, at the first assembly held the next year at the same retreat house in Jamaica, New York, on November 9, 1977, PAN elected a Hispano, Francisco Domínguez, president, and a non-Hispano, John Brogan, vice president. Nonetheless, PAN did not reject an eventual merger with PADRES when that organization would open full membership to non-Hispanos.

The selections that immediately follow are taken from the talks by Bishop Arzube and Padre Roberto Peña, delivered during the Encounter.

Bishop Juan Arzube is especially prepared for this task of bridge-building. Born in Guayaquil, Ecuador, in 1918, he received a degree in engineering at Rensselaer Polytechnic Institute in New York State. Successful in the business worlds of his native Ecuador and Los Angeles, he eventually decided on the priesthood, and was ordained for the Los Angeles Archdiocese in 1954. After years of service as a parish priest and pastor, he was ordained auxiliary bishop of Los Angeles in 1971. At first his Ecuadorian nationality was a drawback in the largely Mexican American community of Los Angeles, but as can be seen from his presentation, he turned it into an asset. Bishop Arzube bridged the gap between liberationist and pastoralist by appealing to the needs of the people.

The presentation by Roberto Peña stressed that cultural, regional, and even biological differences can be overcome by a commitment to struggle for justice in the socioeconomic order. This is a theme dear to the heart of this Brownsville, Texas, native. Peña's was a delayed vocation, as was the case with Bishop Arzube. Serving in the army before entering the Oblates of Mary Immaculate at the age of twenty-three, Peña was ordained a priest in 1955. He filled a variety of posts in Oblate parishes in Texas, and eventually became a strong advocate for social justice in his native Brownsville. He was given the opportunity to study for the Social Justice ministry, and spent a year (1974–1975) at the School of International Studies at American University in Washington, D.C. He was elected to the first of his two terms as president of PADRES in 1974.

74. Multi-Hispanic Urban Solidarity

Bishop Juan Arzube

From Bishop Arzube's keynote address to the PADRES National Encounter, held in New York City in April 1976. Used by permission. Trans. A.M.S.A.

. . . The theme chosen by PADRES for this Encounter, "Multi-Hispanic Urban Solidarity," is likewise indicative of the level of development and growth that we have achieved in the organization and the thinking of the members of PADRES.

In its beginnings, back in the year 1969, due to the special circumstances of that time, the membership and the interest of PADRES was for the Mexican American priest.

Last year, during the National Congress that PADRES had in San Antonio, Texas, from the second to the fifth of February, it was voted upon and favorably decided that the membership would be open to any priest, deacon or religious brother who was Hispano and is dedicated to the service of Hispanos. The active movement of the members of PADRES, however, has been limited almost exclusively to the states of Texas, New Mexico, Arizona and California.

But with this convention taking place in New York and with the central theme of Multi-Hispanic Urban Solidarity, PADRES is clearly opening its arms to all the Hispanic brothers of the country, telling them: We don't want any more "backyards"; we seek a broad vision that takes in the whole country and all Hispano-Americans: let the Cubans, the Puerto Ricans, the Mexicans, those from Central and South America join their efforts, their minds, their energies, their hearts in order to obtain a true multi-Hispanic solidarity.

The truth is that the number of Hispanos in this country continues on a very accelerated curve of growth. According to the latest statistics from the division of the Department of Justice in Washington (the Community Relations Service) the total now approaches 20 million, of which more than 11 million are found in the census figures of the past year, and the Department of Immigration estimates that there are more than 8 million undocumented persons.

Some 40 years ago, during the economic depression which swept the country, the migration of blacks from the South toward the North passed almost unnoticed. In the same way now the migration of the Hispano to urban centers receives relatively little attention and care from the rest of the population, even though there are enormous national and international consequences which this migration brings with it.

Because of this, we have to make others see that, if it is not taken into account, and if Hispanos are not made to participate in the programs and decisions of civil and ecclesiastical matters, the considerable increase in Hispano population can cause great complications in the maintenance of social order in this country. But if, on the contrary, they organize and plan programs for the future by counting on the presence and collaboration of the Hispano, this increase can signify a great richness of cultural and intellectual growth for the country. One might mention here that it is not satisfactory or proper that projects first be developed in English and then a group of Hispano "experts" summoned to translate into Spanish. Rather, it is necessary and indispensable that the collaboration of the Hispano is counted on from the beginning, and not only from some experts but from the grass-roots people, so that this voice can be recognized and properly understood in all its cultural aspects. . . .

We have to convince ourselves that being united with all of the Hispanos in this country will make us into a force with the same kind of impact as an atomic bomb. Because of this we need to count on a true leadership at the parish level, and the diocesan, regional, and national levels. The development of this leadership is for me the number one priority. There are great masses which are like the flock without the shepherd in many parts of the country. Yet the leadership must not be of the "paternalistic" type but like that which comes forth from the people, which is distinguished for its conduct and spirit of sacrifice and commitment and is admired and respected by others, works with and for them.

At times we waste valuable elements of leadership due to the fact that we demand too much of them as far as doctrinal or technical preparation is concerned. The catastrophic effect of this lies in that we let the Jehovah's Witnesses go from door to door with their propaganda, but we don't let ordinary Catholics of good will do the same according to their potential.

In Los Angeles, one priest has had a lot of success publishing some simple flyers with information which offers religious thoughts, articles with a sense of humor, cooking recipes for the housewives, local news, short Bible readings, etc. He found first 10, then 20 and later 30 persons who committed themselves, each one, to distributing these little flyers personally, once a week to 10 houses in the neighborhood. So each one sustains a communitarian spirit in his neighborhood and, at the same time, is able to tell the priest about any physical or spiritual necessity in the barrio. . . .

To close, I would like to share with you a meditation about the day of judgment in which we can imagine Jesus telling us:

I was hungry and you spent millions to send a man to the moon.
I was hungry and you blamed the communists.
I was hungry and you told me to be patient.
I was hungry and you created a committee to study the situation.
I was hungry and you told me, "We don't have bread or work for the illegals."
I was hungry and you assured me with indifference that, certainly, I was to blame because I was lazy.
I was hungry and you got worried about paying more for war weapons.
I was hungry and you quoted the Bible to me, "We will always have the poor with us."
Lord, was it really You who was hungry?

---

75. Concerning Multi-Hispanic Urban Solidarity

Roberto Peña, O.M.I.

Text of Peña's presidential address to the PADRES National Encounter, held in New York City in April 1976. Used by permission.

Solidarity taken as an effort to be united as a *pueblo Hispano* can be obtained through a change of our attitudes, attitudes that seek the well-being and justice for my brother and sister. We need to overcome the tendency to egoism, individualism, and materialism that prevails in our society, which is encouraged by our sociopolitical-economic system through fetish consumerism. To animate this change of attitude, we have to become a people that is concerned with a people's development that is total and authentically human. This commitment arises from a serious "Gospel Reflection" that analyzes Christ's concern and option for the poor, the oppressed poor, who should have the basic human needs to live with human dignity.

PADRES' efforts for solidarity and commitment to the service of our Hispanic people can be determined by our unequivocal identification with *nuestra gente pobre* [our poor people]; one of the purposes of our existence is mutual support to this commitment. We need to offer ourselves, our scarce financial and scientific resources and expertise to continue a creative search for a ministry that is truly missionary and apostolic. We need to be saturated with the Holy Spirit that can lead us to those institutions that enslave *nuestro pueblo* and deny us our religious, social, political and economic rights, and self-determination. Connected to this saturation of the Holy Spirit is the consideration that we be allowed to be responsible through our own leadership to contribute to the justice and peace that the people of God seek. Lastly, this commitment must carry with it the challenge of a Passion, Death and Resurrection so that the "other" may live with human dignity.

In the quest for solidarity, let us become sensitive to the mass media of communication that can provide us the forum through which we can present, clarify, organize and form coalitions in our *lucha* [struggle] for justice. A sense of national unity is lacking in our struggle. We need to know that the problems of the urban West and the urban East are not the same—the barrios of Los Angeles and San Antonio are not the same as the ghettos of Chicago and Brooklyn where our people live. We do not have the luxury of sociologically knowing each other through academia, so every source of communication must be used to bring about a national Hispanic solidarity.

Our cultural identity, which is another element for unity, and is being stressed through the word "Hispanic," should not lead us to a Hispanic melting pot; our cultural strength lies in not losing our identity as Puerto Ricans, Colombians, Spaniards, Cubans, Chicanos or Mexican Americans, to name a few. In our time let us stress less the folklore of the cultural, but accentuate our common effort as a people for a communal life through justice.

The contradictions that exist in the socioeconomic and political arena in an urban situation are so forceful that one feels useless to confront them, such as secularization and the gigantic operative principles of large corporations that determine our well-being and that of the rest of the world. These operative principles are technological rationalization and maximization of profit. "Technological rationalization" means that in the planning of the operation by the decision-making board, all factors of production are considered in terms of their contribution to the total process. Each factor is technologically perfected to make it more efficient in the operation of the whole. These factors include the laborers, who are treated as just another thing among the factors of production. Another operative principle that determines the fate of our poor is "the maximization of profit," a principle of planning and decision-making. It simply states that when the board of directors is confronted with various plans of action and development, it will study them carefully, compare them with the others and eventually choose the plan that promises to maximize the profit of the company; thus, by being faithful to this principle it makes decisions that affect people, especially the working class. The problems that result from the application of these two principles are common to all the poor, including the Hispanic in our urban situation. These common problems for the working Hispanic people are a basic reason for solidarity, since solution to them has to be a concerted effort of the working Hispanic Christian. Modernization in industry and inflation bring great unemployment among our *gente* [people]; economic justice is essential to employment.

To realize our solidarity there must also be a true process through which we truly accept the *mujer* [woman] as an equal partner in our quest for liberation. There can never be a true struggle for solidarity in our Hispanic community and in the total church until *nuestra mujer* becomes an essential part of our ministry to the poor. *La mujer* is as capable and as dedicated to the mission that we as PADRES have chosen.

Lastly, another common element that we have for solidarity is our faith. Our common faith is part of our cultural heritage, which is predominately Catholic. Our present concern is our many brothers and sisters, young and old, who are not identifying with the Catholic church and are leaving it for other denominations, which most of the time separate them from our communal efforts to work for justice and peace through a conscious effort for solidarity.

In conclusion, may I state that we have just scratched the surface of seeking multi-Hispanic urban solidarity and we need to go back to our people and allow them to show us the way.

The 41st International Eucharistic Congress, scheduled for Philadelphia in August 1976, was an opportunity for the pastoralist leadership to demonstrate the power and organization of the Hispano church to the world. The results of the efforts of the Washington Secretariat to orchestrate a mass demonstration of unity and harmony, however, were less than entirely satisfactory. Father Lucien Hendren, invited from Santa Fe to direct Hispano participation from a national level, was surprised repeatedly by complaints and countersuggestions to his program. For instance, the *cursillistas* of the Northeast, largely Puerto Ricans, and led by Mr. Eduardo Kalbfleish from New York, insisted that the preeminent place of host concelebrant at the Spanish-language mass be given to Cardinal Aponte Martínez of San Juan, Puerto Rico. Since he was an American citizen, it was argued, he was the highest-ranking Hispano in the United States. And so, instead of a Mexican American serving as host prelate to Hispano bishops from all over the world, a Puerto Rican took the spotlight.

At the leaders' conference held during the congress, however, none of the Puerto Rican prelates was invited. That meeting was shortened by lack of time, and although it specified some important directions for future development, such as unity in pluralism, youth and lay leadership, it was incomplete. Moreover, the implementation of these goals was left principally in the hands of the secretariat, to the pique of regional offices of the Midwest, Southwest, and Northeast. The regional directors—Rogelio Manrique, Lupe Anguiano, and Mario Paredes—sensed that the grassroots people had so completely absorbed the theological focus upon *el pueblo,* that they could not accept meetings organized from above. As Bishop Arzube had described in his address to PADRES, equal participation was imperative not only vis-à-vis the non-Hispano institution, but also for Hispano leadership.

Typical of mounting grassroots impatience with vestiges of paternalism was the complaint of Haydee Borges against the Northeast Pastoral Center on the question of a woman's conference. The excerpt is taken from a newsletter published from time to time by CHAPJ (see p. 278). The principles of cooperation and equality are well articulated, albeit in a context of rights *within* the church, as one might expect from the framework of the *cursillista* ecclesial model.

76. The Voice of the Laywoman in the Church of the Northeast of the United States of America (excerpt)

Haydee Borges

From El Pueblo Pide, *December 1976. Used by permission. Trans. A.M.S.A.*

On May 5, 1976, the Regional Pastoral Center for Hispanos in the Northeast called a woman's meeting for a small group of ten lay and religious women involved in the Hispano apostolate. The director of the center wanted to hear the women's opinion about how to establish a communications network with all of the Northeast of the United States—something of great importance, since the church is made up of men and women, although men are always the ones who have a voice in what is going on. It is then a rare occasion when we women are asked for our opinion in order to form a more exact vision of what the church is. They asked us for written suggestions and said that these would be taken into consideration in the planning of a pastoral approach for the center. I personally sent my written suggestions, some of which are already being taken care of. For the second meeting, they asked each one of us to invite another person besides ourselves.

On June 9 we met again, the ten women, and talked about how to organize ourselves as women and as Northeast. We decided to continue meeting as a woman's group at the regional center and thus offer our suggestions and ideas for the better operation of the center. On July 6, thirteen lay and religious women came to the monthly meeting and, with a lot of enthusiasm, it was agreed among ourselves to plan a conference on the Hispana woman of the

Northeast. Each one of us agreed to do some "homework," with an eye to organizing the conference. It was agreed that the theme of the conference would be "The Ministries of the Woman in the Church," and the following topics would be treated, four topics by two key speakers: (1) Woman Historically, Considered in the Past (biblically, Mary) and the Present (Scripture); (2) The Pastoral Issue of Today (pastoral dynamics in small groups); (3) The Woman in the Apostolate Today (a panel for each need); and (4) Cultural and Religious Obstacles Which the Woman Faces in the Church (group dynamics).

Women from the Northeast were to be sought for the principal presentations. On September 8, 1976, another meeting was held where different laywomen from the grassroots were excluded for reasons that were scarcely convincing, and in that meeting three committees were formed: (1) Committee for the Program, on which there were only three religious and an American laywoman (who quit); (2) Publicity Committee, formed by three laywomen from Brooklyn and a sister; (3) Committee for Hospitality, formed by three religious women.

It is ironic to think that those left out were lay persons from New York! Those who were not informed of the meeting and thus were absent could join any of the committees. Now, in accord with parliamentary law, committees are named to plan and to study, but then their work should be presented to the whole assembly or group in order to be approved, with changes or additions. Here, the committees plan and it's done! What two or three say is the decision! A meeting was called for each group and only four persons came to continue what had not been either reviewed or approved by a majority. Although the presentations shall be those that the committee had prepared, what happens? Three or four people are making the plans for the conference and this is not democratic, since a conference of this kind in the Northeast should take grassroots laywomen into account, and not be planned only according to a vision seen from the ideas of three religious women. I think that the church is made up of religious men and women, lay persons and priests, etc.

Here can be very clearly seen the third-class role that is given to the woman who is not a member of any religious order. We are discriminated against, first because we are Hispanas, second for being women, and third for being lay persons who do not belong to any religious order. The religious woman—nun—lives a reality very different from ours since she has been lucky enough to get a good education with a great academic title. And speaking of justice, this does not give them the right to speak for all women in the church, since they have to recognize that we nonreligious women live a very different reality. As a laywoman and as a leader, I ask that the voice of all the women in the church be heard. If we want unity, we should respect each other as true sisters, daughters of the same Father God, redeemed by one Lord, Jesus Christ. We don't want a conference where they tell us the problems to challenge us. But let our voice be heard with all united in love to help each other, to look upon ourselves as equals, the women of the church!

We women of the grassroots serve God by a divine vocation through our baptism, without any limitations or bonds to the structures which oppress and stifle the spirit. I, as a single laywoman committed completely to the service of the church, wish to publicly raise my voice from these pages of *El Pueblo Pide* since they don't pay any attention when you speak privately. Two years ago grassroots women asked for a movement of Hispana women in the church and nobody showed great interest in it. This conference offered great hope, but we see with great sadness that the conference—if it is carried out—will be a resounding failure, since they have not taken into account the grassroots women. In order to free others, we first have to be free ourselves from the bonds of selfishness and pride, from complexes of all kinds, and above all be free in Christ, who is the Truth and Justice for all. . . .

As a free woman in Jesus, I speak out loud for the equality of rights of the woman in the church, and as a Christian I ask and demand that our dignity as daughters of God be respected in our diverse states—single women, married, widows, divorcées. We serve the total church—without pay—by vocation and love for God and neighbor, and as laywomen we carry the royal priesthood of Christ, consecrating our femininity day after day on the altars of service to the People of God—church—and in the church we work so that in this world there may be found peace, love, understanding, happiness and, above all, sisterhood and justice for all—equally.

Shortly after the 41st International Eucharistic Congress, some of the Hispano bishops with Father Edgard Beltrán and Pablo Sedillo journeyed to Riobamba, Ecuador, for a historic meeting with leading Latin American prelates. In the ensuing violation of the meeting's privacy and the mass arrest by the government of the participants, the visitors from the United States suffered the same as their Latin American brothers. The Hispano bishops, all of whom fit the general description of pastoralist, were treated as political revolutionaries by the military of Ecuador. It was as if the distinction made within the Hispano church between liberation as pastoral conscientization and liberation as radical political action was meaningless in Latin America. Indeed, Bishop Antulio Parrilla Bonilla had prophetically stated at the 1976 PADRES Encounter, "There are no pastoral questions which are not also political ones."

77. Protests against the Mistreatment of the Hispano Bishops of the United States in Ecuador

From El Visitante Dominical, *September 12, 1976. Used by permission. Trans. A.M.S.A.*

... According to Monsignor William Martin, vicar general of the San Antonio, Texas, Archdiocese, the meeting of prelates in Riobamba, Ecuador, was organized by the Vatican, and the Hispano bishops of the United States were invited as [special] guests of CELAM, the Latin American Episcopal Conference, to help study the social conditions in a cluster of Spanish-speaking countries and to be able to help the suffering poor.

The conference was held in the Retreat House near the city of Riobamba and coincided with the Annual Meeting of the Latin American prelates in a place some 130 miles from Quito, the capital. It was expected that the meeting would last from August 8 to the 14th. The host at that time was Bishop Leonidas Proaño of Riobamba, who is a controversial figure in the eyes of the present Ecuadorian government. According to Archbishop Sánchez of New Mexico, it is very possible that "the arrests were made to discredit Bishop Proaño," since recently he has been actively engaged in programs of agrarian reform against poverty for the benefit of the Indians of Ecuador. All of this has inflamed the wrath of large landholders.

On Thursday, August 9, at five o'clock in the afternoon, members of the Ecuadorian police in plain clothes invaded the meeting room where the priests and bishops were in session, and, armed with machine guns, carried the prelates off in buses to prison. . . .

78. Interview with Pablo Sedillo

From El Visitante Dominical, *September 26, 1976. Used by permission. Trans. A.M.S.A.*

The following is the text of an interview with Pablo Sedillo on the occasion of the military government's "invitation" to leave Ecuador, when Sedillo and church hierarchy and religious leaders attended an international conference for the interchange of pastoral experiences.

1. What was the nature of the meeting and what was discussed there?

The theme of the conference was basically a review of the pastoral work that Bishop Leonidas Proaño of Riobamba has been developing for the past five years. The meeting had its origins in a meeting that took place a year ago in Tula, Mexico, where various Latin American bishops got together. They continued meeting in a friendly way to search for solutions to the particular problems of South America. So the first three days of the conference in Riobamba were dedicated to exploring the pastoral plan of Bishop Proaño. I can add that the meeting was at the invitation of the bishop, who, of course, as Ordinary of a diocese, has a right just like any other bishop to invite bishops to share their experiences.

2. Is it possible that what constitutes an act of subversion for the armed forces is a pastoral concern for a bishop?

No, I don't think so. In the first place, we were dealing with church matters and not with politics, so that everything fell under the religious tenor of the diocese's pastoral plan, as I just mentioned.

3. Concretely what did you deal with?

We dealt with the kind of development that the bishop has had in his diocese, that is to say, the development of leaders from among the peasants of the diocese. I understand that the government interpreted this as a preparation of leaders for revolutionary purposes. As a participant at the meeting, I want to emphasize the fact that this was not any different from meetings held in church circles in the United States. Such meetings create a level of conscientization within Catholic communities regarding individual responsibilities toward church and state. This could have had some influence, but I would say that the word "revolutionary" has particular connotations. I would place these men in a category of being perhaps "revolutionaries of the gospel," of trying to take the gospel to the people, but not in the sense that I

think the government of Ecuador understands "revolutionary," stretching it
as far as subversive attacks or a plot to topple the Ecuadorian government. . . .

---

79. Declaration of the Hispano Bishops on Their Treatment in Ecuador, August 9-14, 1976

From El Visitante Dominical, *September 26, 1976. Used by permission. Trans.
A.M.S.A.*

We, bishops of the United States, together with Mr. Paul Sedillo and
Father Edgard Beltrán of the NCCB, were invited to attend the meeting of
the National Conference of Latin American Bishops in Riobamba, Ecuador,
from the 9th to the 14th of August. The purpose of this meeting was to share
our pastoral experiences with the bishops present. The participation of the
North American bishops offered a better understanding of the great number
of Latin Americans resident today in the United States. We wish to make it
clear that this meeting was not held in secret. We arrived in the country
wearing Roman collars, with American passports and the corresponding
visas. The Episcopal Conferences of the different Latin American countries
had previous knowledge of the presence of the bishops at this meeting. We
wish to make it clear that the meeting had at no time a subversive character. It
was a sharing of pastoral experiences only.

We wish to protest the unfounded suspicions that the Ecuadorian government displayed toward this meeting and most especially against the violent
and forcible manner in which the meeting was interrupted and in which the
participants were arrested. Armed, without identification, and offering no
explanations, the military police, dressed as plainclothesmen, forced all the
members at the Holy Cross Retreat House with the participants of the
meeting into trucks to be transported for some five hours to the city of Quito.
They did not offer the detainées any explanation about this act of violence.
Nevertheless, we wish to emphasize that during the detention we were
treated courteously.

We are grateful for the intervention of the Papal Nuncio, Monsignor Luigi
Acogili, the Cardinal Archbishop of Quito, Cardinal Pablo Muñoz Vega, the
American Embassy, the Ambassador M. Blumfield, and the Mayor of the city

of Quito. We wish to give thanks for the help that they rendered to all those who were detained. We want to make it clear that we were not expelled or deported from the country. All of those who were detained were given unconditional release. We do not harbor any animosity against the Ecuadorian people. We profoundly lament this act, which was so serious and shameful on the part of the Interim Minister of the Government of Ecuador, Javier Manríquez.

August 12, 1976
Quito, Ecuador

> Roberto Sánchez, Archbishop of
> Santa Fe, N.M.
> Patricio Flores, Auxiliary Bishop
> of San Antonio, Tx.
> Gilberto Chávez, Auxiliary
> Bishop of San Diego, Ca.
> Juan Arzube, Auxiliary Bishop of
> Los Angeles, Ca.

In Puerto Rico, the Catholic Bishops Conference, which no longer invites Bishop Parrilla Bonilla to its meetings, issued a pastoral letter that was read at all masses on Easter Sunday 1976. The letter excommunicated any persons "subscribing to the Marxist doctrines of Christians for Socialism." A substantial part of the position paper of Christians for Socialism is provided here, along with the full text of the bishops' condemnation.

80. *Position Paper, Christians for Socialism, Puerto Rico (excerpt)*

November 19, 1975

. . . This captivity of the Christian faith is very palpable in Puerto Rico. The churches have been used in the service of the empire. Despite a supposed neutrality, which in practice presupposes a choice of position, the churches have served as conveyors of the values, symbols and ideals of the empire.

Often the economic dependency of the churches and institutions has been the determining factor in achieving this identification with the empire. Many church-related schools, founded for the benefit of the poor, have placed themselves at the service of the Americanization of the colonial elites. Even today much of the clergy is of a foreign mentality, alienated from our national struggle. With a few praiseworthy exceptions, religious leaders have lent themselves to service as spokesmen and allies of the regime in areas such as worker-employer conflicts, student uprisings and environmental problems. Ecclesiastical organizations and institutions have shared the social, economic and even racial discrimination of the rest of the colonial Capitalist society. They have also been, at times, an important factor in the investments of transnational corporations. Our commitment to the Gospel obliges us to denounce this situation, as part of the process of struggling for the liberation of our people.

The preaching of an abstract kingdom, remote from the historical present, has stunted the growth of a revolutionary consciousness in many of our people. The dominant classes have used the Bible to justify their structures of power. The dominated classes, through a situation of ideological dependence, have internalized that justification. The Exodus history of the Hebrew people has become politically neutral; the prophets have been reduced to mere purifiers of the cult, minimizing their profound message of justice and their condemnation of the oppressors. Jesus has been projected as a meek and mild preacher of bourgeois ideals, obviating his intense revolutionary message. Christian eschatology has been transformed into a land beyond the grave. The illusion of an otherworldly kingdom serves to castrate the impulses of historical renewal, since it concentrates the believer's attention on an afterlife, thus separating it from the tasks of transforming the reality around us.

As a result, the original and correct meaning of Christian faith has been distorted. This has led to a separation between faith and commitment, and to a fear of political involvement in the struggle for justice. Such involvement has been seen as anti-Christian. It has also led to the use of Christian faith as a brake against those who radically question the existing structures of power. Ecclesiastical leaders ally themselves with temporal leaders to carry out repressive measures against the voices of resistance and protest. Priests, ministers and seminarians are threatened, marginalized and expelled for their dissident visions and their conflicting interpretations of the relationship between faith and the present situation. Laity too, when they disagree with official positions regarding the political, social and economic panorama of our reality, confront repudiation, censure and marginalization from our religious institutions.

As Christians who have opted for socialism and national independence, we live in solidarity with the oppressed of our country and of the world, and we condemn injustice and oppression in all their manifestations. We do so fully aware that we are a part of the people of God struggling for our own liberation. We commit ourselves to struggle so that social, political and economic conditions may contribute to the enjoyment by all human beings of the state of dignity and nobility to which God created them. Only in this way can we fully understand the message of Christ to the human being, and in this way the new church can bear its true witness as a sacrament of salvation for all.

CHRISTIANS AND THE STRUGGLE FOR SOCIALISM

Beginning with our commitment to the struggle for the liberation of Puerto Rico, and with our understanding of the development of similar efforts at the international level, we have reaffirmed—together with Christians from other countries, especially in Latin America—the original, authentic, liberating meaning of the Christian faith. We have rediscovered biblical faith as a mobilizing force among the masses on behalf of the oppressed and exploited poor.

We identify ourselves with the history of the Christian faith. The origin of the Hebreo-Christian tradition is found in the liberation of an enslaved people, obligated to manufacture bricks under oppressive conditions. From that time on, that people understood God as redeemer of the poor and oppressed, and understood itself as the vanguard of a kingdom of justice, abundance, peace and brotherhood, which was to be established on earth. The promise of that new order was conceived in different ways by each prophet, precisely because it was seen in terms of the concrete problems of the history of Israel. The historicity of biblical faith and its commitment to justice for the poor, the oppressed, the marginalized and rejected of the dominant system, constituted the center of prophetic preaching.

This is the same tradition that Jesus receives and invigorates. His ministry is characterized by confrontation of the religious, political and economic powers of his time, represented by the Pharisees, Sadducees and rich people. Although his message about the kingdom of God is for everyone, it is limited to the poor and those who live in solidarity with them. The new order of things as represented in the kingdom of God allows no class distinctions, nor a system that produces them. We find a sign of this social revolution in the early church, both in the Magnificat of Mary and in the decision of the disciples to sell their property and live communally, sharing their goods.

Even though we find in the Bible itself and in the history of the church occasions in which oppressive ideologies are triumphant, time after time the history of liberation arises as the lodestone of the Christian tradition. History shows us the continuity of this interpretation of the faith with which we are identified. We are heirs of the Christians who have struggled, in Puerto Rico too, for this new order of liberty, justice and brotherhood.

Theological reflection can clarify the history of faith as commitment to struggle toward this new order in which we place our hope. But before this can happen, theology must itself be liberated from ideological captivity and from the distorting prisms placed over it by the dominant classes.

Christian faith was distorted first by the pressures placed on the church by the political and economic powers, to legitimate them as natural, universal, and representative of general well-being. This necessitated the ideological transformation of the church through the adoption of a cosmic vision which would separate religious consciousness from commitment to a new worldly order for the poor and suffering. The ideological apparatus used for this purpose involved the spiritualistic cosmic vision of contemporary Platonism. For the Bible there is only one history and God is manifest in it, truth is forged and a new reality is built. Platonic metaphysics, in contrast, lays over history a world of ideas wherein the essence and the immutable, universal truth of all things are to be found.

Theology, thus, attempted to develop a Christian life without regard to the imperative of historical transformation or to commitment to the new order of justice and freedom. Into the vacuum created by the spiritualization of theology came the economic, political and social structures of the dominant classes as if they were natural, universal structures, representative of the essence of social being, and they were sacralized. In some cases there were attempts to make religious consciousness apolitical, relegating it to the realms of the private, the personal, the spiritual. In others, there was open legitimation of the existing order, making of theology a direct source of ideological justification of the structures of power. The Protestant Reformation, for its part, identified with the new centers of power that were characteristic of the emerging capitalist system.

One important manifestation of the use of theology and Christianity to support dominant structures has been the hegemony of the man over the woman in the church. Theology has uncritically accepted a patriarchal background for its conceptualization. The priesthood and principal hierarchical positions have been reserved exclusively for men, excluding women or relegating them, as in the case of feminine religious orders, to a secondary and auxiliary level. As a strategic objective of our organization, we envision the total elimination of this discrimination against women in the heart of our ecclesiastical institutions. This objective is focused within the context of the socialist struggle against the exploitation of women and their integration in an equality of rights within society.

We confirm, therefore, that theology became prisoner of the interpretations of the dominant classes. And that is how we received it: as a negation of the biblical concept of history. We must liberate it from that captivity and return it to a function of reflection on the historical praxis of liberation and the building of a new reality.

We are identified with the theologians who have developed in Latin America what is known as the "Theology of Liberation." This theology is a critical reflection on the concrete and historical praxis of liberation. It attempts to restore history to its pristine value, starting with reality itself. It incorporates into theology a scientific, dialectical and global analysis of economic, social and political reality; also into the ideology which represents the best political strategy of liberation. Theological reflection ceases to be merely an interpretation of reality, and becomes a theory of transformation of reality.

We consider useless for theological reflection all dualisms between soul and body, spirit and matter, eternity and history, which remove salvation from the only history which exists. It is in this history that Christians and non-Christians meet, in the struggle to build that new order free of oppression and alienation.

The values and hope of Christian faith are fruits of history. We contribute them to the struggle for human liberation. We understand, however, that Christian faith does not itself provide an instrument of social and historical analysis, nor a political strategy for the concrete realization of those values and that hope. For this, we adopt the analytic instrument and political strategy of socialism. We choose socialism for its scientific nature, its concrete solidarity with the oppressed, and its vision of a future society free of human exploitation. We recognize socialism as a specific contemporary means by which to make our faith historically effective.

We understand that history is an open process, with a future to be made, which moves dialectically. The conflicts found in human social reality come from the development of relations of production which determine, in the last analysis, the type of political organization that upholds the social order and the class content of the law, morality and education which justify it ideologically. We reject as pseudo-science attempts to analyze social reality by taking for granted the established system, imputing social wrongs to a malfunction in that system, claiming a neutral objectivity toward it and suggesting economic and political "efficiency" as the solution to social problems.

We reject the attempts to create "Christian" political alternatives between capitalism and socialism. The parties of what is called "Christian Democracy" have proved to be anti-socialist instruments used by the capitalist system to manipulate Christians, as in the Christian Democratic parties of Chile, Germany and Italy. We must make our contribution of Christian hope and values in the revolutionary process as socialists committed to the future of humanity.

The dominant classes have made use of Christianity to uphold their anti-Communism and defend their privileges. In this way they have tried to isolate the Christian working people from the socialist struggle, creating an emotional and arbitrary antagonism between Christian faith and Marxism. In recent years, however, this attitude has been questioned by both Christians and Marxists. A new search for theoretical common denominators, which can serve as a basis for cooperation in the creation of a new society, has come out of the joint struggle of Christians and Marxists against European Fascism. In several countries, especially in Latin America, political alliances have been established between Christians and Marxists to carry out the popular struggle more effectively. Thus we have come to recognize the possibility and necessity of a strategic alliance between revolutionary Christians and revolutionary Marxists. This has led to a new openness on the part of Christians to Marxism, and on the part of Marxists to the revolutionary potential of the Christians. We reject anti-Communism as a divisive strategy of the dominant classes to impede the development of class consciousness among the working people and their full participation in the revolutionary process. We recognize that just as in the past the Christian faith was critically expressed in the contemporary categories of thought, structures and institutions, it can also be expressed in socialist conceptual categories and institutions. As Christians committed to our people's destiny, we are free to use Marxism as a methodology of social scientific analysis and revolutionary praxis. We insist, too, on our right and responsibility to participate in the organized socialist struggle in labor unions and political parties. We reject the position that atheism is the indispensable condition of a good socialist and participant in the organized socialist struggle.

Christians for Socialism is an autonomous and nonsectarian organization. By autonomous we mean that our group, although independently involved in the process of national liberation and socialist struggle, is not an appendix or front for any political organization. By nonsectarian, we mean that we do not have as a function the propagation of any sect, church or doctrinal system. We are united by the biblical message of freedom and justice and by our choice of socialism.

On the other hand, our group cannot be an excuse for individual failure to participate militantly in political, labor, social or community organizations which in some way are involved in the struggle of the people for liberty and justice. On the contrary, these organizations are the front ranks of our militance. As a group, we consider it useful to meet for reflection, evaluation and criticism of our political action in the light of the Christian and Socialist beliefs which we uphold.

Our organization serves as witness, within the churches and in the heart of our people, to the authentically liberating nature of the Christian faith. We are obliged to fight every manifestation of repression, especially within ecclesiastical institutions. That means being alert to all repressive infiltration by the agencies of imperialism (CIA, FBI, and others). We must also keep watch over the human rights of those who are persecuted, imprisoned and oppressed. It means, too, that we offer our testimony, clearly and firmly, to the authentically liberating character of Christianity in the midst of the revolutionary process.

81. Bishops of Puerto Rico Denounce Socialist Movement (text of statement)

From El Visitante Dominical, *May 2, 1976. Used by permission. Trans. A.M.S.A.*

The Episcopate of this island has issued the following statement:

The bishops of Puerto Rico have followed with great attention and concern the birth and development of the movement Christians for Socialism, as much outside of Puerto Rico as in Puerto Rico itself. A careful study of the documents coming from each international assembly of the movement, not excluding the document prepared by its adherents in our country, has convinced us that the movement is based, if not completely, at least in part, on Marxist doctrine which has been declared repeatedly by the Magisterium of the Church as totally incompatible with Catholic faith, although said doctrines may be presented under the guise of Gospel or theological norms and proposed as a new way, and promoted by persons clothed with ecclesiastical authority (cf. Pius IX, *Divini Redemptoris;* Paul VI, *Ecclesiam Suam,* n. 37; Allocution, 24-XI-1965, *Octogesima Adveniens;* Cardinal Ugo Poletti, Allocution to the Pastors of Rome, 19-X-1975; Allocution to the Priests' Senate of Rome, 30-X-1975; Declaration of the Italian Episcopal Conference, 13-XII-1975; *Osservatore Romano,* 25-I-1975).

Moreover, Christians for Socialism, like other ideologies and theologies based on dialectical materialism, is objectionable to Catholic teaching because of its acceptance and promotion of an ideological and theological monism, also censured by the Magisterium of the Church (cf. "The Document of Christians for Socialism," P. Pierre Bigo, S.J., pp. 4-5; Leo XIII, *Sapientiae Christianae,* n. 13; Pius XI, *Immortale Dei,* n. 21; *Gaudium et Spes,* n. 43, 76; Paul VI, Allocution to the Diplomatic Corps, 10-I-1972).

Because of these reasons, we declare that those who profess, defend and propagate the doctrines of Christians for Socialism, like those other ideologies or theologies based on Marxist doctrine, incur the same censures laid upon those in these systems and ideologies (cf. Canon 2314 in the Codex of Canon Law as provided for those who are apostate from the Christian faith; The Sacred Congregation of the Holy Office, Decree 1-VII-1949, AAS 41, 1949, 334; cf. K. Hormann, *Dictionary of Christian Morals,* 1975, p. 1291).

Hence we exhort all the Catholic faithful, priests and religious, not to belong to the movement Christians for Socialism, nor to any other movement or theology objectionable to the Church, inasmuch as they would run the risk of incurring the same sanctions which the Church has laid upon those who profess dialectical materialism.

The following verses were composed during the conflicts of 1960 between the bishops and Muñoz Marín, then the governor of Puerto Rico. There are references to the Christian Action Party (PAC) of the Irish bishops on the island and the Popular Democratic Party, or *Populares,* of the government, which allowed birth control and sterilization programs. The verses, written in 1960, foreshadow the continuing Catholic indifference to the political consciousness of either Christians for Socialism or the bishops who excommunicated the group in 1976.

82. *"Don't tell us to mix politics and religion"*

Anonymous

Trans. A.M.S.A.

Un cura me dijo a mí
que encribiera[1] su partido
y yo le dije en seguida:
"Padre, esto no es así,
a usted lo mandan aquí
a otra representación,
a predicar su sermón,
como es lo natural
y no nos mande a mezclar
política y religión."

Católico campesino,
no te dejes engañar,
mira que por manejar
hay quien nos tape el camino.

A priest said to me
that I should register in his party,
but I told him right away,
"Father, it should not be so;
what they send you to do here
concerns another order:
Go preach your sermon
as is natural
and don't tell us to mix
politics and religion."

Catholic farmworker,
don't let them fool you!
Look out for the maneuvering:
there's someone hiding the way
from us.

Están haciendo un partido	They're putting together a [political] party
pa' dejarte en confusión.	to leave you confused.
si quieres tu salavación,	If you want salvation,
sigue siendo Popular	keep on being a *Popular*
y no vayas a mezclar	and don't be mixing
política y religión.	politics and religion.
Ya me voy a despedir,	Now I am going to go,
Terminó mi decimita	my *décima* is finished.
¡Pobre de los estadistas	Poor *estadistas* [assimilationists]!
con el triunfo de Marín:	Marín triumphed!
la Acción Cristiana por fin,	The Christian Action [Party] finally
que también se rebeló!	also rebelled.
El cura se equivocó,	The priest was wrong
siguió hablando de partidos;	when he kept speaking of political
porque frente al crucifijo	parties because before the crucifix
no tiene perdón de Dios.	he does not merit the forgiveness of God.

1. For *inscribiera*.

The threat of bankruptcy in the City of New York, beginning in 1975, caused a series of drastic slashes in the city's budget. A decision was reached to phase out of existence Eugenio María de Hostos Community College in the South Bronx. This is an institution which services a high percentage of Puerto Ricans. The crisis provided for a united resistance from leadership as diverse as university militants, city politicians, and Catholic church leaders, pastoralists, and liberationists. After a mass march to the Manhattan office of the governor, the ten thousand participants held a demonstration at which the following statement was delivered by Antonio M. Stevens Arroyo, C.P. In this case the direct political action of the liberationist style united rather than divided the Hispano church and saved the college.

83. Statement (May 4, 1976) on Threat to Close Eugenio María de Hostos Community College, South Bronx, New York

Antonio M. Stevens Arroyo, C.P.

All too often, the churchman is summoned to the scene in order to bless and approve what others have accomplished. The invocation, the benediction, the baptism, the funeral: all are in the repertoire of the priest, minister, and rabbi. Yet the mission of religion is found in the spirit of the prophets who came uninvited at moments of crisis to denounce and condemn sinfulness in a society that had gone wrong. The crisis that is upon the Puerto Rican community of New York requires that a churchman choose not to console or accept this present situation, but to attack, denounce, and condemn it.

The proposed budget of Mayor Beame's administration for the City of New York is immoral, unjust, and sinful. It makes the security of banks and a credit line more important than people. It presumes to shut down firehouses, close hospitals, eliminate schools, and thin police forces in a way that falls unfairly on the politically powerless of this city. Any person who puts more importance upon money and efficiency than upon human beings is sick. It is money, banks, and resources that are supposed to serve men and women, not men and women that are to serve these abstract interests. The viciousness of the present system is clearly evident in the case of Hostos Community College.

Hostos is the best visible sign in the City University because it values bilingual education by making it a thorough and serious goal of the college. It is the only branch of the City University located in a poverty area, the South Bronx, which is largely Puerto Rican. Hostos has the highest minority enrollment (some 94%) of the university branches. It is a small college that has been successful in projecting a family atmosphere for many black and Hispano students who otherwise would not enter college. Its total budget does not exceed one-half of one percent of the CUNY expenses, whose Central Office alone has twice the expenses of all of Hostos. It makes no sense to close this college when there are more pressing priority decisions to be made about the future of higher education in the city. Chancellor Kibbee and the Board of Higher Education should make a responsible decision now about the future of CUNY as an institution, rather than adopt the opportunistic political strategy of cutting Hostos loose. Should not the City University concentrate on educating students who cannot afford to go to private colleges, rather than compete with the Ivy League for specialty departments in history and medieval studies, etc.? It is because saving Hostos says a great deal about saving New York City that the Puerto Rican people have taken and will continue to take direct action to keep Hostos open.

The doctrine of the Catholic church about such conflict is clear. One is always entitled to the use of force in order to defend oneself. Put in another way, self-defense entitles one to use violence sufficient to repel the intruder. The Jesuit scholastic of the seventeenth century, Juan Mariana, elaborated this theory and applied it to the actions of governments directed against religious and racial minorities of the population. He argued then, as Jefferson, Adams, and Franklin would in 1776, that a government that attacks its own citizens is tyrannical and has lost its moral and legal claim upon the citizenry.

In my judgment, such is the case for the Puerto Rican community in New York. The threatened closing of Hostos is the effect of shameful priorities produced by a system of values that is rooted in the basest motives of power, opportunism, and profit. Such a mentality has no moral claim upon free men and women and must be confronted with the righteousness of a holy cause. The Puerto Rican community will defend Hostos. Some persons are at work to save the college by using political strategies. Congressman Herman Badillo is willing to take the issue to Washington and apply the force of federal legislation against the unjust consequences of the proposed budget cuts. It still may be possible to pass legislation being formulated in Albany by Angelo del Toro, Luis Nine, Armando Montano, and José Serrano. Councilman Luis Olmedo wants to use 5 percent of the proceeds from Shea and Yankee stadiums to keep the college open. But none of these or any other measures will succeed unless large numbers of Puerto Ricans and other New Yorkers are convinced of the seriousness of the issue.

To close Hostos is an act of genocide against the Puerto Rican people of New York. It strikes at the emerging vanguard of a rapidly growing and increasingly talented element of the city's multi-ethnic population. Already Puerto Rican children suffer from malnutrition, the elderly from closed hospitals, the families from poor housing, the youth from violence and drugs in shabby schools, the women from mass sterilizations. All of these abuses have advanced to a degree scarcely imaginable in a civilized society. Now the spiritual symbol of the Puerto Rican's right to excellence—a higher education in a bilingual program in a college named after a Puerto Rican—is to be destroyed. We will be told that violence is wrong, that Don Pedro Albizu Campos was a terrorist, and that we are all of us "Americans." But the city administration, with its priorities fixed on the defective perceptions of the banks, grinds on inexorably. The Puerto Rican option is to survive as a "hyphenated North American," or not at all. The only Puerto Rican to be tolerated is like the one described by Nicolás Guillén: someone who says, "Sí in good/ Sí in bad/ Sí in very bad."

I for one will not say, "Yes." I will not allow the power brokers to take me or any other Puerto Rican for granted. It is because I want them to open their eyes to their sinfulness that I march with the Puerto Rican people on May 10 against the Emergency Financial Control Board. And I will not be frightened off by those who are afraid of "Communists" or "violence." A dying man who is being murdered does not play word games. Hostos is our Puerto Rican college and we must keep it open. We can never surrender our right to say, "No!" to those who would eliminate us and our values. And as José de Diego urged, we will say, "No!" with "the sound of a canon roaring" if necessary. For we cannot stop being what God made us to be, because his gifts are more precious than even life itself. Our need is for resistance and for the defense of our right to survival. This is our patrimony, which is unique, genuine, and irrevocable.

The Call to Action Conference culminated a year-long bicentennial celebration prepared by the NCCB and the USCC to mark the anniversary of United States independence with a scrutiny of the meaning of the principle "liberty and justice for all" (see pp. 7-13). Held in Detroit's Cobo Hall in October 1976, the conference provided an opportunity for unity at a national level within the Hispano church. With almost 130 delegates, the small circle of national Hispano church leaders was made much larger. For some of the delegates it was their first meeting with the Hispano bishops and with Pablo Sedillo, Roberto Peña of PADRES, Mario Barrón of Hermanas, and other important personalities in the Hispano leadership. Enthusiasm was generated by this new leadership that was eager to speak for the grassroots. Transcending to the tensions between pastoralists and liberationists, the Hispano caucus of Call to Action closed ranks around the all-important task of speaking with one voice. Stephen Solis, then a staff member of the Washington USCC Secretariat for the Spanish-speaking, administered to the coordination of the Hispano caucus, and although the delegate strength was scarcely one-half the representation due the proportion of Hispano Catholics in the United States, the performance was formidable. The delegates convincingly articulated the needs of the people before a national audience. Moreover, the valuable experience of the many regional and diocesan Encounters enabled the Hispanos to be highly effective within the conference. In an inversion of the stereotype as sleepy Mexicans or emotional Puerto Ricans, the Hispanos proved to be more adept at procedures than the bulk of lay participants. More importantly, the Hispanos themselves realized that if unity was present, they could exercise considerable clout in the entire Catholic church of the United States.

The following is an excerpt from the statement prepared for the Call to Action Conference by Lupe Anguiano, at that time the director of the Southwest Regional Office for the Spanish-speaking (SWROSS).

In her message, Anguiano warns against clericalism and institutionalism within the Hispano church. A liberationist herself, as can be seen from her analysis of migration, she nevertheless shows great respect for grassroots piety and for the bishops. She also recognizes that since the church is one, a pastoral plan for Hispanos is meaningless unless it summons the attention and energies of non-Hispanos as well.

Born in La Junta, Colorado, Lupe Anguiano became a Victory Knoll sister and with her generation was soon swept into the spirit of church reform after Vatican Council II. Resigning from her congregation, she became an organizer for the UFW and emerged a close ally of Robert Kennedy and Andrew Young in their outreach to the Chicano community. She administered programs for the Spanish-speaking in Washington before returning to the Southwest in 1974 to work for the church as a regional director. Since 1977 she has been director of a special program of leadership training for Spanish-speaking women.

84. Statement for Call to Action Conference, Detroit, Michigan, October 1976 (excerpt)

Lupe Anguiano

Used by permission.

Faith is of the Spirit and thus cannot be extinguished by man; that gift of Faith given to our forefathers so embedded in our history and in our culture has been *preserved and shared* through our families, especially through the woman—the mother. If we examine carefully Hispanic participation in the church structures we will find a tremendous gap; I would even venture to say that Hispanics have never truly participated in the church structures. Yes, things are starting to change very, very slowly with the ordination of our beloved Bishop Patricio F. Flores, Archbishop Robert Sánchez, Bishop Gilbert Chávez, Bishop Juan Arzube, and Bishop René Gracida—but we still have a long way to go.

Lack of participation of the Spanish-speaking/surnamed is further verified with the information recently gathered by SWROSS through diocesan surveys and needs assessment in the Southwest.

Spanish-speaking/surnamed Catholics are about 70 percent of the total Catholic population in the Southwest Region:

For Example:

Diocese	Spanish Speaking/ Surnamed Catholics
Amarillo	76 percent
Brownsville	85 percent
Corpus Christi	86 percent
Dallas	46 percent
El Paso	73 percent
San Angelo	75 percent
San Antonio	72 percent
Gallup	75 percent
Tucson	75 percent
Santa Fe	80 percent

(These conservative estimates were derived from information provided by parishes regarding registered Spanish-speaking/surnamed families.)

Very few Spanish-speaking/surnamed Catholics participate in diocesan, pastoral, or parish councils. Worse still is the fact that the true concerns and the unique Christian culture/expression of Spanish-speaking/surnamed people is not found in these councils.

Diocesan programs in general are seriously lacking in bilingual, bicultural staff. Such programs are not adequately reaching the Spanish-speaking/surnamed people because they lack cultural content.

Confraternity of Christian Doctrine (CCD) programs lack the expression of these people's reality or historically how God has revealed himself to them.

There is a critical shortage of Southwest native vocations. Large numbers of Spanish-speaking/surnamed seminarians and religious drop out before they complete their training.

The people hunger for meaningful liturgies embedded in their Christian cultural reality or history.

Diocesan Catholic schools as a whole do not offer meaningful human development programs which are bilingual and bicultural in nature or which deal with a Southwest reality.

The material goods (financial) of the church are not adequately shared with Spanish-speaking/surnamed programs. Diocesan Spanish-speaking offices receive meager budgets—for example, SWROSS receives only $35,000.00 to cover the apostolic work of the laity in twenty dioceses.

Large numbers of Spanish-speaking/surnamed Catholics are leaving the church for another Christian church—very little or nothing is being done by the Catholic church to find out why. For example, many Spanish-speaking are turning to Jehovah's Witnesses.

And most serious is the losing of deep Christian values embedded in their culture, such as close family ties, by a strong assimilation process into the mainstream of United States society, which is strongly prone to attachment to material wealth.

After reviewing feedback from our region, the problem emphasized could be divided into three major areas:

1. *The Hunger for Leadership*

—No people become a people without the recognition of their own leaders. A people without their own leadership are infants.

—For the past few months I have sought and have collected a large list of what can be truly called "our overqualified Hispanic bishop candidates." Yet when Spanish-speaking persons ask for the appointment of Hispanic bishops they receive the response, "There are none who are qualified."

—Our communities hunger to have Hispanic pastors, Catholic college presidents, superiors of religious communities, seminary rectors, CCD directors, school superintendents, pastors, Catholic school principals, chancellors, heads of NCCB committees, etc.

—We hunger for Hispanic lay leadership—recognition of the leadership talents of many men and women in dioceses and parishes.

—Hispanic lay persons hunger for the opportunity to be ministers of the *Word* in the structured parish; instead they are confronted with a strong clerical attitude, which asks them to cut the grass, cook a fiesta meal, run a Bingo, sell tickets, clean the church, wash altar cloths, etc. This attitude is contrary to the teachings of the church.

> . . . Let the laymen/women not imagine that their pastors are always such experts that to every problem that arises, however complicated, they can readily give them a concrete solution or even that such is their mission. Rather, enlightened by Christian wisdom and giving close attention to the teaching authority of the Church, let the layman/woman take on his/her distinctive role (Vatican Council II, Pastoral Constitution *Gaudium et Spes* 43).

> . . . It belongs to the laymen/women, without waiting passively for orders and directives, to take the initiative freely, and to infuse a Christian spirit into the mentality, customs, laws and structures of the community in which they live (Paul VI, *Populorum Progressio* 81).

—Clericalism has greatly retarded the growth and development of our SWROSS diocesan Spanish-speaking councils.

2. The Hunger for Dignity

—To be seen and understood as we are—a people with a rich heritage—our mestizo reality, our Indian and Spanish ties, also highly influenced by an Anglo society; which makes us part of three worlds.
—A great desire to build a culturally and linguistically pluralistic society. However, the structured church is one of many opponents in our efforts.
—A hunger to celebrate our history, our faith in the vernacular. We are not encouraged or allowed to do this; Spanish masses are placed at bad hours. At times our people must even hold special fund-raisers to pay for Spanish-language hymnbooks.
—Great desire to be treated as responsible adult Christians and not as infants.
—We resist strong assimilation social forces—because such forces are taking from us our Christian and cultural values, such as strong united family ties, a spirit of cooperative and community-oriented behavior as opposed to individualistic and competitive behavior.

3. The Hunger for Justice

—Hispanic people are suffering many abuses and even violence at the hands of U.S. immigration officials. Harassment—pitting brother/sister against brother/sister on the false publicity that they are taking away our jobs. Yet little or nothing is said about the fact of 90-million-dollar annual business gains made by U.S. businesses on U.S. border shops. In the U.S. factories, of every 42 cents invested by the U.S., it reaps $5.50—60 percent of salaries earned by Mexican workers in U.S. plants is spent in the United States. Mexican workers pay income tax, social security, state and local taxes—but it goes unnoticed. Oppressive immigration laws are used to divide Hispanos.
—Diocesan and parish finances are seldom used for priority programs of the Spanish-speaking/surnamed. Some dioceses collect as high as $1,000,000 for development and charity programs—yet Spanish-speaking councils or offices do not receive a share of such collections. In some dioceses the program for the Spanish-speaking is supported by federal or state programs. The work of the Southwest Regional Office for the Spanish-speaking and the Mexican American Cultural Center is set back due to scarce funds. Yet a diocese will contribute $5,000 annually to support an ecumenical program.
—Women suffer greatly from a society and church much prone to false male superiority. If you are not a wife, sister, mother, sweetheart to

those in power, you are nothing; intelligent women in a special way suffer the most. *Mujeres* on welfare are trapped in a system which fails to respect the work capabilities of a woman head of a family.

—Violence by police in our communities is a constant source of suffering for our people. Richard Morales is our most recent widely known victim—a young man who died at the hands of a sheriff without due process; the wife and daughter of the sheriff helped to hide the body. Yet the sheriff did not receive a sentence for capital murder and his wife is free and currently seeking to have the case against her dismissed. This is but one of many such cases.

—We give a great deal of lip service to farm workers, yet we do little to confront agricultural sources of power who fight against just legislation that would protect the rights of workers. We are discouraged by various farm worker leadership—it is not an either/or situation but an and/and.

Recommended Solutions

Carrying out or following up the agreed resolutions or plan of action is usually the weakest part of every conference. It will be of little value for us to have developed, discussed and come to an agreement on written resolutions if in fact we do not also create a solid structure to carry out such resolutions.

As a matter of priority, I'd like to suggest that we commit ourselves to strengthening or organizing well-thought-out *national, regional, diocesan and parish* operating structures—which all of us can agree upon to carry out whatever we come to an agreement on. I would like to challenge us to depart from traditional church structures—where orders come from the *top down*—or competitive structures that isolate one program or organization from the other. I see little value in Hispanics trying to organize an Apostolic Plan of Action if in fact such a plan is based on repeating or trying to duplicate what already exists. It seems to me more in keeping with our Christian ideals and cultural values that we organize structures based on a philosophy of *broad participation* completely given to *community, cooperation and service.*

Within such a philosophical framework I'd like to propose that we spell out how we see the National Secretariat for the Spanish-speaking operating, also the regional and diocesan offices, commissions or councils and, of course, the *parish,* which is where the *base* is. . . .

Another side to militancy is solidarity. The following poem, taken from a secular source, expresses some of the feelings liberationists experience in their struggles.

85. In a Moment

Jesús Papoleto Meléndez

From The Rican, *no. 3 (Spring 1973), p. 71.*

you've asked me to love you
to the fullest depth/
to share this thing called love
to fill your heart with my inner passion
to bring an inner peace into you & i/
yet i can't/   not at this moment

for as i look about me
i see tears in a poorman's eyes/
fears/   in his children's cry
pain/   in my mother's sigh   no
i can't love you/   not at this moment

as a human people/   a man of a culture
i must feed my people
liberate them from the chains of poverty
open the doors of solitude   into a unity

in a moment/   (how long of a moment)
i shall love you to the fullest depth

but if   /however/
you cannot wait for that moment
then join me in this movement
& that will be love.

CHAPTER FOURTEEN

THE SECOND ENCOUNTER

The Second National Hispano Pastoral Encounter was held at Trinity College, Washington, D.C., August 18–21, 1977. Not only was the Second Encounter bigger and better known than the first, but the support for the Hispano church had become wider and more substantial. Working through the regional centers, the USCC Secretariat for the Spanish-speaking in Washington had enlisted the support of many bishops and of Pope Paul VI, who recorded a radio message the text of which follows.

The atmosphere of the Second Encounter was more professional than that of the first. As is described in the citation below, the preparation process required substantial coordination from the secretariat and the regional centers through the diocesan directors of the Spanish-speaking apostolate, reaching down to church movements and to the local *comunidades de base*. The list of the local and regional encounters that had prepared the way from the First to the Second Encounters is truly impressive:

Houston, Texas—September 1972
Mid-West Regional—January 1973
Denver, Colorado—March 1973
Dallas, Fort Worth, Texas—April 1973
Four-State Regional (Kansas, Missouri, Iowa, Nebraska)—June 1973
Dodge City, Kansas—June 1973
Rockford, Illinois—August 1973
California—August 1973
Corpus Christi, Texas—September 1973
Kalamazoo, Michigan—March 1974
Detroit, Michigan—January 1974
New York Archdiocese—June 1974
Brooklyn Diocese—June 1974
Chicago, Illinois—November 1974
Northeast Regional—November 1974
Milwaukee, Wisconsin—February 1975
State-wide Indiana—May 1975
Toledo, Ohio—October 1975
Joliet, Illinois—October 1975
Saginaw, Michigan—May 1976

313

The Second Encounter came a few months before the Call to Action Conference in October 1976 and borrowed from the system of representation and procedures planned for the latter. There was a special effort, however, to avoid the radical image that was given to Call to Action. The Encounter organizers insisted on diocesan recognition for delegates and regulated the participation of observers sedulously. This massive organizational process was both the strength and the weakness of the Second Encounter.

On the one hand, the documents of preparation centralized the thinking of millions of Hispano Catholics, but this also strained the bureaucratic efficiencies of the Secretariat. When delays or lack of communications ruptured the flow of the process, the anger of local delegates escalated. The target of their wrath was not the Anglo institutions of the church, but vehicles like the secretariat, which had been created by Hispanos. The problems reached crisis proportions in Washington with the unavailability of rooms and the loss of registration forms, reservations, and the like. These inadequacies are described in the commentary of Ada María Isasi-Díaz. Nor was the secretariat fully responding to ideological diversity in the Hispano church. The shallowness of a folkloric approach to cultural and regional differences is cited by the contributors to *Cara a Cara,* the bulletin from the Mid-West Regional Office. Particularly damaging to the sense of solidarity was the oversight by the staff of the Encounter, which neglected to include a Puerto Rican flag among those that adorned the stage at Trinity College representing the Hispano peoples of the world. This touched off a walkout of some Puerto Rican delegates. A pleasant surprise was the positive effect of the Cuban presence. Far from conforming to a stereotype as middle-class and reactionary Catholics, the Cuban delegations from Florida, under the guidance of Monsignor Agustín Román and the able Father Mario Vizcaino, enriched the Encounter by their presence.[1] The enthusiasm of their participation will surely be counted as one of the principal fruits of the Second Encounter, just as the Puerto Rican underrepresentation will be one of the long-remembered defects.

Conspicuous by his absence was César Chávez, whose *La Causa* had been a part of the genesis of the Hispano church (see pp. 117–22). The Chicano labor leader had been criticized in 1977 by many church leaders for his ill-advised statement while on a visit to the Philippines arranged by Ferdinand Marcos. Previous policies of the UFW leadership regarding patrols of the Mexican border to keep immigrants out of the country and squabbles with the Texas Farm Workers had already tarnished the image of Chávez, now loyal church liberals began to pressure him about his visit overseas. A press release by the Friends of the Filipino People, included in this chapter, describes the controversy. During the Encounter, although the organizers had made special arrangements for the migrant workers, there was a general coolness toward the migrants on the part of other delegates. Consequently, while there might be sorrow at the demythologizing of a hero, it was encouraging that the Hispano church had demonstrated its maturity in outgrowing the one-issue orientation of the first stage of development.

The most challenging ambiguity of the Encounter process was the result of

---

1. In the Spring of 1979, Román was named Auxiliary Bishop of Miami, and Vizcaino became the first director of the Southeast Regional Hispanic Pastoral Office (Miami).

differing models of church. As has been suggested (see pp. 306-307), Hispano leadership sought to minimize the frictions between pastoralists and liberationists by focusing the Encounter upon the grassroots people. However, large numbers of Hispanos had moved beyond the clerical influence exercised to a greater or lesser degree through the *cursillista* and pastoralist model of church. During the Washington Encounter, a Chicano group from Denver distributed a legal brief suing the bishops of the Catholic church for misrepresenting the gospel of Jesus Christ (García, 1977, p. 61). Their basic contention was that the hierarchy had no right to decide who could and could not attend the Encounter as delegates. A youth representative from Project Poder in Rochester, New York, who had attended the preliminary meeting in Chicago, was disqualified as a Youth Task Force member because the director of the local apostolate office had changed his mind about the young man's capacity for participation. In the Midwest, the Farm Labor Organizing Committee (FLOC) had a conflict (previous to the Encounter) with the local director of the Spanish-speaking apostolate (see document 91 below). As a result, certain farm worker delegates were not permitted to attend. These incidents reflect a tension between the need for outreach to the unevangelized and the desire to deepen the formation for those already committed to the church. The Encounter's organizers had further confused the issue by encouraging Catholics who did not work within the ordinary church structures to become delegates to the Encounter by seeking recognition from church structures, personified by the bishop and the local diocesan director of the Spanish-speaking apostolate. This is an unlikely process. In the future, the Hispano church will have to answer the question: How can a movement based upon a prophetic and noninstitutional pluralism avoid the apparently inevitable fate of becoming institutionalized itself?

The defects of the Second National Hispano Pastoral Encounter, however, ought to be put in perspective by recognizing its valid accomplishments. Through the Encounter, the Hispano church achieved an identification with grassroots Catholics that outdistances the rest of the church in the United States. Moreover, this solidarity was national in scope, progressive in politics, and included all levels and types of leadership. Judging from the Call to Action Conference (see p. 306) and the documents prepared by the delegates of the Encounter, the grasp of theology in terms of pastoral innovations is more thorough among grassroots Hispano leadership than in the general United States Catholic laity. On social-justice issues, Hispanos are more politically powerful at the grassroots level than the Catholic left. It can be said that the Hispano church has its own religious orders, because PADRES and Hermanas share a common apostolate, spirituality, and formation program with members stationed in different sectors of the country. Certainly the loyalty given to these organizations by some of their members is stronger than what is felt for their different religious congregations. What remains underdeveloped is a mission to the whole Catholic church, national and international.

The document "Unity in Pluralism" ought to be analyzed in this light. Based on a theme first selected at the meeting in Philadelphia in 1976 as a top priority (see p. 288-89), this is probably the weakest document that the Encounter produced, but it illustrates how the delegates dealt intelligently and honestly with their limitations.

86. *Planning the Second National Hispano Pastoral Encounter, 1977*

From Conclusions *(Washington, D.C.: USCC, 1977). Used by permission.*

On January 13, 1977, the Bishops' Ad Hoc Committee for the Spanish-speaking supports the Encounter and preparations get underway.

The National Coordinating Committee meets in Chicago on January 20 and in Washington, D.C., on February 4. Several possibilities become concrete:

1. The Encounter is clearly seen as a decisive step within the process undertaken by Hispanos.

2. The principal strength of the process lies in the diocesan church, but beginning from the grassroots and reaching out to the regional and national levels. Therefore, it is necessary to include the diocesan directors of Hispanic apostolates in the planning of the process. While only 30 diocesan offices existed at the time of the First Encounter, they now number more than 100.

3. The site of the Second Encounter is changed from Chicago to Washington, D.C.

The National Meeting of Diocesan Directors of the Hispanic Apostolate takes place in Tolentine, Illinois, February 21-24, 1977. The majority of diocesan directors, 82, is present; only a few are not.

1. The meeting has three goals:

—Become conscious of the historic significance of the Second Encounter and of the important role of the diocesan directors and the local church within this process.

—Look for the theme for the Second Encounter.

—Concretize the process and the organization of the Encounter.

2. After continuous reflection and careful work, the following results emerge:

a) The theme of the Second Encounter: Evangelization in itself and describing what concept of church we want.

Five other topics in relation to Evangelization are chosen: Ministries for Evangelization, Evangelization and Human Rights, Evangelization and Integral Education, Evangelization and Our Political Responsibility, Evangelization and Unity in Pluralism. These topics are clearly seen not only as themes for study but also for decisions and commitments.

b) The process for the Second Encounter: it should serve as a historic move from a church of the masses to a church of basic Christian communities. Therefore, it would be the time to intensify the renewal and the creation of these small communities throughout the nation. At an interpersonal level, these small groups would speak about the goals of Evangelization and those of other topics.

From the basic Christian communities the process would move to the diocesan church, then to the regions, thus arriving at a truly national Pastoral Encounter.

No one could take part in this Second Encounter who had not first participated in a group *de base,* in a small community.

Achieving this would itself be a historic contribution of the Second Encounter to the renewal of the church in the whole world.

c) The formation of national working committees: to assure the success of the process, a greater shared responsibility was necessary. This was achieved by setting up different committees to deal with the various aspects of the process. The next meeting of the coordinating committee does this.

The National Secretariat succeeds in naming ad hoc coordinators in those regions where there are none.

Distribution of Work among the National Committees

1. On March 10, 1977, in San Antonio, the Coordinating Committee divides the work of the various committees among the regions, aware that the fulfillment or failure of each would spell out success or difficulties for the Second Encounter:
— Orientation Guides: Rogelio Manrique and the Midwest region.
— Housing, and subcommittees for transportation, reception, infirmary, entertainment, decoration and exhibits: Mario Paredes and the Northeast region, especially Washington, D.C.
— Press and Communication: Mario Vizcaino and Southeast region.
— Liturgy and Music: Pedro Garcia and the Far West region, with collaboration of the Southwest and the Northwest regions.
— Overall Coordination: Pablo Sedillo, Jr., and the National Office.
2. The Encounter Motto is chosen: *Pueblo de Dios en marcha.*
3. The official hymn is chosen: *Un pueblo que camina.*
A Special Coordinator for the Second Encounter is approved: The secretariat sought out Rev. Frank Ponce, from San Diego, for this task; he begins his work at the Coordinating Committee meeting in Chicago on May 3.

Voice and Vote Depending on the Status of the Participant— Creation of Other Committees

On July 5 and 6 the Coordinating Committee meets again, this time at Trinity College where the Second Encounter is to take place.
1. The agenda is carefully prepared as to schedule and participants. The

role of cardinals and bishops is delineated. Participation of observers is unanimously approved. The delegates will have voice and vote in workshops and plenary sessions. The observers will have voice only in workshops.

2. Three other committees are formed: Agenda, Credentials, and Rules, with their corresponding chairpersons and members. The National Secretariat takes the responsibility for finding a place for the plenary sessions. The Housing Committee remains in charge of housing and the other subcommittees, such as transportation and others, as previously established. The Committee on Liturgy will send all the material for the celebrations and songs.

3. The National Secretariat is asked at this time to be in charge of publishing the conclusions of the Encounter.

Several conference calls take place with the members of the Coordinating Committee to achieve a greater sharing of responsibility in important decisions concerning the Encounter.

Most Important: The Process That Took Place from La Base

1. More than 100,000 persons nationwide participate in small grassroots communities. They send their written conclusions to the diocesan pro-Encounter committees. A silent people begins to speak with a sense of responsibility, history, and sound gospel values.

2. Their voice is heard by the dioceses, and the voice of the diocesan church is formed.

3. All the participating dioceses form the voice of the regions, of which there are six.

4. A set of conclusions containing the thinking of the regions is prepared for the nation. This becomes the national "Work Document" used during the Second Encounter. That is why no speeches or expositions were given except by Archbishop Sánchez, who presented the central theme. Others simply presented the conclusions of their region on the given topic.

This process that took place among Hispanos throughout the country has signaled a change in the church: from a silent church to one that is prophetic; from a church of the masses to one made up of basic Christian communities; from a vertical church to one of dialogue and communion firmly rooted in the gospel.

This process may well be at this moment of history the greatest contribution Hispanos have made to the church in this country and in the world.

THE DEVELOPMENT OF THE SECOND ENCOUNTER

With the arrival of the participants at Washington, the Second Encounter is already an ecclesial success: their presence at a national assembly is a concrete manifestation and fruit of a process that God had begun with his people.

The delegates had to be very aware that they came not as individuals but as persons charged with a responsibility given by their local church. They were obliged to leave their particular interests aside and be faithful to the thought of their church at the different levels.

The number and quality of observers were of great value, especially in the workshops. Though not being able to take an active part in the plenary sessions, they nevertheless saw themselves privileged to be present from within at such a historic event of the church. Since 250 persons participated in the First Encounter, possibly that number would grow to 500 in this Second Encounter. Yet, 1200 participated, and many more would have come if the number of observers had not been restricted.

Each participant had to fulfill three conditions: have participated in a reflection group *de base;* be recognized by his bishop and diocesan pro-Encounter committee; and be registered within the specified date.

After some initial difficulties due to the great numbers, everyone proceeded to work with a great spirit. The 600 observers watched the plenary sessions through closed-circuit television.

For the Encounter, the National Secretariat printed more than 42,000 pages to assure that all participants had copies of the documents. During the three final weeks before the Encounter, the secretariat sought the collaboration of 20 persons, growing to 30 persons during the Encounter itself, who worked more than 5000 hours. Many of these persons were volunteers.

Workshops

1. There was a total of 28 workshops: 15 on Evangelization, four on Ministries, three on Human Rights, and two workshops for each of the remaining topics.

2. Each workshop had its coordinating team: a bishop, a representative of the Coordinating Committee, a facilitator, a secretary, and a translator. The secretariat employed five persons who worked for 80 hours to organize these teams and ensure representation of the regions in each team.

3. To distribute 1200 persons into the workshops, five persons worked a total of 300 hours in order to ensure that each participant's workshop preference was respected and that the regions were evenly distributed.

The prayer services that preceded and concluded the plenary sessions, and the eucharistic liturgies which focused and celebrated the events of the day, contributed greatly to the success of the Encounter. They reflected the richness of the various Hispanic cultures and included participation from every part of the country. God was truly present among his people.

The language used throughout was Spanish, a fact which strengthened the unity and sense of identity among the participants. English was spoken at the plenary sessions on only two occasions. The Holy Father's message was in Spanish. Many of the bishops also spoke in Spanish.

The presence of nearly 50 bishops was very valuable, both because of their collaboration in the workshops as well as their respect for the voice of the people in the plenary sessions.

One of the great fruits and values of the Encounter itself, affirmed by many, was the *encounter* which took place among the different Hispano peoples. This meeting of different persons and groups—each of them unique—was a great step toward *Unity*. Although not perfect, it can be said that no other gathering, political, cultural or social, has achieved the sense of unity which this Christian Hispano gathering achieved, in the name and by the power of Christ. The majority of participants came with an awareness of this responsibility and went away with this experience of unity.

The Conclusions

1. Valuable in themselves, as a careful reading will show.

2. Valuable because they are the voice of the Christian from *la base.* They were not prepared by "experts" but by the *pueblo de base.* This is their unique value.

3. Valuable because they are the result of a process: coming out of *la base* in writing, this voice was gathered to produce the first set of conclusions at the diocesan level, which in turn formed the regional conclusions. The six regions sent their conclusions to the national office, where, after 600 hours of careful and delicate work, these conclusions from the nation are integrated to produce the working document for the Encounter. Copies of this document are sent to the 500 participants already registered. At the Encounter the total work document is given to everyone, including those to whom it had been sent previously.

Participants now study and amend the work documents; the workshop secretaries work the amendments into the documents for presentation at the plenary sessions. The plenary sessions themselves offer amendments; these, and the rest of the document that is not amended, are approved as conclusions of the Encounter. Thus approved, the Coordinating Committee, with great fidelity, studies the conclusions as to style, ordering of material, and details of presentation.

The conclusions have now gone through seven steps. The secretariat, at the eighth step, puts the conclusions into final form for publication in Spanish; the final step is for the National Office to translate the conclusions into English along with this introduction.

Perhaps never before had the voice of the grass roots been so well respected, listened to, and heeded: from *la base*, diocese, region, national synthesis, workshops, plenary sessions, Coordinating Committee, translation into English, bilingual publication.

4. Valuable because they express the personal commitment of Hispanos

rather than simply a request for something from the church structure. In those cases where something is requested from the structure, the request implies a prior commitment on the part of the people, and asks for the support of the institution. In others, the institution is asked to implement only what it has the authority to establish, for example, the National Youth Task Force and the creation of a National Episcopal Vicariate for migrant farm workers.

5. Valuable because they underscore the importance of basic Christian communities and give a clear ecclesial orientation, both of which were needed for the pastoral life of Hispanos in the church and were successfully articulated in the conclusions of the Encounter.

SECOND ENCOUNTER: PROJECTIONS FOR THE FUTURE

From the Second Encounter has emerged the resolve to continue the process. This means a return to the basic Christian communities where the process began. These should be established where now they do not exist. For it is at the grassroots that the conclusions must be implemented and made a flesh-and-blood reality.

Dioceses and their offices must ensure that their efforts, priorities, and programs reflect both the spirit and the content of the conclusions.

Regional offices must also do the same, in order to serve as examples of this evangelizing thrust for ecclesial renewal. Understanding and cooperation must exist among the various regions. Where none exists, the ad hoc coordination established in that region for the Encounter should continue, until such time as permanent offices can be set up.

The National Secretariat will be closely linked with this process as a catalyst for support, unity, coordination, and ongoing evaluation. It will also serve as a link with the bishops and with the NCCB/USCC.

Hispanos wish to be united with all the church: in the United States, in Latin America, in the world, with all the bishops and our Holy Father.

In this process, the Hispano people are hopeful that bishops and the NCCB/USCC will give whatever support is needed to accomplish this task.

"With full confidence in Christ present among us through the Holy Spirit, we undertake this task in the name of our people, in the name of Our Father" (from the "Message of the Hispano Bishops"). We are a *Pueblo de Dios en marcha.*

87. Message from Pope Paul VI
to the Second National Hispano Pastoral Encounter,
held in Washington, D.C., August 18-21, 1977 (text)

Trans. A.M.S.A.

Venerable brothers and beloved children:

With great joy We wish to send a radio message of cordial greeting to you, Bishops, priests and Spanish-speaking faithful and leaders of this aspect of the apostolate who are meeting in Washington for the Second National Hispano Pastoral Encounter. We know well that you have come to this assembly after closing five years ago the First Pastoral Encounter, which awakened such hopes and enthusiasms and which has definitely become a valid response to the aspirations of that numerous part of the People of God which is united by close ties of religious ethics, of language and of culture.

It pleases Us profoundly that for this present Encounter you have selected as object of reflection the diverse aspects of Evangelization, a theme which is opportune and current and which opens a wide field for your best efforts of initiative. In effect, you have found the appropriate way to prepare contemporary responses and to offer fitting reasons so that your ecclesial community, which ought to be and to feel itself totally evangelizing, can carry the saving message of Jesus Christ within and without its own boundaries. It is an undertaking which demands committed dedication and which ought to begin with all of man's concrete life, pastoral and social, so that the message of the Gospel may truly penetrate diverse situations and illuminate the existence of different groups with their rights and respective duties.

In this gigantic task, your community ought to be strengthened to develop its own creative activity in accord with its specific necessities, always feeling itself animated by faith, love, and hope in cordial openness to the rest of the Church, above all to that Church with which you live in your country.

In a spirit of intimate union with your pastors and with fraternal collaboration for other members of the flock of Christ, which make for unity in a just pluralism and which integrally liberate man, may you become aware of your responsibilities in the dutiful use of a healthy liberty. We wish the best for you, beloved brothers and children. Hence We invite you to conserve and nourish your own heritage, adapting it to local needs without forgetting, among other things, those valid elements of popular religiosity which, when well oriented, can prepare for an authentic encounter with God in Christ.

We exhort you from Our heart to continue on the good road of fidelity to the Church and of generous commitment to the welfare of others. May Mary, the Star of Evangelization, guide you and protect you always, while with paternal affection We bless all of you in the Name of the Father, and of the Son, and of the Holy Spirit.

---

88. Unity in Pluralism: A Statement from the Second National Hispano Pastoral Encounter

From Conclusions *(Washington, D.C.: USCC, 1977). Used by permission.*

1. Introduction

As Hispanos we feel proud of our identity and cultural heritage, as well as of our rich diversity and our participation in the pluralistic reality of this nation.

We affirm and support the concept of integration within our pluralistic society, and we reject an assimilation which destroys personal identity, impoverishes our people, and does not permit a healthy exchange of values.

2. Integration: Unity in Pluralism within the Nation and the Church

To promote this integration and a unity in pluralism which favors the greatest realization of human potential, we propose:

1. That the church at the grassroots, diocesan, regional, and national levels enforce this concept of *integration*, rather than *assimilation*.
2. That each individual and each Hispanic group have the opportunity to know and develop his/her own identity, in the search for a spirit of unity, with an openness to other ethnic groups, without losing our identity. We ask civil and church authorities to assist us at the local, diocesan, regional, and national levels as we develop our own cultural identity.
3. That we take the responsibility as Hispanos to awaken in our non-Hispanic brothers and sisters a greater interest in Hispanic history and cultural heritage by use of cultural centers, conferences and other means, in order to achieve a better mutual understanding and be able to

live and work within a pluralistic unity.

4. That we assume the commitment to initiate dialogue and collaborate with national groups and organizations which focus on general cultural pluralism (the Office of Ethnic Affairs, NAACP, Bureau of Indian Affairs, and others) to unite forces in *our same message* of unity in pluralism to all the nation.

5. That the church promote and maintain the unity in pluralism through the means of communication she possesses.

6. That bishops and pastors be conscious of their pastoral obligation to include Hispanos in all diocesan structures according to the proportion of Hispanos in the local church.

3. Unity in Pluralism among Hispanos

We recognize the serious problems which exist among our people due to the diversity of our histories and heritages.

Nevertheless, we consider this diversity a richness which we need to know better, and we propose to work for a greater unity among the different Hispano groups in order to be mutually enriched, supported, and strengthened as a people.

To achieve this we propose:

1. To help develop a consciousness within our own Hispanic people, diocesan pastoral offices, parish schools, and the apostolic movements of our distinct cultures, histories, and authentic values.

2. To help our families reaffirm, express, and live these values.

3. That when taking to the people her work, orientational, and doctrinal statements, the church keep in mind the sensitivities and historical circumstances of the different communities which compose the Hispanic mosaic in the United States, not focusing on the concrete experience of only one of these groups. This applies to the hierarchy in teaching officially, as well as to any member of the church in doing pastoral work.

4. To promote parish activities and local movements in small groups: small communities which promote an integral education, knowing who we are and where we come from, with reflection and common action that affirm and solidify the unity which exists among us.

5. To develop at the national level themes which motivate a greater unity at the grass roots.

6. To promote in dioceses, at different levels, creative encounters among Hispano groups. To bring about these encounters, regional and national offices and institutions could offer funding and communications media to the dioceses.

7. To prepare with care and pride an annual, national folk fiesta, with the theme of unity in pluralism, which shows the Hispano people as a

beautiful mosaic and not as a melting pot of races, and use the occasion to present a "literary" or "action" award within the context or theme of the festival.

---

89. Editorial: The Second Encounter

From Cara a Cara 4 (September–October 1977). Used by permission.

The Second National Encounter of the Hispanos is now part of the history of the Spanish-speaking Catholics in the United States. The Encounter represents both the accomplishments and the failures of the Spanish-speaking people in the United States. It illustrates how far we have advanced but it also indicates that we still have a long way to go. Through this national interchange, the Hispanic peoples declared: We are present and have certain specific needs. We have made many valuable contributions both to the church and to the nation and we will continue this participation. To the Church, they said: We are the largest ethnic group in the Church. We are tired of receiving second-rate service. Ministries must now be tailored to fit our particular reality. They must be saturated with our culture and heritage and carried out by priests, deacons, sisters, bishops and laity from our own communities. Evangelization must also be rooted in our culture and emerge from our present reality. We, the Spanish-speaking Catholics of the United States, reaffirm our solidarity with our brothers and sisters in our native lands. Their suffering is not alien to us but rather a part of our experience.

During the Second National Encounter, an embryo of unity was formed among the Spanish-speaking. However, if this unity is based only in cultural terms, it will be extremely fragile. In order to strengthen and expand this unity, the various Hispanic communities here in the United States must realize that they are also closely related in their social and economic situations. These ties are rarely considered, as evidenced by the lack of solidarity between those Hispanos who have escaped the migrant stream and those who are still migrants. Although Spanish-speaking people often state that they do not want to assimilate into the United States society, their alternative has not yet become clearly defined.

The recommendations made in the areas of political responsibility, human rights and integral education indicate that the United States Hispanic Community is still weak in its social and political analysis. This weakness presents a challenge to the Hispanic leaders, especially to the Regional and National Offices which were created as instruments of growth and liberation for the Spanish-speaking people. In a world where justice is an essential dimension of life, the ability to analyze the political and social structures is imperative for a true Christian.

The Second National Encounter reflected the failure of society to allow the poor to speak. Parliamentary procedure, which was used throughout the Encounter, is extremely technical. Without previous experience or extensive study, it is quite difficult to understand. Even many of the facilitators were unclear as to the proper procedure. This methodology limited the participation of many of the delegates. We Hispanos must become extremely conscious of the need to develop methodologies which are consistent with our reality and which also allow the most ample participation possible of our people.

The Encounter was another step on the long road of the history of the Spanish-speaking people in the United States. We must now prepare ourselves for what lies ahead—moments of struggle, of defeat and of accomplishment. We must always keep in mind that we are a people with a history and a destiny.

The staff of *Cara a Cara* would like to take this opportunity to thank everyone who participated in the Encounter and helped to make it what it was. We also look forward to similar Encounters in the future.

---

90. Statement to the Press, July 31, 1977

Friends of the Filipino People (New York City)

THE FRIENDS OF THE FILIPINO PEOPLE VIEW WITH EXTREME CONCERN THE TRIP OF UNITED FARM WORKERS PRESIDENT CÉSAR CHÁVEZ, TO THE PHILIPPINES TO RECEIVE AN AWARD FROM PRESIDENT MARCOS.

Contacted by phone, UFW headquarters in Keene, California denied that Chávez knew anything about the award for "services to the trade union movement" before going to the Philippines. Mark Grossman, UFW Executive Secretary, said that the purpose of the Chávez trip was "to talk to farm workers."

A reliable source within the UFW, however, maintained that Chávez knew about the award and attributed his visit to UFW politics. According to the source, Chávez' trip was arranged by Andy Imutan, a former officer and UFW member, and a Marcos supporter. Imutan is currently heading up a controversial social service project for Filipino farm workers in Stockton, California, which is partly financed by the Marcos government. Chávez has been seeking the support of Imutan and his group of Filipino farm workers, who have had differences with the UFW. Apparently, Chávez' trip to the Philippines was one of the conditions set for a reconciliation.

"To please Imutan," the source said, "Chávez disregarded the feelings and wishes of those Filipino farm workers who do not like martial law, or who do not want the UFW involved in Philippine politics."

Whatever the motivation of Mr. Chávez, it is clear that Marcos is using Chávez' presence in an effort to clean up his government's image as a repressive regime. Marcos is trying presently to battle out of the diplomatic isolation in which his government's reputation as a human rights violator has placed him. In this regard, the Chávez visit is another public-relations effort by Marcos to salvage military and economic aid to him which is currently under scrutiny by the U.S. Congress. Approximately 17% in military aid was cut by the House recently because of human rights violations.

Father Edward Gerlock, a Maryknoll priest who was deported recently from the Philippines because of his work with the Federation of Free Farmers, commented, "Under present conditions Chávez' visit can only cause harm to farmers and farm workers in the Philippines." He noted that the visit is already being used to legitimize Marcos' land-reform program.

Gerlock charged, "The land-reform program of the Marcos government is a sham. Only 2 to 3% of all agricultural lands are covered by it. Even then, land reform in these areas is negligible. This kind of land reform has no practical effect and it would have to take 500 years to have any effect at all."

It is unfortunate that Mr. Chávez has allowed himself to be used for questionable ends by a regime which has shown itself to be totally against all those principles and ideals that he has stood for as a fighter for civil and human rights. Clearly, from recent statements he made to the Manila press, Chávez left for the Philippines with very little information about the strike bans and worker arrests since the declaration of martial law. It is our hope that he returns with a fuller understanding of this as well as of the plight of thousands of political prisoners in Philippine jails.

Church and liberal circles have called the FFP offices expressing surprise and consternation.

91. Local Priest Leads Catholic Opposition to FLOC

From Nuestra Lucha *(FLOC newsletter), March 1977.*

For the third consecutive year, the Farm Labor Organizing Committee has been denied funding by the local allocations committee of the Campaign for Human Development (CHD).

In a letter to FLOC secretary-treasurer Ray Santiago, the allocations committee of CHD cited FLOC's "poor follow-through on past projects, lack of financial accountability," and their "failure to obtain or secure other funds prior to application for funding."

"We have had both private and public audits, and have been given clean bills of health every time," said Santiago in an interview with *Nuestra Lucha.* "This is really an insult to our integrity. Where does the CHD get such documentation? Or do they ever use substantive documentation when they review an organization's proposal?"

A local committee-person refused to make comment on that question, but in an interview with CHD co-chairman Father Robert Haas, personal feeling, rather than concrete, factual criteria seemed to be the controlling factor.

"It has always been my feeling that FLOC is wasteful, undemocratic, naive, overambitious, and in opposition to Catholic principles," said Father Haas in an interview with *Nuestra Lucha.* "I remember the Conference of Spanish-speaking Apostolate several years ago, when FLOC president Baldemar Velasquez stood up and declared that he was an atheist! I also happen to know that FLOC staff members are pro-abortion. . . . Several years ago, FLOC received an Economic Opportunity Planning Association grant to open gas and food co-ops. Whatever happened to that money? I'll tell you. The co-ops were mismanaged, abused, and eventually run bust. Now FLOC comes to us, with that kind of record, and wants more money. And for what? To stipend sixty organizers in three states . . . ludicrous! Why does FLOC tramp all over Indiana and Michigan when there is so much work to be done right here in Toledo? How can FLOC be so unrealistic? . . . FLOC should be building small, but solidly. . . . FLOC could be organizing leadership workshops and be emphasizing the importance of higher education for Chicanos. I hope to see more Mexican-American doctors, lawyers, businessmen and teachers some day; now that is visible progress."

When asked where he had obtained his information about FLOC, Father Haas responded that it was "common knowledge."

One source stated that certain individuals on the committee "just didn't care much for FLOC" and that since each member has an unwritten veto power, FLOC would never be funded by the local diocese.

"I guess you're just not aware of the politics of funding," said Sylvester Duran, Spanish-speaking director of the local diocese, when asked if he thought FLOC had been denied funding. "You see, committee members are devoted church people who are appointed by Bishop Donovan; they then make recommendations back to him. The reason FLOC has no representation on the committee is probably because of the way Bishop Donovan feels about FLOC."

"Sure, I support what FLOC is trying to do," said Celso Rodriguez, Director of the Guadalupe Center in Toledo. "It is a pity that people like Father Haas, with their groundless accusations, still remain on that allocations committee. It seems wrong and terribly unjust that individuals holding a petty vindictiveness can effectively prevent the positive work of an organization like FLOC. I know that it all stems from the Luna Pier affair several years ago. Baldemar doesn't like to soft-peddle the issues, but when you're trying to obtain concession from people like Father Haas, you have to be . . . diplomatic."

In a letter from Arthur S. Johnson, the Associate Director of Budget and Finance for the Economic Opportunity Planning Association, he stated, "Our only contact with FLOC was through the Migrant Community Development Corporation in 1970 and 1971 when EOPA signed contracts for operation of gasoline and food cooperatives. The records and financial reporting were adequate. The auditors had no adverse comment."

Ada María Isasi-Díaz is one of the younger Cubans within the church who are trying to break with the stereotype of reactionary anticommunistic Catholicism that impeded the inclusion of Cuban Americans in the first stages of the Hispano church.

Born in Havana, Cuba, in 1943, she graduated from a Catholic high school in 1960, at the height of the Cuban Revolution's confrontation with the United States. She left her homeland and, after joining the Ursuline Order in the United States, was sent to Peru in 1967, where she studied and worked until 1969. Returning to the United States, she eventually decided upon a new career as a laywoman. She graduated from the State University of New York with a master's degree in history in 1977 and enrolled at St. Bernard's Seminary in Rochester, New York, for the master-in-divinity course. While working as a member of a parish team ministry in Rochester, she attended the Second National Encounter. The following account was originally published in Spanish by *El Visitante Dominical*, September 18, 1977, and the author has graciously translated it for inclusion in these pages. Her commentary reflects the highs and lows of the Washington meeting, the frustration of the Puerto Ricans, and the participation of the Cuban American delegation. At present, Ada María Isasi-Díaz works as a specialist for the Woman's Ordination Conference.

92. *The People of God on the Move–Chronicle of a History*

Ada María Isasi-Díaz

Before being able to get to where I had to register, I hear a woman saying to a teen-ager, "I am so tired! But, I am so happy I came!" And I, I smile and keep on going, singing with great enthusiasm and joy: "This is the day, this is the day the Lord has made; let us rejoice. . . ."

While I wait in line, I think of the day when, back in my diocese, I was invited to become part of the Pro-Encounter Committee. A long time has gone by since then! How very much we have all learned as we shared the different themes of the Second Pastoral Encounter! We listened to each other, we discussed, we meditated and prayed—and now, here we are in Washington at last. Instead of the five hundred they were expecting we are almost a thousand; one hundred have no place to sleep. One experiences great joy at seeing those one knows; there is also that unequaled joy one has when one "feels at home" even among strangers.

We are a people that has journeyed a lot to get here. I greet some Cubans that have spent twenty-six hours traveling to get here and now they are among the one hundred that have no beds. What a pleasure to see Sylvia, a Chicano who has come from New Mexico; and there are the people from San Diego, clapping and laughing. Rosa arrives from New Jersey; with a sisterly *abrazo*, we say to each other all that needs to be said!

The Encounter starts and we are welcomed by bishops and archbishops. Our hearts are filled by the effort of Bishop Kelly, who speaks to us in Spanish. We get up and cheer him. The sister sitting by me dries her tears. We seek *unity* and when we hear Bishop Kelly speaking to us in Spanish, I realize that the unity we, as searching pilgrims, have as our goal begins to become a reality. And we sing, we sing full of joy with the firm belief that, as the song says, "each one in their voice echoes a whole people."

They call us, nation by nation, and we stand proud of what we each are: Argentinians, Colombians and Cubans; Americans, Mexicans, Puerto Ricans. Accepting our plurality as given, starting with what each one is, we seek *unity*. A Cuban priest says to a Mexican sister with whom he is talking: Integration, yes; assimilation, no—never."

The great problems we are faced with are not the lack of beds or the long lines into the dining room. What upsets us is not being able to be together. Only the delegates fit in the auditorium. The observers—well, we make ourselves as comfortable as possible on the floor of a side room, having no option but to watch what goes on in the assembly on videotape.

There is great disorder, mainly because of the great numbers we are. There is frustration due to our lack of understanding of parliamentary procedure and also due to lack of time for talking, discussing, sharing—saying all one wants to say. There are complaints, complaints due to the confusion over credentials. There are hurt feelings, and different groups feel isolated and belittled. I hear a woman complaining to the moderator of one of the workshops. He answers her that his intention was good. With a pained smile, she says, "Yes, I don't question your intentions, but, with good intentions one can kill others."

The first session lasts until 1:00 a.m. The document on "Evangelization," which reflects to a large extent the voice of the people, is amended and approved. The organizers are asked to be more efficient in the future plenary sessions; they respond affirmatively. The second document, the one on "Ministries," is approved in an orderly and efficient fashion.

"Listen, I have learned a lot," a lady tells me. This is the first time she has attended this kind of meeting. And I, I who have been to similar meetings before, I have also learned much. I have learned that the union among Hispanics comes from shared values, not from a mere sharing of language, music, customs. I have learned that the voice of the People of God is heard clearly through the small ecclesial communities. I have learned that the People of God will not allow others to continue to oppress them, to ignore them.

Different groups pressure the General Assembly. The migrants, the military, the agricultural workers, the young adults—each one tries to win the hearts of the delegates, to make them be in agreement with their interests, to get their approval for the recommendations they back. Tired but conscious of the obligation they have as delegates, the General Assembly members gather again to approve the document on "Human Rights." Emotions run high. An American nun in almost perfect Spanish asks me, "Do you think the majority of the delegates understands what they are voting for?" I don't know what to think. The delegates come out from the auditorium. They are frustrated and tired. We all go to the "Hispanic Rainbow"—a presentation of regional music and dances. I don't know if the music pacifies us or calls us to go beyond what we think in search of unity, a unity we feel as we savor the music and the dances.

The last day begins. There are three documents still to be brought to the floor. Tension and frustration can almost be touched. "Never," a Chicano priest tells me, "should we have used this process. Parliamentary procedure frustrates our people." I try to move to another group, but he continues talking to me. "We came to reflect together, to share community. Recommendation, documents—we didn't come for this." Finally I get away from him only to run into a Cuban who, choking with tears, tells me that the delegates have had no time to consider a recommendation denouncing the violation of human rights that political prisoners in Cuba suffer.

The disorder outside the auditorium where the delegates are meeting is unbelieveable. "Let's not fight." "Brother, calm down." "You'll see, all will turn out for the best." Heralds of hope in the midst of confusion. . . .

It is so late. The last document reaches the floor. "Unity in Diversity." The Cubans are able to include the resolution on political prisoners. The document proposes as valid the concept of integration within a pluralistic society while totally rejecting "an assimilation that imposes on us the value system of the dominating group."

A group of Puerto Ricans in the assembly protests the fact that their flag is not included among those on the auditorium stage. Furious, hurt, they abandon the session even as it is explained that the absence of their flag has been unintentional. A young Puerto Rican woman points out to me that the document at present on the floor considers "an enriching element" the diversity of our people—a diversity born of different historical events and cultural heritages. "Right now," she complains sadly, "I don't consider diversity an enrichment."

The moderator asks for a final vote accepting the document as amended. It is impossible to describe the feelings of the delegates, the observers, the organizers—the innermost feelings of all there present when the last vote has been cast. But the Second Encounter does not finish there. Tired out by the process, frustrated by the lack of time, upset by the disorganization, pressured by different groups which "thirst and hunger for justice"—no, the Second Encounter does not finish on such a negative note. The Second Encounter does not end on a violent note because, as Archbishop Flores will remind us in his homily, we are the people that has used violence the least.

"How is it possible for us now to go on to celebrate the Eucharist after so many fights, so many hurt feelings?" I hear a young man asking a priest. The organizers ask me to move and I do not hear the answer. Four abreast we start walking, singing as we go. The question of the young man stays with me. We are going to the Shrine of the Immaculate Conception. I am able to go off to the side and find a place to sit on the floor in front of the first pew. And while bishops, archbishops, and cardinals enter in solemn procession, the answer to the young man's question comes to me: "Yes, we can celebrate Eucharist together in spite of difficulties and differences. Differences, difficulties— they do not divide us. The celebration of the Eucharist makes visible, surfaces what unites us—our value system: friendship, importance of family, sincerity, spontaneity, hospitality, openness, accepting others and, above all, our faith—our common belief. Yes, we are brought together by our faith, a faith we live as we struggle to understand it and which we understand as we live it."

We have not solved differences or difficulties. But we know what we are—a people, the people of God that marches on. Recommendations that will be presented to the bishops have been agreed upon. But much more important is the courage for the struggle that our coming together gives us; the conviction with which we return home is that the Lord walks shoulder to shoulder with us. Armed with what we have experienced, what we have lived in this Second Encounter, we now go back to serve, to strengthen our sisters, our brothers, with the firm hope that our struggle will one day make it possible for us to reach "Another city which knows no end, a city without sadness and difficulties, the eternal city."

National Youth Task Force of the USCC. 1978. Left to right kneeling: Archbishop Robert Sánchez. Chairman-Moderator: Bishop Patricio Flores. Moderator: Bishop John Snyder. Moderator (courtesy Esteban Solis)

CHAPTER FIFTEEN

NEW ELEMENTS IN THE HISPANO CHURCH

The Second National Hispano Pastoral Encounter demonstrated the valuable accomplishments of five years within the Hispano church, but it also revealed the uneven distribution of success and the need for wider representation at leadership posts. Encouragingly, the differences between Puerto Ricans and Mexican Americans, between pastoralists and liberationists are just the sort of regional and nationalistic loyalties that make the Hispano leadership so refreshing and vital. Surely, just as a forum was created to forge unity among all the diversities, the same ingenuity can find a way to express diversity without losing hold of a basic solidarity.

There are positive advantages to these past frictions and they enrich the paradigm of Hispano participation. Among the people who are generally untouched by conceptualization of theological models of church two movements pose important consequences for the Hispano church: the Charismatic movement and the *comunidades de base,* or fundamental grassroots communities.

Hispanos are known to be open, warm, and loving persons who articulately express their feelings. Sometimes this stereotype is caricatured as if the persons with *no* emotions were in control and those who cried, wept, rejoiced, etc., were out of control. But since Aquinas, Catholic philosophy has taught that the display of emotions is part of the full exercise of humanity in its body-soul interplay. The Charismatic movement is asserting this for hundreds of thousands of United States Catholics who have been out of touch with their emotions in a prayer context for many lifetimes. Yet precisely because Hispanos are so culturally preconditioned for such open prayer and feelings, the Charismatic movement carries different implications for future development among Hispanos. How all of this will affect the Hispano church is not yet clear: it is certain, however, that it cannot be ignored.

The *comunidades de base* have sprung up wherever there are Hispanos. It is not only that such grassroots groups are common in today's Latin America, it is also the conscious policy of the Spanish-speaking Secretariat in Washington to develop this movement. As we have seen, Father Edgard Beltran, a Colombian priest with wide experience in Latin America, emphasized *comunidades de base* rather than movements such as the Cursillo in the preparations for the Second National Hispano Pastoral Encounter. In a gradual fashion, inner-city ministries, such as the Catholic Committee for

Urban Ministry (CCUM), have been moving in the direction of such communities. Moreover, the apostolic letter by Pope Paul on evangelization has given impetus to the movement. Once again, it cannot be clearly foreseen what consequences the *comunidades de base* will have, but it should not be doubted that they will be important.

Outside the Hispano community, there are new constellations of influence. The paradigm of Hispano participation at all levels of the church is accepted: indeed, Poles, Italians, and blacks are adopting some of the theology and methods of the Hispano church. Certainly the increased awareness of ethnicity by the whole church will create opportunities for Hispanos to influence general church practice. This is likely to happen not only at the highest levels of church politics, but more and more in local parishes, particularly those with a multi-ethnic constituency. The interest of many dioceses in the Encounter process is an encouraging first step.

The formation of an ad hoc Migration Committee in the NCCB, under the chairmanship of Hispano Bishop René Gracida of Pensacola-Tallahassee, ought to create more theological visibility for the Hispano church. Until recently, this Committee on Migration and Tourism dealt mostly with questions of airport and seaport chaplains. Yet in the Vatican, the Sacred Congregation dealing with migration enjoys much influence in pastoral development. If the Migration Committee of the NCCB were to assume an analogous role within the United States Episcopal Conference, it would reach many more persons than just Hispanos with the paradigm created by the Hispano church. We could expect to see Poles, Italians—perhaps even Irish Catholics—holding pastoral encounters and working through secretariats. Indeed, if ethnicity and race are reinterpreted in terms of a migration experience, all the Catholics in the United States would be grouped under some form of "migrant ministry"! This is the profound implication of applying the norms of *Pastoralis cura migratorum* to the United States.

These then are the elements that are exercising new influences upon the Hispano church; from within, the Charismatic movement and the *comunidades de base;* from without, ethnicity and race in the light of the pope's letter on migrant ministry.

The following excerpt is taken from the award-winning series "Religion in American Cities," published in *New World Outlook.* This article on San Juan by Ana María Díaz Ramírez (see p. 208) highlights some of the political and sociological implications of the Charismatic movement, which enjoys its greatest success worldwide in Puerto Rico.

93. Religion in the Melting Pot of the Caribbean — San Juan, Puerto Rico (excerpt)

Ana María Díaz Ramírez

From New World Outlook, *May 1975, pp. 8-15.*

. . . To some Puerto Ricans, San Juan is closer to being a "boiling-pot" where the Puerto Rican element is, at best, sticking to the bottom or boiling over into the fire. Rather than lowering the flame or changing the pot, those in power are desperately trying to keep all the contents in by merely putting a cover on. The recent explosions in San Juan and around the island from both left- and right-wing groups seem to speak of that general unrest; and the silence with which the U.S. press has treated these happenings could be taken as a sign that someone doesn't want word to get out that "the natives are restless."

In the midst of this environment and atmosphere of materialism, political unrest, and frustration on the one hand, and indifference on the other, the churches try to keep alive and busy about "their work." But one may ask, what is the work of the church?

THE BOILING POT

For certain the church too has its share of unrest, conflict, and misunderstandings. And in an effort to solve or placate these it has become ingrown, keeping a close watch on its own "pot," afraid to involve itself in anything it cannot control, in any struggle it cannot contain within its own walls.

Rev. Victor Torres-Frias, secretary to Luis Cardinal Aponte Martínez of the San Juan Catholic Archdiocese, says that the people suffer from apathy because they lack native representation within the clergy. He is speaking, of course, of the Catholic church in the San Juan area which has only 17 Puerto Rican diocesan priests. Protestant churches have close to 700 ministers. And yet the latest survey on religion shows that 75 percent of the close to 3,000,000 population considers itself Catholic, while 20 percent declared themselves as belonging to the diverse Protestant denominations and the remaining 5 percent as others. Puerto Rican Catholics are questioning, he says, what their role is within the church when they lack voice in the leadership of that church.

THE CURSILLO MOVEMENT

In order to remedy the apathy of which Father Torres-Frías speaks, about fifteen years ago the Cursillos, a movement of lay formation, was brought from Spain and adapted to the Puerto Rican milieu. The Cursillo movement had had considerable success in Spain with professional people. In Puerto Rico it drew more numbers from the middle and professional classes and a more limited number from among the working class and spread quite rapidly in the metropolitan area and throughout the island. But the cure was worse than the ailment, thought some members of the clergy. This feeling seemed to prevail especially among members of the foreign clergy who traditionally have seen Puerto Rican religion as inferior to their own and who now saw a threat to their own authority and power in the newly aroused laity awareness effected by the Cursillo. The laity was coming alive, but it was also asking for active participation and a voice within the church. They had come of age, they claimed. Who would have thought that simple courses on grace and sacramental theology given during a three-day weekend to a group of people ultimately selected by their own parish priests would bring about such effects!

Little by little the Cursillo made its way into the mainstream of Catholic church life, becoming yet another group governed by its structure, thereby losing some of its challenge and appeal that had originally characterized it. With the passing of time, some say, it became stale, and even let itself be used for political purposes. It is further claimed that as certain members began to link the movement with their particular political views and activities, it began to lose membership. In the San Juan area many Puerto Rican members who had been with the Cursillo since its beginning began to fall away, and their places were filled by Cubans. It was no longer the voice of Puerto Rican Catholics communicating with their church, it was felt.

THE CHARISMATIC MOVEMENT

As this was taking place within the Cursillo movement, a new movement was imported from the United States, this one ecumenical in nature. The Charismatic movement on the island has been viewed by some (especially by some *cursillistas*) as an intrusion, and by others as an attempt to keep in check rising political and social unrest. Still others regard it as a blessing.

. . . Whether or not Charismatics are ready to admit it, the claim that both Pentecostalism and the Cursillo movement have had much to do with their own success should not be readily put aside. For it has been claimed that the Cursillo and the Pentecostals prepared the way, making it possible for church communities, not so long ago very conservative and suspicious of anything non-traditional, to open up to new and diverse expressions of faith and religious fervor and feelings.

The tensions between present Charismatics and *cursillistas* are said to be more than a problem of differences—a struggle for power and recognition within the church. Speaking of these movements, Luis Cardinal Aponte Martínez recognized the Cursillo movement as a movement "in good standing within the church"; the Charismatic movement, on the other hand, he says is under "vigilance, observation" by the Catholic Bishops' Conference.

A MATTER OF CLASS

The conflict between Charismatics and Pentecostals seems to be more a problem of class. Pentecostalism was brought to the island by the first Puerto Rican migrant workers returning from Hawaii in the early 1900s. Since then, Pentecostalism has been the "religion of the poor." It has been characterized by its joyful spirit, by what they claim to be the gift of prophecy and healing, but most specially by the gift of tongues. Puerto Ricans, especially the lower classes who are a people apt to express openly their feelings and emotions, found in Pentecostalism an adequate vehicle for expressing and communicating their religious feelings and convictions.

Modeled somewhat upon the Charismatic movement but seeking neither recognition nor adherence to any church or church structure, the Catacumbas, a group of university-age young people, believe that their mission in life is to become like the first Christians, adorers of God in "spirit and in truth," unlimited and unrestrained by church walls, regulations or structures. They come together to pray, to read the Bible, to sing and to give personal testimony, by the roadside, beneath bridges, in the parks, in empty lots. Among followers they have drawn are a number of young people who have had problems in the past with the police, alcohol, drugs, parental or school authorities. "The group is basically doing a good thing," says Dr. Rafael Boissen, United Methodist district superintendent for the San Juan area, "but they suffer from a spiritual euphoria which causes them to disregard the real problems confronting us.". . .

The Reverend Raymond Rivera, pastor of the Melrose Reformed Church in the Bronx, New York City, is the president of the Hispanic Council of the Reformed Church in America and co-founder of Acción Cívica Evangélica, a union of Pentecostal churches. In this statement, the Reverend Mr. Rivera ties the Pentecostal movement to the theology of liberation. The prophetic words of this Puerto Rican minister indicate a horizon for ecumenical action and the possible integration of the Charismatics within the Hispano church with the pastoralists and the liberationists.

94. The Political and Social Ramifications of Indigenous Pentecostalism

Raymond Rivera

Used by permission.

From *Time* magazine to the *Christian Century,* headline stories reflect the rapid rise of the Pentecostal experience to the forefront of America's national religious consciousness. Once the object of intellectual disdain and ridicule, the Pentecostal phenomena of glossalia and Charismatic Christianity have emerged as a source of interest and inspiration among people of every denomination, ethnic group, and economic class. The preeminence of the social ministry propagated in liberal theology of the 1950s and 1960s has been supplanted by a growing movement toward the otherworldly and mystical orientation of Pentecostalism. Yet the faddish attention to those celestial elements of the Pentecostal faith, which has become so acceptable in white middle-class and academic circles, relates to only one part of what this faith has meant among the uneducated, poor, and oppressed peoples of the world who historically embraced and perpetuated its dogma.

The indigenous Pentecostal experience, while emphasizing the spiritual dimension, has evolved as a virtual "theology of survival" for the downtrodden and hopeless. In this sense, Pentecostalism has carried with it significant social and political ramifications that define the full meaning of the religious experience among people whose physical existence and personal development depend directly on their lives in the church community. The influence of the Pentecostal church in the urban Hispanic community demonstrates clearly the sociopolitical relevance of indigenous Pentecostalism.

The urban Hispanic, through years of racist conditioning, suffers from an ethnic stereotype that predetermines failure and self-hate. An Anglo-dominated system of colonialism has crippled the Hispanic soul and effectively isolated him from his own culture, history, and language. As a result of historical oppression, the Hispanic is caught in a cycle of despair—stripped of energy, motivation, and hope for a better future. He is alienated from his own people and from a society that has eroded any sense of self-respect or pride.

At a grassroots level, the Pentecostal church reaches out to an individual who is conditioned to fail. The church offers a new birth in Christ, a new hope for life according to God's plan, and a positive answer to the frustrations of an empty and directionless existence. Outside observers have considered this conversion experience as a solely celestial-oriented escape from sordid reality. In fact, it represents the beginning of a counterassimilation process and the first step in rebuilding the damaged Hispanic psyche in a social and political context. The Pentecostal convert enters an entirely indigenous Hispanic church structure. His past stereotype of fellow Hispanics has been totally negative—the welfare cheats, drug addicts, the street-corner beer crowd. In the church he begins to see his people as industrious leaders, articulate speakers, and members of a mutually supportive fellowship. Hispanic language and culture, belittled by white society, are a source of pride and identity within the Pentecostal church, reinforcing the shared sense of communal pride and understanding between Hispanic peoples.

It is an accepted sociological fact that role models, authority figures, and status symbols are crucial to individual self-development and social assimilation. As the Pentecostal church touches the lives of urban Hispanics, it brings a totally new set of models that contradict the predominantly negative images Hispanics have of their people. The Pentecostal community thus produces self-esteem and self-appreciation at an individual level that translates into political strength and collective growth at a community level. The individual convert believes, and learns from the church, "that for them that believe all things are possible." Obstacles that once discouraged and frustrated him disappear with the faith that with God, all things are possible. The individual is no longer doomed to accept his lot in life as what "must be," but is inspired to the knowledge that with God he can transcend all limitations.

Today, the Pentecostal church is the fastest-growing denomination among Third World peoples. During the past decade, as other church bodies have declined in influence and membership, the revival and explosive growth of Pentecostalism has silenced its long-time critics. But the true implications of this movement remain largely unrecognized among scholars and churchmen who fail to perceive the political and social revolution taking place beneath the dogma of celestialism. The true role of the Pentecostal church is continuing at a community level, whether consciously or unconsciously, where thousands of once-alienated individuals are gaining the strength and confidence that will enable them to confront a system that has long oppressed and divided them.

Ultimately, indigenous Pentecostalism represents the vehicle for liberation of all colonialized and oppressed peoples, not only in a spiritual sense but in all political, social, and economic contexts. *Time* magazine would do well to recognize that the Pentecostal phenomenon does not belong only in its religious pages, but rather, at the forefront of news analysis of the dynamics of political activity among Third World peoples.

The development of *comunidades de base* has been due in large measure to the efforts of the USCC's Edgard Beltrán. There are, however, other *comunidades de base* in the Hispano church which are independent of Father Beltrán's work. One of these independent groups is Naborí, a community of Puerto Rican university students in New York City. This group took its name from the Taino Indians, the original inhabitants of Puerto Rico, and has been instrumental in laying the foundations for a national Hispano youth ministry.

Following is an excerpt from the presentation at the Northeast Regional Encounter (see p. 223), which gave impetus to the Youth Pastoral Council (CPJ) and Operation Solidarity; the Encounter was held in Hartford, Connecticut, in the summer of 1975. Focused upon the struggles of the Puerto Rican migrant farm workers (see pp. 264ff.), it was the first specifically Hispano youth program in the United States to come from the Hispano church. Naborí later helped formulate Operation Understanding during the Eucharistic Congress held in Philadelphia in 1976, the mobile Hispanic Institutes, and the National Hispanic Youth Task Force organized during the Second National Hispano Pastoral Encounter in 1977. In 1978 members of Naborí directed the Latino Youth Training Program at St. Joseph's College in West Hartford, which gathered Chicanos and Puerto Ricans from all parts of the country.

The *comunidad de base,* as exemplified by Naborí, is not only a prayer and support group, but also an apostolic force.

95. Presentation by Naborí, Youth Workshop, First Northeast Regional Pastoral Encounter, November 30, 1974 (excerpt)

Lala Torres, Edna Zallas, Annette Ramos

Used by permission.

The New Testament describes for us the history of the primitive church with these words from Acts (2:44-47, *Good News for Modern Man*):

All the believers continued together in close fellowship, and shared their belongings with one another. They would sell their property and possessions and distribute the money among all, according to what each one needed. Every day they continued to meet a group in the Temple, and they had their meals together in their homes, eating the food with glad and humble hearts, praising God and enjoying the good will of all the people. And every day the Lord added to their group those who were being saved.

Today, unfortunately, in spite of the great number of Hispano youth in our cities, their presence in the church is minimal. Even among those who go to church, there is a rapid and continuous drop off. We ask where the fault lies: is it that the community of the faithful has stopped being a visible witness or is it that the goings-on of the modern world do not let us hear the call? It is certain that once our youth leave the parochial school, once beyond child-hood, adolescence, puberty—the enthusiasm also ends. Sometimes it seems that they forget God. Certainly this is not a local problem, nor a regional one: it is a universal phenomenon. But we live in this region of the Northeast of the United States and it is very important for us to face up to the situation in which we live to remedy it. Youth is the hope of the future. But if this youth does not return to the church, what church will be left for us tomorrow? For example, in the city of New York, half of the Puerto Rican population is nineteen years old or less. But, brothers and sisters, does our church dedicate half of its attention and its resources to us? Does the church commit half of its money for use in programs for us? Are our Hispano children, let alone half of them, admitted to Catholic schools, or to Catholic high schools? The answer to these questions is a firm "No!" We young people wish to share with you our Christian concern for the Christian development of Hispano youth in our region. But first we would like to introduce ourselves.

Some of us are university students and, as such, we know the problems of youth—our problems—by their scientific names. We suffer from social disintegration, from alienation, from exploitation, from a family structure which has been destroyed, etc. But we also know these sad realities because we have felt them in our own flesh. And so we prefer to speak of them in terminology common to everyone; we want to speak *tú a tú* of our personal experiences.

I am a member of Naborí. Naborí is a Taino name, from the tribes of the Indians of the Antilles; that is, of the islands of Boriké, Haití and Cubanacán, today known as Puerto Rico, the Dominican Republic, and the Socialist Republic of Cuba. On these islands lived a class of Indians whose job was to be workers in the fields and—in moments of danger—to defend their homeland. To this class of Indians, a worker-warrior, was given the name "Naborí."

Recognizing our Taino heritage and accepting the responsibility of struggling and working for our values, we have adopted this name. Naborí functions as a *comunidad de base*. Among its principal elements, we would like to point out the following ones to you.

1. We are a family, we love one another mutually, showing affection and interest in the needs, worries, and projects of the members of the group. We study and work together for the good of our community.

2. We have used group dynamics and psychological games to deepen our personal commitment.

3. In Naborí we are all Puerto Ricans. It is not our intention to look down on other nationalities, but we have thought that it was very important that the bonds that join us in this *comunidad de base* should be common to everyone by the similarity in our lived experience, in the ambient and the cultural background from which we come.

4. We are all of us poor, children of *jíbaros*, and we are proud of it. [*Applause.*] We do not feel ashamed at all of having been born outside of our land in poverty, because in like condition was born in Bethlehem the Child of Mary of Nazareth.

5. In Naborí, there is no distinction according to class. We are all equals. We have no president, no dues, nor do we look for prestige or privileges. Once we asked help from a parish and it was denied us. Instead they offered us basketball games and participation in bingo as the apostolic programs of the parish.

6. We study our culture and the history of our Puerto Rican people. We are interested in poetry, theater, literature, and music.

7. We try to keep abreast of all movements which are focused on the destiny of our people.

8. We share our ideas and even the little we have and seek to make life a little more friendly for all of us. . . .

The following two selections are taken from the proceedings of the annual bishops' meeting, November 1976. The words of the apostolic delegate to the NCCB refer to three challenges: the need for lay ministry, for *comunidades de base*, and for an understanding of ethnicity. Whether he realized it or not, Archbishop Jadot urged the assembly of United States bishops to develop along lines that have achieved their most articulate North American form in the Hispano church.

At that same meeting, the NCCB approved a statement on the nature of the pastoral care of migrants in this country. The chairman of the Ad Hoc Committee on Migration and Tourism is Hispano, Bishop René H. Gracida, of Pensacola-Tallahassee in Florida. Once again, a perspective clear to Hispanos was being adopted by the rest of the United States church.

96. Signs of the Times

Archbishop Jean Jadot, Apostolic Delegate to the United States

Address to the Annual Meeting of the National Council of Catholic Bishops, November 9, 1976 (text). Reprinted from Origins *6, no. 22 (November 18, 1976).*

On September 3, we commemorated Pope St. Gregory the Great. The Office of Readings in the new and inspiring Liturgy of the Hours offered us a meditation taken from a homily by this doctor of the church who is rightly considered as an outstanding example and teacher for all pastors.

St. Gregory took as his text the words of Ezekiel: "Son of man, I have made you a watchman for the house of Israel." He tells us: "Note that the man whom the Lord sends forth as a preacher is called a watchman. A watchman always stands on a height so that he can see from afar what is coming. Anyone appointed to be a watchman for the people must stand on a height for all his life to help them by his foresight" (Liturgy of the Hours, Catholic Book Company edition, 1975, vol. 4, p. 1365).

If St. Gregory were speaking in our days, he would perhaps refer to radar, satellites and computers. Our knowledge of history—the *magistra vitae* as Pope John called it—the insights coming from the modern sciences of psychology, ethnology and sociology, our means of communications, all give us the possibility to see further and wider into the future than ever before.

I believe that St. Gregory would insist that we, even more than the pastors of his day, must be "watchmen" for the people of God. For, each one of us is a "man whom the Lord sends forth as a preacher." Vatican II emphasized our role as a preacher and, therefore, in St. Gregory's words, as a "man who sees from afar what is coming."

Now is the time to look ahead. Just as we can look at the sky at night and tell what the morning will bring, so we must be able to read the signs of the times to prepare for the future (cf. Mt. 16:2-3).

This morning, my brother bishops, I would like to share with you some of the signs that I read in our times so that we can see from afar and be prepared for what is coming.

One problem that we will have to face very soon—at most within 10 years—is the shortage of priests. I ask your permission to be frank and candid. I am worried that so many of us—laity, clergy and bishops—do not seem to be concerned that, if not today, then in a very few years, we will not be able to staff our parishes and institutions with priests as we did in the past.

Already, there are parishes in which two priests are trying with the same pastoral approaches to do what four priests did a few years ago. In some regions priests are dying in their 50s from overwork. Others are chronically tired and frustrated because they cannot accomplish by themselves what several priests together accomplished in the past.

I am deeply convinced that we must seriously study the problem. When I say "we," I mean bishops and priests, religious and laity, all together.

There are solutions open to us if we set priorities; if we are willing to give greater responsibilities to the laity, both men and women; if we make more effective use of permanent deacons and extraordinary ministers. I am not in a position to elaborate on these possibilities. But I know that if we do not search for new avenues of pastoral care, in 10 years we will be unable to meet the spiritual needs of the people of God or to bring the light of the gospel to a world that is crying out for the good news of Christ.

Even if there will be an increase in the number of priestly vocations in the next few years—and we have reasons to hope that there will be—nevertheless, we must be prepared for a shortage of priests at least for a generation to come.

Another problem ahead of us which will grow in the coming years is the size of our Christian communities.

The Synod of Bishops in 1974 showed that there is a general move within the whole church to seek smaller communities. In his exhortation on evangelization, the Holy Father underscored and elaborated upon the findings of the synod. "The Church," Pope Paul tells us, "is also conscious of the fact that, if the preaching of the gospel is to be effective, she must address her message to the communities of the faithful which are scattered amid the multitudes, for the action of these communities can and must reach out to the others" (*Evangelii nuntiandi*, n. 57). Having insisted upon this point, the Holy Father immediately proceeds to an analysis of different types of small communities. He goes on to say that the groups which unite themselves to the church and foster her growth will be "a hope for the universal church" (*ibid.*, n. 58).

Even in the United States we see an increasing interest in smaller communities—some having a form of life in common, others being less structured, such as prayer groups, and Bible study classes.

Last year at your meeting Bishop Ottenweller spoke about the problem of parishes that are not responding to the expectations of many Catholics. People today, and especially young people, are searching for a group in which they can find a true communion of faith, of worship and of commitment. Many are suffering from a certain feeling of loneliness. They experience a need to identify with others who share their yearning for a more communal life. They are looking for a truly spiritual community which will have Christ as its center and the church as its framework.

Again, I do not have a simple answer to the problem. Church leaders will have to work with the laity to develop new patterns of parochial life and, perhaps, new forms of parochial organization so that the parish can become "a community of small communities."

I should like to mention a third problem that is with us today and will undoubtedly increase with time. It is the problem of minorities. I refer to pastoral care for ethnic and racial minorities, both Catholic and non-Catholic. Some, such as the blacks and many Hispanics, have been in this country for years, if not for centuries. Others, such as the Vietnamese and the growing number of families coming from Portugal and its former territories, are more recent arrivals.

In the 1800s and the early 1900s the bishops of this country faced the problem of providing pastoral care for the thousands of men and women coming here from Europe. "National parishes" were established to help the immigrants remain faithful to their religious and cultural traditions. Frequently, a group of people from one area in the "old country" settled around their national parish, which became the center of their civil, social and religious life. I am not qualified to express an opinion on the advantages and disadvantages of "national parishes." But I do see them as an attempt in a certain moment of history to meet a pastoral need.

It seems to me and to many observers of the American scene that in the last quarter of the 20th century we are facing a double problem.

First, how are we to give pastoral care to those who do not feel at home with our white, western European ways of public worship and community living, to those who have not adapted and do not want to adapt to what we call our American way of doing things? What is to be our pastoral approach to the blacks, the native Americans, our brothers and sisters who have their roots in eastern Europe, to the Catholics who belong to the Oriental rites? How are we, as pastors, to serve our large and active Spanish-speaking communities and, to some extent, our flourishing Italian communities? How can we help the Irish, the French-Canadian and the German Americans to preserve or to rediscover the best of their national traditions?

Second, how are we to foster the unity of the people of God within the one, holy, catholic and apostolic church while at the same time preserving the diversity that is one of the riches of this great country?

I am deeply aware of the complexity of these problems, as I am aware of the many who are working to promote social justice and respect for all cultures. But at times I wonder if the majority of our priests and people realize our shortcomings in these areas and even our arrogance toward our brothers and sisters in the faith who are in some ways different from ourselves. I wonder if we can ever fully understand the legitimate frustrations that they feel.

Our responsibilities to work for social justice and to respect all cultures are even more serious when they are viewed in the light of our obligation to spread the good news of Christ. As the Holy Father has written in *Evangelii nuntiandi*, "Evangelization loses much of its force and effectiveness if it does not use the language, the signs and the symbols of the people to whom we preach the gospel, if it does not answer the questions they ask, and if it does not have an impact on their concrete lives" (n. 63).

There are other problems either near or far on the horizon. I could mention the question of the role of women in society and in the church or the problems that will come from the rejection of the traditional standards of morality in social, political and business life. But I have already been too long. Much time would be required to put them in their proper perspective or do justice to the bishops and priests, religious and laity who are working hard to solve the problems we inherited from the past.

I would conclude this talk by repeating what St. Gregory said in his homily: "How hard it is for me to say this, for by these very words I denounce myself. . . . So who am I to be a watchman, for . . . I lie down in the valley of weakness? Truly the all-powerful Creator and Redeemer of mankind can give me, in spite of my weakness, a higher life and a more effective speech; because I love him, I do not spare myself in speaking of him."

My brother bishops, let us be confident, courageous and open to the Spirit. Let us build the church of God by our foresight. All is possible "because I love him."

---

97. Resolution on the Pastoral Concern of the Church for People on the Move (excerpt)

Approved by the National Council of Catholic Bishops, November 9, 1976.

"I was a stranger and you made me welcome" (Mt. 25:35).

The movement of people seeking their daily bread and the protection of their human rights is a growing phenomenon of our times. Large-scale international migration is due chiefly to demands for plentiful and cheap labor created by technological progress and patterns of investment or to political unrest. People cross international borders for seasonal work, for temporary work, and for permanent resettlement. In all too many cases human considerations, such as family life and family values, are sacrificed to economic ones.

Massive migration from underdeveloped countries and regions is a special phenomenon of our age. The United States alone receives about 400,000 new immigrants each year. Our country continues to attract immigrants as workers and refugees.

Many of today's immigrants are doubly marginal: they are forced to migrate because of inadequate resources and unequal distribution of goods; then, in their countries of adoption, they are sometimes ignored or subjected to new injustices. Perhaps it is because of such compounded injustice that Jesus specifically promises His Kingdom to those who recognize Him in the immigrant.

In his Motu Proprio *On the Pastoral Care of Migrants* Pope Paul called for a careful balance of the immigrant's rights and duties: to the right to emigration corresponds the duty to serve the common good, especially in developing countries (e.g., the problem of "brain drain"); the right to be accepted as an immigrant is limited by the common good of the country receiving the immigrant; to the right of immigration corresponds the duty to adapt to the new environment; to the duty of serving the common good in the country of origin corresponds the duty of the state to create jobs in the country of origin.

As a leaven in the world, the Church is called to participate in human affairs and to recognize in the poor, the afflicted, and the oppressed the presence of the Lord summoning the Christian community to action.

Seen in this evangelical perspective, immigrants, refugees, migrant workers, seamen and other people uprooted and on the move for survival and human dignity are a theological sign to the Christian community. They are among those signs of the times to which the Second Vatican Council called our attention in order to discern the working of God's will.

While the pastoral care of the Church is directed to all, it is especially imperative that it be extended to newcomers "driven by political or economic forces to move abroad" *(On the Pastoral Care of Migrants, I)*. Their human and spiritual needs are great. Furthermore, the Church has a natural concern in this area, for at least three reasons.

First, a high percentage of the new immigrants to our nation come from traditionally Catholic countries such as Mexico, Cuba, the Philippines, the Dominican Republic, Colombia, Portugal, Haiti, etc. Second, the changed character of the new immigrant population, now predominantly Latin American, Caribbean, and Asian, finds in the transnational character of the Church an appropriate catalyst for a healthy adaptation to a new life. Third, the background of many of these immigrants has accustomed them to look to the Church not only as a source of spiritual guidance, but also as a natural point of cultural and social reference. . . .

The following excerpt from an interview with Bishop Gilberto Chávez, auxiliary of San Diego, reflects the naturalness with which representatives of the Hispano church speak about the failures of the institutional church. Hispanos tend to defend the people first and the institutions second, contrary to what is often expected from church leaders.

Born in Ontario, California, of Mexican parents, on May 9, 1932, Gilberto lost his father in a train-automobile accident in 1947. Following his older brother into the seminary and priesthood, he was ordained for the San Diego Diocese in 1960, and did graduate studies after ordination in philosophy and psychology at the University of California at Riverside. After a few years as a high school teacher, he worked full-time as a parish priest until his ordination as auxiliary of San Diego in 1974.

The bishop graphically describes the differences among Chicanos, Mexicans, and Mexican Americans, almost making them different nationalities. His frankness about the limitation to a clerical ministry is prophetic. It is unfortunate, however, that the bishop confuses statistics that belong to the total Hispano population in his reference to the Mexican, Chicano, and Mexican American segments of that community.

98. The Bittersweet Experience of a Mexican American Bishop—An Interview with Bishop Gilberto Chávez (excerpt)

Interviewed by Father Silvano M. Tomasi, C.S. (Director of the Center for Migration Studies, New York)

From Migration Today, December 1976, pp. 12-13, 24. Used by permission.

INTERGROUP RELATIONS

Father Silvano M. Tomasi: Do you see a big difference between the Mexican-American or the Chicano community and the immigrant community? Do they get along? What kind of positions do they have in the city structure?

Bishop Gilberto Chávez: The great difference is that the Chicano has been living here, and knows that his rights have been violated time and again and is struggling to have equal share with other Americans, while the Mexican comes from Mexico primarily for one purpose, survival. Over there they are starving in misery and oppression, and so they come here to enjoy the right to eat. Since this is their main concern they cannot be involved civically or socially or politically, because this is their basic need, and if they can fulfill it they are satisfying their reason for coming to the United States.

SMT: Are you trying to be a bridge between the two communities?

GC: It is very difficult to unite people with different mentalities. We are working very successfully with the Mexicans because they have a very simple but profound faith. The Chicanos, on the other hand, are very difficult to work with on a religious basis. We work with them more on a social and political basis because of the fact that the Chicanos have left the Church. For many years they have been neglected by the Church; therefore, they see their very absence from the Church as a manifestation of protest against the Church. We are not really concerned with converting them but with treating the Chicano as human individuals, while helping them in the political, social and economic struggles they are engaged in and by assuring that their rights likewise be respected. We are concerned with them on a very human level!

SMT: Do you find it difficult to create and establish credibility between you as a priest and the Chicano community?

GC: It depends upon the individuals. There is a great lack of credibility. This gap has existed for many years. It's ingrown. The Chicano has lost interest in the Church. Therefore, it is difficult to change his mentality or attitudes just in one or two years. It will take some time and real leadership on the part of the Church, the priests and the laity, before these Chicanos can likewise change their mentality. Right now they at least tolerate the Church; they respect the Church, but they are not willing to be counted as part of the Church.

THE FUTURE OF THE AMERICAN CHURCH

SMT: Some people observe that the hope of the American Church in terms of its vitality comes very much from the Mexican-American and Chicano community. How do you see it regarding the future, especially the future of the Southwest?

GC: I think this is true because we are now 25 percent of the Catholics of the nation and we will be increasing every year, first of all by the fact that many don't practice birth control and secondly because of the number of Mexicans coming from Mexico. Likewise, we are becoming aware of our situation, our power and effort for self-determination. By being united I think that we will become actually leaders in the Catholic Church and in the United States. I don't know when; but I know that eventually the process of history and development will take the Mexican-Americans to an actual leadership position.

SMT: Do you see any specific contribution that the Mexican-American community will inject into both the American society and the American Church?

GC: The idea we have tried to inject is the idea of pluralism, that the United States is not a melting pot, that we can still retain our culture, our tradition, our language, our values and by means of these values and culture enrich not only the cities or states where we are, but also the entire country. Variety in life is like the variety in flowers which enriches the different gardens and areas of the world. A variety of traditions and languages is also a means of enriching God's creation. Our mentality is quite different from the Anglo-Saxon mentality. If it is respected, if it is listened to, we can form a pluralistic, a more real Church, and not simply a very static Church that can easily die because it is not permitted to be creative.

SMT: In terms of the future in the Church, one issue that is often brought up is vocation. How do you see the future of Mexican-Americans with regard to their own community, the priests, and Catholic involvement in the community?

GC: First of all, I see that we will not have very many Mexican-American vocations due to the fact that we have been ignored for 150 years by the American Church and, secondly, because of a growing anti-clerical and anti-religious trend in the world. Thirdly, the Mexican people by nature are very human. An aspect of this humanness is sexuality, or expression of being a human individual. Both in Mexico and here we have *machismo*, not in the wrong sense that we are domineering of women, but that we are men with a sexual life to live. Because of this *machismo* and the traditional culture reinforcing it, an increase in the number of Mexican-American vocations is difficult to achieve. Thus, I see the priesthood in the Mexican-American community to be really dying. This is a problem that the Church and the people can address. Unless something is done, the priesthood in the Mexican-American community is going to die out, to be extinct, or to be a rarity.

The following article, reprinted in its entirety from *The Priest*, provides a general description of how ethnicity is understood by different segments of the United States church.

99. What Is the Ethnicity of the American Church?

Antonio M. Stevens-Arroyo, C.P.

From The Priest, November 1976, pp. 37-41.

The meaning of the term "ethnicity" has not yet been fixed. For some, "ethnic" is different from "minority," for others it is inclusive. Occasionally ethnicity includes race; most often it does not, and so it goes. There are, of course, lines of agreement. Ethnicity does embrace the phenomenon of migration. In this way all the people of the United States are ethnic groups, since all have passed through a stage of migration in their American history. Even the native Americans, who were here before Columbus, have been forced to be migrants in their own land, though they were never immigrants. The struggle over ethnicity is like a tug-of-war. Recognizing that the United States church is an ethnic church, various contestants try to pull the others over to a particular definition of ethnicity. The prize is a sort of moral and historical preeminence.

ETHNICITY AS MOTIVATION

Father Geno Baroni is an activist. He uses ethnicity with the general meaning of positive motivations which are not universal in the North American culture because they spring from national origins. Ethnicity is a tool to achieve a better and more just society within and without the church. His focus is upon the urban parish because it is—or used to be—a neighborhood, i.e., a place where the quality of being neighbor is realizable. This "being neighbor" is not a fuzzy psychological state, or induced eschatology caught up in moralizing and feelings. Perhaps because he understands the labor movement, Baroni reflects in his definition a nonidealist, nonacademic, but thoroughgoing practical concept of ethnicity.

In an anthropological way, Brother Ronald Pasquriello says the same thing when he contrasts "head" with "heart" values and describes how ethnics differ from the dominant North American culture. On the question of school busing, however, we have an example of how, at certain levels, this motivational practicality can degenerate into pragmatism. Baroni is certainly correct in asserting that school busing will not work with the ethnic (as distinguished from minority) groups because it is not applied to all sectors of the United States population. But the *goals* of school desegregation are not undesirable simply because the *means* now proposed are unworkable.

CULTURAL SELF-CONCEPTION

Michael Novak is an activist of a different stamp. He thinks of ethnicity in terms of positive motivations, but where Baroni places priority on action in neighborhoods, Novak prefers to describe cultural conceptions and social group interaction at a national level. He is accurate in his detailing the white ethnic self-conception, particularly the Polish and Slovak versions. Novak's fostering of a grand ethnic coalition is a tribute to his capacity as a dialectical political thinker. A great many of his writings, especially those of a polemic nature, reflect an argumentation that attacks the contradictions of liberal urban politics. He shows, for instance, that quotas to make up for under-representation of blacks on university faculties, prejudice a similar under-representation of Slovaks. His target is not black opportunity, but the liberal establishment planners who arbitrarily distribute these "favors" to make what Novak sees as an unnatural political alliance of WASP intellectuals with black working-class people *against* white ethnic working-class. This dialectical reasoning is essential to raising the consciousness of those ethnics, who, because they are white and not Hispanic or black, have been relegated to silent underparticipation in North American society. There is a weakness, however, in this approach to ethnicity. The force of such arguments presupposes a liberal establishment, and depends upon a system where everyone tries to receive "a piece of the pie."

Novak has, in a metaphor, slapped the wrists of any ethnic group trying to take more than its fair share of the pie, but he has not forced the bakers to produce a bigger one with enough for all. Nor has he been able, as yet, to couple neighborhoods to any creative functions. His approach to ethnicity may end up serving as intellectual justification for what is mostly rearguard political action against liberal programs.

ETHNICITY AS CULTURAL DIALECTIC

Virgilio Elizondo, director of the Mexican American Cultural Center, speaks with the expertise of Novak about the Chicanos and other Mexican Americans in this country. But he takes an objective and historical stance instead of a subjective posture. Moreover, by expressing his kind of cultural concept of ethnicity against the background of Latin American Liberation Theology, Elizondo has an advantage over Novak and Baroni. They deal with ethnicity in the context of politics: he includes the sweep of social history in his expositions. At the [USCC] Bicentennial Hearings, Elizondo was credited with the concept of "stewpot" as a definition of ethnicity. In this conception, the various ethnic groups do not amalgamate into some new alloy as the term "melting pot" suggests. But neither do they remain static and separated from each other, like little chunks of stone in a mosaic. The ingredients of a stewpot remain distinct from each other while they cook, but produce a flavoring that is the result of all the elements stewing together.

Elizondo shows how the cooking has been done during United States history and objectifies in rich historical data the explanations of what-is in terms of what-has-been. Where Elizondo's concept demonstrates weakness is in terms of what-will-be. His understanding of the dialectic introduced by Liberation Theology is more Hegelian than Marxian: more focused on ideas than on deeds. For instance, he accepts at face value the promise of the North American Republic's "liberty and justice for all," without stating that the economic structure of the United States will never expand sufficiently to bring about equality because the nature of the expansion is predicated upon inequality. In plain terms, capitalism is an obstacle to Elizondo's concept of ethnicity: he would prefer patiently to nibble away at its ideology, rather than attack the basic structural problem of injustice head-on. In this he differs from many of the theologians he has invited to the Mexican American Culture Center in San Antonio.

ETHNICITY AND RACE

The black Catholic articulators of Liberation Theology, notably Sister Jamie Phelps, have an advantage over all who have been mentioned above. The blacks in this country have a historical Theology of Liberation which antedates Gutiérrez's book by two hundred years. This theology is expressed by music, lifestyle, culture and Christianity so rich that they have passed from the underground into the mainstream of what would otherwise be a barren North American English-speaking culture. The black struggle has borne much fruit in the past decade and a half, and its cultural revival is much richer than a Novak-style rearguard action. Black social activism has been a "praxis" rather than a political tactic: a reflective action constantly measured against and improved by a faith commitment. They also have advantages over Baroni, in that this faith has religious symbols of resistance rather than of nostalgia. By all rights, black Catholics ought to be the leaders in the articulation of a militant ethnicity, but they too have an Achilles' heel. Most black leaders are not Catholic; moreover, black faith traditions are expressed in Protestant confessional forms. Perhaps black ethnicity will be increasingly perceived these days as "American," but it will not often be seen as "Catholic." Black identity is centered, it should be added, around color and race rather than country of origin and language. Hence the dimensions of race, to the degree that they help blacks define themselves as an ethnic group, isolate them from others in the United States and serve to particularize rather than universalize their experience.

ETHNICITY AND CLASS

The third strain of Liberation Theology about ethnicity comes through Puerto Rico. On that sunny island of uncertain happiness, seventy-eight years of United States domination have decided the issue of cultural vs. economic dialectic. Puerto Rican Christians for Socialism have clearly opted for the economic priority as the focus of Christian activity, thus standing Elizondo "on his head," the way Marx did to Hegel. At the Newark Bicentennial Hearings, as a mainland-born Puerto Rican, I outlined a "Theology of Ethnicity" in an effort to relate what has been experienced on the island to the situation in the States.

Puerto Ricans have experienced prejudice against their language and culture, just as other ethnics have. Racial prejudice has not been absent, since Puerto Ricans are as Indo-American as Chicanos and as African as blacks. Moreover, the religious symbols of our faith have been forged out of resistance to the straitjacket of European Christianity. But because Puerto Rico is an economic colony of the United States (a fact recognized by the Democratic-sponsored bill introduced into Congress early in 1976), the Puerto Rican definition of ethnicity clearly includes social class. Puerto Ricans are, after all, largely working class. In New York City, where the majority reside, Puerto Ricans have the highest percentage of blue-collar workers of the three major groups in the city.

This concept of ethnicity includes the other factors such as religious differences, cultural and racial distinctions, but puts them together in class analysis. It is important to avoid minimizing the real injustices suffered in these first three categories, but it must be understood that class has been kept invisible because in the United States sociologists are supposed to tell us there are no classes. North American social science has preferred to describe class in terms of the capacity to *consume* (i.e., income levels) rather than the original determination which discloses a relationship to the *production* of goods and of values.

The class analysis of ethnicity has the advantage of being historical like Elizondo's, of going to a Christian praxis which transcends the Eastern European Marxism that Novak so correctly disparages, and at the same time does not omit the immediacy to experience that strengthens the approaches of Baroni and Phelps. The weakness of such a synthesis is, however, that it is not as easily done as said. Most of the authors mentioned above would probably question these brief generalizations of their concepts of ethnicity (and rightly so!). Not all of them would see the outlines of a Theology of Ethnicity as complementing their own experiences. Another basic difficulty would come at the grassroots, since not many white ethnics, or even blacks, would be attracted to a class analysis which carried strident tones of anti-Americanism. In such a case, this approach would seem to be a rejection rather than an explanation of United States history.

There are, of course, other authors, such as those found in Offices of Peace and Justice, at the Center of Concern and in the various Liberation Theology process groups. Most likely all of these persons would prefer to dialogue with each other rather than dissent. In effect, I have described only the different regiments of one side of the opposing armies. Who then would contest these concepts of ethnicity? They are, I think, of two tendencies: those who wish to ensure transcendence to theology by eliminating all considerations of ethnicity; and those who eliminate transcendence from ethnicity by denying it any theological dimensions. These similar-sounding positions need more explanation.

ETHNICITY BY OSMOSIS

The first group consists of those who would agree with the Hartford Statement [signed by a group of prominent theologians] and seek to prohibit the entry of social science into theology. They denounce evil and encourage good, but do not want to study the concrete manifestations of that evil, or describe its causes. No doubt they are against injustice, but limit the scope of theology to offering positive models of justice based on revelation instead of activism. Ethnicity enters into salvation history by osmosis: Become the new person in Christ, and you will automatically be a new Pole or a new Puerto Rican.

ETHNICITY AS NOSTALGIA

The second group of opponents to ethnic militancy are those who see it as a temporary and passing phenomenon which can be explained by social science, and has little if anything to do with theology. These persons, however, are articulators of a concept of ethnicity that the theologians on whose side they find themselves are not. The most important of these sociologists is Father Andrew Greeley. At the Bicentennial Hearings in Newark in November of 1975, he offered an outline of the sociological literature on ethnicity, and concluded that it should be defined as "national and cultural differences that form a mosaic with permeable boundaries." He said that one can choose to belong or not belong to an ethnic group in any of several ways. While much of his presentation corroborates standard analysis of race and ethnicity, not all of it rings true. For example, Father Greeley declared that an Afro-American has the same kind of option about ethnicity as an Italian-American. Sister Shawn Copeland of the Black Sisters' Coalition was quick to point out that she was identifiably black no matter what her preference. Father Greeley admitted this was her experience, but said that it ought not to be, since we are all striving to eliminate differences of race and ethnicity. He concluded by citing St. Paul that "in Christ there is neither Jew nor Greek."

In effect, Greeley compartmentalizes sociology and theology, thus precluding any theological meaning to ethnicity. His conception of ethnicity is one of nostalgia, which deals with the topic as phenomena and not as causality. Ethnicity is a stage to be passed through, and little more than a sociological variable in the equation of power and politics in the United States. It is not interested in ethnic neighborhoods except as folklore: it is not concerned with mobilizing ethnic voters to a reconstruction of society in order to eliminate injustices. For Greeley, and for many others, ethnic differences are like psychological clothes which individuals tailor to their tastes. This vision defends assimilation into the American system, and, carried to its logical conclusion, will describe as "pathological" those groups which do not conform to a model of upward mobility at the expense of ethnic consciousness.

GREELEY'S SYNDROME

It is unfortunate that Father Greeley's sense of objectivity and the quality of his sociology are so unevenly mixed with both wit and sarcasm. His "tell it like it is" syndrome seems at times to reduce a self-searching dialogue in the church to the level of a Monday-night football commentary. Nonetheless, as a sociologist, Andrew Greeley should be counted on to shed light upon the viewpoints he shares with others and help clarify issues for those with whom he disagrees.

Ethnicity is a key to the pastoral practice of the United States church now, and it always has been. In the future, I believe, it will challenge the creativity of theologians and social scientists. More and more it will resemble an emerging North American theology, as Liberation Theology has become synonymous with South America. And in this process, it could well be the greatest contribution of the Catholic church to the United States experience in two hundred years.

EPILOGUE

THE JOURNEY OF FAITH

It is fitting that the epilogue for this anthology be the prologue of the pastoral letter *Somos Hispanos*, published by the Hispano bishops in August 1977. The developments of the Hispano church chronicled in this book are only the beginning of a stupendous enrichment of Catholicism in the United States by the Hispano people. There is little in this prologue that has not come from the heritage documented in the pages of this anthology, indeed the opening words of the pastoral letter echo the vision of Vasconcelos in his description of the Cosmic Race (see pp. 32-38): "We are a mosaic of hues and traditions: a mestizo people." Significantly, the Hispano bishops decided to write the letter in stages, allowing for ongoing growth in the many facets of Hispano life and activity. The greatest threats to the progress of the Hispano church would seem to lie in the danger of institutionalization. Will the statements on social concerns, on economics, migration, and political participation reject a liberationist model of church? (See Chaps. Ten and Thirteen.) Will the approach to culture and popular religion petrify these dynamic realities and thus produce assimilation? (See Chap. Twelve.) Will the *comunidades de base* become an end in themselves and have their vitality sapped by institutional controls? (See Chap. Fifteen.)

As an individual passionately involved in much of what has been included in this book, I believe that the Hispano church will successfully meet these challenges as long as Puerto Ricans and liberationists enjoy proportionately as many leadership opportunities in the Hispano church as Mexican Americans and pastoralists. It should not go unnoticed that in the pastoral letter the Hispano bishops—most of them Mexican American pastoralists—did not attempt to solve the problems of identity for their own people (see Chap. Twelve). They simply listed as separate groups, "Mexicanos . . . Mexican Americans . . . Chicanos" (1.8). As has been seen (see pp. 250-55), these differences are based on ideologies that produce various models of church. *Mutatis mutandis,* other Hispano groups reflect the diversity that is clearly seen in the three names "Mexicanos, Mexican Americans, Chicanos." When the Hispano church projects more than one regional, cultural, and theological vision, it will have an even greater influence upon the entire Catholic church. Assuredly, one day a Puerto Rican priest born on the United States mainland will be ordained a bishop. But it is important—at least at the beginning—not only that he be Puerto Rican, but that he be Puerto Rican with the spirit of a liberationist.

358

Working in concert with the pastoralists and the Mexican American bishops, such a Puerto Rican will make the hierarchy of the Hispano church a model of unity in diversity. In such a combination, the Hispano church will be able to provide direction to the currents that are taking the United States to new levels of understanding of the motto *E pluribus unum.* And the questions surrounding Puerto Rican decolonization will form an important part of this contribution from a Hispano hierarchy.

In the search for unity in diversity, the Hispano church in the United States enjoys an advantage that the Latin American church does not possess, namely, a stable political climate. The 1979 meeting of the Latin American episcopate (CELAM III) in Puebla, Mexico, revealed divisions among the bishops in defining the meaning of the Medellín documents. These divisions are not unlike those between pastoralists and liberationists in the Hispano church.

However, in the Hispano church the conflicts are being resolved. At the successful Joint Encounter of Hermanas and PADRES held in Las Cruces, New Mexico, August 14-17, 1978, liberationists and pastoralists differed in defining the meaning of "poor." The former argued for identification of the term with an exploited social class, while the latter preferred a symbolic understanding based upon biblical archetypes. Nonetheless, the conflict did not destroy the unity of the meeting. In the statement of vision produced at the Encounter, a pluralistic church was described, one which allowed both models to operate in appropriate spheres of the apostolate. Moreover, the Encounter stressed the male-female aspects of partnership in ministry, producing new perspectives on the elimination of clericalism. Styles of ministry were suggested to complement the models of church. Significantly, the Hermanas-PADRES Encounter preceded a similar joint meeting between the Leadership Conference of Religious Women and Major Superiors of Male Religious, held in August 1978. Once again, the Hispano church was clearly in the vanguard of new trends that will no doubt receive attention from Pope John Paul II.

The creation of the Puerto Rican Catholic Organization (OCP) in the months immediately following the Second National Hispano Pastoral Encounter (see *National Catholic Reporter,* Jan. 13, 1978) demonstrates that the laity are capable of generating much of this new leadership. Launched through the active efforts of four Puerto Rican leaders—Eloy Acosta, David Ferrer, Jorge Ithier, and Eduardo Kalbfleish—the OCP has focused on the promotion of Puerto Rican leadership within the Catholic church. The OCP should help Puerto Ricans take a greater measure of influence in the growth of the church. This is a necessary quality in the "journey of faith" that the bishops describe in their pastoral letter (1.10), "because a loving Father and a compassionate Mother have given us the courage to participate with our people in a process of liberation and salvation."

100. Somos Hispanos: A Message of the Hispano Bishops of the United States to the Hispano Catholics in This Country, to All Catholics of the United States, and to All People of Good Will (August 1977)

1.1   Somos Hispanos.

1.2   We are many peoples with an integrated past, rich in faith, history and cultures. We reveal the blending of the Iberian and the Indian, the Black and the Oriental. We are a mosaic of hues and traditions: a mestizo people. The marriage of our various cultures was at times accomplished violently, at others peacefully.

> The Church is universal by vocation and mission, but when she puts down her roots in a variety of cultural, social and human terrains, she takes on different external expressions and appearances in each part of the world (*Evangelii Nuntiandi* 62).

1.3   But throughout this painful process the faith of our people has sustained them. Our Catholic faith has been proclaimed by our people in this land since the sixteenth century. It nourished us through the colonial era. The same faith animated our struggle for independence from Spain. This faith nurtured us through the territorial period of the United States occupation in the Southwest. This faith has endured to the present. We believe this faith is our greatest gift to the United States.

1.4   We are Hispano bishops. As your brothers, nourished by the same faith which has sustained us all, we are united with you in faith, hope, love, blood, culture, language and history.

1.5   Our mission is to proclaim the Good News of Jesus Christ "to all nations" (Mt. 28:19), but in a special manner to you, our Hispano brothers and sisters dwelling throughout this vast land. Our mission is also to be "the light of the world" (Mt. 5:14), to bring that light of Christ wherever there is darkness. We must announce His Good News to all who are in need, to all who suffer, to the poor (Lk. 4:18-19).

1.6   Aware of a history filled with both pain and promise, struggle and rejection, we hear the voices of Hispanic people crying out in deep faith for liberation from sin and injustice. As Hispano bishops, we make our own the suffering and struggles, hopes and disappointments, sadness and joys of all Hispanos.

1.7 We commit ourselves to work for the betterment of the situation of Hispanos everywhere—those in streets and squares; in factories and barrios; in fields and mines; janitors and maids; the undocumented immigrant living in the shadows and the unemployed. None is excluded from our pastoral concern.

1.8 Our Hispanic brothers and sisters are all who profess one faith and envision one brotherhood, whether Mexicanos, Puertorriqueños, Mexican-Americans, Cubanos, Dominicans, Spanish Americans, Chicanos, Central Americans or South Americans. No matter the flag or national origin—*Somos Hispanos.*

1.9 *Somos Hispanos.* With you we search for a deeper identity in faith, the better to discover Christ revealed more fully in ourselves and in each other. We are a Pilgrim People seeking "the new heavens and a new earth where according to His promise the justice of God will reside" (2 Pet. 3:13).

1.10 In this journey of faith, we have great hope, because a loving Father and a compassionate Mother have given us the courage to participate with our people in a process of liberation and salvation.

1.11 This process means lending our voices to the voiceless in order to announce the Gospel and to denounce the many injustices which continue to afflict our people: institutional and personal racism both from within and from without the Church; discrimination in language, culture and education; political underrepresentation; poor housing and few job opportunities. These and more flow from an economic system which prizes economic advantage over individual human worth.

1.12 Our concern here is not simply to recount the history of misdeeds, but to voice proudly those values which make our people great: the experience of the extended family; the worth and dignity of the person over any structure or institution: the esteem in which the name and honor of the person is held; and an ethic that values persons for what they are, not for what they do; the communitarian dimension of the individual; a passion for life; a sense of celebration typified by *la fiesta*. These values have meaning because they are natural, and supply the dynamism for a way of life that is both harmonious and coherent. Today many of these values are being threatened.

1.13 In expressing our cultural values we do not intend to disparage those of other peoples. Rather we invite them to be enriched by our culture, in the same way that other cultures have enriched our own. Thus we manifest God's Design: a human family created in one image, yet expressing that oneness in a rich diversity. Our very unity in pluralism facilitates the evangelization to which we are called by Christ as members of His Church.

> Evangelization loses much of its force and effectiveness if it does not take into consideration the actual people to whom it is addressed, if it does not use their language, their signs and symbols, if it does not answer the questions they ask, and if it does not have an impact on their

concrete life. But on the other hand, evangelization risks losing its power and disappearing altogether if one empties or adulterates its content under the pretext of translating it; in other words, one sacrifices this reality and destroys the unity without which there is no universality, out of a wish to adapt a universal reality to a local situation. Now, only a Church which preserves the awareness of her universality, and shows that she is in fact universal, is capable of having a message which can be heard by all, regardless of regional frontiers (*Evangelii nuntiandi* 63).

1.14 Rejoicing in the success of the Second National Hispano Pastoral Encounter, and encouraged by the hope it offers, we invite our people to reflect on the Gospel message and our role in salvation history. In days to come, we will seek to develop a Pastoral Letter which will reveal not only the spirit of our people, but also their needs for today and their dreams for tomorrow.

1.15 The Pastoral Letter will articulate the reality and needs of our people viewed in light of the Gospel, and will formulate conclusions and recommendations. It is not a letter that will be written only by Hispanos, but their voices have been listened to, their needs have been seen, their reality has been communicated. The vital areas of concern to be developed in the body of the Pastoral Letter will be: History and Culture; Religion and Faith; Social Concerns; Economics; Politics; Education; Migration; and Family Life.

1.16 With full confidence in Christ's abiding presence and guided by His Spirit, we undertake this challenging task in the name of our people, in the name of Our Father.

(Signed)

+ Roberto F. Sánchez
  Archbishop of Santa Fe

+ René H. Gracida
  Bishop of Pensacola-Tallahassee

+ Patricio F. Flores[1]
  Auxiliary Bishop of San Antonio

+ Juan Arzube
  Auxiliary Bishop of Los Angeles

+ Gilberto E. Chávez
  Auxiliary Bishop of San Diego

+ Raymundo J. Peña
  Auxiliary Bishop of San Antonio

+ Manuel D. Moreno
Auxiliary Bishop of Los Angeles

+ Franciso Garmendia
Auxiliary Bishop of New York

Washington, D.C.
August 22, 1977

1. On October 13, 1979 Patricio Flores was installed as Archbishop of San Antonio.—Ed.

BIBLIOGRAPHY

Acuña, Rodolfo. 1972. *Occupied America.* San Francisco: Canfield Press.

Alvarez, Salvador Enrique. 1973. "Mexican American Community Organization." In Romano V., ed., *Voices,* pp. 205-214. Berkeley, Calif.: Quinto Sol.

Arce de Vázquez, Margot. 1967. *La obra literaria de José de Diego.* San Juan, P.R.: Instituto de cultura puertorriqueña.

Arciniegas, Germán. 1966. *Latin America: A Cultural History.* London: Cresset Press.

Bailey, Frederick George. 1969. *Strategems and Spoils.* New York: Schocken Books.

Balandier, Georges. 1970. *Political Anthropology.* New York: Random House, Vintage Books.

Beirne, Charles J. 1975. *The Problem of Americanization in the Catholic Schools of Puerto Rico.* Río Piedras: Editorial Univ.

Bendix, Reinhard. 1960. *Max Weber: An Intellectual Portrait.* Garden City, N.Y.: Doubleday Anchor Books.

Cabrera, Francisco Manrique. 1969. *Historia de la literatura puertorriqueña.* Río Piedras: Editorial Cultural Inc.

Carrillo, Alberto. 1971. "The Sociological Failures of the Catholic Church towards the Chicano." In *Journal of Mexican-American Studies,* Winter issue.

Centro de estudios puertorriqueños. 1979. *Labor Migration under Capitalism: The Puerto Rican Experience.* New York: Monthly Review Press.

Cole, Mary. 1968. *Summer in the City.* New York: P.J. Kenedy.

Cordasco, Francisco, and Bucchioni, Eugene. 1963. *The Puerto Rican Experience.* Totowa, N.J.: Littlefield, Adams.

Corretjer, Juan Antonio. 1964. *Albizu Campos.* Montevideo: Siglo ilustrado.

Coser, Lewis. 1956. *The Functions of Social Conflict.* New York: The Free Press.

Crawford, Rex. 1961. *A Century of Latin American Thought,* rev. edn. Cambridge, Mass.: Harvard Univ. Press.

Davis, Harold Eugene. 1972. *Latin American Thought.* New York: The Free Press.

Díaz Ramírez, Ana María. 1978. "Puerto Rican Peoplehood and Pastoral Practices of the Catholic Church." Unpublished M.A. thesis, Latin American and Caribbean Center, New York Univ.

Dulles, Avery. 1974. *Models of the Church.* Garden City, N.Y.: Doubleday.

Dunne, John Gregory. 1967. *Delano.* New York: Farrar, Straus & Giroux, Noonday Press.

Eagleson, John, and Torres, Sergio, eds. 1975. *Theology in the Americas.* Maryknoll, N.Y.: Orbis Books.

Elizondo, Virgilio. 1975a. "A Challenge to Theology: The Situation of the Hispanic American." In *Proceedings,* vol. 30, 30th Annual Convention (January 1975), Catholic Theological Society of America.

———. 1975b. *Christianity and Culture.* Huntington, Ind.: Our Sunday Visitor.

———. 1978. *Mestizaje: The Dialectic of Cultural Birth and the Gospel.* San Antonio: MACC.

EPICA. 1976. *Puerto Rico: A People Challenging Colonialism.* Washington, D.C. EPICA.

Fenton, Jerry. 1969. *Understanding the Religious Background of the Puerto Rican.* Cuernavaca: Sondeos.

Fichter, Joseph H. 1960. "The Americanization of Catholicism." In Thomas McEvoy, ed., *Roman Catholicism and the American Way of Life.* Notre Dame, Ind.: Univ. of Notre Dame Press.

Fitzpatrick, Joseph P. 1971. *Puerto Rican Americans.* Englewood Cliffs, N.J.: Prentice-Hall.

———. 1972. "The Role of the National Parish and the Puerto Rican Experience." In *Studii emigrazioni,* June issue.

Flores Magón, Ricardo. 1970. *La revolución mexicana.* Mexico, D.F.: Editorial Grijalbo, S.A.

Freire, Paulo. 1970a. "Cultural Action for Freedom." In *Harvard Educational Review* 40 (May and August).

———. 1970b. *Pedagogy of the Oppressed.* New York: Seabury Press.

García, Rudy. 1977. "The Catholic Church Looks for a New Latino Way." In *Nuestro,* vol. 1, no. 9 (December issue), pp. 60-62

Gleason, Philip. 1969. "The Crisis in Americanization." In Gleason, ed., *Contemporary Catholicism in the United States.* Notre Dame, Ind.: Univ. of Notre Dame Press.

Goffman, Erving. 1963. *Stigma: Notes on the Management of Spoiled Identity.* Englewood Cliffs, N.J.: Prentice-Hall.

Gómez, David F. 1973. *Somos Chicanos: Strangers in Our Own Land.* Boston: Beacon Press.

González, José Luis. 1976. *Literatura y sociedad en Puerto Rico.* Mexico, D.F.: Fondo de Cultura Económica.

González, Rudolfo. 1972. *I Am Joaquin.* New York: Bantam Books.

Grebler, Leo; Moore, Joan W.; Guzmán, Ralph C. 1970. *The Mexican-American People.* New York: The Free Press.

Greeley, Andrew. 1972a. *The Denominational Society.* Glenview, Ill.: Scott, Foresman.

———. 1972b. *That Most Distressful Nation.* Chicago: Quadrangle Books.

Gunder Frank, André. 1973. *Lumpenbourgeoisie—Lumpendevelopment: Dependence, Class and Politics in Latin America.* New York: Monthly Review Press.

Gutiérrez, Gustavo. 1973. *A Theology of Liberation.* Maryknoll, N.Y.: Orbis Books.

Guttentag, Marcia. 1971. "Group Cohesiveness, Ethnic Organization and Poverty." In Wagner and Hang, eds., *Chicanos,* pp. 27-45. St. Louis: C.V. Mosby Co.

Herzog, Stephen J. 1973. "Political Coalition among Ethnic Groups in the Southwest." In De la Garza et al., eds., *Chicanos and Native Americans.* Englewood Cliffs, N.J.: Prentice-Hall.

Hurtado, Juan. 1975. *An Attitudinal Study of Social Distance between the Mexican-American and the Church.* San Antonio: MACC.

Jorrín, Miguel, and Martz, John D. 1970. *Latin American Political Thought and Ideology.* Chapel Hill: Univ. of North Carolina Press.

Kuhn, Thomas. 1970. *The Structure of Scientific Revolution.* Chicago: Univ. of Chicago Press.

LaFeber, Walter. 1963. *The New Empire, an Interpretation of American Expansion.* Ithaca, N.Y.: Cornell Univ. Press.

Levy, Mark R., and Kramer, Michael S. 1972. *The Ethnic Factor.* New York: Simon and Schuster.

López, Alfredo. 1973. *The Puerto Rican Papers.* Indianapolis, Ind.: Bobbs-Merrill.

Maccoby, Michael. 1971. "On Mexican National Character." In Wagner and Hang, eds., *Chicanos.* St. Louis: C.V. Mosby Co.

Maldonado Denis, Manuel. 1972. *Puerto Rico: A Social-Historical Interpretation.* New York: Random House, Vintage Books.

———. 1976. *Puerto Rico y Estados Unidos. Emigración y colonialismo.* Mexico, D.F.: Siglo XXI.

María de Sales, Sister. 1964. "El sentimiento religioso en la lírica puertorriqueña." Unpublished M.A. thesis, Department of Spanish Studies, Univ. of Puerto Rico.

McNamara, Patrick. 1973. "Catholicism, Assimilation and the Chicano Movement: Los Angeles as a Case Study." In De la Garza et al., eds., *Chicanos and Native Americans.* Englewood Cliffs, N.J.: Prentice-Hall.

Meier, Matt. S., and Rivera, Feliciano. 1972. *The Chicanos.* New York: Hill and Wang.

Moore, Donald T. 1969. *Puerto Rico para Cristo.* Cuernavaca: CIDOC Sondeos.

Moore, Joan W. 1970. *Mexican Americans.* Englewood Cliffs, N.J.: Prentice-Hall.

Moquin, Wayne, and Van Doren, Charles. 1971. *A Documentary History of the Mexican-American.* New York: Praeger (Bantam Books edn., 1972).

National Catholic Reporter, September 5, 1975. Editorial, "Stone Throwing."

National Council of Catholic Bishops. 1976. *The Catholic Directory.* New York: P.J. Kenedy.

Negrón de Mantilla, Aída. 1970. *Americanization in Puerto Rico. The Public School System 1900–1930.* Río Piedras: Editorial Edil.

Ocampo, Tarsicio. 1967. *Puerto Rico: Partido Acción Cristiana, 1960–1962.* Cuernavaca: CIDOC.

Pantojas García, Emilio. 1974. "La iglesia protestante y la americanización de Puerto Rico, 1898–1917." Unpublished manuscript, Department of Social Sciences, Univ. of Puerto Rico.

Paz, Octavio. 1959. *El Laberinto de la soledad.* Mexico, D.F.: Fondo de Cultura Económica. Published in English as *The Labyrinth of Solitude* (New York: Grove Press, 1961).

Peñalosa, Fernando. 1971. *Class Consciousness and Social Mobility in a Mexican-American Community.* San Francisco: R & E Research Associates.

Rendón, Armando B. 1971. *Chicano Manifesto.* New York: Collier Books.

Romano V., Octavio Ignacio. 1973. "The Historical and Intellectual Presence of the Mexican-American." In Romano V., ed., *Voices: Readings from El Grito*, rev. edn. Berkeley, Calif.: Quinto Sol.

Russell, Philip. 1977. *Mexico in Transition.* Austin: Colorado River Press.

Sáez, Florencio, Jr. 1969. *De Jesucristo al Che Guevara.* Santurce: Editorial La Palma.

Sánchez, Villaseñor. 1949. *Ortega y Gasset existencialista.* Chicago: Henry Regnery Co.

Sandoval, Moisés. 1975a. "Spanish-speaking versus Church." In *National Catholic Reporter*, January 17 issue.

———. 1975b. "Teología de la liberación avanza en los Estados Unidos." In *El Visitante Dominical*, September 21 issue.

Sexton, Patricia Cayo. 1965. *Spanish Harlem: Anatomy of Poverty*. New York: Harper & Row.

Shockley, John Staples. 1974. *Chicano Revolution in a Texas Town*. Bloomington: Indiana Univ. Press.

Silén, Juan Angel. 1970. *Hacia una visión positiva del puertorriqueño*. Río Piedras: Editorial Edil.

———. 1973. *La nueva lucha de independencia*. Río Piedras: Editorial Edil.

Silvert, Kalman H. 1961. *The Conflict Society*. New York: Harper Colophon Books.

Simmons, Ozzie. 1961. "The Mutual Images and Expectations of Anglo-Americans and Mexican Americans," *Daedalus*, XC (Spring, 1961) 286–299.

Smith, Anthony D. 1971. *Theories of Nationalism*. New York: Harper Torchbooks.

Soto, Antonio R. 1975. *Chicano and the Church*. Denver: Marfel.

Stevens Arroyo, Antonio M. 1974a. *The Political Philosophy of Pedro Albizu Campos: Its Theory and Practice*. New York: Iberoamerican Center.

———. 1974b. "The Religion of Puerto Ricans in New York." In Edward Mapp, ed., *Puerto Rican Perspectives*, pp. 119-130. Metuchen, N.J.: Scarecrow Press.

Taller de Migración y de Cultura. 1979. *Labor Migration under Capitalism*. New York: Monthly Review Press.

U.S. Bureau of the Census. 1975. *Persons of Spanish-Origin in the United States (1970)*. Series P-20, March 1975. Series No. 283, August 1975. Washington, D.C.: Government Printing Office.

U.S. Commission on Civil Rights. 1976. *An Uncertain Future. Puerto Ricans in the Continental United States*. Washington, D.C.: Government Printing Office.

Vallier, Ivan. 1967. "Religious Elites: Differentiations and Developments in Roman Catholicism." In Seymour Martin Lipset and Aldo Solari, eds., *Elites in Latin America*. London: Oxford Univ. Press.

Van Alstyne, Richard W. 1965. *The Rising American Empire*. Chicago: Quadrangle Books.

Varo, Carlos. 1973. *Puerto Rico: radiografía de un pueblo asediado*. Río Piedras: Ediciones Puerto.

Vasconcelos, José. 1925. *La Raza Cósmica*. Barcelona: Espasa Calpe.

———. 1927. *Indología*. Barcelona: Espasa Calpe.

———. 1963. *A Mexican Ulysses*. Bloomington: Indiana Univ. Press.

———, and Gamio, Manuel. 1926. *Aspects of Mexican Civilization*. Chicago: Univ. of Chicago Press.

Wagenheim, Kal. 1970. *Puerto Rico: A Profile*. New York: Praeger.

———, and Jiménez, Olga. 1973. *A Documentary History of the Puerto Ricans*. New York: Praeger.

Wagner, Nathaniel M., and Hang, Marsh J., eds. 1971. *Chicanos: Social and Psychological Perspectives*. St. Louis: C.V. Mosby.

Weinberg, Albert K. 1963. *Manifest Destiny*. Chicago: Quadrangle Books.

Wells, Henry. 1969. *The Modernization of Puerto Rico*. Cambridge, Mass.: Harvard Univ. Press.

Williams, William Appleman. 1966. *The Contours of American History*. Chicago: Quadrangle Books.

Wolf, Eric. 1969. *Peasant Wars of the Twentieth Century*. New York: Harper & Row.

INDEX

Other Orbis books . . .

THE MEANING OF MISSION

José Comblin

"This very readable book has made me think, and I feel it will be useful for anyone dealing with their Christian role of mission and evangelism." *New Review of Books and Religion*
ISBN 0-88344-304-X CIP   *Cloth $6.95*

THE GOSPEL OF PEACE AND JUSTICE

Catholic Social Teaching Since Pope John

Presented by Joseph Gremillion

"Especially valuable as a resource. The book brings together 22 documents containing the developing social teaching of the church from *Mater et Magistra* to Pope Paul's 1975 *Peace Day Message on Reconciliation*. I watched the intellectual excitement of students who used Gremillion's book in a justice and peace course I taught last summer, as they discovered a body of teaching on the issues they had defined as relevant. To read Gremillion's overview and prospectus, a meaty introductory essay of some 140 pages, is to be guided through the sea of social teaching by a remarkably adept navigator."

National Catholic Reporter

"An authoritative guide and study aid for concerned Catholics and others." *Library Journal*
ISBN 0-88344-165-9   *Cloth $15.95*
ISBN 0-88344-166-7   *Paper $8.95*

THEOLOGY IN THE AMERICAS

Papers of the 1975 Detroit Conference

Edited by Sergio Torres and John Eagleson

"A pathbreaking book from and about a pathbreaking theological conference, *Theology in the Americas* makes a major contribution to ecumenical theology, Christian social ethics and liberation movements in dialogue." *Fellowship*
ISBN 0-88344-479-8 CIP   *Cloth $12.95*
ISBN 0-88344-476-3   *Paper $5.95*

CHRISTIANS, POLITICS AND VIOLENT REVOLUTION

J.G. Davies

"Davies argues that violence and revolution are on the agenda the world presents to the Church and that consequently the Church must reflect on such problems. This is a first-rate presentation, with Davies examining the question from every conceivable angle."

National Catholic News Service

ISBN 0-88344-061-X   *Paper $4.95*

CHRISTIAN POLITICAL THEOLOGY A MARXIAN GUIDE

Joseph Petulla

"Petulla presents a fresh look at Marxian thought for the benefit of Catholic theologians in the light of the interest in this subject which was spurred by Vatican II, which saw the need for new relationships with men of all political positions." *Journal of Economic Literature*

ISBN 0-88344-060-1   *Paper $4.95*

THE NEW CREATION: MARXIST AND CHRISTIAN?

José María González-Ruiz

"A worthy book for lively discussion."

The New Review of Books and Religion

ISBN 0-88344-327-9 CIP   *Cloth $6.95*

CHRISTIANS AND SOCIALISM

Documentation of the Christians for Socialism Movement in Latin America

Edited by John Eagleson

"Compelling in its clear presentation of the issue of Christian commitment in a revolutionary world." *The Review of Books and Religion*

ISBN 0-88344-058-X   *Paper $4.95*

THE CHURCH AND
THIRD WORLD REVOLUTION

Pierre Bigo

"Heavily documented, provocative yet reasonable, this is a testament, demanding but impressive." *Publishers Weekly*

ISBN 0-88344-071-7 CIP   *Cloth $8.95*
ISBN 0-88344-072-5   *Paper $4.95*

WHY IS THE THIRD WORLD POOR?

Piero Gheddo

"An excellent handbook on the Christian understanding of the development process. Gheddo looks at both the internal and external causes of underdevelopment and how Christians can involve themselves in helping the third world." *Provident Book Finder*

ISBN 0-88344-757-6   *Paper $4.95*

POLITICS AND SOCIETY
IN THE THIRD WORLD

Jean-Yves Calvez

"This frank treatment of economic and cultural problems in developing nations suggests the need for constant multiple attacks on the many fronts that produce problems in the human situation."

The Christian Century

ISBN 0-88344-389-9   *Cloth $6.95*

A THEOLOGY OF LIBERATION

Gustavo Gutiérrez

"The movement's most influential text." *Time*

"The most complete presentation thus far available to English readers of the provocative theology emerging from the Latin American Church." *Theological Studies*

"North Americans as well as Latin Americans will find so many challenges and daring insights that they will, I suggest, rate this book one of the best of its kind ever written." *America*

ISBN 0-88344-477-1   *Cloth $7.95*
ISBN 0-88344-478-X   *Paper $4.95*

THEOLOGY FOR A NOMAD CHURCH

Hugo Assmann

"A new challenge to contemporary theology which attempts to show that the theology of liberation is not just a fad, but a new political dimension which touches every aspect of Christian existence."

Weekly

IS ... h $7.95
IS ... r $4.95

Fl

Tl

Ig

"E ... elation
ar ... essage
m ... salva-
tic ... out in
hi
ISl ... $8.95
ISl ... $4.95

TI

Ju

"It ... ng the
sh ... rity of
vis ... writes
wi ... politi-
ca ... work
of ... s the
m ... eces-
sa ... orary
th ... erical
re

an ... ng in
IS ... 10.95
IS ... $6.95